CW01151464

LAND-ROVER
THE FORMATIVE YEARS
1947–1967

The *Real* Story Behind
The World's Most Versatile Vehicle

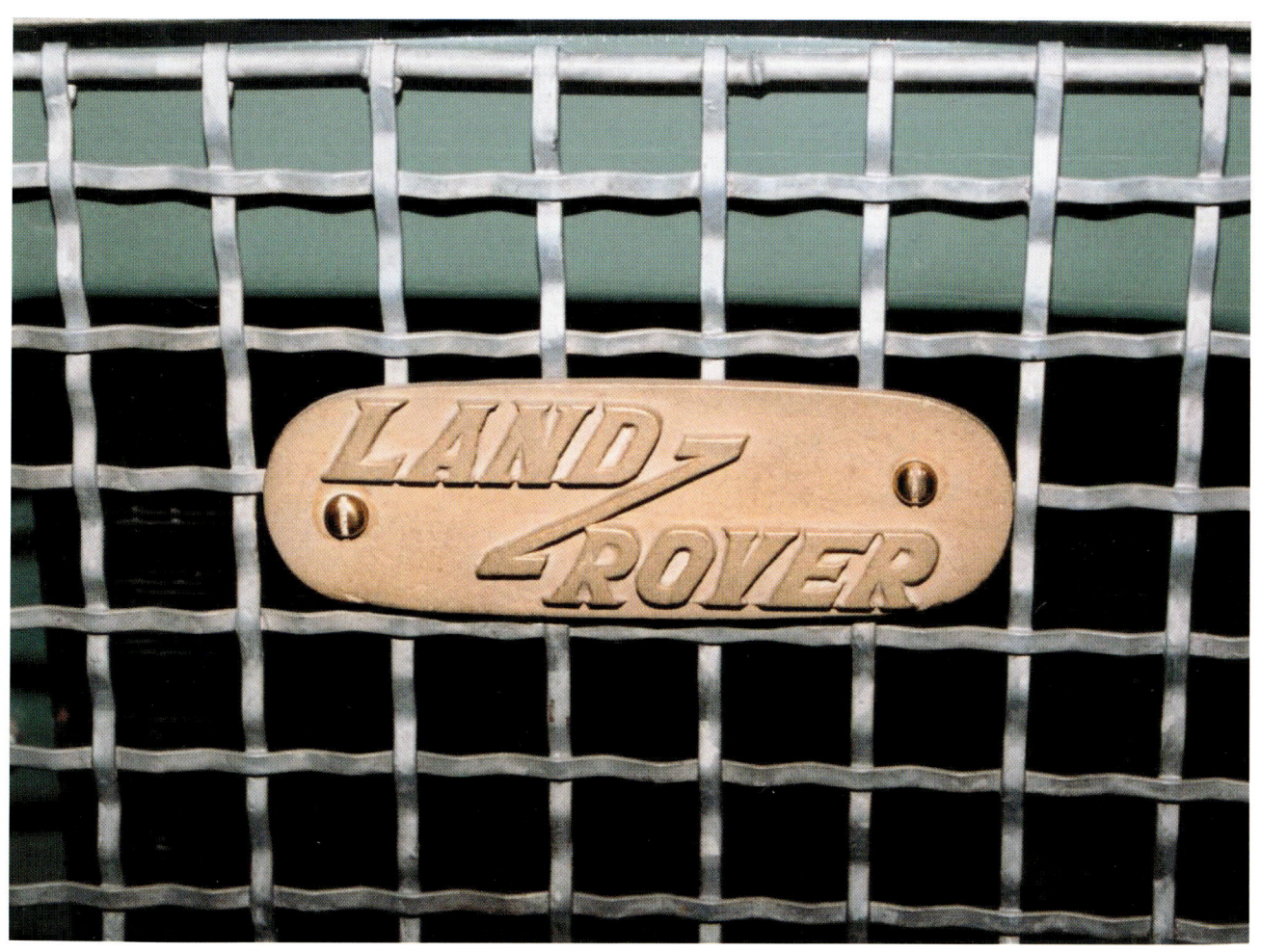

1948 pre-production Land-Rover grille badge

Dedication

To the memory of all those Rover employees responsible for taking the Land-Rover project from a Jeep-based hybrid prototype concept vehicle to an initial pre-production batch of 48, and then into full-blown production, all in a matter of months.

Spencer Wilks (MD)
Maurice Wilks (Technical Director)
Robert Boyle (Chief Engineer)
Arthur Goddard (Assistant Chief Engineer)
Tom Barton (design)
Gordon Bashford (design)
Joe Drinkwater (engines)
Roland Seale (production drawing office)
Frank Shaw (transmissions)
John Cullen (project co-ordinator)
Sam Ostler (body stylist)
Geoffrey Savage (jig shop)
Olaf Poppe (Works Manager)

And not forgetting Jack Swaine whose sloping-head i.o.e. engine became the power plant.

If Maurice Wilks was the Father of the Land-Rover,
then Spencer Wilks was the Godfather

LAND-ROVER
THE FORMATIVE YEARS
1947–1967

The *Real* Story Behind
The World's Most Versatile Vehicle

NAC 747, Pre-production 86

John Smith

Published by

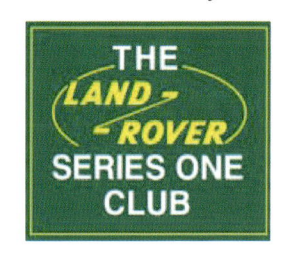

Land-Rover Series One Club Ltd.
is a member of the
Association of Land-Rover Clubs Ltd.

First Edition, March 2009

Copyright © John Smith 2009

The right of John Smith to be identified as the author of the work has been asserted by him in accordance with the Copyright, Designs, and Patent Act of 1988. All rights reserved. No part of this publication may be reproduced, stored in a retrieval system, or transmitted, in any form or by any means, electronic, mechanical, photocopying, recording or otherwise, without permission of the publisher or copyright holders, nor be otherwise circulated in any form of binding or cover other than that in which it is published and without a similar condition, including this condition, being imposed on the subsequent purchaser.

A CIP catalogue record of this book is available from the British Library

The Land-Rover Series One Club Ltd. gratefully acknowledge permission from Land-Rover Ltd. to reproduce material for which it holds copyright.

Land-Rover is a trade mark of Land-Rover Ltd.

ISBN 978-0-9561708-0-4

Book Design

Warren Leavens

Printed in Great Britain by

Wincanton Print Company Ltd
Wessex Way
Wincanton Business Park
Wincanton
Somerset
BA9 9RR

Land Rover Series One Club Ltd. Lavender Cottage, 49 Over Lane, Almondsbury, Bristol, BS32 4BL

Contents

Acknowledgements 6

Foreward 8

Author's Note 10

Prelude 12

INTRODUCTION ... 4x4 .... An Opening Door 16

CHAPTER 1 .... Post-war Austerity .... 'Export or Bust' 20

CHAPTER 2 .... Middle Class, or Muck and Grass? .... Historic Day at Red Wharf Bay 28

CHAPTER 3 .... Birth of the Legend .... A Batch of 50 Sanctioned 38

CHAPTER 4 .... Prototypes and Chassis Frame Tests .... The Centre Steer Hybrid 44

CHAPTER 5 .... From Hybrids to Highway .... Pre-Production Models 58

CHAPTER 6 .... A Pattern for Progress .... Drawings and Designs 80

CHAPTER 7 .... Factory to Farm .... The Late 1940s 96

CHAPTER 8 .... Marketing and Modifications .... Some Early Changes 110

CHAPTER 9 .... Land-Rovers in the Making .... Solihull and Tyseley 120

CHAPTER 10 .... Identity Crisis .... Tractor or Transporter? 126

CHAPTER 11 .... Overseas Adventures .... The Early Expeditions 132

CHAPTER 12 .... A Closer Look .... Into the 1950s 140

CHAPTER 13 .... Soft Seating for Hard Going .... The Early Station Wagons 154

CHAPTER 14 .... The 1951 Season .... 4x4 goes 4x2 162

CHAPTER 15 .... Put On and Take Off .... 'Britain's Most Versatile Vehicle' 178

CHAPTER 16 .... From Cattle Field to Battlefield ...... The Military Manoeuvre 198

CHAPTER 17 .... Under Licence .... Minerva and Tempo 212

CHAPTER 18 .... Bigger and Better .... More New Models 224

CHAPTER 19 .... A Sweeter 2.0-Litre .... The Mid-1950s 244

CHAPTER 20 .... Forward Area Vehicle .... MoS Land-Rovers 256

CHAPTER 21 .... A Change of Heart .... The Diesel Option 264

CHAPTER 22 .... End of the Beginning .... The Close of an Era 274

CHAPTER 23 .... Into the Sixties .... The New Series II 284

CHAPTER 24 .... IIA and Beyond .... Widening and Deepening the Range 296

CHAPTER 25 .... Air-Portable Lightweight .... The Closing Chapter 310

The Illustrations 316

The Rover Company 318

The Land-Rover Series One Club 320

Acknowledgements

My sincere thanks to Stephen Wilks, and Nicholas and Gillian Wilks, without whose co-operation, encouragement and personal contacts, much historical accuracy would have been lost. Kathleen Griffith, nanny to Maurice Wilks' three sons in the late 1940s, was the only remaining 'grown-up' able to recall that all-important day at Red Wharf Bay when Maurice Wilks had his first vision for a Land-Rover, and I am most grateful for her memories.

The late Gordon Bashford kindly lent his personal records concerning the activities of the Rover Company between spring 1947 and spring 1948, including previously unpublished detail on the Land-Rover's chassis tests and other material. James Taylor and Ian Thompson kindly provided material from their own personal research concerning early Land-Rovers.

I am also indebted to various members of the Land-Rover Series One Club, particularly, David Bowyer, Brian Cherrett, Andrew Cross, Jamie Fairchild, Derrey Ferdinando, Mike Hardiman and Les Lawrence, all of whom provided the necessary encouragement from the time the idea for such a book first began to materialise a quarter of a century ago. The Club's Vice President, Reverend Andrew Stevens, made the necessary contact with Bishop Warren Hunt, who knew Patrick Wilks, and through Patrick, I was able to contact Stephen and Nicholas Wilks.

My thanks also go to the many enthusiasts, past and present, of the Land-Rover Register (1948–1953), especially Andrew Bullas, Michael Bishop, Brian Carvey, Jim Cooknell, Dave Davies, Tim Dines, Peter Galilee, Chris Goodyear, Tony Hutchings, Howard Jones, Richard Lines, Tom Pickford, Ivor Ramsden, Chris Stern, Pete Stringer and Marco Tasselli, all of whom lent photographic or other material, or were a constant source of reference in various areas.

I should also like to thank Fernand Van de Plas, President of the Minerva TT Register, for his assistance with the Minerva chapter, and the late Bart H. Vanderveen, of the Olyslager Organisation NV, for his valued correspondence over the years.

Warren Leavens, past editor of the LRSOC's excellent newsletter 'Legend', undertook the all-important task of setting out the text, and overseeing the book into print. Judy Hartley kindly undertook the mammoth task of proofreading the final text.

Finally, my thanks to all those club members, far too numerous to mention by name, whose contribution may simply have been to draw attention to points of detail, either by asking the right questions, or providing the right answers. Their observations have been most valuable.

Foreword

The 'Series I' Land-Rovers were very much part of my childhood – they were the Land-Rovers that my brothers and I grew up with. We were still just young boys when the first pre-production models were being assembled in the factory in early 1948. Even so, I can still vividly remember my father, Maurice Wilks, experimenting with these early Land-Rovers. He would examine every detail of their construction to see what improvements could be made, then notify his team, so they could effect the necessary changes. The Land-Rover project had, in fact, gone from drawing board sketches into production in under 12 months, made possible by the concerted efforts of Rover's dedicated development team.

Today, these early Land-Rovers are a cause for much childhood nostalgia. Around the time production began my father made a fishpond in the garden. He used a Pegson's pump attached to the back of the Land-Rover, driven by a PTO unit, to fill the pond from a nearby well. Dad allowed us three boys to hold the fire hose nozzle, but as the pressure was so high, we could barely control the hose because of the pressure reaction. This resulted in a powerful arc of water not going in the pond, but skywards, high up into the trees.

I can also remember the time we were sitting in the rear of a Land-Rover, along with the children from next door, when we were stopped by the local 'bobby', who was concerned about the lack of seating in the back, and threatened to book my Dad. Not long after that, optional rear seats were made available for the Land-Rover.

I remember going on various cross-country trips with our father. Although we boys didn't realise at the time, Dad was testing the Land-Rover's capabilities, and would often push it to its limits. Any shortcomings would be noted, and suitable modifications introduced. On one occasion we were driving down a particularly steep incline when the Land-Rover's deep-sided fuel tank grounded on a hillock. This resulted in the fuel tank becoming much shallower on subsequent models.

As young boys, we loved the Land-Rover, and every year enjoyed going on holiday in the latest model, which was always better than last year's Land-Rover. Mum, however, was not quite so enthusiastic, and used to say that the Land-Rover was *"made by men, for men"*. She disliked the sharp edges and heavy steering. Dad took such criticisms to heart, not least because mum did a considerable number of miles in the Land-Rover herself, and it was not too long before the vehicle was made more comfortable.

One day we were on Anglesey, where we had a holiday cottage, when Dad managed to get a Land-Rover stuck, attempting to cross the mudflats at Newborough Warren. It was not long before the tide came in and the Land-Rover was soon under six feet of water, making it impossible to recover. The next day we went back to see the Land-Rover and, amazingly, Dad managed to start the engine and effect a full recovery.

In the words of the late Bishop Warren Hunt *"To be a passenger in a Land-Rover when Maurice Wilks drove it over seemingly impossible land and through the sea was an experience never to be forgotten"*. It is a credit to my father, that 60 years on, hundreds of dedicated enthusiasts throughout the world are still enjoying the same experience evoked by these sentiments.

John's excellent book traces the real story surrounding these early Land-Rovers, from the first embryonic hybrid prototype of 1947, and on through the production model's continuous development over the following 20 years. Throughout this time, the Rover Company was still an independent car manufacturer, and for most of that time, my father, together with his brother, Spencer Wilks, was in charge of everything that went on at Rover's factory. These were the formative years of the Land-Rover that were to firmly establish its reputation as 'The World's Most Versatile Vehicle'.

I can think of no better person to write such a book.

Stephen Wilks,
President of the Land-Rover Series One Club

East Grinstead, 2009.

Author's Note

The story of the Land-Rover has appeared in print in a great many publications over the past decades, and the vehicle is now legendary. Nevertheless, the present author believes that much of the embryonic period has been inaccurately and inadequately treated. More than 60 years have passed since the Land-Rover's original conception, so this is perhaps a good time to rectify this situation, before too much of the true story is lost forever. The contents of this volume have been carefully pieced together using a wide and varied selection of first hand documentary and other evidence, the result of which is a tale that may not be entirely in accord with the legend.

This is not a volume for the feint hearted, but is dedicated to the ever growing band of enthusiasts of the early Land-Rovers, built between 1948 and the early 1960s, when Rover was still an independent company in the capable hands of the two Wilks brothers, Spencer (SB) and Maurice (MCW). No apology is made for any excess of detail contained within these pages, nor is it the author's intention that this volume should be, of necessity, read from cover to cover. Instead, it should be savoured in the manner of a delicacy - a small taste here, a small taste there, with perhaps the occasional larger bite, depending, of course, on one's appetite. If, per chance, the contents of its pages should bring the reader half the delight the author had in writing them, then much will undoubtedly have been accomplished.

Prelude

Looking back over 60 years to the summer of 1948, when the Rover Company first turned its recently acquired Solihull premises over to Land-Rover production, it seems unlikely anyone could have envisaged the long-term success their new workhorse would come to enjoy over the ensuing decades, or that it would be owned, first by a German, then an American car manufacturer before the end of the Millennium, and then a car manufacturer from the Indian sub-continent in the following decade.

By 1948 more than a dozen cross-country cars had already seen quantity production at some time or other since the mid-1930s, and not even the idea of a four-wheel-drive vehicle for agriculture was new. So on what grounds do we base the Land-Rover's success? Was it just a good copy of Willys' wartime Jeep, or is there more to its fortune than that?

Ward Canaday of Willys-Overland Motors, Toledo, Ohio, first began examining the agricultural potential of the ubiquitous wartime Jeep as early as 1942, and the US Department of Agriculture showed considerable interest in Canaday's ideas. A 20-page booklet by L.J. Smith and O.J. Trenary, entitled 'The Jeep as a Farm Truck-Tractor for the Post-War Period' was also published by the Agricultural Experimental Station of the State College of Washington. However, flooding the home market with war surplus vehicles was the last thing either Canaday or the US Government wanted, as such a policy had already proved a disaster for the American motor industry after the First World War. The US Government decreed therefore, that when the war ended, all military Jeeps would remain at their last post.

When Ford's contract with the US Government came to an end on 31 July 1945, all rights to Jeep production reverted back to Willys-Overland, who intended to capitalise on the situation. Preparations for a civilian model had long been underway, and even a fortnight before the contract with Ford came to an end, a peacetime model was revealed to the press. Capitalising on the Jeep's wartime image, changes made were to be minimal, but included a tail board, side-mounted spare wheel, column gearshift, sealed beam headlights, and provision for power take-off equipment. Willys' 2.2-litre 'Go Devil' side-valve engine and 6-volt electrics would still remain.

When the new civilian Jeep became available in September 1945, there was certainly no shortage of takers for the new model, particularly among demobilised troops returning to the land. Very soon thousands of new Jeeps were in use on small farms throughout America, ploughing the land well ahead of anything the Rover Company was eventually to have in mind.

So far, however, every cross-country car that had reached volume production before 1948, including Willys' Jeep, owed its existence to a military need to replace the horse and mule as transport in an age of mechanised warfare. All attempts to put a 4x4 light car into volume production, without a military market, had simply come to nothing. With the introduction of their new Land-Rover, the Rover Company would be the first to change all that.

From the very start their Land-Rover had been designed specifically for the agricultural market, not military use. The war was seen as a thing of the past, and Rover was looking to the future. Besides, the British Army's own plans for a vehicle to replace the US Jeep – the FV 1800 project – were already at the prototype stage. If Rover were unable to sell Land-Rovers as a peacetime utility vehicle to the world's rural communities, then it would have little chance of success.

That, surely, is what sets the Land-Rover apart from its predecessors in the history of cross-country cars. Exports, not military orders, were what Rover desperately needed, if not only their Land-Rover, but also the whole of their car concern, was to survive into the second half of the 20th Century. With neither military backing nor background, in Rover's hour of need, the Land-Rover would have to stand entirely on its merits as a civilian off-road utility truck. If it did, it would become the first cross-country car ever to do so. Rover was now poised to show the world that it had not only got the name right, but the rest of the vehicle too!

So what then, were the initial ingredients of the Land-Rover's overwhelming success? Apart from the historical circumstances surrounding the closing years of Britain's colonial empire, dealt with in this story, the answer is to be found in key areas of the vehicle's design: the method of body construction; the materials used; the engine design; the type of transmission; quality of components; ease of servicing; and finally, the vehicle's overall versatility. These were all unique features to the Land-Rover and clearly made it different from any Jeep. To understand the true significance of such features, it is necessary to take a close look at the Land-Rover's design.

Prelude

When any four-wheeled vehicle negotiates a bend, the front wheels travel further and faster than those at the rear. With only rear-wheel drive, this presents few problems, but when power is transmitted through all the vehicle's wheels, as in the early Land-Rover, this can produce mechanical stresses in the transmission, known as 'wind-up'. The experience gained from tens of thousands of wartime vehicles showed these stresses to be relatively harmless, as they work their way out as tyre slip, but with one unfortunate consequence – excessive tyre wear, especially on metalled roads.

To overcome this problem, Rover experimented with selectable two- or four-wheel-drive on the very earliest pre-production Land-Rovers, incorporating a split shaft and locking dog in the front output housing – similar to that on the Jeep's 'Spicer' transfer box. They soon discovered, however, that the Land-Rover could stay in four-wheel-drive without any detrimental effect on the tyres. How was that possible? Already present in the Land-Rover's transmission system were two important features able to prevent these stresses building up in the first place, although it appears that Rover were initially unaware of this fact.

The first of these was Rover's own 'Freewheel' device that had been incorporated onto the rear of Rover gearboxes since 1932, to facilitate smoother gear changes on pre-war non-synchromesh gearboxes. A similar device was incorporated into the Land-Rover's front output housing of the high/low transfer gearbox. This allows the front wheels to travel further and faster than those at the rear, whenever a bend is negotiated. When the vehicle returns to a straight path, as the front wheels slow down, power will automatically be re-applied. It's a bit like a frantic cyclist's legs 'catching-up' when his cycle slows at the end of a downhill gradient, allowing him to usefully power his machine again.

Unlike the 'third' differential commonly used today, on engine pull in a forward direction, the 'Freewheel' is permanently set to give 4x4 traction on any surface. It only needs the 'Freewheel' to be "locked-in" if maximum engine braking is required on a steep descent, or when 4x4 traction is required in reverse motion. At all other times, it has the distinct advantage of always being permanently ready for action.

The second important feature in the Land-Rover's transmission design concerns the front driven axle. In 1924 the Frenchman, Pierre Fenaille designed the world's first true constant velocity, or homokinetic, joint, which his friend, Jean A. Gregoire, then used for his front-wheel-drive car, called the 'Tracta'. Fenaille's Tracta c.v. joint was, and still is, a truly masterful piece of engineering.

Gregoire exhibited his car at the Paris Salon in 1927 and the Societé des Automobiles Tracta went into production. Tracta cars competed at Le Mans no less than eight times from 1927–34, winning their class in both 1929 and 1930. A few hundred Tracta cars were sold between 1927 and 1932, but they never managed to sell a car or chassis for more than it cost. Gregoire was forced to sell the patent on the Tracta c.v. joint to Bendix in 1934 (ironically, the very year André Citroën's 'Traction Avant' took off with a vengeance), and it was not long before Tracta joints started to appear on a variety of British and American four-wheel-drive vehicles being developed for war.

With Europe now engulfed in war, in 1940 the American Bantam Car Co. engaged Spicer for the design and manufacture of a transfer box and axles for their US ¼-ton 'Command Reconnaissance' car that preceded the Jeep. However, when Ford and Willys became involved in quantity production of the final design in December 1941, a variety of drive joints began to appear – Bendix-Weiss, Rzeppa, and Tracta – but only Willys used Tracta joints. Maurice Wilks, the man responsible for the overall design of the Land-Rover, by coincidence, just happened to have a war surplus Willys MB at home, which he decided to use as the basis for the Land-Rover project.

Tracta joints had been widely used on British military vehicles, and quantity production of the design was already available in the UK. They would also continue to be used in the British Army's post-war FV 1800 "Jeep replacement", the Austin 'Champ', then under development. Using Gregoire and Fenaille's 'Tracta' c.v. joint meant the problem of snatch at large steering angles, associated with the 'Hooke' joint, such as the Hardy Spicer u.j. used on car propeller shafts, would be avoided. It was this Tracta joint that enabled early Land-Rovers to handle properly in constant four-wheel-drive, even when cornering at high speeds on the open road.

Despite the advantages offered by the Tracta joint, it was a costly piece of engineering and was eventually superseded by the much simpler Hardy Spicer universal joint in 1953. But by then, the Land-Rover was no longer a constant four-wheel-drive vehicle. Nevertheless, it was the Tracta joint that enabled the Land-

Rover to have a permanent four-wheel-drive transmission at the point of conception. Although the early split output shaft and locking dog arrangement, used to provide selectable 4x2 on the earliest pre-production Land-Rovers, was retained on the first 2,000 production gearboxes, it was totally unnecessary, and so after the first 16 pre-production models, Rover inserted a distance collar on the selector shaft to prevent the locking dog from disengaging 4x4.

Rover's 'Freewheel' device, together with Gregoire's Tracta joint, put the Land-Rover on the right track for both off-road and highway use. Although both these components had disappeared by the time the original 80-inch wheelbase Land-Rover went out of production in 1953, they helped set the Land-Rover on a path that led in only one direction – forward. By that time the Land-Rover was already well placed to take the Rover Co. into the second half of the 20th Century.

Rover also decided to produce a 'Station Wagon' on the Land-Rover chassis at the pre-production stage, and this too would leave its mark on motoring history. Although Willys-Overland had been making 'Jeep' station wagons since 1946, they failed to give them four-wheel-drive – in fact they were not even built on a Jeep chassis, but on their pre-war 104-inch-wheelbase failed 'Americar'.

Apart from the fact that it was all steel, the Jeep station wagon was really no different from any other "woody" wagon of the period, which made it a great disappointment to many potential buyers. It took Willys three years to rectify this situation and produce optional 4x4 for the 4x4-63 model of 1949. But by this time Rover had already pipped them to the post.

Land-Rover 4x4 Station Wagons were exhibited at both the London and Paris Motor Shows in October 1948, and were officially available from December. Their coachbuilt bodywork, by 'Tickford' of Newport Pagnell, was based on the standard 80-inch Land-Rover chassis, and it immediately became the first fully enclosed civilian cross-country car for both off-road leisure and family use, as well as daily transport on the highway, to go into volume production.

Confirming this in their preview published 12 October 1948, 'The Autocar' described this new type of vehicle as *"...nearer the car of the future for the countryman than anything which has yet been produced"*. Certainly an outspoken remark, but after 60 years it has stood the test of time. More than half a century on, every major motor manufacturer still copies the idea, this category of vehicle seeing its greatest expansion in output in the 1980s.

Land-Rover Ltd's own modern equivalents – the Range Rover, the '90', '110' and '130' Defender, the Discovery, and more recently, the Freelander – have already taken Rover's original concept into the 21st Century, and look set to lead the field for generations to come,

By December 1948, Rover's management already knew they were heading in a new direction. No longer were they simply the maker of 'One of Britain's Fine Cars', but manufacturers of

"The World's Most Versatile Vehicle"

Introduction
4x4 : An Opening Door

Around the turn of the century when most roads were little more than cart tracks, four-wheel-drive was already being considered as a means of providing traction for the infant motor car. The earliest example was to come from one of the motor industry's greatest names – Ferdinand Porsche. In 1900, while Porsche was still a young man working for the Viennese coach builder, Jacob Lohner, an Englishman, E.W. Hart, ordered an electric car from the firm. Porsche's talent was already recognised and Lohner gave him responsibility for the car's production. In his design, Porsche incorporated four electric motors – one at each hub – to give four-wheel-drive. The car's name, 'Toujours Contente' (forever satisfied), was to prove something of a misnomer, as the excessive weight of the batteries and electric motors severely restricted its performance.

Across the Atlantic, in Illinois, Charles Cotta also built and patented a 4x4 in 1900. This was a steam car designed to cope with America's backwoods and used a separate chain set to drive each of the four independent half-shafts. Again only one was built, but in 1903 he sold the patent to the American Four Wheel Drive Co. of Milwaukee, Wisconsin, and the following year they produced the world's first 4x4 commercial vehicle, a 7-ton forward control truck appropriately named 'Mogul'.

A further landmark in 4x4 development also took place in 1903. At the Paris Show that year, Jacob Spijker of Trompenburg, Amsterdam, exhibited the world's first four-wheel-drive motorcar with an internal combustion engine, which he intended entering in the 1903 Paris-Madrid race. The car's '50 HP', 8.7-litre power plant incorporated six cylinders – another world first. As well as permanent four-wheel-drive, it boasted a three-speed gearbox that could be operated in high or low ratio range. The propeller shafts were also offset from the centre-line, with a transmission brake on the front shaft to give four-wheel braking, a further feature not found on any other motor car at that time.

Spijker's car appeared at several motor shows, including the London Show at Crystal Palace in 1904, where it gained considerable publicity by climbing the steps of the main hall. Spijker planned to export his car to the Dutch East Indies where his firm (Holland's only motor manufacturer until the advent of DAF in 1957) was already sending trucks. But with a price tag of almost £1,000 it was unlikely to be a commercial success. He changed the name to 'Spyker' for the benefit of the English in 1903 – the Elsworth Automobile Co. Bradford, having contracted to take the entire output of Spijker's more conventional cars for the next three years – but the name change did little for sales.

Nevertheless, Spijker's car did manage to strike an invidious blow at the heart of Britain's embryonic motor industry, when in 1906 it became the only competitor to successfully complete the hill climb held by the Birmingham Car Club in exceptionally muddy conditions, and conclusively proved the worth of four-wheel-drive. No further 6-cyl. 4x4 Spykers were ever built, but a handful of 4-cyl. models went to the East Indies. Spijker's ideas were simply too far ahead of their time. His original car, now the only surviving example, is still in Holland today.

The first attempts to produce an armoured car also took place around this time, but were based on two-wheel-drive. Consequently they were incapable of travelling on really rough terrain. Possibly as a direct result of Spijker's ideas, Captain von Tiaskal-Hochwall of Austria designed the first purpose-built 4x4 armoured car which Paul Daimler built at Weiner-Neustadt in 1903, and followed it up with an artillery tractor built by Magyar Vagones Gepgyer. He demonstrated the armoured car to the Austro-Hungarian Emperor, Franz Josef, the following year. This was very much the era of 'pomp and circumstance', and when a nearby general's steed took fright, throwing him to the ground, all hopes of what promised to be a lucrative contract abruptly came to a close. It did not, however, deter Archduke Leopold Salvator Habsburg-Lothringen, Inspector of the Artillery, from also designing a 4x4 artillery tractor which was built in 1905. Other 4x4 tractor designs followed, including two from Porsche, most of which were built by Austro-Daimler.

In Germany, Kaiser Wilhelm was somewhat more enlightened and, following Britain's example, a German Volunteer Motor Corp was set up in 1905. Two years later, Mercedes produced a 4x4 six-seater car for the Reichskolonialamt which was used in German South West Africa.

During the Second Boar War (1899–1902), the British successfully employed both steam (Fowler B5) and internal combustion engine vehicles. This gave them great confidence in the new internal combustion engine and they set up a Mechanical Transport Committee to organise competitive trials

INTRODUCTION – 4x4 : An Opening Door

in 1901. Despite four of the five entrants being steam powered (and taking the prizes), the potential of the internal combustion engine over steam was fully appreciated, and an MT Company was set up at Woolwich. However, when David Roberts demonstrated his design for a petrol-engined moving track vehicle to the War Office in 1907, little interest was shown, although such machines were eventually to determine the outcome of the First World War.

A major step forward was then taken in 1911 when the Secretary for War surprised Britain's Parliament by announcing that horses were to be replaced by mechanised transport on a grand scale. But things moved too slowly to stop Ruston Hornsby & Sons from selling their patent on David Roberts' moving track vehicle to an American concern, Holts, in 1912 (see below).

Further initiative was shown by the British War Office with the introduction of the 'Subsidy' scheme in 1913. This offered a retainer to any commercial operator enlisting a suitable vehicle, and for a relatively small initial outlay, thousands of vehicles became potentially available for use in an emergency. Then in 1923, at their HQ in Aldershot, the Royal Army Service Corps constructed a 'Haithi' (Elephant) artillery tractor from a captured German Daimler, and Ehrhardt 4x4 vehicles. A further 24 examples were then subsequently assembled by Thornycroft in 1924, together with some later Italian Pavesi artillery tractors built under licence by Armstrong Siddley in 1927/9. But despite such innovative thinking the British actually made no attempt to develop any 4x4 vehicles of their own design for a quarter of a century, until just prior to the Second World War.

Across the Atlantic it was an entirely different story. In 1908, Otto Zachow of the Four Wheel Drive Auto Company, Clintonville, Wisconsin, produced a similar car to Spijker, called 'Badger'. There was no volume production, but the US Army was also starting to look for a mechanical alternative to the horse-drawn covered wagon. Prior to 1910 there was no co-ordinated transport policy, but in 1912 Capt. A.E. Williams of the Q.M.C. decided to run competitive trials with Zachow's vehicle against conventional two-wheel-drive trucks.

Five trucks were entered, but only three completed the arduous 1,500 mile drive from Fort Washington DC to Fort Benjamin Harrison in Indiana. The Badger's performance was outstanding and led directly to the development of a 4x4 truck for military use – the famous 'FWD' – and by mid-1914 the US Army possessed 35 trucks and 17 cars. These numbers almost doubled by the end of the year.

Once applied to military trucks, four-wheel-drive vehicles began to make considerable headway and were used in Gen. 'Jack' Pershing's Campaign against 'Pancho Villa', in New Mexico in 1916, and also the 'Great War' of 1914–18. By the end of the First World War, 12,500 of the 16,000 FWD trucks manufactured (many under licence) had arrived in Europe, and were nicknamed 'Flirt With Death' by the troops. A further 700 FWD trucks were made in England by the 'British Four Wheel Drive Tractor Lorry Super Engineering Company Limited'. Another numerous American 4x4 vehicle to arrive in Europe by the thousand was the 'Quad' lorry, manufactured by Thomas B. Jeffery Co. of Kenosha, Wisconsin. Many Quads were armoured and also had four-wheel steering, as did the French 'Latil' 4x4 artillery tractor.

Staff Captain Pavlavko of the Imperial Russian Army saw the potential of these vehicles and turned a number of them into armoured cars – the first 4x4 armoured cars to go into production. Thirty Pavlavko-Jefferys were ordered by the British War Ministry in 1916, and a number of similar armoured 'Quads' built by the Canadians were also used by the British for security operations in both Ireland and India during the 1920s. The German Army built three experimental 4x4 armoured cars based on the Daimler BAK-Wagen, and Bussing, and Ehrhardt chassis, which were completed by 1915. A further 32 Ehrhardts followed by 1917.

To combat the severe winters in Imperial Russia, in 1910 the Tsar's chief automobile engineer, Adolphe Kegresse, devised a new vehicle with tracks at the rear. Just before the Bolshevik Revolution of October 1917, Colonel Gulkievich started using Kegresse's track system on Russian Army vehicles, and during the civil war these proved far superior to any wheeled vehicle of the time. But by that time, Kegresse himself had already prudently returned to France, where he joined Citroën. The new Red Army, however, continued converting British Austin and American Packard vehicles to his half-track system.

The First World War certainly highlighted the need for military vehicles capable of traversing the most arduous terrain and, as head of Britain's Royal Naval Air Service, Winston Churchill insisted on having a vehicle capable of bridging the trenches. In February 1915 trials took place using various track systems, including a Holts tractor, but without success. Churchill, however, was determined it should be done and took personal responsibility for the expenditure of £70,000 on the 'landship' project. This resulted in the development of a new 'Tritton' track system to solve the problem. The first landship, the 'Tritton Machine' (or 'Little Willie', as it was more popularly known) was completed in December 1915. The world's first armoured 'Tank' had now been born.

The superiority of tracked vehicles during the First World War persuaded the American, J.F. Livingstone of New Virginia, to convert a number of Dodge trucks and Ford 'Model T' cars to half-track. Interest was further stimulated when between December 1922 and January 1923, a number of Citroën vehicles fitted with the Kegresse system made the first vehicular crossing of the notorious Sahara Desert. Citroën followed this up with a Central African Expedition (Croisiere Noire) between October 1924 and June 1925.

Trial demonstrations arranged for the British Army in 1924, only served to confirm the superiority of the half-track system over conventional wheeled vehicles when confronted with marshland and bog. To all intents and purposes four-wheel-drive had been stopped dead in its tracks as the major powers – Britain, France, Germany, Japan, Russia, and the USA – all began using half-tracks for military purposes. In Britain, Crossley and Burford used the original Kegresse system, but Lt-Col Henry Johnson, who had been involved with tank track development from 1915, registered his own Roadless Traction Company Ltd. in March 1918. He then began work on his own track system and in 1923 acquired premises in Hounslow, Middlesex, for production. His half-track design, known as 'E-tracks', was used on FWD, AEC, Guy, Morris Commercial and Morris Mantel vehicles.

By the mid-1930s the tide again began to turn once it was realised that size and weight can be a distinct disadvantage when it comes to general cross-country performance. Attention now began to focus away from military heavyweights to smaller vehicles for use as field-tractors, personnel and cargo carriers, ambulances, command cars, etc. and four-wheel-drive again became an attractive option. Even Massey-Harris' first agricultural tractor, the General Purpose of 1932, would be given four-wheel-drive.

General improvements in the transmission, such as true constant velocity drive joints (in the mid-1920s, 'Tracta' and 'Rzeppa' c.v. joints became available) made all-wheel-drive vehicles more acceptable to the British War Office. Even more to the point, compared to half-tracks, they were finding favour on grounds of cost and ease of maintenance, as opposed to outright cross-country performance. The ever-increasing number of good highways in Europe also gave a strong advantage to the wheeled vehicle. The first of this 'new breed' to enter service in the UK was the British Meadows powered 'Quad-Ant' artillery tractor in 1938. It was based on the Guy 15-cwt chassis, and was soon followed by the Morris Commercial C8 Mk1.

As early as 1924, the US War Department made a recommendation that a class of light vehicle weighing not more than 900 lbs, with a carrying capacity of 450 lbs, for *"...cross-country work of a general military nature"* should be introduced. Prior to 1920 the US did have an enormous number of 4x4 medium trucks, and by the early 1930s the US Army itself had managed to accumulate over 17,000 vehicles. The trouble was, more than 16,500 of them were now well over 10 years old. From 1 January 1935, Congress forbade all further expenditure on repairs to all pre-1920 military vehicles, providing the necessary impetus for a complete re-think of US military vehicle requirements.

The first serious attempt at a new 4x4 US Army vehicle was carried out in 1937 by a civilian firm, Mermon-Herrington of Indianapolis, using Ford 1/2-ton trucks, which they converted to 4x4. Type named 'LD-1', a year later 64 of these vehicles entered service with the US Army. The production model, however, was based on the Dodge T202 4x4 chassis, and designated 'LD1-4'. This quickly paved the way for a wide range of new 4x4s in the 1/2 to 3/4-ton category from familiar names such as Dodge, Chevrolet, and International.

The exceptionally low profile of the original 'LD-1', or 'Darling', as it became known, gives it pride of place as the true ancestor of the ubiquitous US Jeep. At the same time as Mermon-Harrington began experimenting with 4x4, Col. Robert G. Howie designed a low silhouette MG carrier, which was constructed by Master Sergeant Melvin C. Wiley, using an American Austin engine. It became known as the 'Belly Flopper'.

By 1938, under the 'Schell Programme', Germany began rationalising her military vehicles into four main categories, the smallest of which was 1500 kg (30-cwt). The US War Dept. followed suit the following year, grouping their vehicles into

INTRODUCTION – 4x4 : An Opening Door

five categories, with the smallest at 1/2-ton (500 kg). The requirements for a light cross-country vehicle did not stop there, and further specifications were quickly drawn up for an even lighter 1/4-ton 'Command Reconnaissance' 4x4 low profile forward area vehicle that could be physically manhandled by its crew out of the worst situations.

Only two US car manufacturers, Willys-Overland and Bantam, accepted the challenge. But even Willys confessed that they had grave doubts about meeting the 49-day deadline. Bantam, under their previous name of 'American Austin' had already produced a field car in 1933, based on a modified 'Midget Truck' chassis and were not, therefore, entirely unfamiliar with military vehicles. By mid-September 1940 they came up with the 'Bantam 40 BRC', and this became the immediate forerunner of both Willys' MB and Ford's GPW Jeeps. Even so, the US War Dept. was a long way from being first in this field.

As early as 1935, Nippon Nainenki Seiko of Japan produced the first pre-war 4x4 scout cars on a 2-metre (78 in.) chassis using a 1.4-litre V-twin air-cooled engine. Originally available as a two-seater 'doctor's coupé', it was developed into the three-seater scout car known as the 'Kurogane' type 95 'Black Medal' 4x4 car and also a light pick-up truck. Mitsubishi and Isuzu also produced 4x4 command cars in 1938.

Germany also had two light 4x4 cars. The Tempo G1200, was a private venture from Vidal & Sohn in 1936, and used a separate engine for each axle. It sold well for military use to some 40 countries. Then from 1938, BMW, Hanomag and Stoewer all produced the Wehrmacht standard specification 'Kdz 1'.

Britain had nothing herself when in May 1937, a prototype Czech Tatra V750 entered the British Army field-trials at Trawsfynydd, the Army's proving ground in North Wales. Then in October 1938, two British light reconnaissance cars became contenders in the North Wales trials – an Alvis 'Dingo', powered by a 12/70 1.8-litre 4-cyl. engine, and a much heavier Daimler 2.5-litre 'six', both vehicles developing 62 bhp.

Although heavy, slow, and expensive, Daimler's vehicle proved more stable on inclines and was subsequently adopted by the British Army, though ironically, Daimler adopted the Alvis name, 'Dingo' ('Rhino' would probably have been more appropriate). An unusual feature of the Daimler was its use of four propeller shafts, one to each wheel, all driven from a centrally located gearbox. Humber also developed a 4x4 light reconnaissance car, based on an 8-cwt. chassis and sporting independent front suspension. This was used in Britain from 1941.

By 1939, in Germany, the Auto Union/Horch V8, Kfz 15, had become the standard command car. Like the Jeep, it relied on a second source of manufacture, in this case Opel, to increase output and reduce the effect of sabotage. Russia entered the field slightly later, but having been supplied with the original Bantam 40 BRC early in the war, used these to develop her own GAZ 67B field car in 1943.

Certainly by the time the war came to its final conclusion in September 1945, there was a proliferation of light field cars in use by the various belligerent powers. Nevertheless, drive to all four wheels was not entirely the prerogative of the military and commercial truck. Ettore Bugatti in France and Harry Miller in the USA had both built four-wheel-drive racing cars, with some measure of success. Bugatti's 'Type 53' hill climb car took the record at La Turbie in 1932 and 1934, while Harry Miller broke international records at Bonneville Salt Flats. Then after the war in 1947, Piero Dusio commissioned Porsche to design a 1.5-litre supercharged rear-engined GP car using four-wheel-drive, which he called Cistalia, but sadly the money ran out and it never actually raced.

The greatest achievement in this field, however, goes to the Englishman, Reid Railton. Commissioned by wealthy fur broker John Cobb, Railton's car used two 24-litre Napier aero-engines centrally off-set, and facing for-and-aft, in this enormous beautifully streamlined 4x4. As the 'Railton-Mobile Special', Cobb took the World Land Speed Record on no less than three occasions – 1938, 1939, and then again after the war in 1947, exceeding 400 mph on the return run on this final occasion. Cobb's record stood for an unprecedented 17 years. With the coming of age of jet propulsion, it would be the last time the W.L.S.R. went to a piston-engined vehicle.

Between them, Railton and Cobb pushed British motor vehicle technology to the forefront of the world. It only remained for British car manufacturers to do the same for the rest of Britain's motor industry. With gas turbine engine development, 'Quality First' motorcars, Meteor and Meteorite military engines, and their four-wheel-drive Land-Rovers, the Rover Co. was certainly about to play its part.

CHAPTER 1
Post-war Austerity
'Export or Bust'

Reconstruction of the tale that launched a motoring legend would be incomplete without consideration of the economic situation this island nation of people, the British, encountered in the aftermath of the Second World War. Needs must when the devil drives. The difficult days that followed would force those responsible for Rover's future prosperity to rethink the company's entire strategy. They would have to come to terms with the harsh reality that it might no longer lay with that for which they were now so well established – motor cars for England's middle classes – at least, not for the time being. But where, they had to ask themselves, *should* it lie?

The cost of this global conflict had totally demolished Britain's currency reserves. In September 1945 dollar debts for goods received from the United States stood around £5,000 million net, and by 1946, payments were already in deficit to the tune of £650 million. At the same time, overseas expenditure had risen to $300 million, but invisible earnings remained at their pre-war level. Britain was broke. On 15 July 1946, US President Harry Truman signed a credit agreement with Britain for $4,400,000,000 of which $600,000,000 had been drawn by the end of the year. All this debt was only finally paid off to the US 60 years later, in January 2007.

In an attempt to reduce the burden of imports, the pound sterling had been deliberately overvalued at $4.0, but as every British industrialist knows, such policy only serves to make export targets more difficult to achieve. The dollar crises and associated problems of obtaining foreign exchange, meant not only cuts in food imports, but all other goods as well. Wartime austerity would continue to rule the day for the foreseeable future.

In 1946 the British Iron and Steel federation reported to the Ministry of Supply with its plans for reconstruction. War-worn industry was to be re-equipped over the next five to seven years, with steel output to be increased by over 30% during the period. But with all imports now severely restricted, every attempt had to be made to substitute 'home-produced' goods for imported materials. As there were precious few substitutes for iron ore, the whole of Britain's industry became dependent on scrap for its steel.

While traditional exports went into decline in the inter-war years, the motor industry had flourished, redressing any imbalance in trade, and in the documents submitted to the War Cabinet's Reconstruction Committee it was clearly recognised as *'...one of the most prosperous and successful of our industries'*. Led by Lord Woolton, the Ministry for Reconstruction now firmly believed Britain's motor industry held the key to Britain's future economic prosperity through the export of motor cars. In response to these beliefs, the Minister of Economic Affairs, Sir Stafford Cripps, gave a hard hitting message to Britain's motor manufacturers – *'Export or Bust.'*

There would be no compromise. The Board of Trade stipulated that only motor manufacturer's able to export 50% of their output would now receive any further allocations of steel. From now on exports alone were to determine each individual motor manufacturer's allocation of steel with which to build the cars they hoped would take them into the second half of the 20th Century. For Rover, this news was bad enough – but worse was still to come.

In 1947 Britain's gold and dollar deficit plummeted to an all-time low of more than a billion. A looming adverse balance of payments (the difference between import and export earnings) – reported to be £675 million, though corrected figures give £381 million – caused the government to decide in late 1947 that only motor manufacturers exporting 75% of their output would continue to qualify. This decision was officially announced in February 1948 by George Strauss, the Minister for Supply, in Birmingham, the heart of Britain's motor industry. It was certainly scant reward for the motor industry's superb effort during those dark war years, and seemed a far cry from the praises given less than four months earlier by the self-same minister in the 'Autocar', 28 November 1947, when he stated that *'...the magnificent efforts of the motor industry are fully appreciated'*.

Maurice Wilks (MCW)

CHAPTER 1 – Post-war Austerity – 'Export or Bust'

Although 'Purchase Tax' had been introduced in October 1940, it was a time when no cars were being produced in Britain. With a rate set at $33^1/_3\%$, by 1945 its impact on new cars was suddenly realised. In 1940 Rover's popular 12 HP 'six-light' saloon cost £300, but in 1946 it cost £646 inclusive of Purchase Tax. In just six years car prices had more than doubled. And worse was to come. Chancellor Hugh Dalton's last budget of November 1947, announced that anything with a basic price tag of over £1,000 would be viewed as unnecessary 'luxury goods' and pay a double Purchase Tax rate of $66^2/_3\%$. The pressure was now on all Britain's quality car makers to keep their basic prices below £999.

Rover, now well established as a manufacturer of motor cars for the middle classes, was in a particularly ominous situation. They had returned to car production in October 1945, and new cars began leaving the factory in January 1946, but from the range of models being produced, it was hard to believe six years of war had ever intervened. Output was initially very slow – just six cars per day – hardly enough to generate sufficient income to pay both Rover's workforce and Rover's component suppliers.[1] By June output reached 20 cars a day, but not until the beginning of 1947 was a respectable production rate of 200 units a week finally reached.

In this transition from manufacturing aircraft components 'for the Duration', to motor cars 'for the Peace', there had been little time to produce a new model specifically designed for the export market. That was Rover's big problem. An 'Export Department' had been set up in 1945 – the first in the company's long history – and a number of cars were provided with left hand drive (LHD),[2] but the only model to make any progress in this direction was a pretty little sports tourer based on the P2 'Twelve', 200 of which were made in 1947. Quite simply, it wasn't enough. An entirely new model was needed for export, but at the same time Rover still had to consider the future needs of the home economy, if they were also to retain their share of that market.

In the meantime their competitors had been turning to agricultural vehicles to solve the problem. Both were areas where Rover had precious little experience.

Rover's problems now lay squarely on the shoulders of Spencer Bernau (SB) Wilks, Rover's Managing Director, and his younger brother Maurice Fernand Cary Wilks (MCW), their technical man. Born in 1891 in Rickmansworth, Hertfordshire, and educated at Charterhouse, Spencer Wilks trained as a lawyer between 1909 and 1914 and then served as a Captain in the Great War. There he met a young ambulance driver who just happened to be one of bicycle millionaire William Hillman's six daughters. They married, and SB soon found himself working for Hillman's car concern. His brother Maurice was born in 1904 and educated at Malvern College. Spencer had always shown a caring paternalistic attitude towards his younger brother, and despite a 13 year age gap, the two remained close friends. It seemed almost natural that Maurice should now join him at Hillman.

At the time of William Hillman's death in 1926, Spencer Wilks had become joint MD with his brother-in-law, Captain John Black, who had also married one of Hillman's daughters. Maurice Wilks had the title 'Planning Engineer' at Hillman. But what seemed like an idyllic situation was all too soon to change. The Maidstone car dealers, Rootes Ltd., had prospered in the hands of the two brothers William and Reginald Rootes, and were now Britain's largest car distributor. Not content with that, the company was clearly on the prowl for an actual car manufacturer. Abortive attempts had already been made to take over, first Standard, in 1924, and then Clyno, in 1927. Having already acquired Humber's export distribution network, with the financial backing of Sir George May from the Prudential, they gradually increased their ordinary shareholding, until, in 1928, they had a controlling interest.

William Rootes immediately took over as Deputy Chairman and Reginald became Managing Director. They straightaway increased the company's capital and now made a successful bid for Humber's next-door neighbour – Hillman. Had the two brothers only wanted financial control, things might have been different, but when they took on the day-to-day running of Hillman, both SB and John Black knew it was time to go.

As luck would have it, that very same year,1928, the Rover Company found itself in a financial crisis, losing £2,000 a week (sounds reminiscent of more recent history). Lloyds Bank pegged their overdraft at £235,000, and advised Rover's two main creditors, Lucas and Pressed Steel, to insist on an independent financial advisor being appointed to the Board from the Birmingham firm of accountants, Messrs. Gibson & Ashford. Howe Graham, one of the firm's partners, was appointed to the new position of Financial Advisor.

After an unsatisfactory shareholder's meeting, Colonel W.F. Wyley, Chairman since 1909, resigned, and the largest shareholder, W.E. Sudbury,

---

[1] *In 1946, on average, 2/3rds of car costs were for bought-in components (National Advisory Council for the Motor Manufacturing Industry).*

[2] *Several 1946–7 P2 LHD saloon cars survive in Belgium and Norway.*

CHAPTER 1 – Post-war Austerity – 'Export or Bust'

took over. On the recommendation of Sir Alfred May-Smith, an influential member of the Board, Sudbury appointed an outsider, an ex-Tank Corps Colonel, Frank Searle, as Rover's MD. Almost immediately, Searle recommended Captain Spencer Wilks join Rover as General Manager, a position accepted by SB on 3 September 1929. It would not be long before SB's colleagues at Hillman – brother Maurice, Robert Boyle, Geoffrey Savage, and Jess Worcester – all followed, and when E. Ransom Harrison was appointed Chairman 18 months later in April 1931, the corner stones for Rover's long-term future were virtually now all in place.

Colonel Searle then set up a 'Secret Projects Department' in a well-equipped workshop at Braunstone Hall, his home near Rugby. Together with Robert Boyle and Maurice Wilks, a small economy car called the 'Scarab', was developed using a rear mounted 839cc o.h.v. air-cooled V-twin engine. Searle saw Rover's future in quantity production and hoped the Scarab would be the solution to the company's financial problems. On the 25 September 1931, it was *'...resolved that the 7 HP car should be exhibited at Olympia with a list price of £89'.*

Things, however, were soon to take an entirely different turn. Towards the end of 1931, Col. Searle failed to return from a trip to Rover's recently opened new factory in New Zealand. It appears that Sudbury was suing Searle for 'slanderous' statements. During Searle's prolonged absence Spencer Wilks remained in charge of the day-to-day running of Rover and was given twelve months in which to prove himself. He was officially appointed as Rover's Managing Director in January 1933.

SB's philosophy was completely different from Searle's. In the wake of a depression he saw Rover's hopes not in a small car of quantity, challenging the likes of Herbert Austin and his well-established 'Seven', or William Morris' recently introduced o.h.c. 'Minor', along with its highly successful sporting derivative, the MG J2 'Midget'. That would be financial suicide. No, what Rover needed was a *'Car of Quality'*, specifically aimed at England's middle classes – a gap previously filled by Humber. That was where SB saw Rover's future, and in Searle's continued absence, SB cancelled the Scarab project. It was a decision that would not only save Rover from extinction, but at the same time, pave the way for the company's long-term future.

As early as August 1932 SB began to implement changes at Rover, and soon 'four-speed' gearboxes replaced earlier three-speed boxes and the 'Freewheel' device, introduced for smoother gear changes and fuel economy. Engines and gearboxes were now rubber mounted, and Moss Gear Co. spiral bevel drives replaced worm final drives. From now on, six-cylinder cars also got greater priority. SB also implemented the rationalisation of under-utilised premises, selling off the original Rover factory, the 'Meteor Works' in Queen Victoria Road, Coventry, concentrating all work in their Tyseley, Birmingham and Helen Street, Coventry premises. Following these changes, a loss of around £80,000 at the end of 1931, had already been changed into a profit of £7,511 by the end of 1933.

By 1935/6 Rover was building over 8,000 cars a year – more than double the number of cars (3,766) made in 1928, the year before SB joined Rover. He was now on a salary of £10,000 a year, plus commission. To everyone's delight, demand for Rover's cars continued to exceed production and by the time war broke out in September 1939, yearly output was in excess of 11,000 cars, providing Rover with a healthy annual profit of more than £200,000.

With 'VE' day almost in sight, on 18 January 1945 the Wilks brothers advised the Board that when the company did return to car production, there should be an immediate expansion in output, *'...and that to achieve this we should not look primarily to our pre-war models, but that we should add to our range by the introduction of a 6 HP model'.*

This was based on the expectation that after the war, petrol would continue to remain in short supply for the foreseeable future,[3] and under these circumstances, it was concluded that an economy car might now not be such a bad idea.

On the night of 14/15 November 1940, Rover's Helen Street premises were severely damaged in the horrendous air raids on Coventry. All design work was subsequently moved to the ballroom of the Chesford Grange Hotel just outside Kenilworth, in Warwickshire. It was in these rather salubrious surroundings that Gordon Bashford, who originally joined Rover as a schoolboy apprentice in 1930, began work on the new miniature, code-named 'M1'.

Many of Rover's post-war concepts would be embodied in the M1 project: light alloy bodywork; full-width styling;[4] and a new i.o.e. (overhead inlet, and side exhaust valves) engine. The new 699cc power unit was the brainchild of Jack Swaine, and had the unusual arrangement of a cylinder head inclined

---

[3] *Confirmed on 8 April, 1948, when Hugh Gaitskell, Minister for Fuel and Power, informed Parliament the basic ration, about 90 miles per month, would be cut as a result of a Balance of Payments deficit the previous year.*

[4] *Something Rover failed to get right for their first new post-war production model, the P3, announced in early 1948, and which consequently perpetuated the use of the old pre-war P2 body style until the advent of the P4 'Rover 75' introduced in the Autumn of 1950.*

to the block at 22°, with the combustion chamber situated in the crown of the piston. The engine's design combined excellent breathing, enabling low-octane fuels such as post-war 'pool' petrol, to be used at relatively high compression ratios – and was clearly a forerunner of today's modern lean burn engines. Rover used this design for more than 30 years, the origin of which is quite entertaining, and goes back to the 1930s when MCW was keen to replace the current P1 car engines with a more powerful unit of 'V' formation.

When Robert Boyle left Rover to join Morris in 1934 (he would return later), a young engineer by the name of Jack Swaine joined Rover as MCW's new assistant and was put in charge of the engine's development. After toying with the idea of a 60° V8 he eventually settled for a 90° V6. It was a good design, but as it was not intended that P2 bodywork should be revised at this particular point in time (cars and engines were rarely developed simultaneously into a production model during the 30 years of the Wilks brothers stewardship of Rover), any new engine would have to fit within the confines of the current P2's narrow side-opening bonnet. Under these circumstances it was decided a 'straight' six was what was needed. But Jack Swaine's new V6 i.o.e. design was simply too good to be discarded.

The 90° V6 engine's cylinder heads were inclined at 22° to the block. It has been written that this was to do with keeping the engine width down so as to fit within the confines of the Rover car's narrow bonnet. In his reply to a letter from this author, published in the Rover Sports Register newsletter ('Freewheel', April 1991), Jack Swaine points out that *"The inclination of the head face to the cylinder axes was dictated to the design of the combustion chamber"*. This makes more sense. The wide 90° 'V' meant the camshaft could be located in the base of the V, with inlet valves in the head activated by push rods, while exhaust valves remained down in the block. The former could then be almost unrestricted in size, giving the engine excellent breathing and enabling a relatively high-compression ratio to be used with existing pre-war fuels.

Jack Swaine immediately began working on a new in-line design of his 'sloping head' engine, based on just one side of the 'V'. This latest design was filed with the British Patent Office on 10 January 1939. Eight months later it was registered with the US Patent Office on 5 September 1939 – just two days after Prime Minister Neville Chamberlain declaration that Britain *"...is at war with Germany"*. It is on official record that *"...4-cylinder versions were on the test bed and running before the outbreak of war"* but would now have to wait in the wings. Whenever car production resumed, it was intended that Jack Swaine's in-line engine's design should be used in whatever new cars Rover had planned for brighter days ahead. To this end, a 'sloping head' engine of *"...around 1.2-litres..."* was run throughout the war in a 'Rover 10' car, and is purported to have covered over 100,000 miles.

Although the sloping head and piston crown were unusual, the idea of an i.o.e. or 'F-head' engine, as it was more generally known, was not new. Humber, next door to Hillman, where the Wilks brothers had worked, built their reputation for quality on an i.o.e. engine first introduced in 1923, and only dropped in 1932 under Rootes' programme of 'badge engineering'. Even the last 'WO' Bentley, the 4-litre 'six', dating from 1931, had a Ricardo-inspired i.o.e. configuration. After Rolls-Royce's acquisition of Bentley, Jack Phillips, at their Crewe factory, also embarked on the development of an i.o.e. 'F-head' engine in 1935, based on the Bentley design, to replace the troublesome Rolls-Royce V8. This engine was up and running by 1938, with four-, six-, and eight-cylinder versions all developed before the outbreak of war. (Ironically, after the war, the 'four' found its

First P2 car to be powered with new P3 'Rover 60' engine, registered 'GAC 915' on 2 October 1947

1946 'M1' car prototype, 'FNX 799'

CHAPTER 1 – Post-war Austerity – 'Export or Bust'

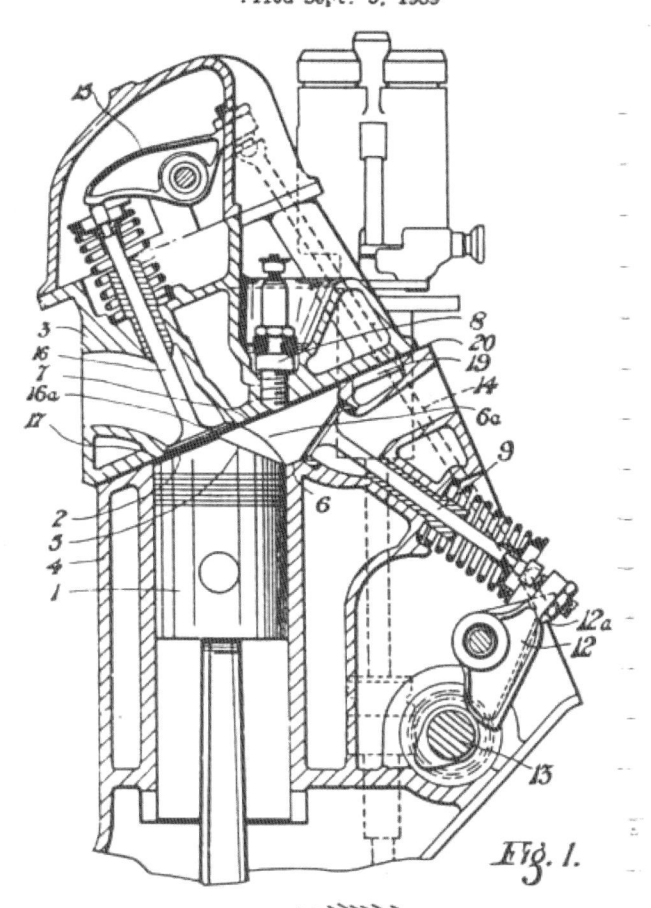

i.o.e. engine patent filed 5 Sept 1939

699cc i.o.e M1 engine

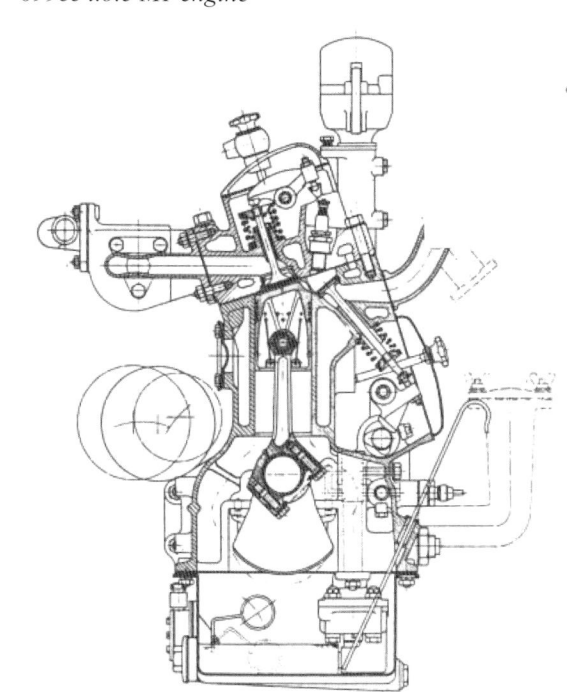

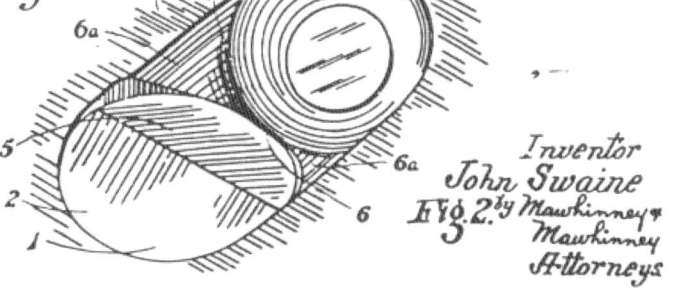

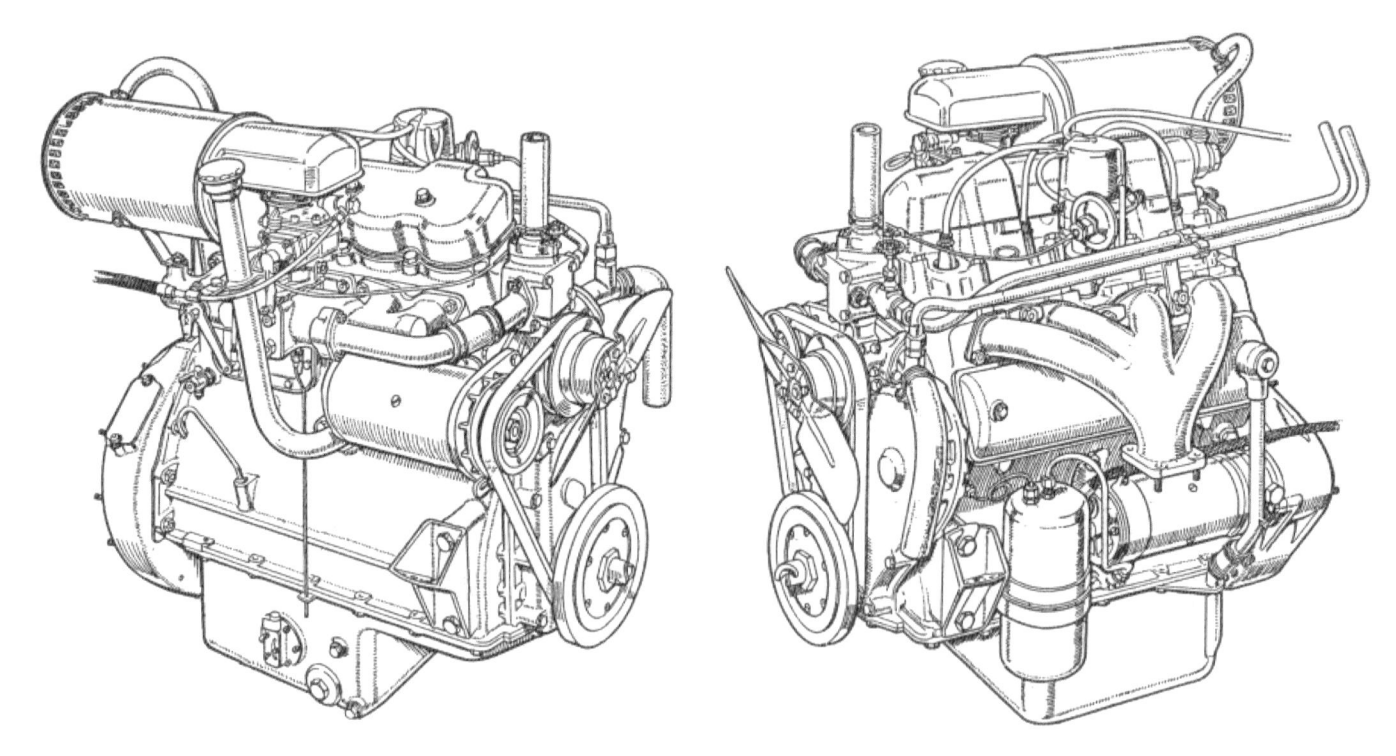

1948 P3 'Rover 60' car engine

'P3' Rover 60' engine as installed in the 1948 Land-Rover

way into 33 Ministry Land-Rovers,[5] though in this writer's opinion, Rover's, or perhaps I should say, Jack Swaine's, i.o.e. engine was of superior design to the Rolls-Royce engine that now replaced it.)

Like the Scarab, Rover's 'M1' never went into production. As an additional model it was eventually considered inappropriate, as Rover's current allocation of steel was barely sufficient to build 1,100 units of the existing P2 model. There would also be the expense of tooling up, the M1 having little in common with any other design. The War Cabinet's Reconstruction Committee had also shown concern over the number of models being produced by Britain's motor industry before the war. They now firmly believed that if Britain's cars were to succeed in overseas markets, larger cars able to compete in the American market would need to be the order of the day. They also believed that a considerable degree of standardisation would be necessary in order to cut costs and give a competitive edge, particularly in the area of components and accessories. The component manufacturer, Joseph Lucas, was certainly behind them, and to make the point, arranged a special exhibition for journalists. In it were displayed: 133 different headlights ranging from the 12-inch 'King of the Road' all the way down to 5-inch tractor types; 98 variations in windscreen wiper units; and 68 different distributors.

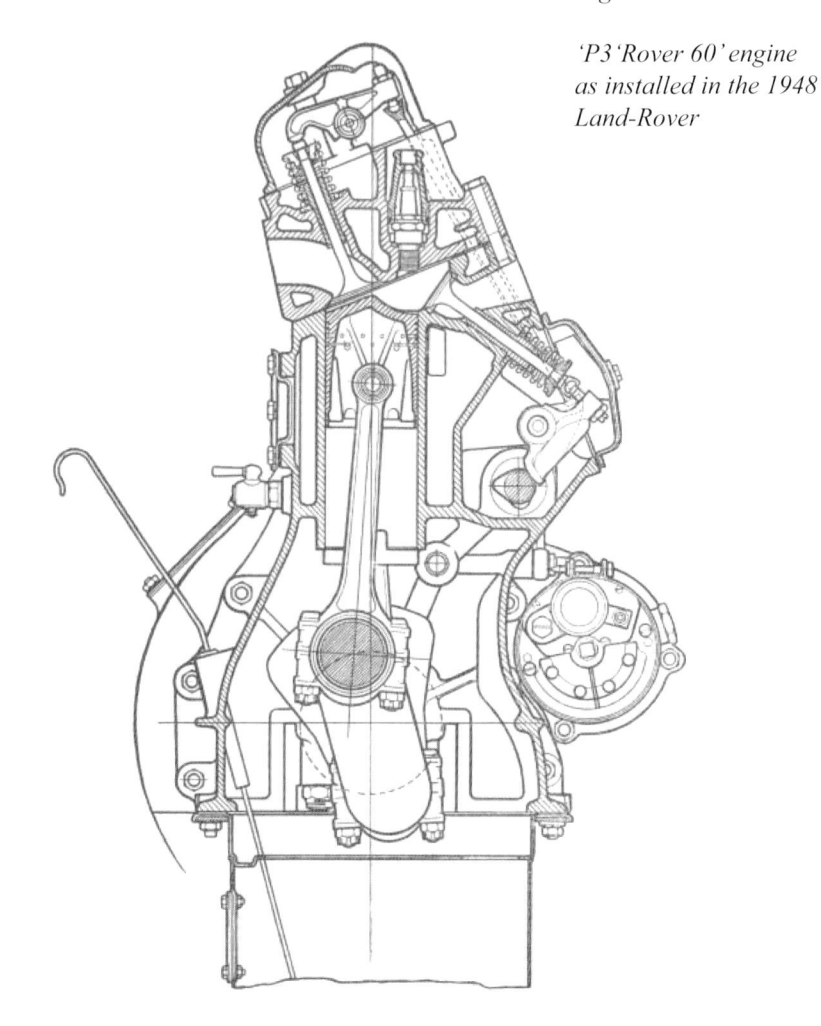

[5] *See Chapter 16*

CHAPTER 1 – Post-war Austerity – 'Export or Bust'

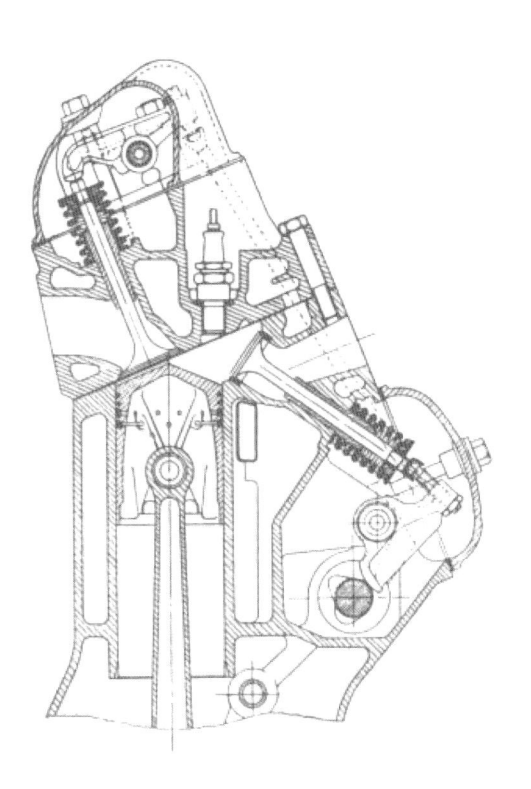

P3 i.o.e combustion chamber

Motor manufacturers themselves had shown little enthusiasm for either rationalisation or larger cars, though on the latter point the government had only themselves to blame, because the current Horse Power tax penalised larger engines. The Cabinet's final overall conclusion was that the motor industry was far too important to leave to the mercies of manufacturers, and what could not be achieved by co-operation would be done by compulsion.

Mr Wilmott, the Minister of Supply, made the official recommendation – *"One make, one model"*. Then on 4 February 1947 (officially confirmed four months later, on 4 June 1947), the government announced to the motor industry that it intended to restructure the Road Fund Licence (i.e. abolish the Horse Power tax altogether) from 1 January 1948. The M1 project's fate was sealed. As it stood, the Road Fund Licence penalised larger cars in the belief that the medium-sized car represented the demands of the export market. That had now changed.

Not long afterwards, Maurice Wilks expressed the overall situation in an interview with Harold Hastings, published in 'The Motor', 10 August 1949.

"First, we found that we could not get adequate supplies of steel for the planned production of the existing range, let alone for an additional model. Then there came the government call for rationalisation – you know, the one make one model cry – coupled with an official emphasis on medium sized cars in the belief that such models represented post-war requirements in the export field.

These political influences, backed by the changes in the taxation scale which took place, all tended to reduce the emphasis on the really small car. In the face of so many external influences, we reluctantly decided that the place which we had foreseen for the M1 in the post-war market would not materialise."

MCW was not alone in this assessment of the situation. W.A. Robotham, Rolls-Royce Chief Engineer, had also been developing a 'Junior' range, known as the 'Myth' project, and this too was abandoned in 1947.

CHAPTER 2
Middle Class, or Muck and Grass? Historic Day at Red Wharf Bay

By 1947, Britain's motor industry as a whole was well on the way to recovery, reaching the pre-war 1938 level of output of 445,000 vehicles by the end of the year. Any fall in car output had been made up by an increase in commercial vehicle output, and by the last quarter of 1947 vehicle exports had risen from 46% to 64% of total output, an increase of 40%. Out of a total of 287,236 cars produced, 140,691 – almost half – had gone overseas. Austin's new A40 Dorset and Devon models set the pace, with over 47,000 of the first 50,000 going abroad, mainly to America, and 20% of Abingdon's MG TC – which was nothing more than a slightly widened version of their pre-war TB – would also be destined to go to the USA between 1945 and 1949.

For the Rover Company, however, it was an entirely different story. Currently their future was now very much in the balance, and another 12 months would pass before they too could share in this success. It was during this uneasy period that the idea of a 'stop-gap' utility vehicle for agriculture and light industrial use slowly began to emerge. Various factors appear to have influenced the Wilks brothers' thinking in this direction.

A particular consequence of the war was a worldwide shortage of foodstuff. The County War Agricultural Executive Committee, set up by the government in 1940, was given the power to take over all waste land for cultivation, and planned an increase in food production of 50% to 60%. With government grants providing for 7 million acres (2.8 million hectares) of land to be reclaimed, upgraded, and improved for arable use – mainly for the production of grain, potatoes, sugar beet and milk – many farmers suddenly found their farms doubled in size over the next decade.

There was however, a serious shortage of labour. To solve the problem new machinery was to be introduced from North America under the United States' Lease-Lend Bill of March 1941. Suddenly, American tractors, such as the Allis-

Early 1947; Maurice Wilks uses his Jeep for snow clearance

CHAPTER 2 – Middle Class, or Muck and Grass? – Historic Day at Red Wharf Bay

MCW and Loyd carrier prepare to move trees

Chalmers' 'Model B', became a familiar sight on Britain's farms. In just six years Britain's tractor population increased four-fold from 50,000 in 1939 to 200,000 by the end of 1946. Such mechanisation also released a further three to four million acres of land previously used just to support the farmer's workhorse.

Of even more significance on the English landscape was the Massey-Harris self-propelled 'Combine Harvester' from Toronto in Canada. Since the turn of the century, Europe had depended on the Canadian prairies for much of her wheat. But Britain's present need was for self-sufficiency in food production. Her patchwork of small fields, remnant of a bygone age when man and horse ploughed but an acre a day, did not however lend themselves to wholesale mechanisation, and widespread uprooting of hedgerows now took place. A centuries-old traditional pattern of English farming was about to be obliterated from the landscape for ever.

Immediately after the war, Britain's agricultural harvest of 1946 was a complete disaster – the poorest and latest for more than thirty years. Even then it depended on German PoWs to supply a quarter of the necessary labour force. In April, Sir Ben Smith, Minister of Foods, was forced to resign, and despite bread never having been on ration during the war years, his successor John Strachey now implemented bread rationing, which came into force on 21 July.

The various measures of self-sufficiency and agricultural support introduced during the war years were extended and consolidated under a new 1947 Agricultural Act, and scientific mechanised farming became the order of the day. Farmers were encouraged to plant disease-free high-yield crops, use lime and nitrogenous fertilisers, and in return, receive guaranteed income from their crops. In under a decade British agriculture had undergone nothing short of a major revolution.

Interestingly, in a book entitled *'Farming Today and Tomorrow'* published in 1947, within the Chapter headed 'Transport' we find these prophetic words:

"Few farmers own all the necessary farm transport... The most pressing need is for an improvement in internal transport for carrying goods into and out of the farm premises. At present most of this work is done by horses or by tractors and trailers. The former are slow, expensive in labour and of limited endurance. The latter have none of these disadvantages, but there is a tendency to underload tractors, thus detracting from their usefulness...

"Wheel spin is bad for the wheels and the tractor engine, and may also be dangerous for the driver. There will be some difficulty if operating tractors for haulage during rainy seasons. Pneumatic tyres are almost essential for road work, but when the tractor leaves the road to cross the field or meadow these tyres may prove useless...

"What most farmers need is some kind of vehicle of dual-purpose character which can be used for road or field work, private and business needs. Something after the style of the American jeep would answer the purpose. Various modifications could make it more useful and weatherproof...

LAND-ROVER – The Formative Years, 1947–1967

May blossom at Blackdown

"This runabout could be used for taking small livestock to market or butcher, for all kinds of farm produce to merchant, market etc. or for taking members of the family on business journeys. When not needed for any of these purposes it could be used for various haulage work in and around the premises or to be hitched to a harrow, roll, grass-cutter, cultivator or even a small plough. With its manoeuvrability and its quickness the average farmer could, by its use, speed up and simplify much of his routine farm work and field work. The younger and more adaptable members of the family would find many new uses for such a vehicle."
(Michael Spurr, LRSOC Newsletter 23, 6/84)

During the 1930s Spencer Wilks purchased a charming old schoolhouse at Glenegedale on the Isle of Islay, part of the Inner Hebrides off the west coast of Scotland. He had the suspension of a P2 'Rover 10' car raised in order to travel across the island's rugged and untamed heathland terrain. This attracted the attention of a local keeper named Iain Fraser, who was not over-impressed, suggesting that what Mr Wilks really needed was *"...a proper 'land' Rover"*. So even pre-war, both the name and the general idea had been given at least some consideration.

After Rover handed over their gas turbine work and premises at Bankfield Shed, Barnoldswick, and Waterloo Mill, Clitheroe, to Rolls-Royce in July 1943, in exchange for production rights to the Rolls-Royce V12 Meteor tank engine, MCW returned to the Midlands and began the search for a new family home. He found Blackdown Manor sitting but a short distance along the road from Rover's wartime offices at the Chesford Grange Hotel. It was the ideal location.

MCW driving Loyd carrier at Blackdown Manor

If nothing else, history has taught us all too frequently that prevailing weather conditions can be the determinant of major events. And they are now about to play a major part in this particular story. In his book 'The Land-Rover. Workhorse of the World', published in 1976, Graham Robson states that *"Maurice Wilks sparked off the project in the spring of 1947"*. This gave some sort of authoritative confirmation to rumours already circulating among club enthusiasts by the late 1960s, concerning the Land-Rover's 'conception' date, and would be a useful starting point. But what evidence is there to support or refute this dating?

On 23 January 1947 snowfalls began that would last for 60 days, and were of a magnitude not experienced by these mild islands since January 1814. Snow drifts exceeded 15 feet in places, and

30

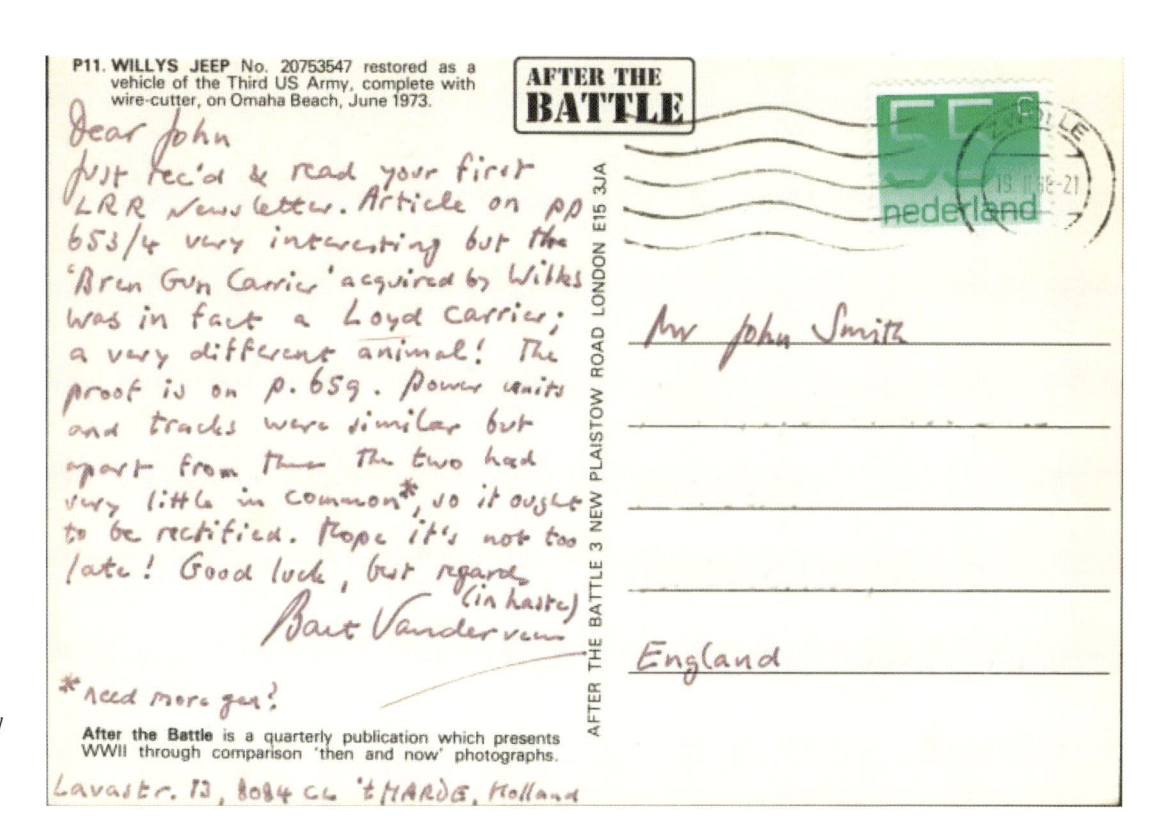

CHAPTER 2 – Middle Class, or Muck and Grass? – Historic Day at Red Wharf Bay

The late Bart Vanderveen's postcard to the author dated 19.11.1988

temperatures plummeted to as low as –21°C. For many areas of the UK, February was to become the coldest ever recorded. Eventually, on Wednesday, 5 March, this severe cold winter spell culminated in what became known as 'the great Midlands snowstorm', when 22 miles of the Great North Road, Britain's main artery of commercial activity, was blocked by continuous snowdrifts.

During this treacherous period, Maurice Wilks, and his wife Barbara, had been unable to drive their Rover P2 cars up the 500 yards of sloping driveway that lead up to Blackdown Manor, and so a war-surplus Willys Jeep was borrowed from Colonel Nash, at nearby Bericote Wood. The Jeep was then used to fill in between road and house. On the opposite side of Cuddington Road to Blackdown Manor, where a neighbour called Banon had a farm, Maurice Wilks' son Stephen still clearly remembers his dad skating on Banon's field, while the boys went sledging. Stephen also remembers it being b****y cold. With its four-wheel-drive and low-ratio gears, throughout this difficult time the Jeep proved an invaluable tool, and MCW attached an improvised blade to the front bumper to use it as a snowplough.

The Rover factory itself was forced to close down for two and a half weeks, and even when car production did eventually resume, output had to be cut for a further three weeks as a consequence of the resulting fuel crises. All this has been further corroborated in a letter dated 10/3/47, that Land-Rover Register committee member Chris Goodyear turned up in an old Rover Car handbook.

The letter is handwritten by well-known Rover employee Alec Joyce, interestingly from his home address, 97a Warwick Road, Kenilworth, and is addressed to 'Dr Neighbour'. The letter informs Dr Neighbour that *"The works are only working 3 days per week…"* and this is why he is having to wait for his new Rover 14 HP, which was soon to be delivered through Rover's agent, Anna Valley Motors (Salisbury). Mr Joyce goes on to say that he is looking forward to seeing Dr Neighbour and his wife at the works. How different things were in those days.

But snow was not the only hazard the country had to contend with that year. On Sunday 16 March 1947 *"A widespread and severe gale occurred in England and Wales"*, with gusts from the south-west reaching 98 mph. According to MET office records, the Midlands weather station at Honiley, just three miles west of Kenilworth, recorded a 'Force 9' at 18.00 GMT, and was only exceeded by a 'Force 10' at Exeter. The south-westerly gales that began on 16 March continued until 24 March, and were accompanied by a rise in temperature, and torrential rainfall. By 21 March, almost all snow had disappeared. The rise in temperature, peaked on 28 and 29 March to a maximum of 12.2°C, and was accompanied by 13 mm of rain on 29 March. The equinoctial gale had brought a sudden and abrupt end to winter, but the ensuing thaw, coupled with the highest rainfall ever recorded for March – 151.7 mm (just 0.7 mm less than 6ins.) – now left much of the country under flood.

31

LAND-ROVER – The Formative Years, 1947–1967

Stephen Wilks still remembers the ravages of the storm, when at least a dozen fallen trees blocked the driveway at Blackdown Manor, preventing a visiting aunt from departing. Once again, the borrowed Jeep and trailer were pressed into service, this time to help clear away the fallen debris. George Middleton, then a young lad in the employ of a decorator working at Blackdown Manor, takes up the story:

"The trees that came down were mostly up the drive. We cut them up with the help of the handyman from the house who drove the Jeep, which now had an ex-forces trailer. We only cleared the drive. Some of the trees were old and big and hung around for a while until Maurice got hold of another piece of ex-surplus, a bren gun carrier. As I recall, he had a great time running up and down the field pulling these trees back into the field where they could be dealt with later."

Wartime Jeeps were not generally fitted with such things as power take-off equipment, or even a simple crankshaft-driven Capstan winch, and without such facilities the Willys MB was clearly unable to shift the huge fallen trunks beyond the edge of the drive.

To acquire his next piece of ex-government surplus equipment, Maurice Wilks went along with his friend and colleague Alfred Jesse Worcester, then Works Manager of Rover's Tyseley Factory, to the WD Disposal Depot at Upper Hill, near Hereford. This time a full-track Loyd Infantry Carrier was purchased and brought back to Kenilworth by train. Following Maurice Wilks 'death in 1963, in a fitting tribute to his friend, A.J. Worcester, now Rover's Production Director, writes about this very event, and comments on the *"...very low cost"*. That was written more than 40 years ago when the Land-Rover itself was a mere 15 years old, and memories still quite fresh.

The Loyd Infantry Carrier was what George Middleton described as a 'bren gun carrier', but judging from photographs of it at Blackdown Manor, on 19 March 1988, the late Bart H. Vanderveen, editor of the Olyslager Auto Library and the 'After the Battle' military enthusiasts 'publication, 'Wheels & Tracks', assured me that it was an Infantry Carrier. Among the differences he listed was the four bogie wheels seen, not three, as found on a Bren Carrier. It was based on British Ford 15-cwt 4x2 truck components and, depending on era, was powered by either a British, American, or Canadian Ford V8 engine. Bart Vanderveen is the only person known to this author to have actually been at the RIA building in Amsterdam when the Land-Rover was launched there in 1948, and he recalled how the demonstrator had more than a little trouble with the Land-Rover's gearbox at the time, but that's a story for later.

According to Stephen Wilks, his father then had to obtain special dispensation to drive the tracked infantry carrier the short distance home from the station, and all bridges had to be bypassed along the way.

Soon after the trees were moved, Maurice Wilks had little use for such a cumbersome beast as the Infantry Carrier, and so a little horse trading now seemed appropriate. Colonel Nash could have the Infantry Carrier for further tree clearance at Bericote Wood in exchange for his Jeep which MCW had previously borrowed, and a three-phase circular saw.

We don't know the exact date the Loyd Carrier was purchased, but it has to be soon after the trees had fallen, and all photographs, film, etc. show reasonable weather, so this puts it at sometime in April 1947 at the earliest, and May at the latest. The light clothing worn by Maurice Wilks and the colourful blossom on the trees, indicates MCW was still driving the Loyd Carrier at Blackdown Manor in May or early June 1947. As the Jeep was registered with Warwickshire County Council in MCW's name on 11 June 1947, this would all seem to indicate the timing of the Jeep/Carrier 'swap' to be in early June.

Clearly the Jeep had proved an extremely useful tool both during and immediately after the extreme weather conditions experienced at Blackdown Manor throughout February and March 1947. But the tree clearance episode had also shown up some serious shortcomings in the Jeep's ability to be a really versatile workaday vehicle, and very soon this would influence Maurice Wilks' ideas concerning his future plans to overcome the difficulties the Rover Co. was then facing. It no doubt also influenced MCW's decision to retain the borrowed Jeep, and the events that were to follow.

Following the horrendous weather conditions of February and March 1947, Easter then arrived in early April (Easter Sunday was 6 April), and Maurice Wilks decided to take his young family to Red Wharf Bay on the Isle of Anglesey, off the north-west coast of Wales, for a much-needed break during the holiday period. For the journey, one of the two new 1947 model Studebaker Champion Regal De Luxe 4-door Sedans, then currently being evaluated by Rover, was used. Why a Studebaker?

By 1941 Studebaker had become America's top-selling independent car manufacturer. They had used a 'Freewheel' device in their cars since 1930, which Rover introduced in their 1933 'Meteor', and then the Speed 16 and Speed 20 models. Studebaker had also been using independent front suspension (IFS) since 1935. Rover themselves billed IFS in their brand new 1935 Streamline 'Speed 14' brochure, but unfortunately failed to pull it off. Not for another 13 years, until the P3

CHAPTER 2 – Middle Class, or Muck and Grass? – Historic Day at Red Wharf Bay

Jeep leaves Blackdown Manor for Anglesey

Grass being cleared from around Trosy

Jeep now used for leisure pursuits

All hands on deck

Now off to the beach

Rover '60' and '75' of 1948, would any Rover cars have IFS.

Interestingly, Studebaker's car acquired its torsional stiffness from a box section chassis, as would the Land-Rover. The 1947 model 'Champion Regal De Luxe 4-door Sedan', currently being evaluated by Rover, was Studebaker's latest model, and had been acquired specifically for Rover P4 car development purposes – the dollar crisis making it virtually impossible at that time to import any cars from the USA for any other reason. Later in 1947, one of the Studebaker cars was stripped down at the factory, and every individual component's weight recorded.

Why Anglesey? Well, before the days of MIRA and Rover's own test circuit at the Solihull factory, with not too many prying eyes, Anglesey was frequently used as a quiet corner of Welsh countryside in which to test Rover's new models. Pre-war, MCW had often driven there with his friend and colleague A J Worcester. Maurice Wilks also kept a motorboat named 'Kestral' at

CHAPTER 2 – Middle Class, or Muck and Grass? – Historic Day at Red Wharf Bay

MCW at Blackdown in a Land-Rover with a Pegson pump attached

Land-Rover R28, car and dingy at Trosy

Anglesey, moored at Beaumaris on the opposite side of the Menai Straits to Bangor, about four miles from Red Wharf Bay. MCW and his brother Spencer had designed the long 28 ft motor boat, which was made of 'Birmabright', and installed two Rover 12 HP engines with Vee drives that MCW designed and had made at Rover's Tyseley factory. The two brothers launched the boat on the Trent and then took it up the east coast. MCW, along with Geoffrey Savage and Jesse Worcester, then continued through the Caledonian Canal to the Isle of Lismore, meeting up later with SB at Ardrishaig.

After the war MCW decided to purchase two cottages and about 1,000 acres of land near Newborough Warren on the island's southern peninsular. The land and one cottage 'Glan-yr-afon', he continued to let out to a local farmer, but the other, 'Tros-yr-afon' (affectionately known as "Trosy"), was to be renovated for holiday use. At this time, however, Barbara Wilks considered the current state of the property unsuitable for the children, and so they stayed at 'Wern-Y-Willan', a local hotel, close to Red Wharf Bay. As soon as they began using Trosy, Mrs Wilks kept a diary of events there, but the cottage took a little time to renovate, and so unfortunately for our story, this only began in 1948.

MCW's brother, Spencer, also kept an ex-ministry air-sea rescue craft, named 'Torquil' moored at Beaumaris, which was a convenient sail to his holiday retreat on Islay. As Beaumaris was only a stone's throw away from Red Wharf Bay, SB sometimes took time off to visit brother Maurice and his family. On this occasion, with the events of the past two months still fresh in their minds, both brothers were apparently sitting on the beach at Red Wharf Bay, when MCW began to romanticise about his vision for a 'land' Rover. His good friend, the late Bishop Warren Hunt takes up the story in a letter to 'The Times', published on 24 February 1986:

Sir,

Mr Pearson Phillips (Spectrum Feb. 13) gives a vision of how the Land-Rover was conceived and born. The account I have came from Maurice Wilks himself as we were on holiday in Anglesey.

He had taken his young sons down to the beach at Red Wharf Bay and as he sat there dreamed of something that would take him and the boys across vast stretches of sand and sea to wherever they wanted to go. Then it would take them up the steep, rough stony track, through the trees back to the hotel.

Dreams turned into ideas that he jotted down on that day's page of his diary. As the first Land Rover stood in the factory yard, he looked back in his diary – it was nine months to the day he had first made his notes.

To be a passenger in a Land Rover when he drove it over seemingly impossible land and through the sea was an experience never to be forgotten.

Yours faithfully,

+ Warren Hunt

It was a like schoolboy's dream of an adventure car that could go anywhere and do just about anything you wanted it to do. It all fitted in well with MCW's sense of adventure. He had his boats and his Westland Wigeon aeroplane. What he wanted now was a 'Go Anywhere, Do Anything' cross-country car.

LAND-ROVER – The Formative Years, 1947–1967

Jeep and dinghy at Red Wharf Bay

The 'Spectrum' story, published in 'The Times', continued to tell the same old myths surrounding the birth of the Land-Rover, which, unfortunately, are still being perpetuated even to this day. When this author spoke to Bishop Warren Hunt, he made it clear it was for this very reason that he felt compelled to write his letter in response to the article in 'The Times'.

The Jeep had not yet arrived on Anglesey at this point in time, which explains why Maurice Wilks *'...dreamed of something that would take him and the boys across vast stretches of sand and sea to wherever they wanted to go. Then it would take them up the steep, rough stony track, through the trees back to the hotel'*. This would have been highly unlikely if the Jeep was already there at this particular time, as it was certainly capable of doing that job.

All photographs of the Jeep on Anglesey show the registration FWD 534 to be in place, but as Warwick records clearly show, it was not registered with that number until 11 June 1947, so it could not be before mid-summer 1947 that it was taken to Anglesey.

Once on Anglesey the Jeep was used to go to the beach, acting as transport for "Pan", a small alloy dinghy made of 'Birmabright', that would be perched above the windscreen of the Jeep to take it from 'Trosy' down to the beach. As 'Trosy' was not habitable around this time, a caravan had been taken to the cottage and Maurice and Barbara Wilks would overnight in it.

Bishop Warren Hunt's account also provides some useful confirmation of dates. If we go to the factory photographic records, the first photographs of a 'proper' Land-Rover (not the centre steer), entitled 'New Body' Nos. 394–395, are dated 29/01/48. Working backwards, *"...nine months to the day..."* at Red Wharf Bay, we arrive at the Easter school holiday period of 1947.

Kathleen Griffith, nanny to Maurice Wilks' three sons, William, Patrick, and Stephen, was also on the beach that fateful day. When I spoke to her about the occasion, she vividly remembered MCW drawing in the sand as he enthusiastically explained his ideas. Before her death, Barbara Wilks also independently relayed a similar account of these events to her son Patrick, and the hotel, *'Wern-Y-Willan'*, *'the trees'*, and *'the rough stony track'* leading down to Wern Farm and the beach where Maurice Wilks drew in the sand, still remain in evidence today, and can be seen on the 'Anglesey' 1:50,000 First Series OS map of 1974. Grid reference SH 561 804 gives the location of the beach end of the track. In the summer of 1948, Maurice Wilks was able to fulfil his 'dream' and take a pre-production Land-Rover, R28, registered GWD 745 on 15/6/48, onto the beach below Wern Farm at Red Wharf Bay.

Both Wilks brothers were now firmly convinced that an off-road utility car was exactly the sort of vehicle the Rover Co. could easily produce and also be successful in the export market. The immediate problem now was how to present such a project to a boardroom likely to resent any idea of Rover – an established manufacturer of motor cars for England's middle classes – making some sort of basic utility vehicle. It was therefore decided to present it to the Board, not as a long-term solution, but something quite temporary – a 'stop gap' – until middle class cars could once again become the staple diet of the company.

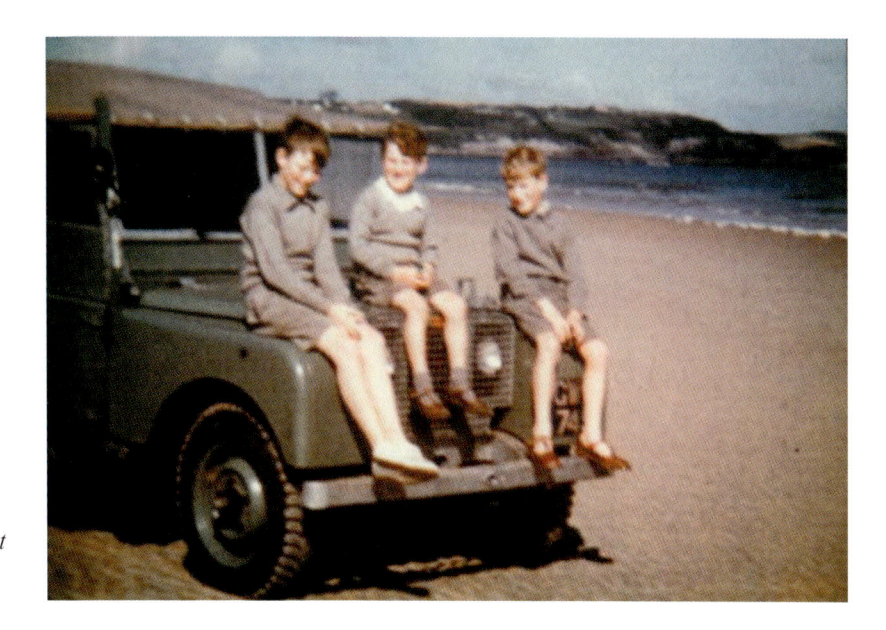

CHAPTER 2 – Middle Class, or Muck and Grass? – Historic Day at Red Wharf Bay

MCW's three sons, William, Patrick and Stephen, on the bonnet of R28

R28 leaving the stony track up from the beach

Fun on the beach with R28

37

CHAPTER 3
Birth of the Legend
A Batch of 50 Sanctioned

The sun had not yet set on Britain's colonial empire, and in 1947 Britain still had a Commonwealth of some 70 different countries ranging from vast Canada to the tiny Oceanic island of Nauru – a quarter of the world's population spread over a quarter of the earth's land surface. During the war, many of these peoples experienced the ubiquitous US Jeep in action, in places where metalled roads were almost non-existent – here "Vinegar Joe" Stilwell's famous 'Road to Burma' immediately springs to mind. Even the best roads of Britain's far-flung empire had suffered as a result of the war, and most were now in very poor condition.

Huge dollar debts were incurred as a result of the war effort and that meant civilian Jeeps were unlikely to be available outside the USA for several years to come – a fact, no doubt, at the forefront of both brothers' minds. There can also be little doubt that their thinking had been influenced by the success their brother-in-law, John Paul Black, now MD of the Standard Motor Co. was having with Harry Ferguson's little grey tractor at their Banner Road works in Coventry. And Ford was even managing to make a success of the new Fordson Major, despite its ageing 1917 side-valve engine. By 1948 both these concerns were selling over 50,000 tractors a year.

Under the Colonial Development and Welfare Act of 1940, Parliament had already voted £55 million to be spent on the colonies over the next ten years. A second Act in 1945 gave a further £120 million, plus another £10 million for the reconstruction of Malta. And that was by no means all. On 25 October 1947, a bill was presented to Parliament establishing the Colonial Development and Overseas Food Corporation, with the power to borrow up to £100 million, plus a further £10 million for temporary requirements. The purpose of the corporation was to develop colonial resources, expand the production of foodstuffs and raw materials, and increase trade. Just think what a nimble little 4x4 utility vehicle could offer to such an enormous programme of reconstruction and development. The Wilks idea of a 'land' Rover had surely come at just the right moment in time.

It is clear that Maurice Wilks now believed a small utility 4x4 such as the proposed Land-Rover, could sell well overseas under these circumstances, particularly in areas where preferential trade terms already existed and sterling was the common currency. The manufacture of such a vehicle would also make sure there was sufficient work to keep the large labour force occupied at Rover's 'No.2 Shadow Factory' at Lode Lane, Solihull, until car production could be increased to a more realistic level.

Nevertheless, the idea of a Land-Rover was far removed from anything Rover were accustomed to manufacturing. Their only previous attempt at anything agricultural had been a tracked plough back in 1931, and that had little in common with the proposed Land-Rover. At the same time, design work on both Rover's post-war P3 and P4 cars was still not finalised, and neither of these had been a particularly straightforward matter.

In order to gain experience with modern styling, Rover acquired two new 1947 Studebaker 'Champion Regal' cars, the first really new post-war design from America. Best described as a medium-size family saloon, it was small by American standards, with a 2.6-litre side-valve engine, but was selling well on the Continent – the main reason why Rover were taking it so seriously. The car's elongated boot and wrap-around rear window, was the work of Raymond Loey and Virgil Exner, and signalled a new 'coming or going' style in automobile bodywork.

Already acknowledged by the pundits as setting a new trend in the world's motor industry, Studebaker's 'Champion Regal' had evolved almost by accident as a result of examining the possibility of optional front or rear engine layouts using a specially constructed box-section chassis. Rover made a very thorough analysis of the new Studebaker, and not only was every part stripped down and examined, but every individual component was weighed – right down to the last nut and bolt. After being stripped down, one Studebaker was then rebuilt on a Rover P4 chassis, fitting almost perfectly, and it soon became known

CHAPTER 3 – Birth of the Legend – A Batch of 50 Sanctioned

The 1947 Studebaker

as the 'Roverbaker'. It was retained in this form as a works hack at the factory for several years before finally being rebuilt back again into a Studebaker.[1]

At the Solihull works, Rover's new i.o.e. engine and two new cars were now both in hand, but MCW still had to get to grips with the Land-Rover project. It was to be an exceptionally busy time for Rover's design team and something eventually had to give. With time fast running out, there could be no protracted design period for the proposed new Land-Rover. MCW knew that his Jeep would be the ideal starting point for the project. Gordon Bashford stated that he was then given the job of bringing *"a couple"* of roadworthy Jeeps from a war-surplus dump in the Cotswolds. These were then stripped down at the factory; their axles, transfer boxes, steering parts, and chassis frames would then all be used in the development of the Land-Rover. MCW's own Willys Jeep would play a more essential role.

Kathleen Griffith recalls it was about this time that, on entering the bathroom at Blackdown Manor, she was both surprised and amused to discover various detailed drawings of MCW's proposed new Land-Rover all over the tiles of the bathroom wall. The idea of a Land-Rover was eventually presented to Rover's Board on 4 September 1947. Under the circumstances, they

[1]*Many Studebaker car parts, including the back axle, had also been used in the original 'Bantam' Jeeps.*

probably had no alternative but to accept it, and a trial batch of 50 Land-Rovers was sanctioned. The first official factory photograph of a 'Land-Rover' was taken on 23 September 1947, and by early October 'No.1' had been completed. This was the now famous hybrid centre steer prototype, which, apart from its new P3 'Rover 60' engine, Rover main gearbox, and new alloy bodywork, was Maurice Wilks' Willys Jeep.

Three months later, and before even a single pre-production Land-Rover had been constructed, Spencer Wilks decided it was now time to seek the Board of Directors' full approval to go ahead with production of the new utility vehicle. The minutes of the Board meeting for Wednesday, 4 December 1947, tell their own story:

"The Board considered the position, and also the numerous alternative product lines which had been under consideration since car manufacture had recommenced. Mr Wilks said that he was of the opinion that the all-purpose vehicle on the lines of the Willys-Overland post-war Jeep was the most desirable.

The P3 engine, gearbox and back axle could be used almost in their entirety: little additional tooling and jigging would be necessary, and body dies would not be required, as facilities had already been provided in our Shops for the necessary pressings. Considerable research had been carried out on this vehicle by our Development Department.

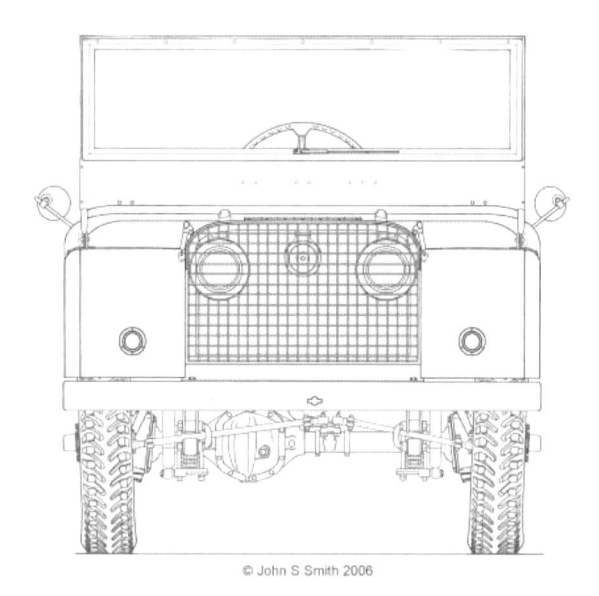

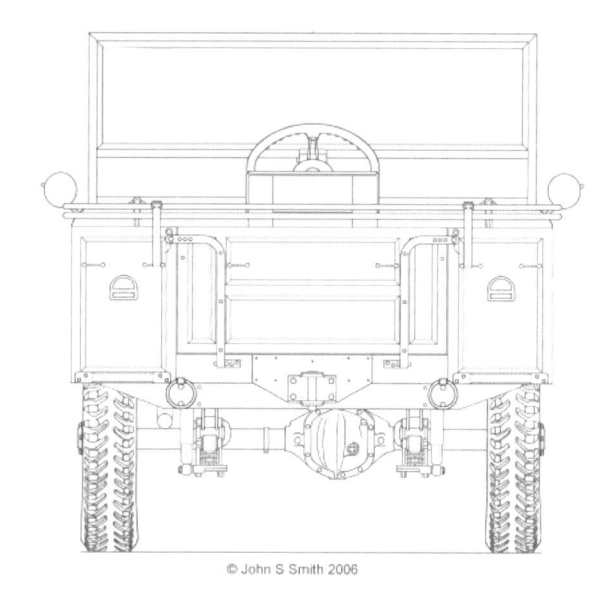

Centre steer front, rear and side view

It was, therefore, agreed that this should be sanctioned for production."

The way it was presented certainly made it sound as if the power source and transmission system were already taken care of. Nobody questioned the fact that there was no front wheel drive system, no offset axle casings, no suitable front drive shafts, no transfer gearbox, no steering gear, no power take-off (PTO) units of any sort, and certainly no chassis or bodywork. But the idea was sanctioned for production, and that's all that mattered.

Spencer Wilks had deliberately centred the discussion around the *"...Willys-Overland post-war Jeep..."*. This was the CJ-2A *'Universal Jeep'*, a civilian model that became available from 4 September 1945, and not the original wartime Willys MB or Ford GPW.

As early as 1942, car designer Brook Stevens had presented the idea of a peacetime Jeep to the American 'Society of Automobile Engineers' (SAE). Technical illustrations, dated April 1942, were then published in 'Popular Mechanics'. It was not to be based on the wartime Jeep's 80-inch chassis, but on the longer 104-inch chassis of Willys-Overland's "failed" Americar. To keep costs down, Willys intention was to avoid involving any

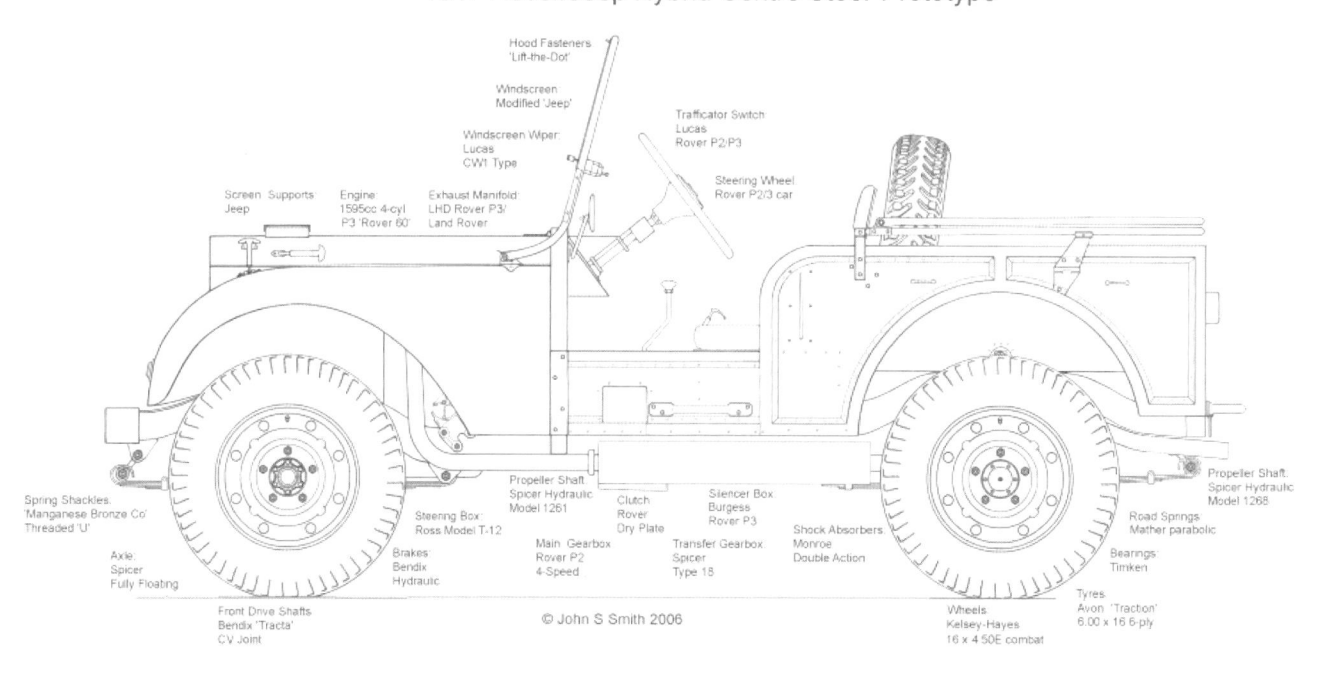

CHAPTER 3 – Birth of the Legend – A Batch of 50 Sanctioned

Centre steer nears completion in Rover's "Jig Shop"

of the "car body" firms. That meant there were to be no deep pressings, so that all body panels could be stamped out by any of the firms previously involved in the production of ammunition cases.

Since the early 1940s, Willys had also been experimenting with farm and commercial implements fitted to their wartime MB Jeep, and to this end their employee, Bob Green, had jury-rigged a whole range of agricultural devices such as crop sprayers, post-hole diggers, and even fire-fighting equipment, all designed for use in America's backwoods.

The new civilian Jeep, the CJ-2A, was based on these ideas, and only differed from the wartime MB by having a column gear shift, tail board (the spare wheel was now mounted at the side), larger sealed beam headlights, and power take-off facilities. The old 'go devil' side-valve engine and 6-volt electrics would still continue to rule the day. The first civilian Jeeps, produced in June 1945, were simply demilitarised MBs, but by August, production of the new CJ-2A had begun. The 104-inch chassis, however, would be reserved for the Jeep Station Wagon, a two-wheel-drive car that went into production in 1946.

The total number of wartime Willys Jeeps built had been 362,841. They had saved Willys from receivership. The civilian CJ-2A 'Universal Jeep' would prove just as successful. Costing just $1,146 (less than £300), before the end of 1946 sales had already reached 71,445 with 75% going overseas. By April 1947, they had passed the 100,000 barrier, as Jeeps began to appear on thousands of small farms scattered throughout America, enabling Willys-Overland to beat their previous 'all-time' sales record of 1929 (more than 38,000 would be sold in 1950).

For the Wilks brothers, Willys-Overland's success with their 'Universal Jeep' could not have come at a better time if it was to have any influence on the Rover Co. Board's decision to go ahead with the Land-Rover project. The other factor was the Wilks brothers' track record. If Rover were to become involved in the production of a farmyard utility vehicle, there was one thing the Board could be sure about – it would be better than anything anyone else would have to offer – a fact that almost holds true of Solihull's products even today.

The use of light alloy body panels, rather than steel, would not only avoid eating into Rover's

41

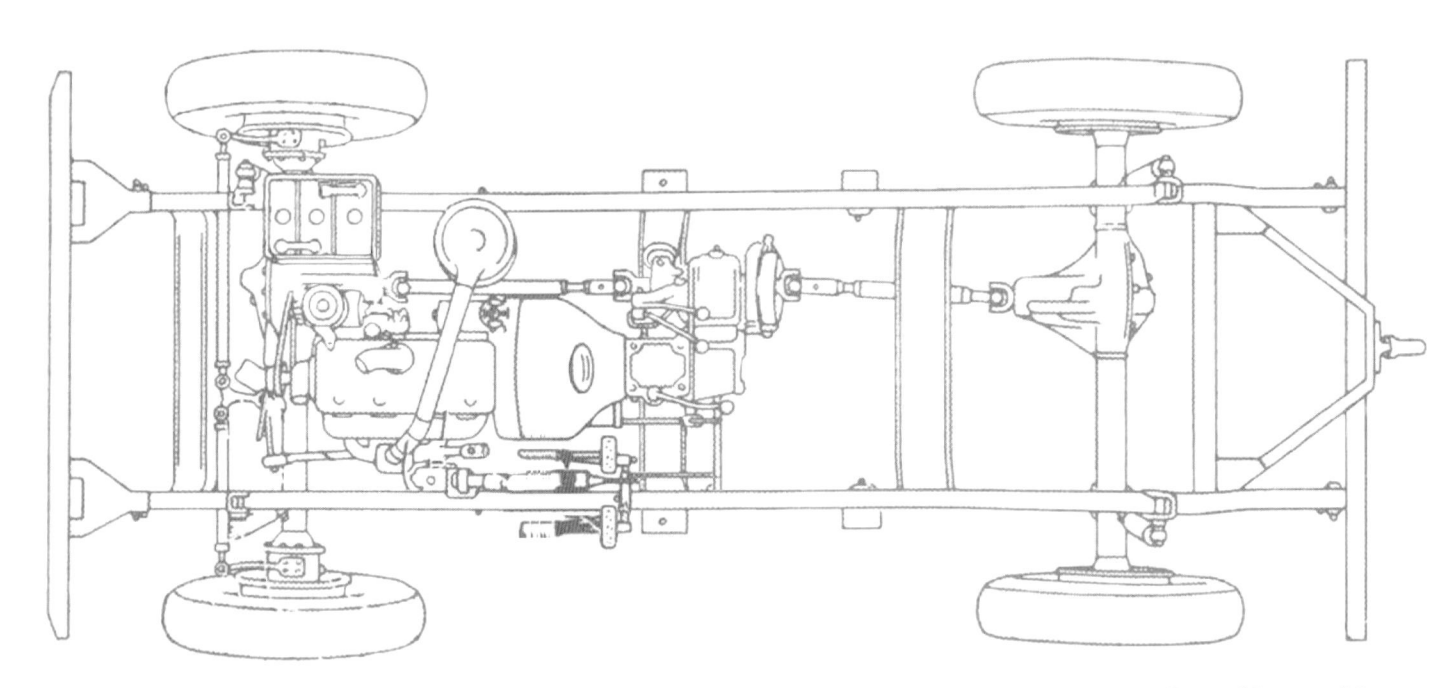

General layout of Jeep chassis

precious allocation of steel, but as SB was careful to point out, it meant existing presses, previously used for the construction of light alloy aircraft body parts, would be suitable for the job. There was no shortage of aluminium, and early pre-production models would in fact be constructed from Duralumin left over from Gloster, Lancaster, and Bristol airframes and wings, which Rover had been busily manufacturing during the war years. They also had a wealth of experience to draw on with this lightweight material, and knew it could be shaped in simple plywood jigs. All this would avoid the expense of heavy pressings for bodywork, and finished panels could be simply spot-welded, riveted, or bolted together. But what would they use for a chassis? That problem still had to be resolved.

Had SB been entirely honest in the picture he had portrayed to the Board? Certainly the P3 engine and its main four-speed gearbox *"...could be used almost in their entirety"*, but even the gearbox had to have all its selector rods repositioned, so as to operate from the front and not the rear, as on Rover's cars. And it certainly was not true of most other parts there were no offset axle casings; half-shafts would need to be two different lengths; there was no front wheel drive system (this would involve expensive constant velocity joints); only the car's differentials could be used. There was no transfer box for high and low ratio, and no front output housings. Neither was there any suitable steering gear, and certainly no power take-off equipment.

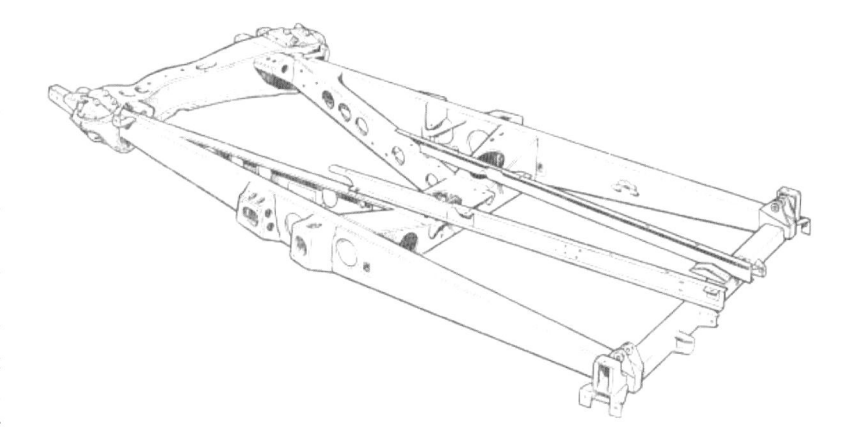

P3 car's 3/4-length box section chassis

The practical realities of this situation suggests that SB may have been more than just a little economical with the truth. He was, however, shrewd enough to know that this was probably the project's only chance of getting the Rover Board's approval, and at the end of the day little else really mattered if the company was to have any future beyond the first half of the 20th Century.

Certainly the Board's decision would have been influenced by the lack of any suitable alternative on the table so, like it or not, they were more or less forced to go along with the project. But what they privately thought of the Rover Company, a well-established manufacturer of motor cars for the middle classes, turning to a humble agricultural utility truck for their survival, is a matter of pure conjecture. This was their one chance to stay in business, and they had little alternative but to take it.

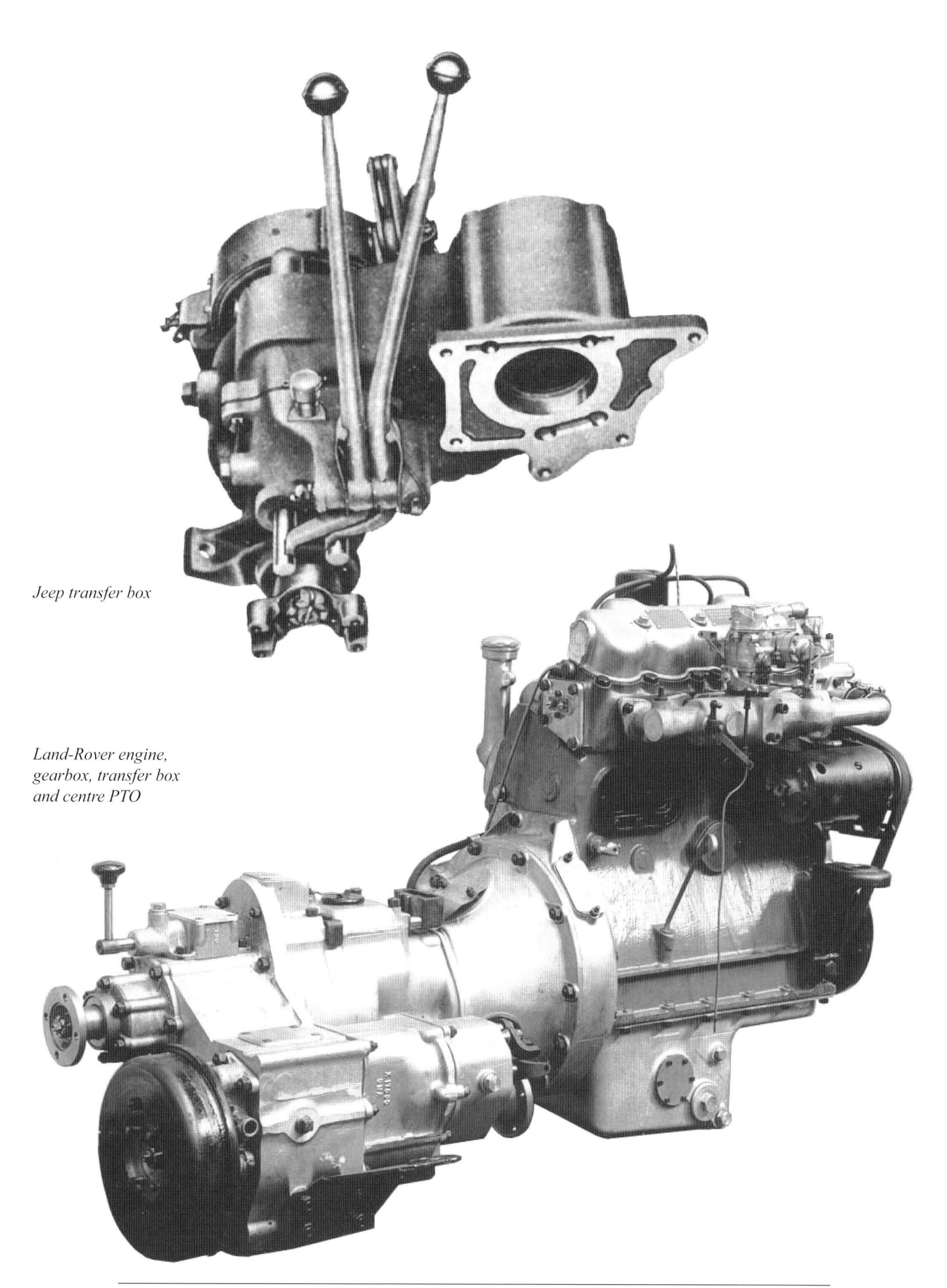

CHAPTER 3 – Birth of the Legend – A Batch of 50 Sanctioned

Jeep transfer box

Land-Rover engine, gearbox, transfer box and centre PTO

CHAPTER 4
Prototypes and Chassis Frame Tests
The Centre Steer Hybrid

Instead of wasting time on an entirely scratch-built prototype, Maurice Wilks appears to have used his own 1943 Willys MB Jeep as the basis for the Land-Rover project. The fact that it was in excellent working order would avoid unnecessary hiccups, and his son Stephen still remembers its sudden disappearance from Blackdown Manor at that time. Two more ex-surplus Jeeps acquired for the project were dismantled for use by Gordon Bashford in the Design Department, many parts finishing up in a second 'mule' prototype, as Rover had neither offset driven front or rear axles, nor a transfer box at that time.

Under the direction of Geoffrey Savage, construction of the first prototype – generally referred to as 'The Centre Steer' – then commenced in Rover's Jig Shop in late September 1947 and was completed within three weeks. On 15 October 1947 it was officially photographed and the following day Rover's MD, Spencer Wilks, optimistically announced to the Board that:

"...a pre-production batch of fifty was already in progress, and the first prototype was at present on test".

That very same day, 16 October 1947, the Board also gave the un-hyphenated name 'Landrover' their official blessing. It looked as if the adventurous little utility car that Maurice Wilks dreamt up on the beach at Red Wharf Bay, just six months earlier, was now about to be born.

Spencer Wilks had already told the Board that the new Rover P3 car engine and gearbox could be used for the Land-Rover. It is certainly clear from Rover's photographic record dates that the 12 HP P3 'Rover 60' engine, which would later be used in the 48 pre-production models and production models, was now available, and Rover's first car to have the 1595cc i.o.e. 'Rover 60' engine, GAC 915, had been registered with Warwickshire authority in the company's name on 2/10/1947.

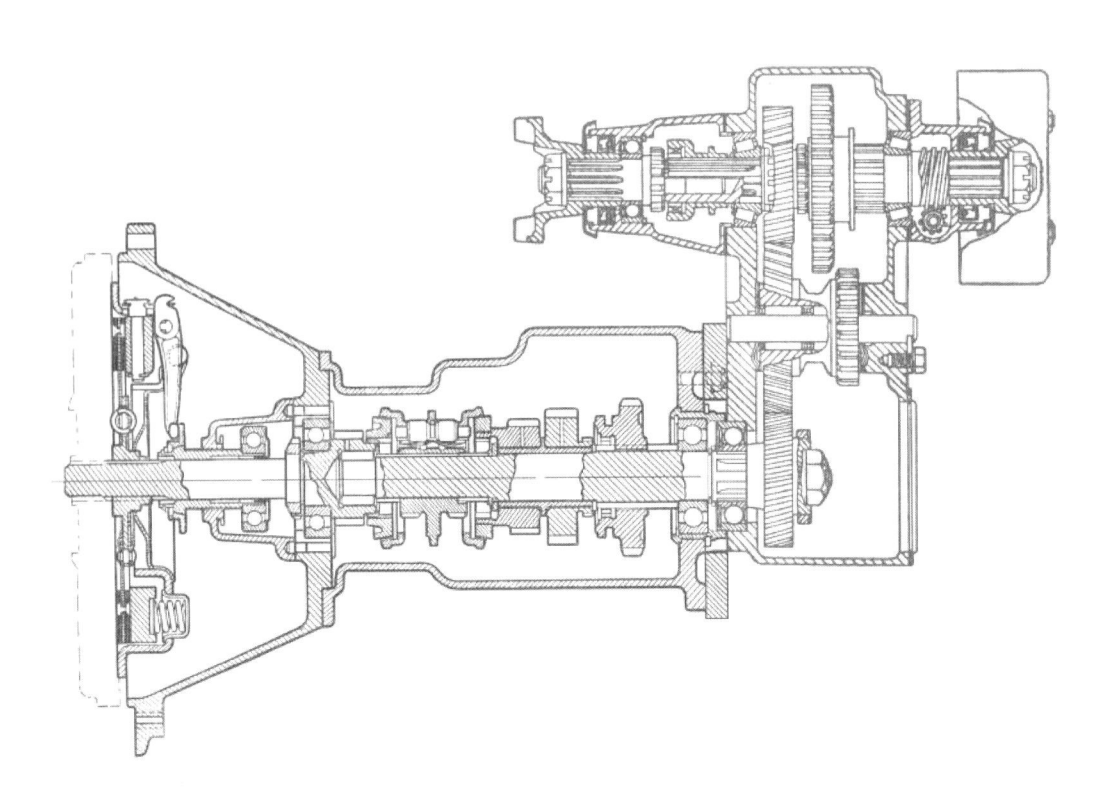

Rover's clutch, short bell housing, and P3 gearbox with special mainshaft, connected, via an adapter plate, to a Jeep 'Spicer' transfer box, as used in the centre steer hybrid

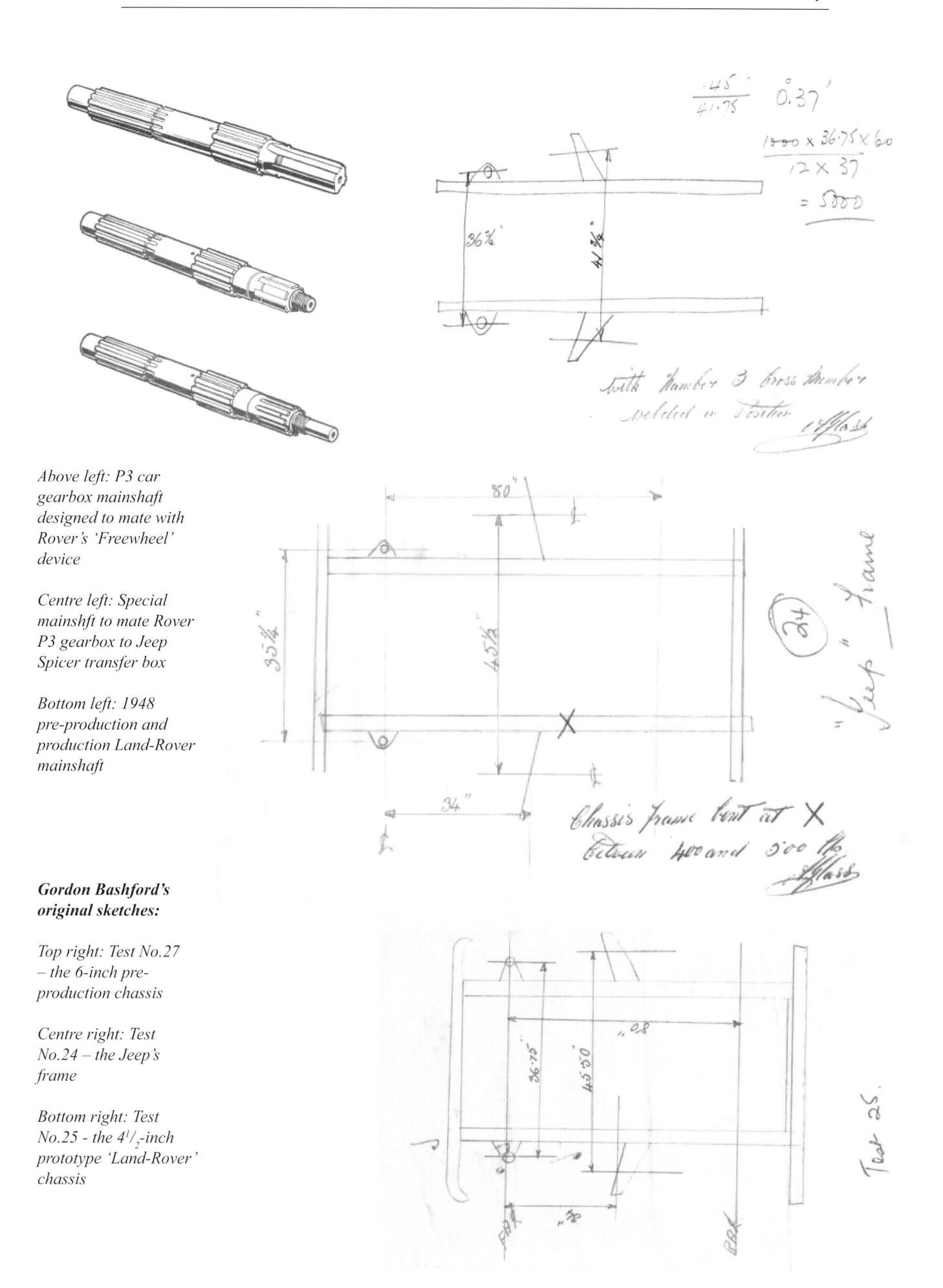

CHAPTER 4 – Prototypes and Chassis Frame Tests – The Centre Steer Hybrid

Above left: P3 car gearbox mainshaft designed to mate with Rover's 'Freewheel' device

Centre left: Special mainshft to mate Rover P3 gearbox to Jeep Spicer transfer box

Bottom left: 1948 pre-production and production Land-Rover mainshaft

Gordon Bashford's original sketches:

Top right: Test No.27 – the 6-inch pre-production chassis

Centre right: Test No.24 – the Jeep's frame

Bottom right: Test No.25 - the 4½-inch prototype 'Land-Rover' chassis

45

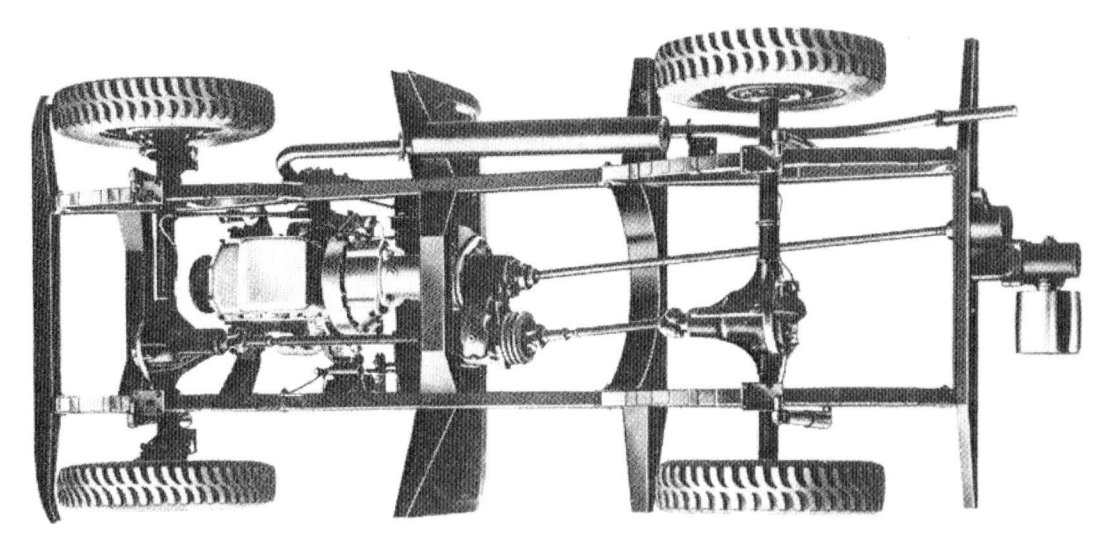

Tom Barton then set about grafting the new P3 engine and gearbox onto the front of a Jeep 'Spicer' transfer box. In order to keep the gearbox in the same position in the new 4-cyl. P3 'Rover 60' car's chassis, a long bell housing was used to make up the space lost by the two absent cylinders, compared to the 6-cyl. engine used for the 'Rover 75'. But in the new Land-Rover, the shorter 'Rover 75' bell housing would be used in conjunction with the 4-cyl. engine.

In Rover's P3 car gearbox, the locking dog and inner member of Rover's 'Freewheel' device, were located on four splines at the end of the gearbox mainshaft (Pt. No. 09921). The Jeep's Spicer transfer box input gear, however, required a longer mainshaft with six splines at the output end, not four, followed by a threaded section, with a small hole drilled, to take the Jeep type retaining nut and split pin.

A new mainshaft, Rover Part No. X17190, was therefore specially designed to mate up with the Jeep's Spicer transfer box's existing input gear. This appears to be the only factory drawing designated purely for the construction of the 'Jeep'-based hybrid centre steer development model. A 1/2-inch thick adapter plate was used to enable Rover's gearbox to mate up with the Spicer transfer box case, before relocating it all into a Jeep rolling chassis.

Rover's own transfer box used in the 1948 pre-production and production Land-Rovers, had an entirely new mainshaft (Pt. No. X17501). The number of splines was increased to ten, and a special cone-shaped nut with tabbed lock washer retained the input gear in position. This was followed by a further plain section supported by a rear bearing located in a cast aluminium end cover. The Jeep's Spicer transfer box offered no such support at this location to either the standard Jeep mainshaft or Rover's special mainshaft (Pt. No. X17190), and it had just a simple pressed steel end cover.

For the centre steer model, the Jeep's steel body was discarded, and a new light alloy structure was created. By moving both the seating position and bulkhead forward by three inches, the new rear body bin's length – the payload area – was increased from 31 to 34 inches. (On later pre-production and production Land-Rovers it was increased still further to 37.5 inches). This would have placed the original gear control in the centre of the floor area, between the driver's legs. So instead, Rover reverted to a remote gear shift placed on the right side of the gearbox, in pretty much the same manner as previously used by Rovers for the 14/45 and 16/50 HP Rover's of the 1920s.

Rover's 4½-inch chassis, used for the second hybrid development model

Rover's 4½ inch chassis showing the adapter plate mating Rover's gearbox to the Jeep's Spicer transfer box

CHAPTER 4 – Prototypes and Chassis Frame Tests – The Centre Steer Hybrid

The new bodywork included a tail board for load access – something not normally found on the wartime veteran. Close scrutiny of factory photographs reveals some interesting features, including the sump of the P3 engine and the exhaust discharging down the left side – Rover's previous engine's exhaust on the P2 had discharged from the bloc on the right side. The alloy bodywork was reinforced not with steel galvanised cappings, as on later pre-production and production models, but with external boxed alloy sections spot-welded into position on the return fold – no doubt a technique learnt from Rover employees' wartime experience making aircraft frames.

Like Jeep bodywork, there were no doors, but a very high sill. To allow water to drain, either from wading, washing or rainstorm, a 5" x 4" rectangular cut-out was provided on either side, which also doubled as a toehold. The Jeep locker boxes were kept behind the rear wheels, and were accessed from a top panel immediately behind the wheel arch. Trafficators were mounted inboard of the rear body sides, where they would be no more vulnerable than on any other car of the time – so long as you didn't use them off-road. Their operating switch was Rover's standard Lucas car part attached to the steering column.

The windscreen, although similar to the Jeep, had become one piece, and a single wiper motor operated across the middle section of the glass. There was no transmission tunnel within the cab, and the clutch pedal remained on the left side, but brake and accelerator were repositioned to the right side.

The Jeep's left-hand steering position was also replaced, but not its steering box. Instead, a new centrally located steering wheel would be relayed across to the original 'Ross' left-handed steering box by means of a Reynolds chain and sprockets – an agricultural arrangement for an agricultural machine. The steering box also had to be relocated to outside the chassis rail to accommodate the P3 engine. Initially an apron was placed between the vehicle's front dumb irons. This was later replaced by a mock Capstan winch and rope guide mounted on the front bumper. The Jeep's original PTO equipment was used at the rear.

There are no known colour photographs of the original centre steer concept vehicle, but George Middleton, who saw this vehicle at Blackdown Manor, has described the colour as 'grey'. The 'duplicate' log book of R01, and the original buff RF 60 log book of this author's pre-production Land-Rover L11, also give the colour as 'grey'. But both L11 and R01 have always been 'light green', a colour which this author believes to be aircraft 'Cockpit Green' – the paint applied to all internal alloy surfaces of wartime aeroplanes to prevent condensation corrosion.

Research by Ian Duddy in Australia has revealed that Rover's light green paint does have the same characteristic Antimony (Sb), a bluish-white element used for flame proofing paints, as light green paint samples from a 1941 Avro Ansen. Rover had been heavily involved in making airframe sections for Gloster, Lancaster and Bristol warplanes during the war, so they knew that this paint had been formulated to adhere to aluminium alloys. This makes it highly likely that this was not only the paint mix used for pre-production models, but at a good guess, would have been used for the hybrid prototype centre steer model too.

Careful study of the many factory photographs of the centre steer prototype indicate that only one model of this type was actually constructed. Company employee H.B. Light, Rover's unofficial historian at that time, also only refers to just one with *"...steering in the centre"*. Ralph Nash, who took responsibility for R02 when it was 'despatched in' at the factory on 15 March 1948, and later had it built into a station wagon for his personal use, was also adamant there was only one centre steer. The centre steer was, after all, simply a concept vehicle for an agricultural runabout, and little purpose would have been served by producing further hybrids using what was essentially, a Jeep chassis and Jeep running gear. Besides, there was an impending sense of urgency to keep the project moving forward as quickly as possible.

The host of contemporary factory photographs of this Willys-Rover hybrid on trial clearly indicate Maurice Wilks' desire to produce a vehicle that, more than anything else, could make a substantial contribution to the world's farming communities. Jeep running gear and general layout would certainly assure the vehicle of its general off-road capability. But it was also able to pull a two-furrow plough, power agricultural implements such as a reaping machine, tow a sizeable trailer, and drive various pieces of stationary equipment such as an elevator or saw bench using a pulley drum mounted on the rear power take-off facility. At the front end a Capstan winch could also be available for such things as grubbing out trees and self-recovery.

So what happened to the original hybrid centre steer? There have been many 'hoax' findings over the past thirty years, but not so much as a photograph has ever been forthcoming. It was last officially photographed at the factory on 28 January 1948, and it seems reasonable to assume it was then broken up around the time R01 was completed. Tom Barton has also confirmed that both prototypes were broken up.[1]

[1] Details of the second prototype, appear below.

LAND-ROVER – The Formative Years, 1947–1967

Front view showing layout of body-bin

Close-up of instrument panel

Rear view showing interior layout of the centre steer

This author is fully convinced that under the centre steer prototype's new bodywork was Maurice Wilks' own Willys Jeep. MCW's son Stephen Wilks also thinks this could be right. What evidence is there to support this theory? We know from factory photographs that the Jeep trailer used with the centre steer hybrid carried the registration mark FWD 534, the number belonging to Maurice Wilks' own Jeep, which he used both at his home, Blackdown Manor in Warwickshire, and on Anglesey. As it was definitely his Jeep trailer, it seems quite reasonable to assume that it was also his Jeep; after all, it was a well-sorted vehicle and, according to Warwick Records, was still road taxed up to 31 May 1961.

We also know from Maurice Wilks' son Stephen's recollection of the time, that both Jeep and trailer disappeared rather suddenly from Blackdown Manor. This may have been when they were taken to the factory. The very fact that the centre steer hybrid is known to have been kept at Blackdown Manor at some stage also lends credence to the theory that it was Maurice Wilks' personal property – namely, his own Willys Jeep.

Stephen Wilks also recalls his father taking him round the factory and pointing out a pile of light

CHAPTER 4 – Prototypes and Chassis Frame Tests – The Centre Steer Hybrid

Sawing logs with Maurice Wilks' trailer

alloy body parts by a wall, telling him quite clearly that they had belonged to the very first Land-Rover. They were certainly nothing to do with R01, the first Land-Rover to be 'despatched in' at the factory, as this vehicle went to Francis Adcock at Dairy Farm, Kenilworth, on 4 January 1949 – just a short distance from Blackdown Manor, where, no doubt, Maurice Wilks could keep a general eye on its performance. R01 stayed at Dairy Farm until 1956 before returning to the Rover factory. Apart from occasional refurbishment – once for the 21st Anniversary, and again for the 50th, it has always remained in one piece either at Donnington, Syon Park or at the 'Heritage' museum at Gaydon where it can be seen today.

All this tends to suggest the body parts Maurice Wilks pointed out to his son Stephen could only have come from this hybrid centre steer development vehicle, the rest of which was returned back to a Jeep. We certainly know from Warwickshire County Records that Maurice Wilks' own Jeep was road licensed right up until 31 May 1961. Such action would have been entirely in character with Maurice Wilks and there was no shortage of Jeep parts at the factory with which to do the job. It could also be argued that this was a convenient way of disposing of any hard evidence as to what had actually taken place – particularly important if the Land-Rover was to establish itself as a vehicle in its own right, rather than as a Jeep replica, which chassis tests, method of construction and materials, power unit, etc. clearly showed it was not.

So much importance was attached to the new project that production of the P3 saloon car, planned for September 1947, was delayed until February 1948, the following year, now that Maurice Wilks (Technical Director), Robert Boyle (Chief Engineer), Arthur Goddard (Assistant Chief Engineer), and the five section leaders, Tom Barton[2] and Gordon Bashford (design), Joe Drinkwater (engines), Roland Seale (production drawing office), Frank Shaw (transmissions), together with John Cullen (project co-ordinator), and Sam Ostler (body stylist) who sketched up the bodywork, had all now been transferred over to Land-Rover development.

[2] *Following a major difference of opinion between Robert Boyle and Arthur Goddard, Tom Barton was appointed Assistant Chief Engineer. He was later given charge of Land-Rover development when John Cullen left Rover to develop a 4x4 vehicle for the David Brown organisation in 1954. As 'Mr Land Rover', Tom Barton held this position until his retirement in 1980.*

Centre steer with hood and rear PTO pulley drum

Maurice Wilks had grappled unsuccessfully with the concept of 'full width' styling for the new P3, and decided the existing P2 body design from the current '6-light' Saloon and '4-light' Sports Saloon cars would have to be re-used. Other areas of design were, however, more successful.

Rover knew their latest engine intended for the P3 car would be a success, as it was based on Jack Swaine's 'inlet-over-exhaust' design used earlier in the abortive 'M1' project. Now it was in much larger sizes – a 1.6-litre 'four' and a '2.1-litre 'six'. Suddenly, however, the whole business had become more complicated with the introduction of the Land-Rover project at this critical point in time. All new P3 four-cylinder engines were now earmarked for Land-Rover use, so when the P3 finally arrives in February 1948, it is initially only available as the more powerful 'Rover 75'. Fortunately, this worked out better than might be expected, as the deliberate delay of the P3 had been engineered to coincide with the abolition of the old 'horse power tax' from January 1948. Rover's customers would no longer be penalised for buying the larger engine. Even when they were given the choice, a few months later, the 'six' always remained in greater demand.

The real significance of the P3 car's delay becomes even more apparent when we consider the P3 itself was only intended as a temporary 'stop-gap' between Rover's P2 pre-war models, then currently still in production, and the P4 (Auntie) 'Rover 75', the company's true post-war model for the 1950s, now under full development, which would replace the P3 as early as September 1949.

The advent of flexibly mounted engines and gearboxes in the early 1930s meant traditional open chassis frames lost much of their torsional stiffness, and on cars with coachbuilt bodywork, flexing became a problem. To overcome this, in 1933 Rover, in conjunction with Wilmot-Breeden Ltd., came up with the idea of the 'Harmonic Stabiliser Bumper'. This consisted of a pair of transverse spring leaves, the width of the car, mounted by 'Silentbloc' bushes onto the car's dumb irons. Lead weights, cleverly incorporated in a rolled mounting eye at the ends of the bumper, were then added to the extremities of the springs.

But even this modification was insufficient for Maurice Wilks to offer independent front suspension on their 'Speed 14' model for 1935, as originally promised. Rover would now have to overcome this problem of torsional stiffness if they were to offer independent front suspension on the proposed new post-war P3 car.

Immediately after the war Rover began to research into chassis design. Studebaker had

CHAPTER 4 – Prototypes and Chassis Frame Tests – The Centre Steer Hybrid

Centre steer ploughing

Trailer detail showing MCW's Jeep's registration plate

used a 'Freewheel' device since 1930 and had independent front suspension since 1935. From 1941 they were America's top-selling independent car manufacturer. The Studebaker had acquired its torsional stiffness from a box section chassis, and Rover were currently evaluating their latest model, the 1946 Studebaker Champion Regal De Luxe 4-door Sedan. Although Rover had added a fourth side to their pre-war P2 car's 'U' channel chassis, it was only to the middle section. The section above the suspension remained entirely open.

Rover's proposed new cars, the P3 '60' and '75' would, however, be simply 'stop-gap' models bridging the gap between their ageing pre-war P2 models and the planned P4. In the P3, they wanted to try out Jack Swaine's new i.o.e. engine, together with Girling's new independent front suspension.

The P3 would only be in production from February 1948 to September 1949, so there could be no lavish expense on tooling. Instead most of the old body pressings from the P2, both 'four-light' and 'six-light' models, were used, with bonnet and wings coming specifically from the P2 'Rover 12'. For Pressed Steel to have provided a new body, the tooling alone would have cost Rover a cool three-quarters of a million pounds, when total sales of P3 cars would hardly top five figures.

To provide the necessary rigidity for Girling's independent front suspension, Rover's P3 car required an entirely new strengthened chassis. The cost of a channel pressing would be prohibitive for such a low-volume short-term model, and so the idea of a 3/4-length fabricated box section chassis was hit upon. By running longitudinal members for only the front three quarters of the car would avoid the need to arch them above the rear axle. The front ends of the rear leaf springs could still be attached to the chassis, but their rear end would be attached to the floor pan using a tube and reinforcing floor pan plates. If this was done, the top edge and sides of the longitudinal chassis rails could then all be perfectly flat.

To do this simply, each longitudinal member was constructed from a single sheet of 16 swg (1.625 mm) mild steel folded into a narrow box section just $1^1/_2$ inches wide and 6 inches deep at the centre, tapering to 3 inches at either end. All that was then needed to fabricate each member was a single seam weld along the entire length of the underside centre line. Previously all Rover car chassis had been bought in from John Thompson Motor Pressings of Wolverhampton, but such a simple chassis could now be constructed 'in house'. Unwittingly the whole idea would now provide the necessary lead for the development of the first Land-Rover chassis that were soon to follow.

As an agricultural runabout, the Land-Rover, had no 'official' long-term future, so the expense of a heavy channel pressing was again out of the question. The 3/4-length box section chassis of the P3 car could be of no use, and so an entirely new design was clearly required.

To help determine the Land-Rover's chassis design, Gordon Bashford arranged for 'torsional stiffness' tests to be carried out on a Jeep chassis. These tests produced a torque strength figure of 260 ft/lbs per degree twist, with collapse taking place between 400 and 500 ft/lbs/° (officially recorded as 'Test No. 24'). Much of the Jeep's structural strength came from an all-steel body pressing, but the new Land-Rover's bodywork was to be constructed in thin aluminium alloy sheet, simply folded as necessary, then bolted, riveted or spot-welded into place. It was therefore unlikely to provide any of the structural rigidity necessary for such an open-top cross-country car. Every ounce of strength would have to come from a rigid chassis if Rover's cross-country car was, quite literally, not to fall apart at the seams. Based on the groundwork already done for both the P3 and P4 chassis, Gordon Bashford, the man responsible for much of the Land-Rover's general design, was now able to determine a torsional stiffness figure of not 260, but 4,500 to 5,000 ft/lbs per degree twist – almost 20 times that of the Jeep.

The encouraging news was that experimental tests already carried out had shown such a figure to be readily obtainable if a box structure was used. To give the required torsional stiffness, it was thought that the Land-Rover's chassis needed to be in heavy '12 gauge' (2.65 mm) steel, – over 1 mm thicker than the P3 car chassis – and run the full length of the vehicle, arching over both front and rear axles. Clearly a totally different approach to the P3 chassis design was required, but the general idea was there. Here Rover's Works Manger, Olaf Poppe, who was responsible for tooling and jigs, takes credit for coming up with the answer. Why not simply use four separate lengths of flat 12 swg mild steel sheet to form a box section? The two side sections could first be cut to the required profile, and then the top and bottom sections could be simply welded on to these along their entire length, using a jig to assist alignment. By using this fairly simple construction technique, Rover would also be able to build Land-Rover chassis 'in house' at their Lode Lane premises in Solihull.

Construction now began on a second Land-Rover development vehicle. Within it two highly significant developments in the direction of an 'all Rover' Land-Rover would take place. Whereas the Jeep chassis had previously been used for the centre steer concept model, this time a Rover-built chassis frame would be used. Using Olaf Poppe's 'four plate' concept, in September 1947 work began on this first ever Land-Rover chassis in Rover's Manufacturing Engineering Department. Longitudinal members $4^1/_2$ inches deep and 2 inches wide – exactly the same as a Jeep's chassis profile – were cut from 12 swg material and assemblesdtogether. To complete the ladder frame structure of this very first 'Land-Rover' chassis, items such as engine mountings, crossmembers and outriggers, all needed to be positioned correctly to accept Rover's new P3 1.6-litre four-cylinder i.o.e. engine and four-speed gearbox, as these would be used in the Land-Rover if it went into production.

This first Land-Rover chassis would now be built up into a second prototype model, but Rover would still be using the Jeep's 'Spicer' 4x4 high/low-ratio transmission, axles, wheels, and PTO system, as Rover still had no 4x4 transmission parts of their own. Along with Rover's new P3 engine and gearbox grafted onto a Jeep's 'Spicer' transfer box, the P3's radiator, exhaust manifold, silencer and pipe work would also be installed in this new chassis. In this second prototype model the clutch pedal was mounted for left-hand drive, so in theory it could still be used with centre steering, but as no steering gear was provided, it could never actually be driven. It was already apparent that if the Land-Rover's steering gear was not to be unnecessarily complicated, it would have to be mounted either left or right of the P3 engine.

No bodywork was ever provided on this prototype either, so it never became a complete Land-Rover, and after the chassis was completed and the power plant and running gear all installed, its development was taken no further. In fact, quite the reverse took place. Unlike the earlier centre steer hybrid that preceded it, this was not a concept vehicle, but simply a development model, so none of that mattered at this early stage of Land-Rover development.

Having made sure all supporting brackets and crossmembers etc. were in the right place, this first Land-Rover chassis still had a further important job to do, and for that purpose it would have to be stripped back down to just a bare chassis frame. It would then be subjected to the same type of torsional stiffness test as previously carried out on a Jeep frame. The test results gave this very first Land-Rover chassis a torsional stiffness figure of 4,000 ft/lbs/° twist per foot length (Test No. 25), and proved beyond doubt the additional strength of a box section chassis, compared to the Jeep's open frame. But it still fell short of Gordon Bashford's minimum requirement. An even stronger chassis was now required.

CHAPTER 4 – Prototypes and Chassis Frame Tests – The Centre Steer Hybrid

Chassis tests recorded in Gordon Bashford's ledger

Torsional Stiffness Tests on Frames

Test Nº	Frame Type	Matl. SWG	Weight (lbs)	Load (lbs)	Angle °	Torque (lbs/ft/°)
1.	14.1P. Std Saloon			600	2° 19'	690.
2.	14 1P. Std. frame with body. all openings closed.	"	"	1300	1° 23'	2500.
3.	as No. 2.	"	"	1600.	1° 35'	2688.
4.	As No. 2 with openings open	"	"	1600	2° 1'	2110.
5.	as No. 2.	"	"	1800.	1° 48'	2660.
6.	as No. 4.	"	"	1600.	1° 45'	2377.
7.	Expl. box 5"x4"	Reanf. 14.SWG.		2030	0°-24'	3999.
8.	" "	"	"	DIST. 26 cuts	0°-24'	3999.
9.	1st. P4. tripl. minus x members			1600	1°-27'	2942.
10.	" minus Rear x members			1600	1°-16'	3230.
11.	" comp.			2000	1°-22'	3742.
12.	Studebaker. minus x members		190	600.	3°-32'	551.
13.	2nd P4. like Stude.	16.SWG		1000	2°-48'	1070.
14.	" front x members only	"		1000	2°-13'	1365.
15.	" Front + Rear floor	"		1000	1°-48'	1666.
16.	" complete.	"		1000	1°-40'	1820.
17.	3rd P4. like Stude. 4½ deep	14.SWG				2092.
18.	as above ½" deeper	"				2246.
19.	as 18. Rear end locked	"				6640.
20.	As Tests 7+8. Rear locked					7750.
21.	Swept front X member to 4¼" deep box. as 17.	14 SWG.				2640.
22.	Rear members swept Attachment as #21.	"				3040.
23.	4¾ deep frame as 18 new swept type crossmembers.	"		1000	0°-59'	3090.
24	Am. Jeep.		184	300	3°-23'	260.
25.	"Land Rover" 4½" Deep	12.SWG.		1000	0° 47'	4000
26.	"Land Rover" 6"Deep	12.SWG	277.	1000	0°.26'	7000
27.	"Land Rover" 6"Deep	14.SWG	235	1000		5000
28.	"Land Rover" 6"deep without No. 3. x member. as test 27	14 SWG		1000	0°.53'	3500.
29.	Std. 12 P. Frame.			500.	4°	320.

53

With seed drill

To increase torsional stiffness still further, a '2nd frame' was constructed, again using 12 swg (2.65 mm) mild steel. But instead of using the Jeep's cross-section of 4½" x 2", the longitudinal rails were increased substantially to a depth of 6 inches and a width of 3 inches. For the first trial chassis – the 4½-inch frame – Rover had been able to keep to the same basic dimensions as the Jeep chassis. This was possible because the width between the chassis rails was sufficient to accommodate Rover's new P3 engine and gearbox, which all sat on the left side, while the Jeep 'Spicer' transfer box, transmission brake and front output housing, all sat further back on the opposite side. This latest chassis would now be specially designed to accommodate only Rover's own engine and transmission components.

When put under test, the torsional stiffness of this second Land-Rover chassis produced a figure of 7,000 ft/lbs/° (Test No. 26). This was 40% over target, and although way over the top, it was excellent news. A third Land-Rover chassis immediately followed, only this time using lighter 14 swg (2.05 mm) mild steel. Under test, the '3rd frame' came out at 5,000 ft/lbs/° (Test No. 27) - the top end of Gordon Bashford's requirements. Not only was it adequate for the job, but chassis weight had fallen from 277 lbs to just 235 lbs – a reduction of 42 lbs or more than 15%.

Apart from the overall weight loss, which would improve the Land-Rover's power to weight ratio, steel supplies to the motor industry were under tight government control, and instead of eight Land-Rover chassis per ton of steel, based on this latest figure they could now make nine and a half chassis per ton. More precisely, from 1,000-tons of steel, instead of 8,086 chassis, 9,532 could now be made – that's an extra 1,446 Land-Rovers.

Still not totally satisfied, a further test was carried out on this 3rd Land-Rover frame, only this time with 'No.3 X-member removed' (Test No. 28). That is the substantial box section crossmember located immediately beneath the gearbox bell housing. The resulting figure of 3,500 ft/lbs/° was far too low, and worse than the figure produced by the original 4½-inch chassis. Clearly no further gain in weight could be easily made and the crossmember was welded back into place.

Alongside 'Test No. 27', the letters *'O.K.'* were then inscribed in Gordon Bashford's ledger. This became the final design and no further Land-Rover chassis tests are recorded. All subsequent chassis would be based on this pattern. Increasing the chassis box section dimensions in this way did, however, have certain implications. Rover still kept the chassis longitudinal rails on the same centre line as used for the Jeep, but increasing the rail width to three inches added an extra half inch to each side of

CHAPTER 4 – Prototypes and Chassis Frame Tests – The Centre Steer Hybrid

Deep wading

the rails. This left a gap of just 25 inches in which to fit the engine, starter motor, gearbox, transfer box etc. and things became extremely tight. The overall external width of the longitudinal rails had also increased, from 30 to 31 inches.

Up to this point Jeep axles had been used. These had a track of 49 inches. If this dimension was kept for the Land-Rover, its turning circle would be considerably reduced, the vehicle's front tyres coming into contact with the chassis too soon, reducing steering lock by several degrees. To compensate, the Land-Rover's track was therefore correspondingly increased by 1 inch to 50 inches. Only after such calculations were completed could final dimensions for the new Land-Rover's running gear be at last determined.

The original $4^1/_2$-inch Land-Rover chassis frame used for this hybrid prototype development model had become the second vehicle from the batch of 50 Land-Rovers initially sanctioned by Rover's Board, and has provided much of the mystery essential to a good tale. It was, in fact, the 'missing link', previously so often talked about in the 1970s, between the original Jeep-based centre steer hybrid and 'R01' – the first 'all Rover' Land-Rover to be 'despatched in' at the factory.

These first two hybrid prototypes took very little time to develop, but from now on progress would be much slower. Rover's own 4x4 transmission components still had to be developed and manufactured before construction of the remaining 48 pre-production models could get underway. In consequence, at the next Board meeting on 12 November 1947, there was nothing more exciting to record than:

"Mr Wilks informed the Board that work on the pre-production batch was proceeding."

There can be little doubt that the original $4^1/_2$-inch Land-Rover chassis was scrapped after testing had finished, but the second Land-Rover chassis, which was also made of thicker 12 swg steel, seems to have been put to one side – at least for the time being. There can also be little doubt that the third Land-Rover chassis, which became the final design, was used in a pre-production model after its No.3 X-member was reinstated. However, as very early pre-production Land-Rover chassis were not stamped with a frame number – only their 'car' number (generally referred to as the chassis number) – there is no obvious way of identifying which Land-Rover used this third 'definitive' frame. It appears to have been first photographed on 24 February 1948, and may well be that sitting under R01, in the 'Heritage' museum at Gaydon.

After initial stress tests, the original 12 swg chassis was probably used as a jig to determine bodywork design detail and the exact location of various other component parts, ready for the first

LAND-ROVER – The Formative Years, 1947–1967

Showing off-road capability

batch of pre-production chassis to arrive back after being galvanised. Once the first few pre-production Land-Rovers had been completed, it seems likely that this 12 swg chassis later joined the line as a complete vehicle. The chassis on L11 is made from 12 swg and could well be this original test chassis.

The earliest chassis to be stamped with a frame number is '16', belonging to pre-production Land-Rover L29. Conversely, the earliest known Land-Rover with a stamped frame number is pre-production L12, which is stamped '23'. Based on extant pre-production chassis, it has become clear that the very earliest frames were never stamped up either before or after galvanising. Although L12 has a frame number, this author's 1948 pre-production Land-Rover, which immediately precedes it, only has 'L11' stamped on the chassis – there is no frame number. Pre-production Land-Rover R04 has no frame number, just R04 on a 'cover-up' plate, which was temporarily removed during its restoration to reveal 'R05' underneath. Currently R19 is the last known pre-production Land-Rover not stamped with a frame number. However, as R16 has frame '38' it would seem there were quite a number of chassis from which to choose by then.

Confused? You're not the only one. My guess is that it has something to do with chassis frames being stacked at random when they arrived back after being galvanised – forget frame numbers, just grab the first one off the pile. We can only deduce from all this that maybe the first 15 or so chassis frames constructed went unnumbered, and only when they were being assembled into a complete vehicle was any number stamped on them. We do know from contemporary photographs that many pre-production models carried their number stencilled on their front crossmember, but no 'L' or 'R' preceded it, so it's possible that was the only way in which early chassis frames were originally numbered. After that, both car and frame numbers would be stamped alongside one another on all remaining pre-production Land-Rovers, and also production Land-Rover chassis, for the next few years.

Delivering the milk

That well known photo with 'Timber' Woods and Bill Whale

56

CHAPTER 4 – Prototypes and Chassis Frame Tests – The Centre Steer Hybrid

CHAPTER 5
From Hybrids to Highway Pre-Production Models

There was now the small matter of marketing the Land-Rover. It was a vehicle designed specifically for the export market, but apart from Britain's colonial empire, this was an area in which Rover had almost no experience. So to give the Land-Rover as much publicity as possible it was decided its debut should take place at one of the world's major international motor shows.

When the time came to produce an advance publicity handout for the proposed launch of the Land-Rover, it seems that only the two hybrid prototypes were sufficiently developed to feature in a brochure. Even then, the second prototype was never given a body (something noted later of the first 'prototype' specialist military Land-Rover), as it was neither necessary nor particularly desirable at this stage of development. Consequently, it was left to an artist to 'complete the picture' for the first publicity brochure.

This early brochure was printed in English, Dutch and Spanish, giving some idea of Rover's intended markets outside Europe. It carried various illustrations, including a photograph of the original $4\frac{1}{2}$-inch 'Land-Rover' chassis frame (used for the second prototype), turned on its side, as if viewed from beneath, complete with P3 'Rover 60' engine, coupled to an internally modified P3 'Rover 75' gearbox and bell housing, but still showing the Jeep 'Spicer' high/low transfer box and running gear in use. A further illustration shows clearly how Tom Barton grafted Rover's own P3 gearbox to the Jeep transfer box. Also illustrated are the radiator, exhaust manifold, oil filler tube, and side cover from the P3 'Rover 60' car engine, none of which stayed with the Land-Rover beyond the pre-production stage.

Land-Rover axles were given a track two inches wider than the Jeep axles illustrated. This is accounted for by the increase in Land-Rover chassis cross-section width from two inches to three inches after the 'experimental' $4\frac{1}{2}$-inch chassis – an extra inch on either side being necessary to maintain wheel lock. Land-Rover axles also differed from those of the Jeep by sensibly having

L11 under construction in Rover's Experimental Department

The Land-Rover is announced to all Rover's main agents

CHAPTER 5 – From Hybrids to Highway – Pre-Production Models

Ref: No.529

THE ROVER COMPANY LTD.

London Showroom
DEVONSHIRE HOUSE
PICCADILLY LONDON W1
Telephone Grosvenor 2072

METEOR WORKS
SOLIHULL BIRMINGHAM

London Service Depot
SEAGRAVE ROAD
FULHAM LONDON SW6
Telephone Fulham 1221

TELEPHONE SHELDON 2411
TELEGRAMS ROVER SOLIHULL

All communications to be addressed to the company and not to individuals

REF. 2/AOH/MC   19th April 1948

TO ALL DEALERS & RETAIL DEALERS
- - - - - - - - - - - - - - - -

Dear Sir (s),

The Land-Rover

With this letter we are very pleased to send you a leaflet so that you may have particulars of the Land-Rover, a new and most interesting vehicle which will be on view for the first time at the Amsterdam Motor Show, to be open to the public from 30th April to 9th May inclusive.

We have also arranged for Land-Rovers to be exhibited at the four Agricultural Shows which have been approved by The Society of Motor Manufacturers & Traders Ltd., for the display of Light and Medium Commercial Vehicles. They are :-

    Royal Ulster Show Belfast   ...   May 26th to 28th.
    Bath & West Show, Cardiff   ...   May 26th to 29th.
    Highland Show, Inverness   ...   June 22nd to 25th.
    The Royal Show, York   ...   July 6th to 9th.

In addition of course we shall have them on our Stand at the Commercial Exhibition, Earls Court, October 1st - 9th 1948.

Production is planned to commence during June, but owing to the controlled material position and the need to export, it seems we may not be able to supply more than one Land-Rover to your Distributors during this calendar year.

The retail price of the Land-Rover is shown on a seperate enclosure which also sets out a list of "extras", the prices of which will be available in the near future.

It is our present intention that discounts shall be the same as for Rover Cars, that extras and special equipment will be subject to a discount of 10% only, and that Dealers with wholesale rights shall pass the whole of this to the Trader selling, except of course in the case of a Repairer who will be entitled to his 5% introductory commission only on the list price of extras and special equipment as well as on the list price of the vehicle.

After the middle of May a Land-Rover will be available for inspection in our Showrooms, Devonshire House, Piccadilly, London, W.1. and we hope you will make this known to all those who may be interested in seeing it there.

Yours faithfully,
THE ROVER COMPANY LTD.,

A.O.Hollick
Sales Manager

detachable housings for the swivel pin bearings at the front, while at the rear, the axle was no longer fully-floating. Unlike the Jeep, which had both differentials built up into the axle casings, Rover differentials also had their own separate housings. This meant they too could be easily replaced as a complete unit, should the need arise. Similarly, the brake drums on Land-Rovers could be removed as a single item, whereas the Jeep brake drums could only be removed by removing the hub and exposing the wheel bearings and grease to the elements. After that, the wheel studs had to be driven out (requiring new replacement on reassembly), to separate hub from drum. Wheel nuts on the left side on the Jeep also had the added complication of being left-hand thread. All this helped make the Land-Rover a far more suitable car to maintain in the field than the wartime Jeep, especially in remote locations. One thing that did remain exactly the same was the size and thread of those large special nuts (Pt. No. 217355) retaining the front hub bearings on the stub axle.

Other illustrations in the first brochure, based on factory photographs, show the original centre steer hybrid cleverly disguised with 'artist's bodywork' to make it look more like the Land-Rovers that would eventually emerge from the Solihull factory. A good deal of trouble was also taken to add detail already found on the second prototype,

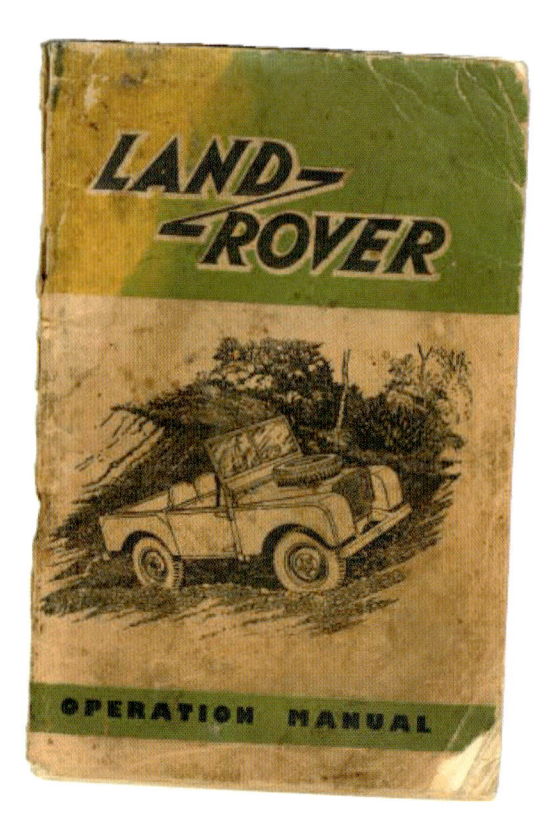

R02 in the Solihull factory – note side-screen hinges bolted on

TP/108/A June 1948, the first driver's handbook

Right: First brochure, published in English, Dutch and Spanish

Far right: The Land-Rover was first unveiled in England at the 'Royal Show' York.

CHAPTER 5 – From Hybrids to Highway – Pre-Production Models

R01 as it appeared in the announcement in 'The Times'

"All roads lead to YORK"

The 'ROYAL' is there July 6 to 9

Mark these dates on your calendar — for they are the days of this year's 'Royal' at York. As always the cream of Britain's pedigree stock will be there. You'll see, too, the last word in agricultural implements, from combines to simple hand tools; a glorious flower show, a forestry exhibition, and of course, horse jumping and other attractions in the show ring.
Don't miss the 'Royal' this year: it is better than ever.

Remember: on 'opening day' — July 6th — the show ring is reserved exclusively for stock judging; Horse jumping and other competitions will take place during the three subsequent days.

THE ROYAL SHOW
YORK, July 6, 7, 8, 9

THE ROYAL AGRICULTURAL SOCIETY OF ENGLAND
16 BEDFORD SQUARE, LONDON, W.C.1

The LAND ROVER
FOR THE FARMER, THE COUNTRYMAN AND GENERAL INDUSTRIAL USE

such as conventional spring shackles instead of the American 'Manganese Bronze Co.' threaded 'U' type used on the original Jeep framed hybrid. The usual Land-Rover fuel tank is not seen below the body line. This is because the first fuel tank design, as depicted in Gordon Bashford's ledger, was only $11^1/_2$ inches deep, but 25 inches long, and 'L' shaped to go forward under the floor panel. This shallow profile 'L' tank had good ground clearance and was to have been fitted under the passenger seat, where there were no foot pedal levers. It would have been fine on a LHD model, but on a RHD model its location was too close to the exhaust pipe work. It was therefore dropped in favour of the now familiar short deep tank of similar capacity.

With production of the new P3 saloon car underway by January 1948, all efforts were concentrated on the Land-Rover. With chassis dimensions now determined, a special jig, known as 'the Christmas tree' (its many toggle clamps stuck out like branches) was built for its construction. Then as soon as the 4x4 transmission became available, the Experimental Department began constructing the first pre-production Land-Rovers.

Apart from the road springs, which because of the Land-Rover's unbelievably short propshafts, took some time to get right, the last calculations in Gordon Bashford's ledger concerning Land-Rover development, refer to the hand-brake cross-tube (an item specific only to LHD models and not illustrated in the original Spare Parts Catalogue), and are dated 22 January 1948. Other pointers to the Land-Rover's earliest possible construction date are the factory photographic records: the 'new galvanised chassis frame' is dated 24 January; 'new body' 29 January; and 'new pattern grille', 19 February 1948.

All the drawings for the Land-Rover's early 'push-pull' selector mechanism for engaging 4x2/4x4, high/low ratio, and engaging/disengaging the 'Freewheel' device also survive. The earliest drawing, dated 1 January 1948, was for the black knobs (the drawings for two of the 'bronze' bosses supporting the rods as they pass through the bulkhead are dated 13 January 1947, but these were an existing Rover P3 car part and so not peculiar to the push-pull system). All these dates tie up nicely with the timing – as recalled by Maurice Wilks' friend, Bishop Warren Hunt – of the very first Land-Rover being finished nine months to the very day MCW had his vision at Red Wharf Bay back in April 1947.

The last dated drawing for the push-pull control system, Pt. No. X18179 – 'support for the control lever bracket' – on which the push-pull vertical control levers were mounted on the engine side of the bulkhead, was 1 April 1948 (don't let that fool you). But by then two of the pre-production Land-Rovers, R01 and R02, had already been completed and 'despatched in' at the factory, suggesting that the design may have taken some time to perfect. The 'X' preceding these part numbers indicates an experimental part. Eventually, the 'X' would be replaced by a '2', if subsequently a part went into full production. The last recorded modification to the push-pull control system was to Pt. No. X18191, 'sub-assembly tube and link control', dated 23 April 1948.

The first 'all Rover' Land-Rover, R01, had taken just six weeks to construct. Its body was considerably different from the centre steer model and altogether much squarer and modern in shape. The rear body appears, however, to have remained unpainted, keeping it unfinished, possibly to avoid the minor technicality of being 'despatched in' and accountable as a 'completed car' on the factory records until all initial trials were satisfactorily completed. Who knows? Newsreel film covering these trials still exists today, and the front cover

R01 Almost as good as a mountain goat

CHAPTER 5 – From Hybrids to Highway – Pre-Production Models

R01 demonstrates its fording capabilities

This picture of R01 was used for the cover TP/108/A

Pre-production Land-Rover ready for use as a demonstrator

of the first two owner handbooks, TP/108/A and TP/108/B are based on a still photograph of what must have been quite an occasion.

On Thursday, 11 March 1948, this first 'all Rover' Land-Rover was finally 'despatched in'. Although it was the third of the batch of 50 models sanctioned by the Board on 4 September 1947, the previous two were both hybrid prototypes; as the first real Land-Rover it was officially entered into Rover's Despatch Book as '01'.[1] Four days later '02' followed, but Rover were already too late for the first international motor show of 1948 at Geneva. They now fixed their sights on Amsterdam, just seven weeks away. With two Land-Rovers satisfactorily completed, the minutes of the Board meeting for 23 March put on record that:

"...the first prototypes of the Landrover are now on test, and the Directors made a personal inspection of one of these".

Six weeks after 02 was 'despatched in', and with just three days to go to before the Amsterdam show, three more vehicles – L03, R04, and L07 – were 'despatched in' on 27 April, closely followed by L05, a 'Welder'; R06, a 'Fire Engine'; and R08

[1] *There was no prefix 'L' or 'R' in the Despatch Book for these first two Land-Rovers.*

Pre-production model uplifted for handbook diagram

CHAPTER 5 – From Hybrids to Highway – Pre-Production Models

R02 undergoing field trials

R02 on trials in Wales

R02 on trials in Wales

R02 on trials in Wales

65

LAND-ROVER – The Formative Years, 1947–1967

R06 up to the job

R06 Fire Engine

the following day – the same day the Land-Rovers left for Amsterdam. According to 'The Motor', 28 April 1948, only two vehicles were scheduled to appear at Amsterdam – one a standard version, possibly L03 as it is left-hand drive and known to have been used as a demonstrator on the Continent, the other, *"...equipped with an arc welding unit"*, could only have been L05. In 1950 this 'Fire Tender' received a prototype 2.0-litre engine and went to Dewars Garage and Engineering Works, Calcutta, one of five Rover distributors on the Indian sub-continent.

The late Bart Vandeveen, editor of the Olyslager Auto Library and the 'After the Battle' military enthusiasts' publication 'Wheels & Tracks', attended the show, which was held in the old RAI buildings on Ferdinand Bolstraat between 30 April and 9 May. He later recalled the event in a letter to one-time Secretary of the Land-Rover Register, Peter Galilee:

"On the stand of Messrs H. Englebert NV of The Hague, was one Land-Rover and there was another one outside, as a demonstrator. The latter was parked, with other vehicles, according to my diary, in the street right opposite the RAI's main entrance. To the best of my recollection it was a light green one, open, with RHD. What I recall most vividly is that when I was looking it over, a rep got in and after firing it up, tried to engage first or reverse gear: this produced considerable grating noises, as if the clutch would not disengage, or not properly anyway. It caused considerable embarrassment, too! (In retrospect, what a way to remember one's first encounter with a particular vehicle!)"

The incident is not altogether surprising as Rover had little time to prepare the vehicles, which at this time were still equipped with troublesome 'bulkhead controls' for high/low-ratio selection, 'Freewheel' engagement, and 4x2 selection, which were soon to be abandoned. It is currently believed that of the 48 pre-production Land-Rovers assembled in the factory, only the first 16 were ever fitted with push-pull bulkhead controls and selectable 4x2.

CHAPTER 5 – From Hybrids to Highway – Pre-Production Models

R06 the Fire Engine

R17 the 'Crop Sprayer'

LAND-ROVER – The Formative Years, 1947–1967

L03 demonstrating in Spain

L03 demonstrating in Spain

CHAPTER 5 – From Hybrids to Highway – Pre-Production Models

L03 demonstrating in Spain. Note badge on the wing

L05 Push-pull controls and engine governor quadrant

Although only the 48 'all Rover' pre-production Land-Rovers were 'despatched in' at the factory, a full set of 50 parts were made (gearboxes No. 49 and 50 and at least one set of bronze hubs having since been discovered in early production models). The purpose of these pre-production models was several-fold. Initially they were used to determine the final layout of the Land-Rover itself, including the various variants such as the 'Welder', 'Fire Engine', 'Crop-Sprayer' and 'Station Wagon'.

After completion of the first 20 pre-production Land-Rovers, the construction of the remaining 28 examples was then used to determine the layout of the factory production line and the positioning of the sub-assembly feeder lines. Many then went on to be used for trials as demonstrators both around the factory and elsewhere, providing advanced publicity at shows etc. to test public reaction to the vehicle. They also provided Rover with a reasonable number of Land-Rovers for overseas distributors for showroom and demonstration use, soon after the initial launch.

Using the general layout of a wartime Willys Jeep, and Rover's new P3 'Rover 60' engine as a power plant, enabled Land-Rover development to come a long way in a very short time. An indication of the pace is revealed by the 'Girling' brake master cylinder's bracket being welded on after chassis frames were galvanised on all pre-production chassis – the only item not duplicated on both sides of a pre-production chassis frame for 'handing'. Prior to being galvanised, all pre-

CHAPTER 5 – From Hybrids to Highway – Pre-Production Models

R23, L24, L25 and L26 ready to leave for Switzerland

L05 the 'Welder' went to the Amsterdam Show

L25 and glider about to leave Redhill Aerodrome for Samaden, Switzerland

R01 coping with floods

R01 showing 'lift-the-dot' hood fixings. Both sections of side screen slide with finger grab

production Land-Rovers chassis had been properly equipped on both sides with special distance tubes to take a Lockheed brake master cylinder, which had its own integral reservoir, and not the Girling unit. L09, the only LHD pre-production Land-Rover to remain in the UK and still retain left-hand drive,[2] is also the only pre-production model to have the original Lockheed braking system still in place.

Rover adopted the new Girling 'Hydrastatic' system for the Land-Rover at the eleventh hour. The system's light contact of shoe linings on the drum offered a cross-country car, such as the

[2] *Accounted for by the fact that it was never officially 'sold off' from the factory.*

Land-Rover, a number of advantages, including: automatic brake adjustment; good braking under varying loads; minimal brake fade after wading; no space for the ingress of foreign matter between lining and drum, preventing drum score.

The original Lockheed braking system was considered technically superior, but unfortunately was far too sophisticated for a cross-country utility vehicle such as the Land-Rover, and clogged up in off-road conditions, which made braking a hopeless affair. Rover's only previous experience with Lockheed hydraulic brakes was on their pre-war 1934/35 P1 'Speed 14'. All Rover's other pre-war and post-war cars had Girling mechanical brakes, until the advent of the P3 of 1948, which

71

LAND-ROVER – The Formative Years, 1947–1967

L26 at Samaden

CHAPTER 5 – From Hybrids to Highway – Pre-Production Models

LAND-ROVER – The Formative Years, 1947–1967

L29 on trade plates

R23 door is sign-written for Brussels distributor

used hydraulic brakes at the front end for its independent front suspension layout.

To speed things up, only those features of the Jeep which did not fit in with Maurice Wilks' original vision at Red Wharf Bay in April 1947 were abandoned. In his ledger, Gordon Bashford had even based his calculations for the Land-Rover's steering final ratio on Jeep figures – variable between 17.2:1 at centre and 20:1 on maximum lock, although the Land-Rover's 18.4:1 was a fixed ratio. The central steering position was not continued beyond the development stage – clearly a correct decision, as it would have made the Land-Rover far too agricultural for the many roles it was eventually to play.

One feature not kept was the Jeep's facility to direct its headlight beams into the engine bay – a considerable convenience in those moments of darkness when not everything was as it should be. But such an arrangement might have implied that Rover did not have every confidence in their new product, and furthermore, that if anything was to go wrong, it would be at the least convenient moment. Rover's new Land-Rovers only needed to see where they were going, not why they weren't going, and so it was never adopted.

The galvanised steel chassis fitted in nicely with Maurice Wilks' plan for a vehicle able to cross *"...vast stretches of sand and sea..."*, yet capable of withstanding the corrosive effects of salt spray. However, only the 48 pre-production Land-Rover chassis were given this treatment. The suggestion that the process was discontinued because of excessive accumulation of zinc in the box section can be discounted, as this had been overcome by placing two large drain holes beneath the chassis rails at the rear end. Distortion would not have presented any serious problem either. It was simple economics that prevented the process being continued as it meant either transporting heavy chassis frames elsewhere, or an expensive investment in plant at the factory. In either case, what was the point of galvanising a chassis that was already likely to outlast the rest of the vehicle in both off-road and agricultural use?

CHAPTER 5 – From Hybrids to Highway – Pre-Production Models

R28 at Kent Show with Winston Churchill

The 48 pre-production Land-Rovers became the flagships of Rover's new venture. Frequently used as demonstrators, they would receive a good deal of rough treatment off-road. And with the eye of 'Everyman' upon them, it was imperative that a quick hose-down could return them to showroom condition. A galvanised chassis enabled this to be easily achieved. Every motor manufacturer likes to give that bit of extra spit and polish to his latest offering, and Rover was no exception, even if it was only a 'Land' Rover.

The weight of the earliest production models was officially put at 1-ton 3-cwt, including water, fuel, and oil, but most of the pre-production models have recorded weights of around 1-ton $3^1/_2$-cwt – galvanising, no doubt, accounting for some of the extra $^1/_2$-cwt. Whether they had been weighed with spare wheel, door, etc. which were not standard on the earliest production models, is not known. The recorded weight of R04, now at the National Motor Museum, is 1-ton 4-cwt, but the official figure for L11, this author's example, is only 1-ton 2-cwt. Was L11 empty of water, fuel and oil and perhaps carried no spare wheel? Maybe R04 carried a prototype front winch? It has the necessary five distance tubes inserted in the chassis No.2 crossmember.

Altogether, ten pre-production models were 'despatched in' during May, and according to factory records, the first of these, L09, was eventually 'despatched out' to Spencer Wilks as late as 23 January 1963, soon after his retirement as Chairman of the company. It remained lefthand drive and seems to have spent its early life as a factory hack.

Six vehicles from the May batch are recorded in the company despatch book as the first LandRovers to be shown to the British public between 26 and 29 May 1948. They are: L11, R13 and R14 – Royal Agricultural Show, Belfast; L12, R15 and R16 – Bath and West Show, Cardiff.

The Land-Rover's debut in England came slightly later at the Royal Show, York, from the 6–9 July, where L11 and R14 were again exhibited. One other vehicle from the May batch worth mentioning is R19, as this was in Spencer Wilks' name.

Fourteen more Land-Rovers appeared in June. The first of these, L20, was 'despatched in' to 'Tickfords' of Newport Pagnall, where it was provided with a prototype coachbuilt Station Wagon body before being 'despatched out' in October to Franco Britannic Autos of Paris, Rover's distributor in France, in time for the Paris Show, replacing L26, which was returned to the factory. Another

Field Tests

vehicle in this batch, R22, was used on trade plates by Maurice Wilks between 10–23 June, and colour home movie of this still exists.

Six others from the June batch also went to distributors, four to A. Douglas A/L Export, Redhill in Surrey, eventually for loan to Rover distributors in Europe. They were: R23 and L25 to Ets. Paul Sterckx Ing. S.A., Brussels; L24 to N/V. H. Engleberts Automobielhandel, The Hague: L26 to Franco Britannic Autos, Paris.

Initially, however, all four had been lent to the British Gliding Association and towed gliders across France to Samedan in Switzerland for the first post-war World Gliding Championship, the connection being with Redhill Aerodrome, home of Surrey and Imperial College Gliding Clubs. In return, Ann Welch (née Douglas), British team manager, was given responsibility for feedback to Rover on the vehicles' behaviour. MCW's nephew, Peter Wilks, had to be sent out to sort out minor problems with the gearbox – but nothing too serious.

The next two, R 27 and R 28, both went to MacRae & Dick Ltd., Inverness, in time for the Highland Show, held on 22 to 26 June. Later, R28 returned to the factory. It was then driven

R32 in the field

CHAPTER 5 – From Hybrids to Highway – Pre-Production Models

Rover's Turbine Team alongside R38. Rover's Chief Turbine Engineer, R.F. Bell, is second from right

L46 Undergoing 'Tilt Test'

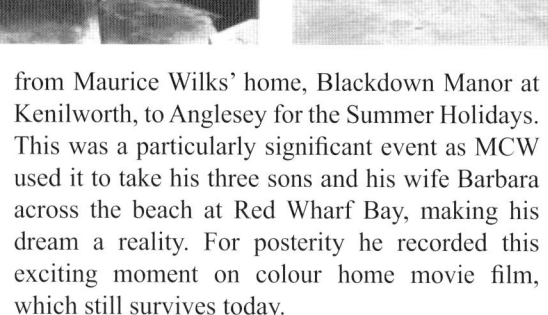

from Maurice Wilks' home, Blackdown Manor at Kenilworth, to Anglesey for the Summer Holidays. This was a particularly significant event as MCW used it to take his three sons and his wife Barbara across the beach at Red Wharf Bay, making his dream a reality. For posterity he recorded this exciting moment on colour home movie film, which still survives today.

The last two vehicles of the June batch also deserve special mention. These were pre-production Land-Rovers L29 and R30. Both were 'despatched in' at the Rover factory on the 23 June, and went out the following day, to the Ministry of Supply at Chertsey in Surrey, for Army field trials, ensuring the British Army had an early opportunity to try out Rover's new cross-country utility truck.

By June everyone involved on the Land-Rover project was engaged in a concerted effort to get production underway, and a gap of three weeks passed before any more Land-Rovers were 'despatched in' at the factory. From now on their construction would mainly be used to determine the layout of the production line and the positioning of the sub-assembly feeder lines. Non-production

LAND-ROVER – The Formative Years, 1947–1967

Early pre-production at Blackdown Manor

items, such as the original 'integral' bumper became less common, while other features, such as the bulkhead gearbox controls, disappeared altogether. During this time Rover's employees were already busily engaged assembling production Land-Rovers, the first of which, R860001 and R860002, were finally completed on Monday, 19 July 1948. For all those involved in the initial development of the Land-Rover, it was the end of the beginning.

Along with these first two production models, seven more pre-production models were also 'despatched in'. Two of these, L31 and R32, were immediately sent for extensive trials with the National Institute of Agricultural Engineering and Scottish Machinery Testing Station.[3] The other five, R40 to R44, all went out the following day, heading for the Overseas Development Corporation's ill-fated 'Ground Nut' scheme in Tanganyika (modern Tanzania), providing an ideal opportunity for the Land-Rover to establish itself in East Africa.

With the Land-Rover production line now ready to roll, Rover's employees then took their annual fortnight's holiday, and another three weeks

3 See 'The British Society for Research in Agricultural Engineering, Report RT 1/49034 on test of Prototype Land-Rover, 27.8.49'

intervened before the remaining pre-production models were finally 'despatched in'. It was now the second week of August. The first vehicle, 'despatched in' on Monday 9th, was an early vehicle, R17, that had undergone conversion into a crop-sprayer by Dorman Simplex of Cambridge. It may also be the first Land-Rover to use floor controls instead of the original push-pull bulkhead controls. Other pre-production Land-Rovers 'despatched in' that day were L36, R37, and R38.

The following day, Tuesday 10 August, another three pre-production Land-Rovers appeared. These also went to overseas distributors: R39 to Puzey & Paine of Salisbury, Southern Rhodesia (modern Zimbabwe); L47 and L48 to Alberto Fahling of Buenos Aires, Argentina. On Wednesday 11th, L45 was 'despatched in', followed by L46 – the last of the pre-production models to be 'despatched in' at the factory – on Thursday 12 August. Today L46 is best known by contemporary photographs of Rover's 'tilt test' establishing the Land-Rover's 30° angle of safe operation. The Solihull factory was now geared for full-scale production – albeit on a limited basis for the next few months.

CHAPTER 5 – From Hybrids to Highway – Pre-Production Models

Field Tests

Ploughing

CHAPTER 6
A Pattern for Progress Drawings and Designs

Nearly all pre-production Land-Rovers that have survived into the 21st Century were models sold off in the home market after their use as demonstrators. Being embryonic models, Rover generally updated them with various 'improvements' before they left the factory, and that often included a replacement engine. In consequence it is necessary to refer to early factory photographs and drawings, and contemporary articles in the motoring press to reveal details of items either removed by the factory or subsequently lost.

Despite the late Gordon Bashford organising a thorough factory search immediately prior to his retirement, the original 1/4-scale drawings for the Land-Rover, Pt. No. X18030, have never been re-discovered. Generally such drawings are a useful guide to modifications undertaken, as they are normally updated, with dates of modifications given.

Of the early batch of 20 pre-production Land-Rovers, R01 to L20, which were probably all originally constructed by Rover's Experimental Department, 11 have so far come to light, providing a first-hand opportunity to study the structure of these embryonic models in some detail. Of these extant models, many have been restored to their former glory and are now in the hands of the more serious collectors.

The Rover Co. never actually parted with R01, and after spending seven years as a working vehicle with William Francis Adcock of Dairy Farm, Ashworth, near Blackdown Manor, it went back to Rover and was refurbished by apprentices in 1956. Only eight years had passed, but memories were already fading and, for some time, R01 was thought to be the first production rather than pre-production model (the first production model was to have a less fortunate fate). Rover then lent R01 to the Birmingham Museum of Science and Technology, where she was appropriately positioned across the main isle from that giant of four-wheel-drive vehicles, the Railton Mobile Special, which in 1947 became the last car with a piston engine to take the World Land Speed Record.

After Rover became part of Leyland Motors R01 was re-acquired and given a replacement log book on 11 May 1967, in plenty of time for the '21st Birthday' celebrations. It was then displayed in the motor museums at Donnington and at Syon Park, Middlesex, until the opening of the British Motor Industry Heritage Trust collection at Gaydon, Warwickshire, in spring 1993. This author had an opportunity to drive R01 in Belgium in 1998, during the 40th Anniversary celebrations, and again in 1990 at the ARC National Rally at Trentham Gardens, Staffordshire.

The next extant pre-production model, L03, is the first left-hand drive Land-Rover, and was re-discovered in 1974. It was in excellent condition, with only the engine having been replaced. Its owner, Tim Dines, restored it just in time for the 50th Anniversary celebrations of 1998.

A further early vehicle, R04, was acquired in December 1976 by Tony Hutchings, founder of the 'Land-Rover Register', and after an extensive restoration, was lent to the National Motor Museum at Beaulieu, where it is now a permanent exhibit,

HNX 950: R04 at Beaulieu

Pre-pro diagrams, copyright John S Smith, 2009

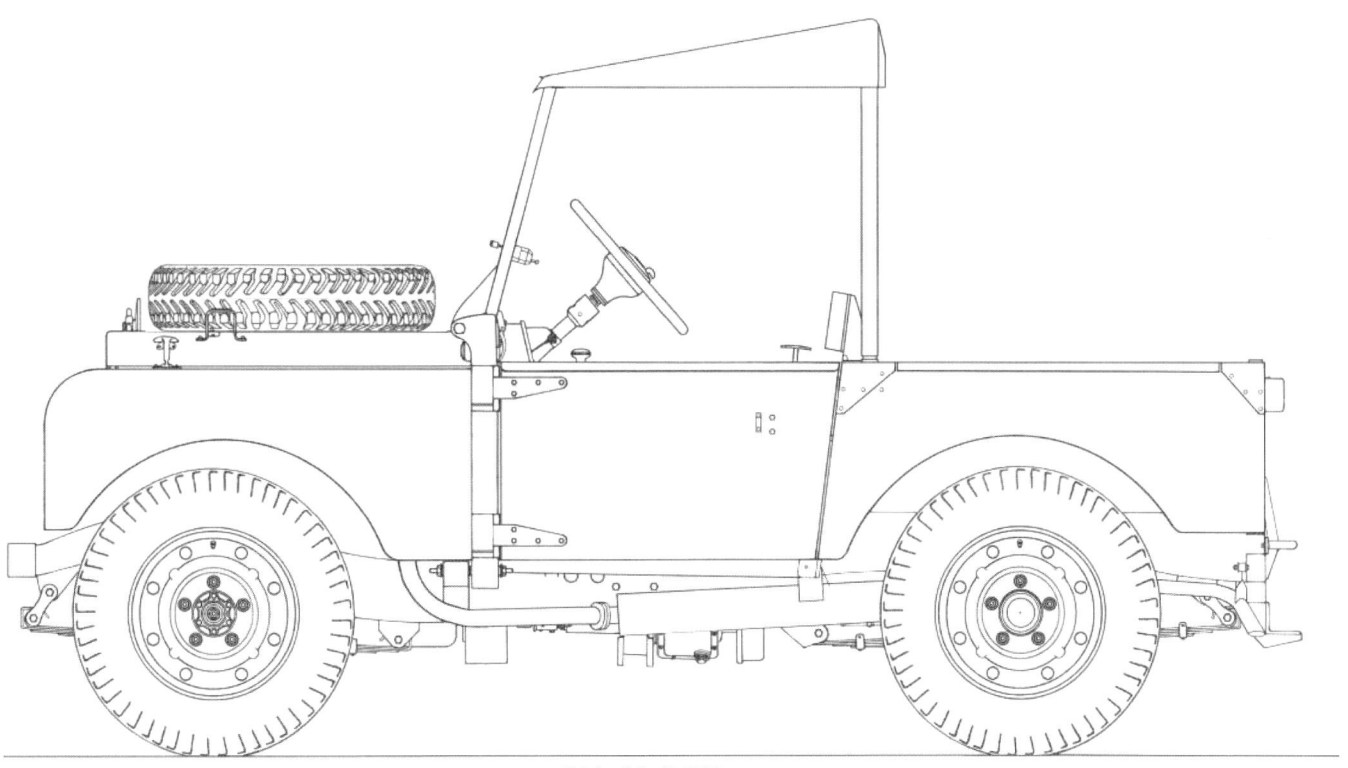

CHAPTER 6 – A Pattern for Progress – Drawings and Designs

© John S Smith 2008

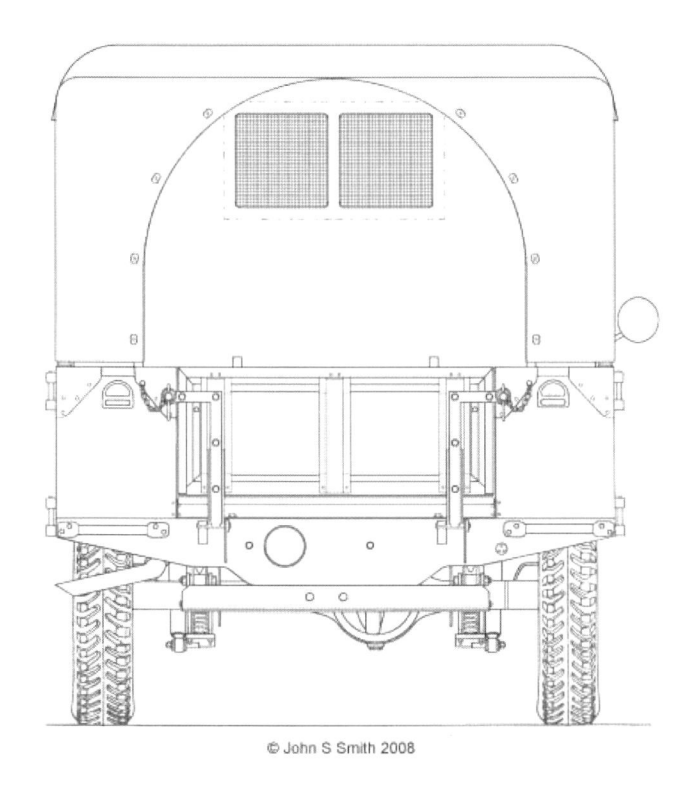

© John S Smith 2008

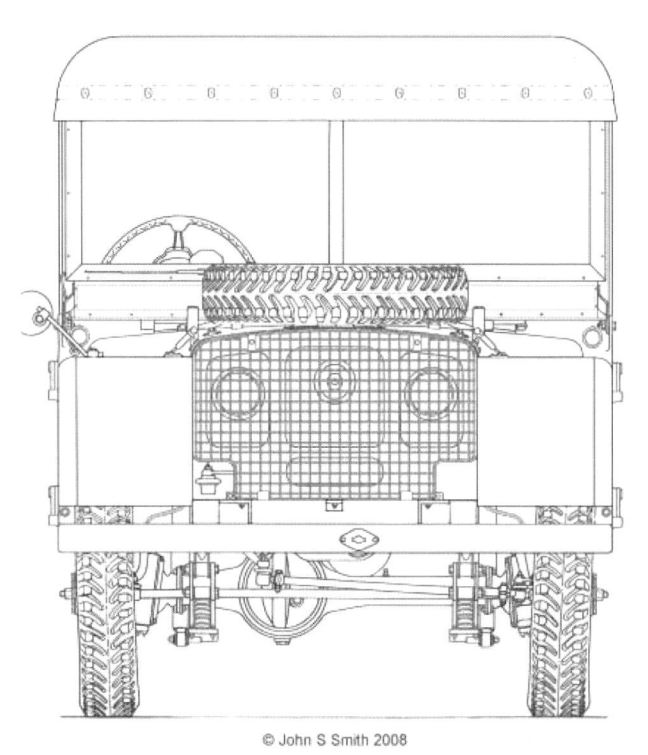

© John S Smith 2008

R01 'despatched in' as completed on 11 March 1948

having been purchased in 1980, with the aid of funds from the Science Museum.

The chassis and gearbox of R08 were discovered in Northamptonshire in August 1987, by Robert Ivins, one-time technical writer for 'LRO International'. Undeterred by its condition, its new owner managed to find sufficient early production parts to turn it into a running vehicle.

When L09 turned up in Warwickshire in early 1992 it was acquired by the Heritage Museum, in exchange for a working Land-Rover, and prior to the opening of the BMIHT museum at Gaydon, was housed at Studley Castle. Although no more than a rolling chassis, it still had the original Lockheed braking system (used by Morris), and left-hand drive steering levers in situation. Ken Wheelwright, currently Chairman of The Land-Rover Register, acquired it from the BMIHT in 1997 and has since restored it, using a replica bulkhead and bodywork from L26. The Dunsfold Collection acquired L09 in 2008.

The next extant pre-production Land-Rover is L11. This is the earliest recorded show model, and unveiled the Land-Rover in both England and Ulster, and has been owned by this author for more than 20 years. It is an extremely original example and one of the few pre-production models to still have its original engine, No.'11'. When L11 left the factory, after conversion to RHD, it went to Charles H Pugh Ltd., of Birmingham – maker of the famous 'Atco' mower, and boat impellers. After that L11 spent most of its working life in the Fens of East Anglia, before being discovered by Roger Parker in Cambridgeshire in 1984. A year later, it was acquired by this author, and in March 1986, led the then successful 'Keep Land-Rover British' campaign to No. 10 Downing Street. This was the first time a pre-production Land-Rover had appeared in 'The Times' since the original announcement back in 1948. Engine, body and chassis of this Land-Rover remained in excellent condition, and the gearbox has never been rebuilt.

As part of the 40th Anniversary celebrations, Land-Rover Ltd., gave full sponsorship to L11 to do a 10,000 mile trek around the peripheral edge of Europe, via the Arctic Circle, in the winter of 1988. Without any form of heating and only a canvas hood for protection, daytime temperatures of –20ºC were regularly experienced in the cab. It took eight weeks to complete the journey, with brief stops at Helsinki, Leningrad, Moscow, Kiev, Odessa, Istanbul, and Venice. Thankfully, both author and Land-Rover survived to tell the tale.

Three more pre-production models recorded as show models also survive – L12, R14 and R16. For many years L12 remained in north Devon until it was auctioned by Sotheby's at the RAF Museum, Hendon, in September 1995. Completely unrestored, it was bought for an inclusive figure of almost £12,000. Its new owner, Alan Wheelwright,

Drawing, topside of pre-production Land-Rover for handbook

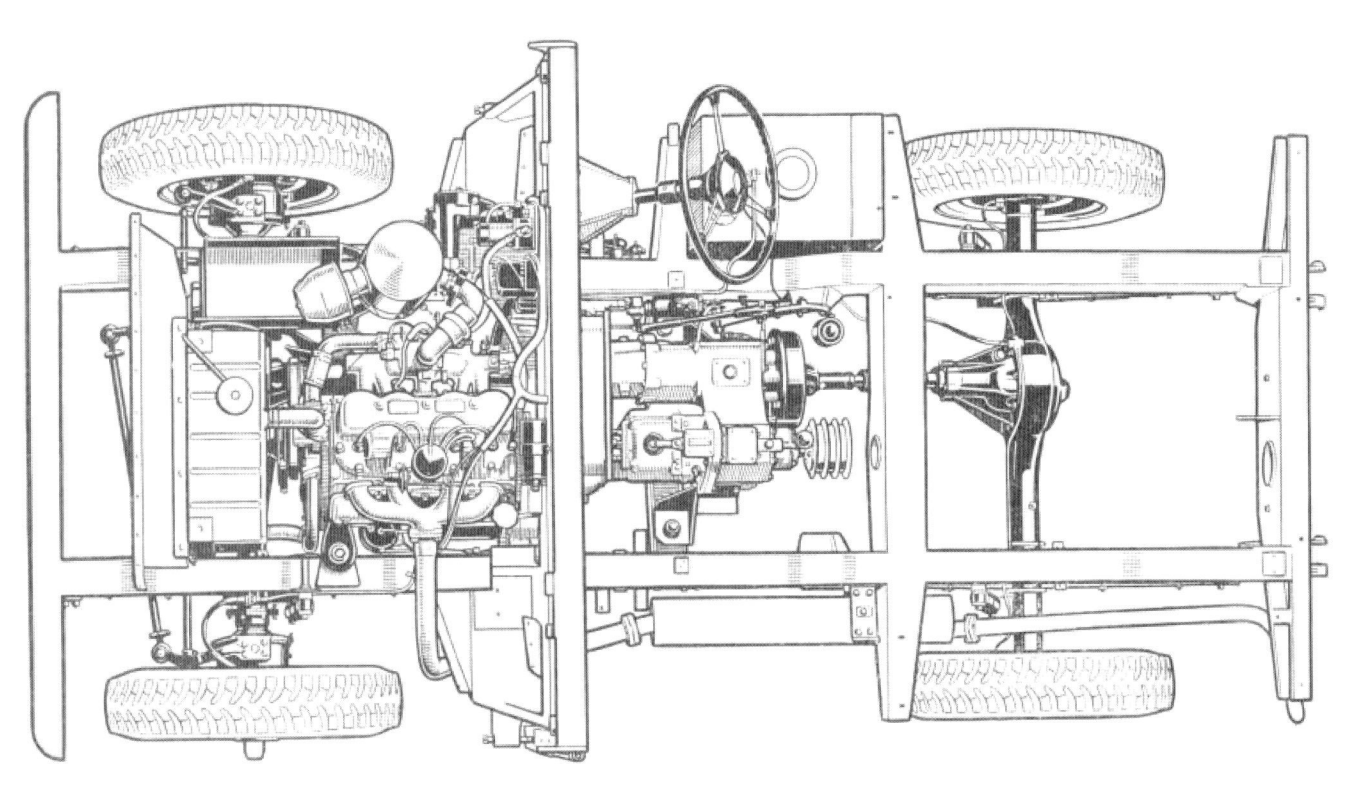

CHAPTER 6 – A Pattern for Progress – Drawings and Designs

is nephew of Ken Wheelwright, long-standing Chairman of The Land-Rover Register. The restoration of L12 was completed in 1997, in time for the 50th Anniversary celebrations.

The show model R14 has never been restored, but continues to be used regularly. Land-Rover Register committee member Michael Rivett purchased it from enthusiast Gavin Howell in 2004. At that time it had the 'aluminium'-type bulkhead frequently used by Rover when the press die broke for the later pressed steel bulkhead at various times from 1949–1953. Could it be the original jig frame used for the initial set-up of the steering box and column for the early Land-Rover?

The last recorded show model used for the Land-Rover's debut in the UK is R16. For many years it was used by the Rover Co. as a factory hack, and was never road registered before its more recent restoration, which past Secretary of the Land-Rover Register, Richard Lines, managed to complete just in time for the 50th Anniversary celebrations in 1998.

A Dorman-Simplex Crop Sprayer was fitted to R17, and this Land-Rover also survives, but sadly, without any crop spraying equipment. Owned by Nigel Withers, R17 has many original features, but is currently rumoured to be in pieces, and has yet to be restored.

The restoration of R19 was begun by Jim Cooknell, one-time Membership Secretary of The Land-Rover Register, but it was later purchased by Ken Wheelwright in June 1986. Ken completed its restoration in the mid-1990s, in time for the Land-Rover's 50th Anniversary celebrations. In 2003 Ken sold R19 to enthusiast Bill Newport, who already owns L24.

Of the last 28 pre-production models, only nine survive – R23, which is little more than an abandoned chassis, L24, L25, L29, R30, R32, L45, L46, and L48. Five of these have now been restored: L29, the ex-Ministry demonstrator belonging to past Treasurer of The Land-Rover Register, Guy Pickford; R30, owned by the Land-Rover main dealer, Roger Young; R32, which was restored by John Taylor and now belongs to the Houben Family, in Holland – mainland Europe's largest collection of historic Land-Rovers; L46, which after being auctioned off from the John Craddock collection, was acquired and restored by Andrew Ings of Specialist Car Services; and L48, which was found in Argentina, and has been restored by Marco Tasselli. After a brief spell in the UK, L48 now resides in Perth, Australia.

Many pre-production Land-Rovers received a replacement engine as a matter of routine, before being sold off. Others lost theirs with the ravages of time, and of the 20 pre-production models so far discovered, only four – R01, L11, L12, and R19 – from the first batch of 20, and another two – R25 and R45 – were found with their original P3 car engine still in place under the bonnet.

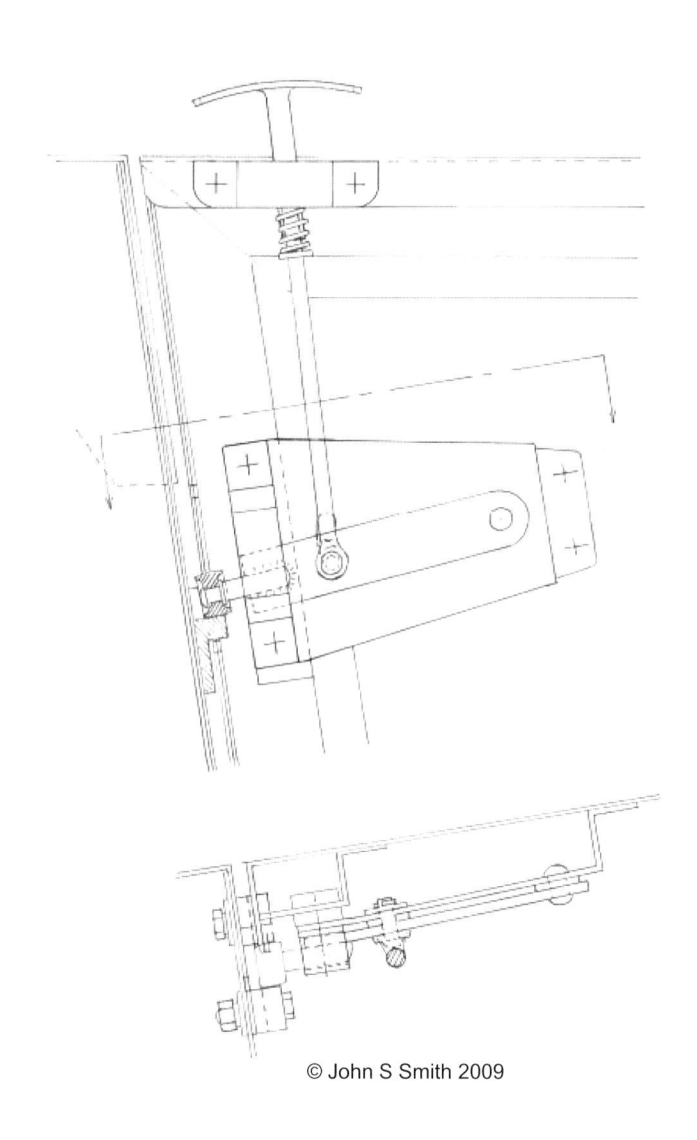

Among the modifications made to the P3 'Rover 60' engine for installation into the Land-Rover was the use of 'Specialloid' and 'Lo-Ex' low compression pistons, which were otherwise only available as an option on 'Export' Rover P3 cars. Their use in the Land-Rover necessitated a slightly different distributor. However, when production Land-Rovers started in earnest in August 1948, these pistons became standard for all current Rover car engines. Ironically, this meant that the four-cylinder P3 'Rover 60' car now had a Land-Rover engine, rather than vice versa.

The standard two-blade fan used for the car gave way to four blades, again optional on export cars, to improve cooling in hot climates. The car clutch and gearbox were used but the 'Rover 75' bell housing was fitted and the selector rods were adapted to operate from the front end, rather than the rear, as on the car. The P3 car exhaust manifold seen on the $4^{1}/_{2}$-inch chassis prototype possessed very good gas flow characteristics, but now had

© John S Smith 2009

Diagram illustrating detail of early door catch mechanism

Overleaf left: The early 'Lucas' wiring diagram

Overleaf right: Gordon Bashford's early 'L'-shaped fuel tank and final fuel tank

CHAPTER 6 – A Pattern for Progress – Drawings and Designs

Photograph topside of production model for TP/108/B, 10/48

Photograph underside of production model for TP/108/B, 10/48

85

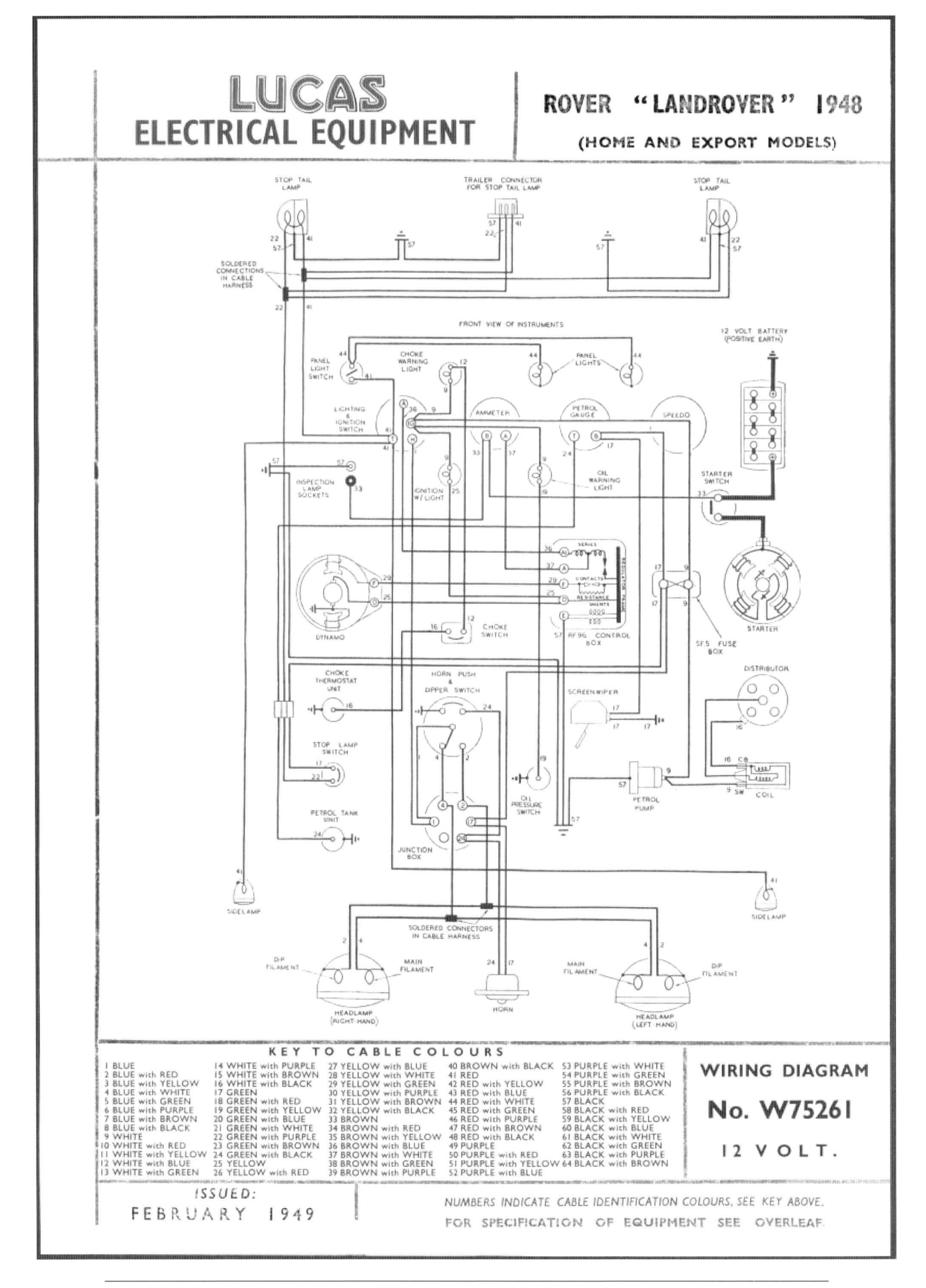

LAND-ROVER – The Formative Years, 1947–1967

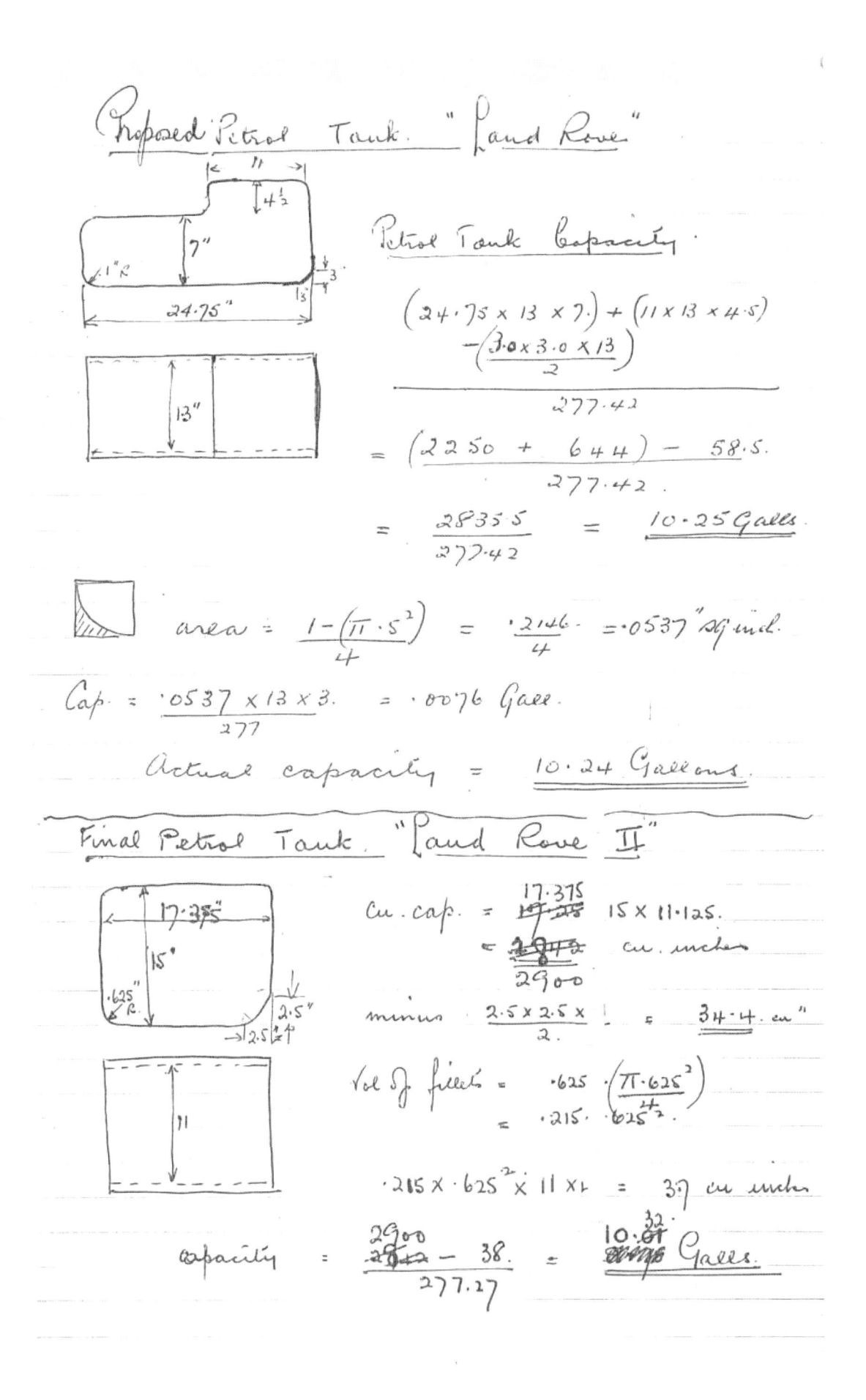

CHAPTER 6 – A Pattern for Progress – Drawings and Designs

Proposed Petrol Tank. "Land Rover"

[Diagram: L-shaped tank profile, 24.75" wide, 7" high main section, 4½" upper step 11" wide, 1"R corner, 3/3 chamfer; end view 13" deep]

Petrol Tank Capacity.

$$\frac{(24.75 \times 13 \times 7) + (11 \times 13 \times 4.5) - \left(\frac{3.0 \times 3.0 \times 13}{2}\right)}{277.42}$$

$$= \frac{(2250 + 644) - 58.5}{277.42}$$

$$= \frac{2835.5}{277.42} = \underline{10.25 \text{ Galls.}}$$

[Diagram: fillet corner]

$$\text{area} = \frac{1 - \left(\pi \cdot 5^2\right)}{4} = \frac{.2146}{4} = .0537 \text{ sq ind.}$$

$$\text{Cap.} = \frac{.0537 \times 13 \times 3}{277} = .0076 \text{ Gall.}$$

Actual capacity = $\underline{10.24 \text{ Gallons}}$

Final Petrol Tank. "Land Rover II"

[Diagram: tank 17.375" × 15", .625" R, 2.5" × 2.5" corner, end view 11"]

$$\text{cu. cap.} = 17.375 \times 15 \times 11.125 = 2900 \text{ cu. inches}$$

$$\text{minus } \frac{2.5 \times 2.5 \times 1}{2} = \underline{34.4 \text{ cu"}}$$

$$\text{Vol of fillets} = .625 \cdot \left(\frac{\pi \cdot .625^2}{4}\right)$$
$$= .215 \cdot .625^2$$

$$.215 \times .625^2 \times 11 \times 4 = 3.7 \text{ cu inches}$$

$$\text{capacity} = \frac{2900 - 38}{277.27} = \underline{10.32 \text{ Galls.}}$$

Factory drawing illustrating push-pull controls

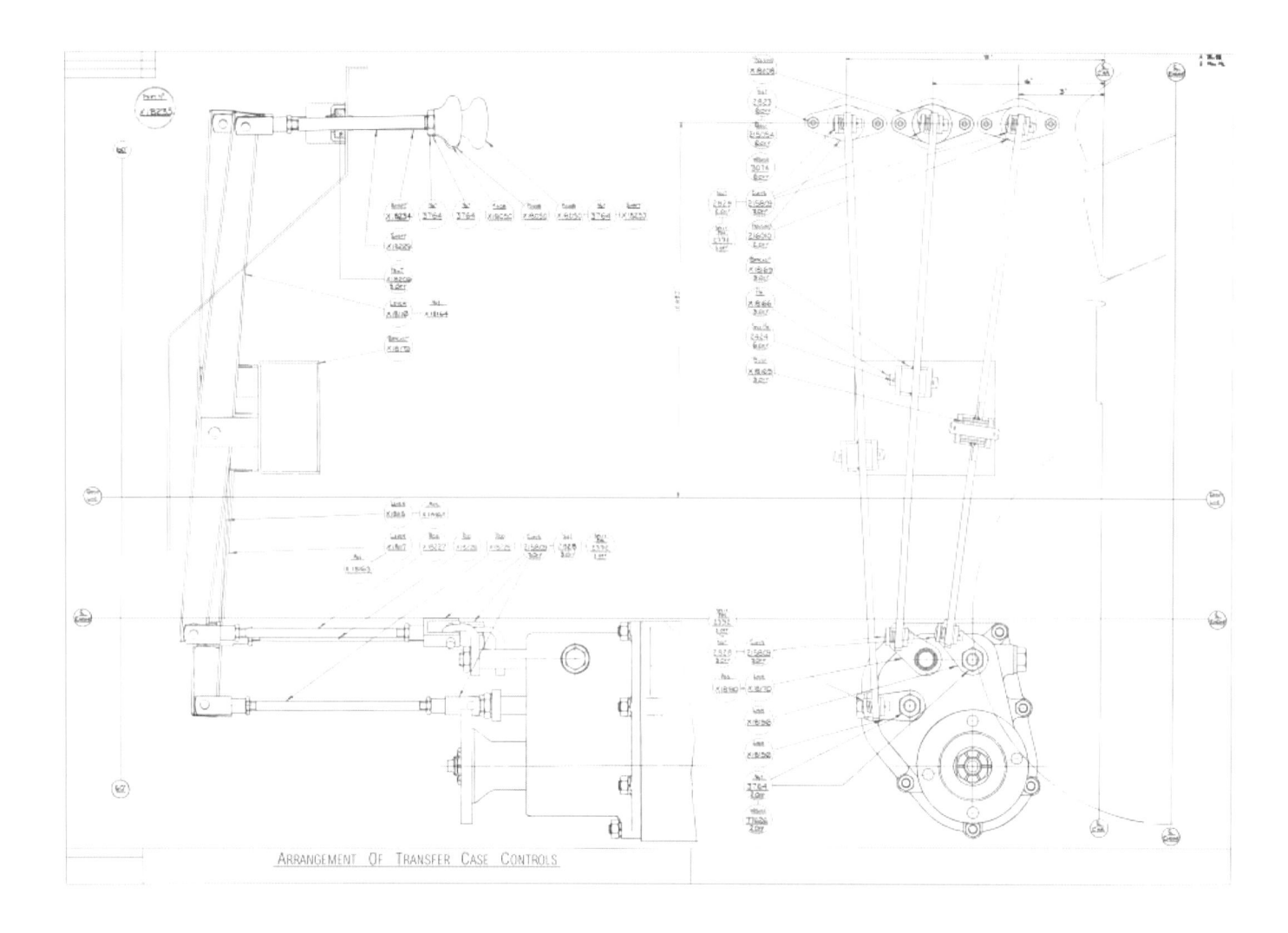

to be replaced as there was insufficient clearance for the down-pipe once the chassis box section was increased from 2 inches to 3 inches in width. The car's normal horizontal air cleaner was also replaced by an upright 'AC Sphinx' type with oil bath and centrifugal pre-cleaner. On cars, the fuel gauge doubled as an oil level indicator by means of a push-button switch, but on the Land-Rover the oil sender unit was removed, its position in the sump covered by a blanking plate, as wires to the unit might easily be torn away in the bush or other vegetation such as long grass, scrub, or farm crops.

Much of the engine's original layout, as it first went into the Land-Rover, can be seen in three excellent contemporary technical illustrations by: John Ferguson in 'The Autocar'; S.E. Porter for 'The Motor'; and Attwood in 'The Complete Book of Motor Cars, Railways, Ships and Aeroplanes', published by Odhams Press Ltd., in 1949. All show the car oil filler tube mounted on the two inlet manifold studs. This was replaced by a cast aluminium oil filter mounted on the opposite side at the rear of the cast aluminium side cover, where previously a crankcase breather pipe was located.

A new crankcase breather then went where the oil filler tube had been, and led to the carburettor air intake, providing a mist of oil to the combustion chambers – in much the same way as a wartime Jeep.

Many features found only on the earliest pre-production models can be seen in these drawings, making them significant historical documents. But there is one important difference between them. The illustration in 'The Motor', based on R02, clearly shows an integral boxed bumper but the other two artists both show the bumper as bolted on to 'fish-plates' located on the chassis. Contemporary photographs of L03 and later production models bear this out as correct. Although on inspection it appears the integral bumper was sawn off when damaged, many pre-production Land-Rovers appear to have been fitted this way from new – sometimes after the chassis had been galvanised and the original bumper sawn off either side of the dumb irons. This could give the impression it was a later addition. L03 is particularly interesting because the fish-plates are bolted to both the chassis and the bumper, so as to prevent weld damage to the galvanising, whereas later pre-production

CHAPTER 6 – A Pattern for Progress – Drawings and Designs

models have the fish-plates welded to the chassis in the same way as the early production model, suggesting their modification took place before galvanising.

Unlike the production models that followed, less than a handful of pre-production Land-Rovers appear to be identical. Those used as publicity demonstrators within the British Isles were generally updated before eventually being sold off to one of Rover's 96 home distributors. Rover were not keen to supply second-hand pre-production Land-Rovers overseas, so any left-hand drive models used within the UK, such as L03 and L11, were converted to right-hand drive before being sold off in the 'home' market.[1]

Plenty of other modifications also took place. 'T' door handles, seen in contemporary photographs, were always removed, along with the push-pull bulkhead controls for transfer box, 'Freewheel', and 4x2 selection, which in any case had only been fitted to the earliest pre-production models. Certainly they were no longer being fitted by the time the first handbook TP/108/A, published in June 1948 to accompany the first demonstration models, was put together.

Bulkhead controls, intended to keep the floor pan free from obstruction, had their problems too. Their vertical control rods pivoted on a rigid fixture at the bulkhead which, in turn, relayed to a flexibly mounted gearbox. With no spring loading provided on the front output selector shafts for this arrangement, difficulty was often experienced retaining selectors in their desired position when anything but level ground was being negotiated. It has been rumoured that on initial trials, early vehicles often exhibited stout pieces of wood jammed between the control knobs and the rear body in an attempt to retain selectors in their desired position. A further, more serious problem for the vehicle itself was the driver's ability to inadvertently select both low-ratio gearing and 4x2 in rough going or under heavy load, with possible dire consequences for the rear axle's differential.

Rover soon realised that their use of 'Tracta' constant velocity drive joints for the front axle, combined with their 'Freewheel' device in the Land-Rover's front output housing, made the option of 4x2 selection (as provided on the earliest pre-production models) totally unnecessary. So instead, the array of bulkhead controls was simply replaced by a single lever on the floor for high/low ratio, with a 'pull ring' set into the floor pan to lock the 'Freewheel' to provide engine braking to all four wheels, or for reverse 4x4 traction, when this was required.[2] With the bulkhead controls now abandoned, cover plates were provided to hide all redundant holes.

It now seems that R17, the 'Dorman-Simplex' Crop Sprayer, was the first Land-Rover to use floor controls instead of bulkhead controls. Now too late to alter before production, the first 2,000 transfer boxes on production Land-Rovers still retained the original split output shaft and locking dog mechanism to enable 4x2 selection. Having conceded at an early stage that 4x2 was totally unnecessary, no provision was then made for disengaging the locking dog on either late pre-production or early production Land-Rovers. Henceforth, all road wheels remained permanently under power in the forward motion on every new Land-Rover for the first two years of production.

Land-Rover body construction was also entirely different from the wartime Jeep. Life expectancy of the Jeep, under combat conditions, was less than 24 hours. Even so, it had an army of skilled mechanics for maintenance purposes. The Land-Rover, on the other hand, needed to be easily maintained by almost anyone, anywhere, often single-handed, and perhaps with little more than the rudimentary set of hand tools provided with each new vehicle. Life expectancy was certainly greater than 24 hours – in fact, pre-production models, with their galvanised chassis, might just last forever.

Instead of being welded into a single structure, Land-Rover body parts could be easily unbolted for maintenance of the engine, transmission, and chassis. Body panels, being made of light alloy, would not rust, and could also easily be reshaped by hand after damage. This made the Land-Rover the ideal vehicle for outback off-road work, and was unquestionably, a major part of the Land-Rover's design concept – something certainly overlooked by Willys when they revamped their faithful wartime MB into the post-war CJ2A 'Universal' Jeep.

Unlike production models, pre-production Land-Rover bodywork was made from Duralumin, a remnant from Rover's Air Ministry days, suitably painted in 'Cockpit Green' – a paint previously used for internal surfaces on airframes. Initially coded as 'No.2 Green', it was renamed 'Light Green' when it became the standard colour for all production Land-Rovers. The 'Perspex' used for side screens was also a wartime aircraft material, and the hand throttle used for production models was also another war-surplus aircraft part.

On pre-production Land-Rovers, every surface was painted, just as if it had been an airframe. The body bin bolted down onto the chassis instead of having mounting plates, and wooden packing pieces were often used to give correct alignment to doors

[1] *L09 remained left-hand drive, as it was not officially sold off from the factory.*

[2] *See 'Introduction', concerning the Land-Rover's transmission system.*

and tail board. External bump stops mounted on the doors were intended to protect new paintwork, but soon began to dent the wings, so were transferred to the wing before completion of the first batch of pre-production models. There they could bump the door harmlessly on its reinforced edge. No luxuries such as rubber draught excluders were fitted at this stage, so internal doorstops, held by a simple metal strap, were provided on the body bin's transom panel to minimise door rattle. Even doors and side screens would be marketed as optional extras.

Attwood's drawing clearly shows inset tail board hinges integral with the retaining eye, but by L11 these had become separated items, though not galvanised but nickel plated. This modification allowed tail board hinge adjustment without upsetting the position of the retaining eye. L11 does not have the usual wooden packing pieces under the body either. This may have something to do with the new hinge coupled with the two halves of L11's chassis being better aligned than most. Previously, with back body height determined by chassis alignment and no adjustment to the early 'L' hinges, which pivot on a fixed bracket on the chassis, if the 'fixed' locating pegs on the body were to line up with their 'eye', 'L' hinges would need some individual tailoring. Pre-production tail boards themselves had three wide external 'top-hat' strengthening ribs similar to those found under the body. Unlike production models, the body floor was spot-welded to the wheel arches only as far as the jaws of the machine would reach – the rest was simply hand riveted.

It was quickly discovered that at night the wing mirror reflected light from the bulkhead-mounted sidelights, and so the mirror was soon repositioned to the windscreen frame, making it totally useless if the screen was folded down. Original hoodstick sockets at the top corner of the windscreen are occasionally found on surviving pre-production models, along with a wider centre divide. There were no side-screen stays at the start, and when eventually added, they were only a simple bent wire affair, initially simply bolted on, and not the more familiar 'Y' used on production models.

Door handle access flaps were first mounted on the inside. This allowed easy water penetration. The hood itself, on early pre-production models, was confined to covering the cab, and no staples for a full-length hood were fitted along the outer rear body. The front edge of this hood was held in position by nine 'lift-the-dot' fasteners, which also

Chassis R 861201 showing early production bulkhead

CHAPTER 6 – A Pattern for Progress – Drawings and Designs

R01 showing early hood detail

served as fixing's for the top glass retainer. At the rear was a curved arch opening to which a curtain with two large rectangular mesh rear windows was attached by means of nine turn-buckle fastenings.

In Ferguson's drawing for 'The Autocar' the stubby hinges on the passenger seat-box locker lid can be seen, but none of the drawings show the pre-production Land-Rover's pear-shaped access cover to the fuel tank under the driver's seat. Certain other features found only on pre-production models can also be seen. They include: the angular wraparound to the spring leaf; four extra set screws for the battery box; a large header tank for the radiator; a bonnet stay bracket; a shroud for the ignition coil; a small wheel-knob for the hand throttle; an earlier pattern starter button; and a simple keyless 'ON' knob for the ignition.

Another feature of particular interest on pre-production chassis are the longitudinal members, which are constructed from two box-section lengths, both a little over 5 feet long, with large drain holes for the galvaniser's hot zinc to drain out, placed at the back on the rear length's underside. The rear cross-member is also fabricated, rather than the usual pressing, and the chassis has distance tubes on both sides to accommodate the Lockheed brake master cylinder with its integral reservoir and brake switch. Only one chassis, L09, has ever been rediscovered with the Lockheed brake system still in place. As L09 stayed at the factory as a works 'hack' well into the 1960s, there was probably no need to update it. All other pre-production chassis had a handed bracket welded on after galvanising, to take a Girling brake master cylinder.

Bulkhead outriggers were fabricated from five separate pieces of sheet and retained the 2-inch end section found on the prototype $4\frac{1}{2}$-inch chassis. This gave their outer end a square appearance, but tapered out to 3 inches where they joined the main frame. Very early production models still have these outriggers, but once production was well underway their width became a full 3-inch section constructed from a single sheet. The pre-production body outrigger forward of the left rear wheel was given a large rubber block for the exhaust mounting – it's sometimes still found in position.

The P3 silencer box was still being used at this stage and passed below the left floor panel to discharge immediately behind the left rear wheel. This left little space in the vicinity of the wheel area. Later pre-production models have the early production exhaust system. Some vehicles, such as L11, had only a pair of holes in the rear crossmember, offset to the centre line, for a towing plate or ball hitch. Where this was the case, the left hole doubled as the lower PTO mounting hole, but on other chassis, these were centralised, with a smaller separate hole being provided for the PTO, the same as on production models.

Pre-production bronze hub and swivel housing

Several pre-production parts were cast in aluminium-bronze. These included: front hubs; swivel pin housings; foot pedals; steering box; and steering relay body. This material has a high corrosion resistance due to the formation of an alumina (aluminium-oxide) film on the surface, making it ideal for marine propellers. The very first drive flanges for the front hub were machined from solid stock, but by R04 were being cast with two pairs of the six bolt holes linked – exactly the same as a Willys Jeep.

At the rear end, there was originally no protection for the vulnerable 'D' lights, so on R01 Jeep bumperetts were added as protection. These were replaced by Jeep grab handles which might enable the Land-Rover to be manhandled, should it became stuck. Divided 'combat' or 'split rim' wheels, were fitted in order to assist removal of the unidirectional 6.00 x 16 Avon 'Traction' tyres, as these would not necessarily be facing the right direction whenever a spare was pressed into service.

The earliest bonnet spare wheel support plates were fabricated, rather than pressed. Wooden packing blocks were then used to support the edge of the wheel, with larger wooden blocks used on the bonnet to support the windscreen in the down position. The steering column support brackets also consisted of three separate pieces welded together, the side plates, no doubt, having been added as an afterthought – a strengthening modification at an early stage.

Seat bases at this stage were just flat squabs held by small forward-mounted circular locators, while the accompanying seat back was just a rudimentary curved rectangular pad in matching green leather-cloth. The seat base was later modified on some early models to incorporate a slope, with leather-cloth hinge and securing flap added to hold it up against the transom panel while re-fuelling. The hinge and flap parts did not reach the production stage, but the general style and slope were retained.

There are no hard and fast rules about the parts on pre-production models, and a number of later models completed after 19 July 1948, when the first production models were being 'despatched in' at the factory, are known to have been fitted with production parts for trial purposes. This was precisely what pre-production models were all about, and makes them just that little bit more interesting. None have remained exactly as first built, and of the survivors, each one is now unique, but the number that still have more than 80% of their original parts amounts to less than a handful.

Some of the later pre-production models have a production seat box and windscreen, and one contemporary photograph shows 'spade back'

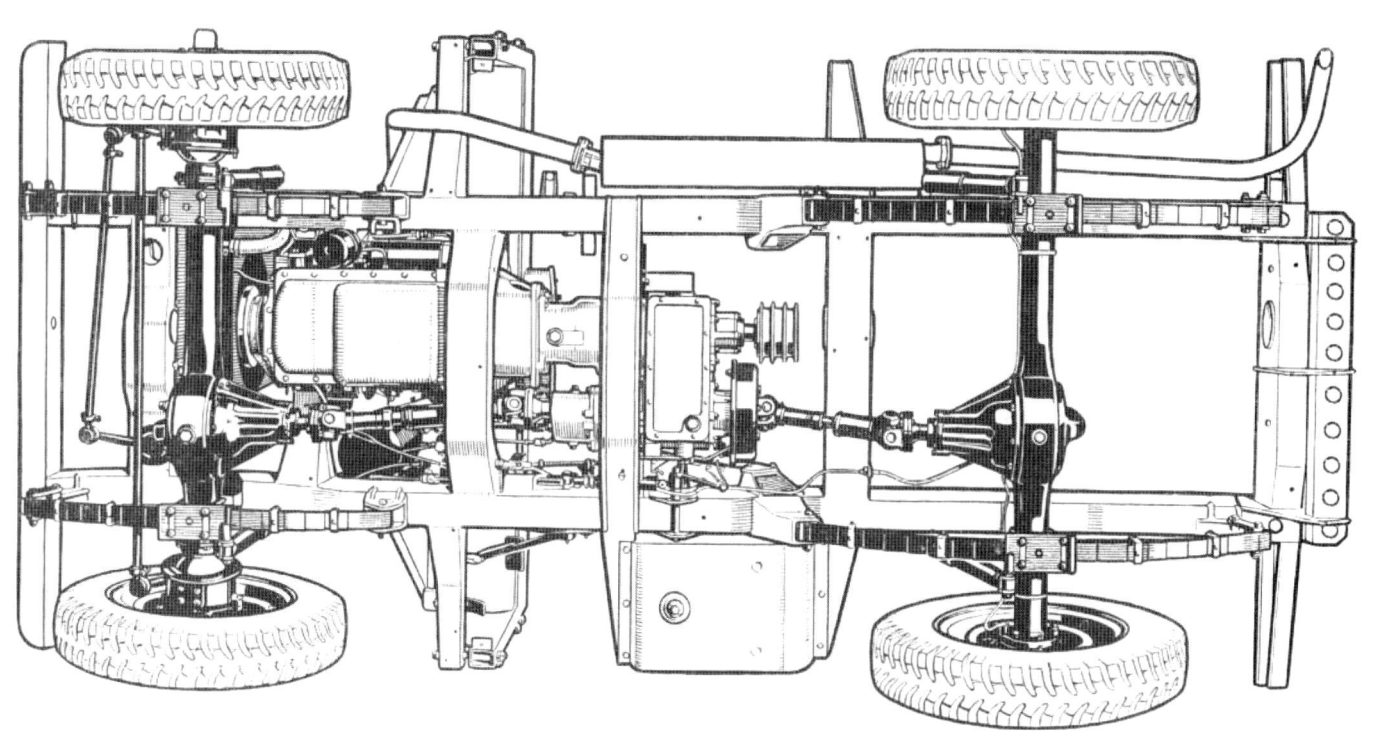

CHAPTER 6 – A Pattern for Progress – Drawings and Designs

Underside view of pre-production model shows spring shackles at front close to steering levers where they would contribute most to wheel wobble. Also note early push-pull control linkage to front output housing is present in this diagram.

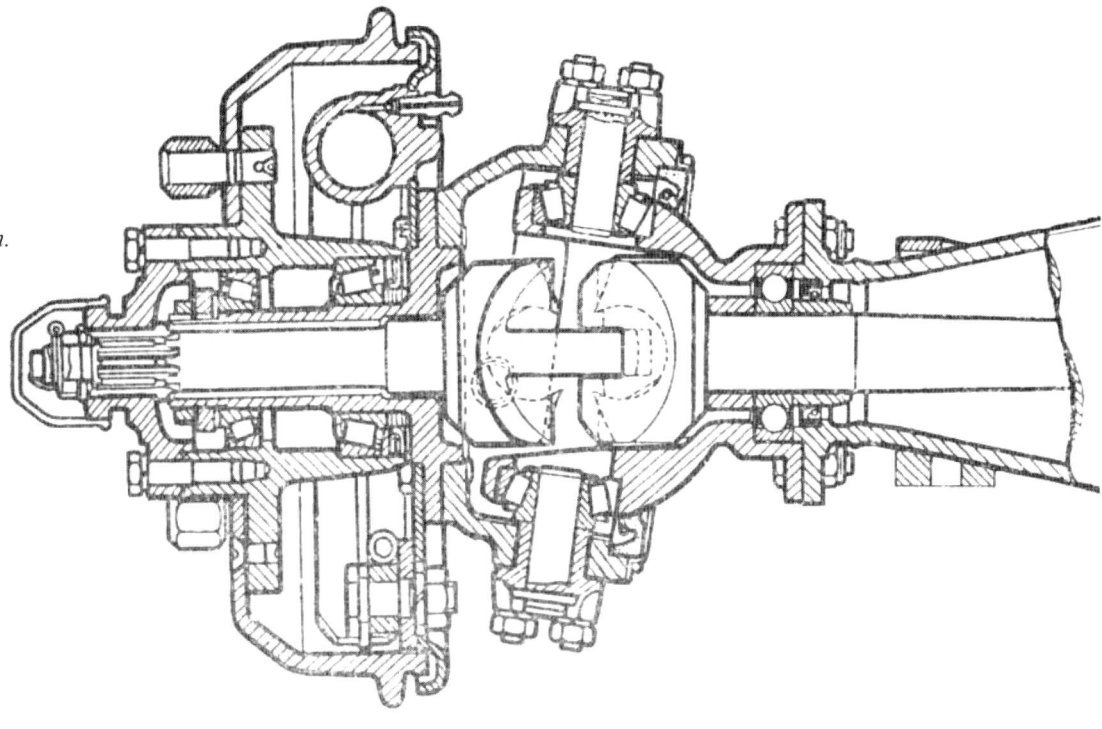

The 'Tracta' true constant velocity joint

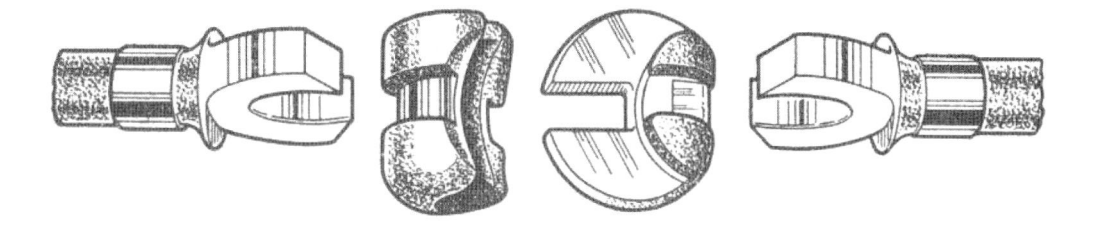

LAND-ROVER – The Formative Years, 1947–1967

L11 fitted with push-pull bulkhead controls

seats, so in one way or another they often became a mixture of pre-production and early production parts quite early on. R45 has production gearbox, No. 860009, and L48 No. 860064 – both probably fitted from new. At the same time, gearboxes R37 (in R860004), R46 and R50 (in R8665806) have all turned up in early production models. Land-Rover R860053 has bronze wheel carriers and various chassis parts are still similar to pre-production models.

A proper logo was needed for the Amsterdam show, so the two words 'Land-Rover' were cast in brass, with the now familiar 'Z' simply added to hold the letters together. First chromed, it was then painted red to give a greater visual impact against the Land-Rover's light green bodywork. Today, the only surviving example of this early badge remains on the front wing of L03. Such a frail casting in this location would be vulnerable on an agricultural vehicle. It was quickly decided to announce the Land-Rover's 'purpose and pedigree' with a much more solid oval brass casting, in keeping with the character of the vehicle, with raised red lettering on the same light green background. The new badge was attached to the front grille, but there was no rim as yet – that would come later – and the 'Z' now only separated the two words.

Despite all these various changes, the detail which has set these embryonic models apart from all production models remains clearly visible to the discerning enthusiast. It is this that has given the pre-production models their select position among the ever growing band of enthusiastic followers of what can only be described as Britain's greatest post-war motoring success – the Land-Rover.

Land-Rover badge used for Amsterdam show models

94

CHAPTER 6 – A Pattern for Progress – Drawings and Designs

L11 as found in 1983

L11 enters Lapland in 1988

John Smith driving L11 at Chepstow in 2008

CHAPTER 7
Factory to Farm
The Late 1940s

On Tuesday, 20 April 1948, the Land-Rover's imminent arrival was heralded by the following announcement in 'The Times' newspaper, under the heading 'Home News':

NEW VEHICLE FOR AGRICULTURE FROM OUR MOTORING CORRESPONDENT

"A special vehicle designed for agriculture and industrial work is to be made at the rate of 200 a week by the Rover Company at Birmingham. Called the Land-Rover, it bears a strong resemblance to the jeep and is designed to be equally at home on main roads and across-country. It has the same four-cylinder engine as the Rover 60 car, eight forward speeds, and a power take-off for driving agricultural machinery. It has a non-corrodible light alloy body and weighs just over a ton with an overall length of 11ft. The price has been fixed at £450, no Purchase Tax being payable. The Land-Rover will be shown publicly for the first time at the Amsterdam motor show, which opens next week."

A few days later on 23 April, the 'Farmer's Weekly' also gave a glowing account of the Land-Rover to Britain's farming community:

AN ANSWER TO THE JEEP

"Under severe testing it has been almost impossible to find going or gradients where it loses traction or stability. Four-wheel-drive gives maximum surface grip and a transfer gearbox in combination provides eight forward speeds. A free-wheel incorporated with the front wheel's propeller shaft, acts as a differential to deal with varying ground conditions. A PTO is fitted at the rear and another can be fixed centrally, if needed. Provision is also made for a power driven Capstan winch at the front of the vehicle."

Prior to these public announcements of Rover's new Land-Rover in the press, a letter, dated 19 April 1948, had been sent out from the Solihull factory to all Rover agents and retail dealers, informing them that the Land-Rover would *"...be on view for the first time at the Amsterdam Motor Show, to be open to the public from 30 April to 9 May inclusive."* Dealers were also informed that the Land-Rover would also *"...be exhibited at four Agricultural Shows..."*, listing these as:

Royal Ulster Show, Belfast .... May 26th to 29th
Bath & West Show, Cardiff .... May 26th to 29th
Highland Show, Inverness .... June 22nd to 25th
The Royal Show, York .... July 6th to 9th

The same letter also announced that *"After the middle of May a Land-Rover will be available for inspection in our Showrooms, Devonshire House, Piccadilly, London W.1."* In addition Land-Rovers would also be appearing *"...at the Commercial Exhibition, Earls Court, October 1st – 9th 1948"*.

Uncluttered lines and aircraft 'cockpit green' paintwork gave Rover's new all-purpose vehicle a clean fresh look, far removed from the usual black bloated bulbous pressings of a post-war motor industry so intent upon the masses.

To coincide with the Amsterdam debut, the two established motoring journals 'Autocar' and 'The Motor' each published their own account of the new Land-Rover, with every detail of construction being described in the usual excellent manner associated with these two publications. In particular, John Ferguson's technical illustration for 'The Autocar' left almost nothing for the imagination.

Spring had indeed arrived. By April 1948 a cool refreshing breeze was already blowing through most of Britain's motor industry, but for Rover, the air was about to turn particularly sweet, when just ten days after 'The Times' announcement – the last day in April – the Land-Rover made its world debut at the Amsterdam show. Rover's famous Viking sail looked set to billow once again.

As well as Amsterdam, the Land-Rover was scheduled to appear at various other international shows in 1948. These included:

CHAPTER 7 – Factory to Farm – The Late 1940s

Land-Rover stand at the Bath & West show

Toronto Motor Exhibition; August 27th to September 11th

British Exhibition, Copenhagen; September 18th to October 3rd

Paris Motor Show; October 7th to 17th.

London Motor Show, Earls Court; October 27th to November 6th

Commercial Motor Show, London, October 1st to 9th

In the UK, on 26–29 May, the Land-Rover made its debut simultaneously, at the Royal Ulster Show, Belfast, where my own pre-production Land-Rover, L11, along with R13 and R14 appeared, and the Bath & West Show, Cardiff, where L12, and R15 and R16 appeared. The Scottish debut followed a few weeks later, at the Royal Highland Show, Inverness, from 22–26 June, where R27 and R28 were shown. England came a little later at the Royal Show, York, from 6–9 July, where again, L11 and R14 appeared. According to the 'Farmer's Weekly', it was something of an international affair with *"Over 230 overseas visitors from the Dominions and Colonies, USA, Scandinavia, Denmark, Holland, France, Czecho-Slovakia, Malaya, etc."* all having a first-hand opportunity to see the new Land-Rover in action.

In Paris the left-hand drive Station Wagon, L20, made its debut, before going on to Brussels. With L20, still on the Continent, a second 'prototype'

LAND-ROVER – The Formative Years, 1947–1967

John Ferguson's illustration, as it appeared in The Autocar

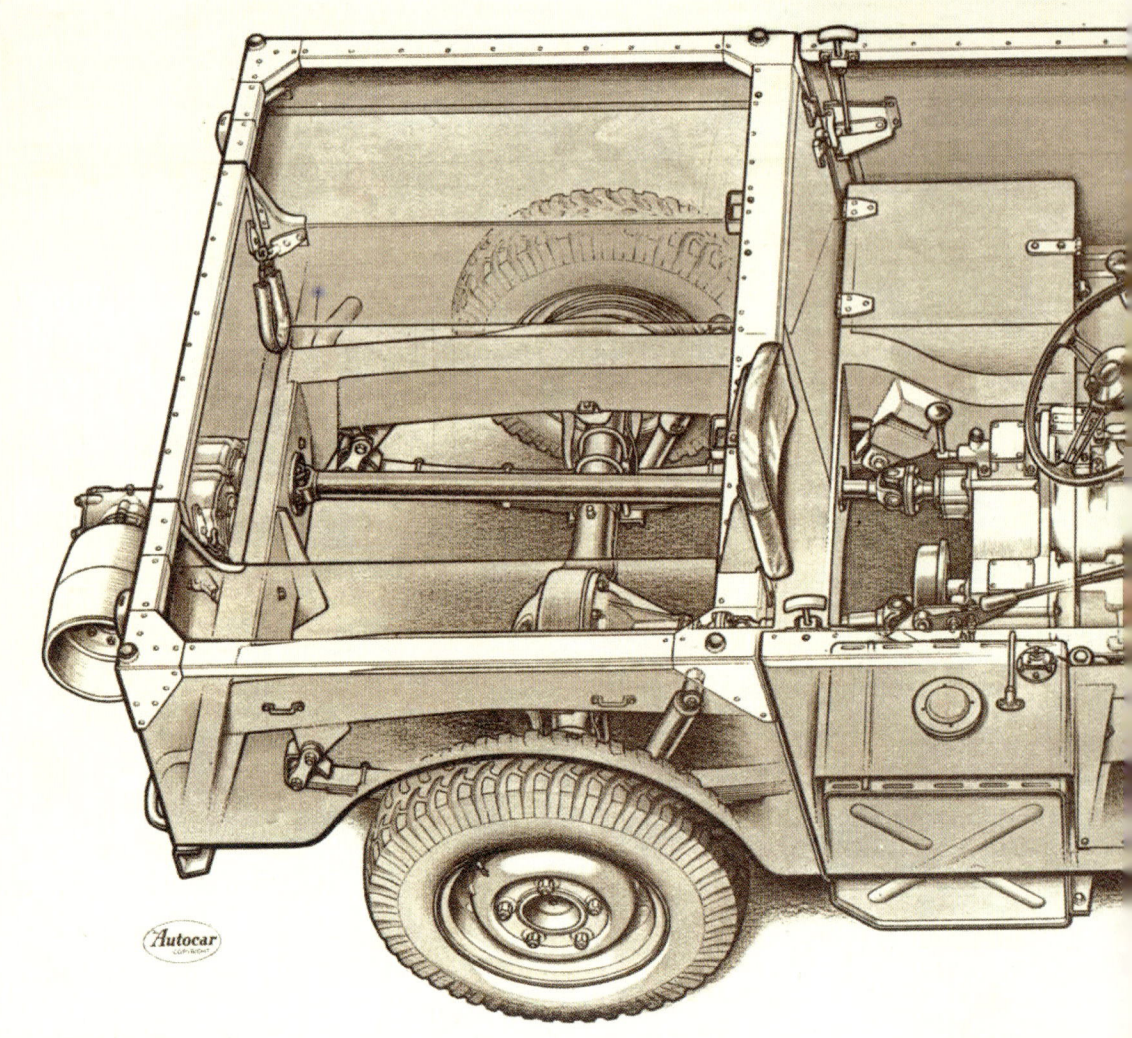

An All-purpose ROVER

ALTHOUGH these pages are normally devoted to the many aspects of the purely private car and its usage, there is now something to describe which can either be regarded as a private car able to perform many most valuable duties other than sheer transport, or as a general purpose countryside worker which is also capable of providing comfortable and efficient transport. This dual role of the new Land-Rover, regardless of which range of duty is of the greater value to the owner, cannot be too highly stressed, because it opens up possibilities of the greatest value to those who live in the country, whether under cultivation or in the wild state. So much has been said and written in the past about the so-called People's Car, much of it nonsense, that the advent of a really practical British vehicle which goes far beyond that over-publicized proposal should be hailed with genuine acclamation.

Let us consider the new Land-Rover in a sharp perspective, and see what it offers. It is a car with a wheelbase of 6ft 8in and a track of 4ft 2in; the overall length is 11ft, and the width 5ft. It has an open body able to seat three in a row on the front seat and four, wagonette-style, in the back—seven in all. It can have doors, side panels, and a complete all-weather equipment. It has a modern design high-efficiency four-cylinder engine developing 50 b.h.p. On main roads it can average as high as 40 miles within each hour, and its fuel consumption at that fast average is round about 27 m.p.g. It weighs 22½ cwt. It has been designed and built by the Rover Company, and that in itself is a guarantee of quality which will be instantly accepted by any British motorist.

Its appearance is starkly practical;

CHAPTER 7 – Factory to Farm – The Late 1940s

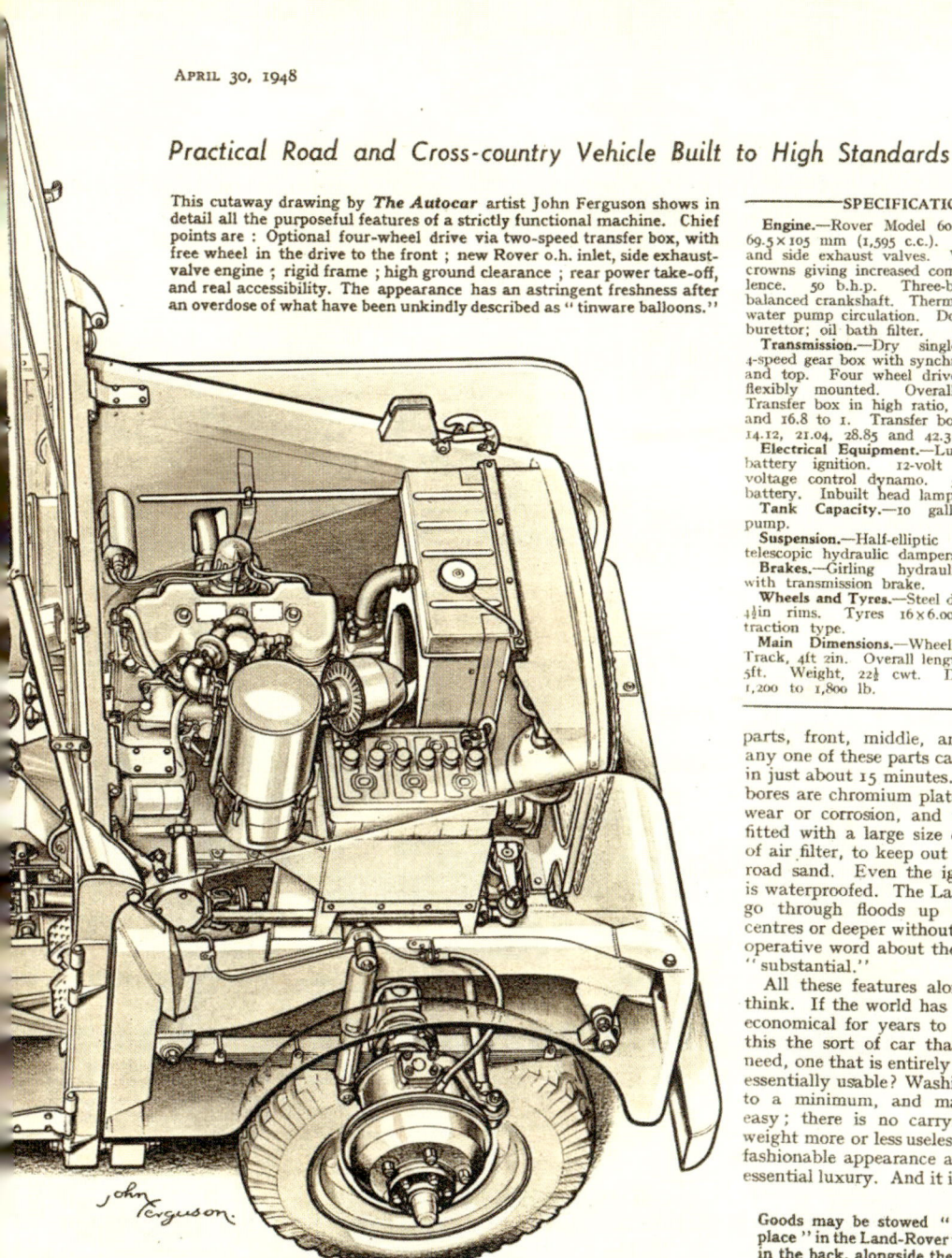

APRIL 30, 1948

Practical Road and Cross-country Vehicle Built to High Standards

This cutaway drawing by *The Autocar* artist John Ferguson shows in detail all the purposeful features of a strictly functional machine. Chief points are : Optional four-wheel drive via two-speed transfer box, with free wheel in the drive to the front ; new Rover o.h. inlet, side exhaust-valve engine ; rigid frame ; high ground clearance ; rear power take-off, and real accessibility. The appearance has an astringent freshness after an overdose of what have been unkindly described as "tinware balloons."

---SPECIFICATION---

Engine.—Rover Model 60. 4 cylinders, 69.5 × 105 mm (1,595 c.c.). Overhead inlet and side exhaust valves. V-shaped piston crowns giving increased compression turbulence. 50 b.h.p. Three-bearing counter-balanced crankshaft. Thermostat controlled water pump circulation. Downdraught carburettor; oil bath filter.

Transmission.—Dry single-plate clutch. 4-speed gear box with synchromesh on third and top. Four wheel drive. Power unit flexibly mounted. Overall gear ratios: Transfer box in high ratio, 5.6, 8.36, 11.46 and 16.8 to 1. Transfer box in low ratio, 14.12, 21.04, 28.85 and 42.3 to 1.

Electrical Equipment.—Lucas. Coil and battery ignition. 12-volt with constant voltage control dynamo. 52 ampere-hour battery. Inbuilt head lamps.

Tank Capacity.—10 gallons. Electric pump.

Suspension.—Half-elliptic springs with telescopic hydraulic dampers.

Brakes.—Girling hydraulic four-wheel, with transmission brake.

Wheels and Tyres.—Steel disc wheels with 4½in rims. Tyres 16 × 6.00in heavy-duty traction type.

Main Dimensions.—Wheelbase, 6ft 8in. Track, 4ft 2in. Overall length, 11ft; width, 5ft. Weight, 22½ cwt. Draw bar pull, 1,200 to 1,800 lb.

parts, front, middle, and rear, and any one of these parts can be removed in just about 15 minutes. The cylinder bores are chromium plated to prevent wear or corrosion, and the engine is fitted with a large size oil bath type of air filter, to keep out fine dust and road sand. Even the ignition wiring is waterproofed. The Land-Rover can go through floods up to its wheel centres or deeper without trouble. The operative word about the whole car is "substantial."

All these features alone make one think. If the world has to be strictly economical for years to come, is not this the sort of car that most of us need, one that is entirely practical and essentially usable? Washing is reduced to a minimum, and maintenance is easy ; there is no carrying about of weight more or less uselessly devoted to fashionable appearance and not really essential luxury. And it is a car usable

Goods may be stowed "all over the place" in the Land-Rover when open— in the back, alongside the driver, and, no doubt, on the bonnet when there are "just a couple of sacks left over."

there is nothing of the luxury vehicle about its looks. Nevertheless it is not ugly and has a distinctly attractive appearance all its own. Everything necessary for travel is there. Accessibility reaches a degree which does not exist in an orthodox modern car, and the finish inside and out is of a kind which permits the owner to leave the vehicle in the open in any weather without fear of deterioration. All the exposed steel parts, including the chassis frame, are heavily galvanized with zinc, and the body panels and flooring are of a non-corroding hard aluminium alloy. The body is in three

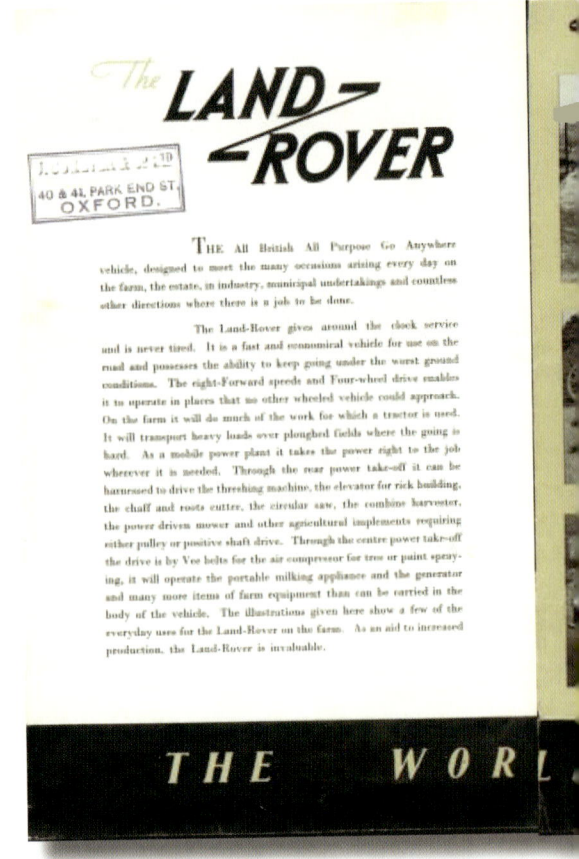

Station Wagon was built on right-hand drive production chassis R860071, in time for the London Motor Show. This was Britain's first motor show after the war and the opening alone was attended by 562,954 visitors. The left-hand drive 'Welder', L05, and the 'Fire Engine', R06, also appeared at the Commercial Motor Show.

Pre-production models R23, L24, L25, and L26 also gained considerable publicity in Europe when they were used to tow four gliders, to be used by the British glider team, from their base at Redhill Aerodrome in Surrey, over to Samaden in Switzerland, in time for the first post-war World Gliding Championship held from the 19–30 July 1948. The route taken was via Dover, Rheims, Basle, and Zurich, returning via Lausanne, Paris, Boulogne, and Dover. In Switzerland they were used to retrieve the gliders from Chur, Lake Constance and Lake Como in Northern Italy, successfully climbing the Alps to as high as 8,000 feet, while towing glider trailers of around 30 feet in length. This was the first overseas expedition ever to be undertaken by Land-Rovers, and was commemorated 50 years later by a return visit by members of the Land-Rover Register in 1998.

In the same edition of 'The Times' that heralded the coming of the Land-Rover, under 'Imperial and Foreign' news, was the story that some 300,000 acres of Crown lands, near Albany in Western Australia, were to be offered for development in 400-acre lots, ex-servicemen being given preference in the allocation of farms. The Australian government also let it be known that they intended to investigate the possibility of a further settlement scheme in co-operation with the British government, and that a planning committee had been working on such schemes for review by the Government. Australia was about to become Rover's biggest overseas market. It comes, therefore, as no surprise to learn that the fourth production Land-Rover, R860004 – the earliest to arrive in the Southern Hemisphere – turned up some 40 years later in a wrecking yard in Perth, Western Australia.

Early brochures

CHAPTER 7 – Factory to Farm – The Late 1940s

Throughout both the motoring and agricultural world, publicity for the Land-Rover was extremely favourable. On 30 June, 'The Motor' reported that *"the Overseas Food Development Corporation, who were responsible for the East African groundnuts scheme, have placed an order for 500 Land-Rovers"*. And that was even before the four pre-production models R40–44 were sent there.

Rover's official press release of 19 April 1948 had stated Land-Rover production would begin in June. Confirmation of this schedule comes from the first two issues of Rover's 'Service Bulletin', referring to 'Numbering' and 'Specification', being dated 16 June 1948. The first driver's handbook, TP/108/A is also dated June 1948. Although Land-Rover production began around this time, a whole new assembly line had to be set up in the large Solihull building and many mechanical parts not shared with Rover's P3 cars had to be manufactured and machined at Rover's Tyseley plant and then assembled together.

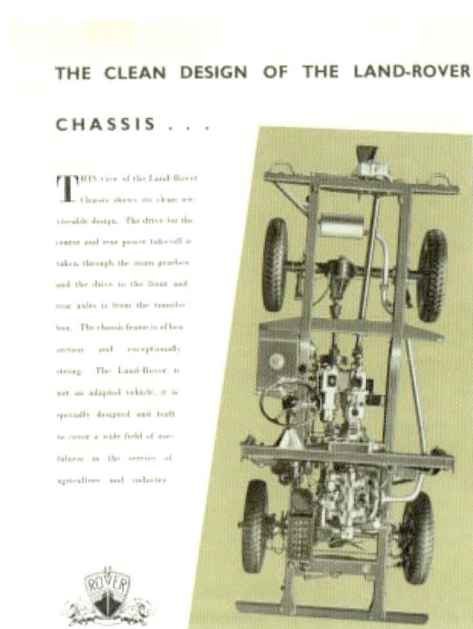

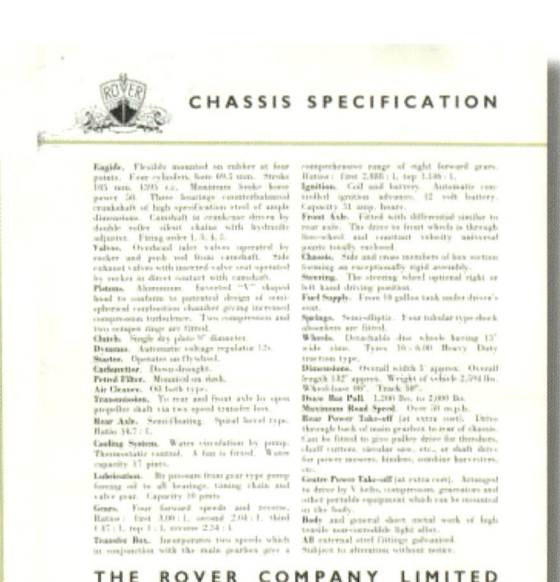

Left: Early brochure

Below: Dutch stand advert

Right: Advertisement in 'British Farm Mechanisation', July 1949

On July 19, the day when the first two production models, R860001 and R860002, were 'despatched in', seven pre-production models were also completed, but that still only took the overall total of all Land-Rovers produced to 41. With only three production models actually completed, on 21 July 1948 Rover's MD, Spencer Wilks, had sufficient confidence in the potential of future sales to report to the Board of Directors that *"...it was becoming more and more apparent that there was a very extensive demand for the Land-Rover both at Home and Abroad, and that the export orders and firm enquiries on hand at the moment amounted to approximately 8,000 of these vehicles"*. What he did know for certain was that Rover's order book was now sufficiently full to keep the assembly lines busy for at least the next 12 months.

At that same July Board meeting Spencer Wilks also acknowledged that planned output should reach 150 Land-Rovers a week by December. The minutes recorded that, on the basis of those orders so far received, Spencer Wilks immediately put in a plea to expand production to 500 Land-Rovers a week, *"...in order to be in a position to satisfy the potential demand that there was for this type of vehicle, and also with a view to reducing costs so that we might be in a position to meet competition which he felt we might have to face from other manufacturers"*. That day, Spencer Wilks not only secured the fate of Land-Rover production, but also that of the Rover Co. for the foreseeable future.

CHAPTER 7 – Factory to Farm – The Late 1940s

July, 1949   BRITISH FARM MECHANIZATION   11

Britain's most versatile vehicle!

EVERY FARMER will appreciate the value of this tough little go-anywhere vehicle. Its low-geared four-wheel drive takes it over the roughest going, yet it is a fast and economical vehicle on the road. By using the power take-off it becomes a mobile power unit for rick-building, root cutting and a score of other jobs.

Write for full particulars of the new 15 cwt. steel trailer — light, but strong and roomy — specially designed for use with the Land-Rover.

Wherever there's work to be done —you'll find the
LAND-ROVER

MADE BY THE ROVER COMPANY LIMITED · SOLIHULL · BIRMINGHAM

L05 pre-production at Amsterdam

At the Kent County Agricultural Society show. HAC 939 (R860049) on loan to Alfred Day MBE, Honorary Director of KCAS

Cooper's Kenya. Land-Rovers arrive for the groundnut scheme

CHAPTER 7 – Factory to Farm – The Late 1940s

Production line, June 1948

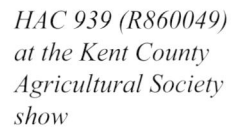

HAC 939 (R860049) at the Kent County Agricultural Society show

Below left: R861547 (HUE 730) undergoing trials

Below right: Convenient livestock truck

105

Interestingly, the first production model to actually leave the factory was not R860001, as might be expected, but R860003, which went to the Piccadilly showrooms of Henlys', Rover's main agent in London, on 23 July 1948.

R860004 (which carries pre-production gearbox '37'), went out to Faulls Ltd., in Perth in Western Australia, on 26 August, making it the earliest numbered production Land-Rover to go overseas, and the earliest Land-Rover to go to the southern hemisphere. R860005 went to Regent Motors in Melbourne, Victoria, even earlier, on 17 August, but technically, R860014, which went to C.A. Darmanie in Trinidad on 9 August, was the first production model to go overseas.

Altogether, just ten production Land-Rovers were completed before the end of July 1948. Along with nine remaining pre-production models, a further 66 were completed in August, so in reality few production models actually left the factory much before the beginning of September. But then things started to gather momentum, and by the end of September production exceeded 50 vehicles a week.

By the beginning of November that figure had doubled to 100 a week and by the second week in December, output was again up, this time to 150 Land-Rovers a week – exactly as Spencer Wilks predicted back in July – enabling total output to pass the 1,500 mark on 22 December 1948. From then on the early fabricated bulkhead was replaced by a new pressed steel structure, with various other modifications becoming necessary to accommodate it. The Land-Rover was clearly here to stay.

Despite the apparent slow start, the fact of the matter was that Rover had managed to get an entirely new vehicle from an initial prototype into full production in less than 12 months – truly a remarkable achievement. But not everything in the garden came up roses. In September Rover received the devastating news that, based on the company's poor export performance earlier in the year, their allocation of steel was to be cut back for the last quarter of 1948.

A further increase in Land-Rover output now became imperative, and Spencer Wilks recommended immediate steps be taken to increase production to 250 Land-Rovers a week, stating it would be necessary to raise £100,000 to finance this expansion. To double that number to 500, his original figure, together with an extra 200 P3 cars, would require a further £1,000,000 – serious money in those days.

Despite such problems, in a matter of weeks, and with less than 1000 Land-Rovers out of the factory, it was already apparent that Maurice and Spencer Wilks had secured the Rover Company's

Letter to Alfred Day MBE announcing Rover's scheme to lend Land-Rovers to the NFU

CHAPTER 7 – Factory to Farm – The Late 1940s

1948	month	July*	August				September					October				November				December					1949
Chassis Numbers	week	1	2	3	4	5	6	7	8	9	10	11	12	13	14	15	16	17	18	19	20	21	22	23	24	
861451	861500																						29	15	5	1
861401	861450																						35	13	2	
861351	861400																					5	42	2		1
861301	861350																					22	20	6	1	1
861251	861300																					26	19	5		
861201	861250																					1	32	13	2	2
861151	861200																				18	19	12			1
861101	861150																				23	23	4			
861051	861100																			4	33	11	2			
861001	861050																			11	26	9	2			2
860951	861000																		1	23	21	5				
860901	860950																		3	34	11	1				
860851	860900																		32	17	1					
860801	860850																		46	3		1				
860751	860800																	27	20	1	1					1
860701	860750																		45	3	1	1				
860651	860700																	23	26	1						
860601	860650																	44	6							
860551	860600																12	28	10							
860501	860550																45	5								
860451	860500														1	29	20									
860401	860450														16	34										
860351	860400													6	34	9	1									
860301	860350													39	10	1										
860251	860300										1	36	12	1												
860201	860250									28	18	4														
860151	860200								1	37	10	2														
860101	860150			1				8	23	16	2															
860051	860100					5	12	16	13	3	1															
860001	860050	9		7	11	8	10	5																		
Weekly Land-Rover output		9	1	7	11	13	22	29	37	47	41	56	61	62	73	78	100	114	106	94	136	154	178			

*Week commencing 19 July 1948.   Note: Ignore last three columns, as their totals would include post-1500 Land-Rovers, not shown in table   © John S Smith 2009

Chart showing weekly increase in output to Christmas 1948

future for a second time during a period of crisis. Everyone involved with the Land-Rover project soon realised they had more than just a 'stop-gap' vehicle on their hands and on 26 November 1948, Rover's Chairman, E. Ransome Harrison, prepared a statement which announced to shareholders on 20 December:

"The orders and inquiries we have already received, particularly from overseas, indicate that the vehicle will be something very much more than an additional source of production. It may well equal – and even exceed – our car output in quantity."

Rover's main dealer down under

His forecast could not have been more accurate, and for the Wilks brothers it would no doubt be a memorable Christmas.

Apart from the success the vehicle was having overseas, in the home market a number of factors were working in Rover's favour. In May 1948 petrol, which had previously been unavailable to the ordinary motorist since the outbreak of war in 1939, went on general ration, and the ordinary motorist was, for the first time since the outbreak of war, free to drive his motor car. Ironically, those already on 'essential and supplementary ration', such as doctors, received no further allowance for

Roll your own field

Ploughing for pleasure

The old cart gets a new workhorse

social and domestic use. To ensure new cars would continue to be available primarily for export, ordinary individuals were currently restricted to purchasing not more than one new car every two years. But this did not apply to commercial vehicles. A farmer, or anyone else who could afford it, could have both a new car and a new Land-Rover.

At the same time, under the Finance Act of 1936, farmers could also take advantage of an existing licence concession and use their Land-Rover duty-free on an adjoining highway, provided they did not exceed six miles in any week. There was also a further incentive. The price of the 'Basic' Land-Rover had been set at £450, but as a commercial vehicle, it did not attract Purchase Tax – then $33\frac{1}{3}\%$ – although legally this did appear to restrict it to 30 mph on the open road. Finally, a business could offset the whole cost of a new Land-Rover against tax in those days, and that included any extras such as PTO equipment.

The British Army was also taking a serious interest in the Land-Rover. Having had an early opportunity to test two of the pre-production models, L29 and R30, a small order for 20 Land-Rovers was placed in September 1948, under Ministry of Supply Contract 6/Veh/2854. Delivery of these took place on 16 December 1948.

A further increase in Land-Rover production, to 200 a week before the end of 1948, doubled output within two months, the 3,000th model being 'despatched out' on 23 February 1949. All 8,000 Land-Rovers that initial enquiries suggested would be necessary, were consequently completed within the first financial year, which ended on 30 September 1949.

In the same period P3 car output, which stood at 5,700 units, had been exceeded by more than 40%. But to be fair, the minutes of the December Board meeting do suggest car production had been deliberately cut back so that Rover's reduced quota of steel for the last quarter should not interfere with their expansion in Land-Rover output. Cars, or no cars, nothing could be allowed to stand in the way of Land-Rover production and that all-important export drive upon which Rover was totally dependent if the company was to survive into the 1950s.

CHAPTER 7 – Factory to Farm – The Late 1940s

CHAPTER 8
Marketing and Modifications
Some Early Changes

When it came to marketing the Land-Rover, what was surprising from a company such as Rover, with its reputation for quality above all else, was the number of items which the ordinary motorist had come to expect as standard now being offered as optional extras on the Land-Rover. Just about anything that might conceivably be considered as surplus by someone, somewhere in the world, was an optional extra – and that included the canvas hood, both doors, side screens, passenger seats, starting handle, even the tyre and inner tube for the spare wheel supplied.

Clearly, Rover's policy had been influenced by the expectation of an agricultural market, where such items may well have been superfluous. But as orders flooded in, it soon became obvious that this was not the vehicle the vast majority of customers wanted. Rover were quick to recognise their mistake. At the factory, time was being wasted fitting items individually that demand clearly warranted should be fitted as standard on the production line. Rover's distributors also had the unenviable and embarrassing task of explaining to potential customers that what they considered to be a complete vehicle was going to cost a lot more than the list price – despite the fact that it would still be an extremely basic motor vehicle.

In terms of both Rover's overall prestige as a luxury car manufacturer and the new Land-Rover's image, the benefits of such a policy were clearly dubious, and many, no doubt, considered it little short of miserly. Aware of the damage that might be done, this policy quickly changed. Before October 1948, passenger seats, doors, hood, etc. were all included in the deal at no extra cost – at least for the time being. In addition, a new passenger grab rail, a towing pintle, and a trailer lighting socket, were also provided. The latter was intended for use with a new trailer, specially developed by J. Brockhouse & Co. Ltd., for the Land-Rover, which Rover marketed in early 1949.

Only trafficators still remained optional from the ordinary motorist's kit (fittings for these were not provided on very early Land-Rovers, but were included in the listing of optional extras). As the '7-seater' hood was usually ordered, this too was provided as standard, replacing the '3-seater' which now became optional. Both hoods were a different pattern from those fitted to early pre-production models.

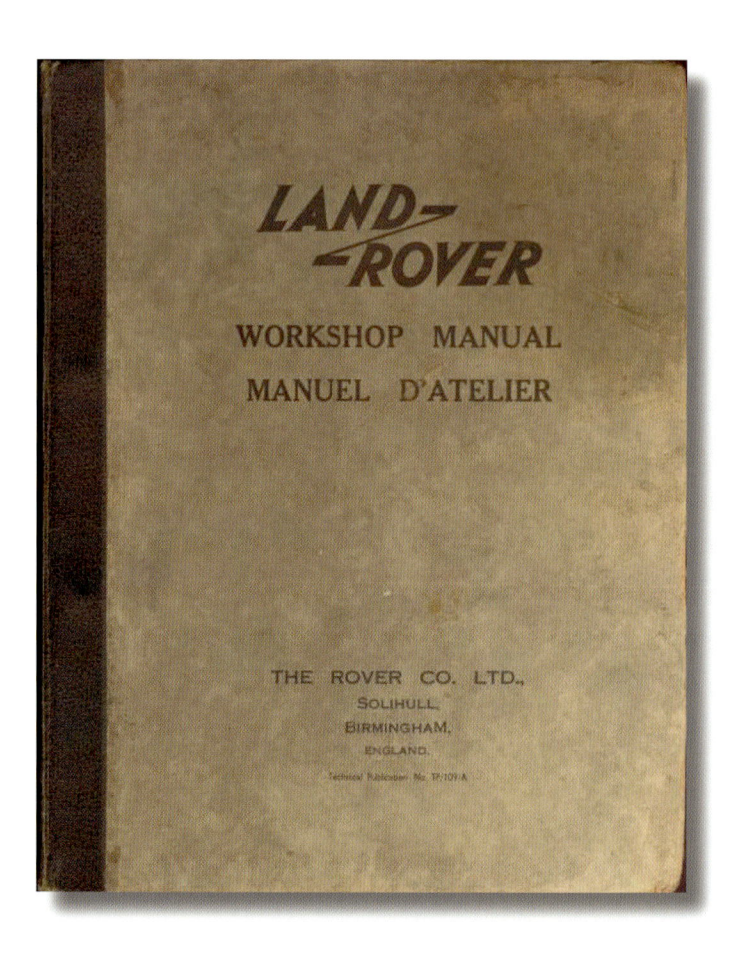

Despite such shortcomings, in terms of sales, the Land-Rover was, without question, an overwhelming success, and Rover had little hesitation in implementing a 20% price increase from £450 to £540 in late October 1948 to cover the extra cost of these additional items.

There is little evidence to suggest that the population at large had much idea of the problems faced by Rover in 1947/8 when the rest of Britain's

The first Workshop Manual for the Land-Rover, TP/109/A, published in December 1948

CHAPTER 8 – Marketing and Modifications – Some Early Changes

Ref;No.233.
London Showroom
DEVONSHIRE HOUSE
PICCADILLY LONDON W1
Telephone Grosvenor 2092

THE ROVER COMPANY LTD.

METEOR WORKS
SOLIHULL BIRMINGHAM

TELEPHONE SHELDON 2461
TELEGRAMS ROVER SOLIHULL

London Service Depot
SEAGRAVE ROAD
FULHAM LONDON SW6
Telephone Fulham 1221

All communications to be addressed to the company and not to individuals

October, 1948.

To simplify production, we have decided to adopt a standard specification for the Land-Rover, and in future this vehicle will be supplied with the following extras and equipment :

    Two Aluminium Doors with Perspex Sidescreens.
    Full Hood with Rear Panel.
    Cushions and Backrests for two front seat passengers.
    Spare Wheel and Tyre, 600 x 16.
    Starting Handle.
    Towing Plate for Rear Draw Bar.
    Pintle Hook.
    Socket and Cable for Trailer Light.
    Hand Rail.

We have made general improvements in the chassis and from November 1st, the price of the vehicle to the above inclusive specification will be £540.

Other extras will be supplied if required at the prices shown on our published list of extras. We would mention that if driver's hood is required it can only be supplied as an extra and no allowance will be made for the hood which is part of the standard equipment.

October 1948 Letter announcing Land-Rover now to be sold with certain Extra Equipment

The 1948 Land-Rover as it will now be sold

motor industry was successfully building up their export trade. Rover's employees, on the other hand, had been all too well aware of the situation. But by mid-1949 the immediate crisis was well and truly over. No matter what their first thoughts may have been of building an agricultural utility vehicle, Rover employees certainly now felt they had good reason to be thankful for the Land-Rover, and the idea of celebrating the Land-Rover's first birthday was put forward through the works suggestion box. In all, nearly 4,000 employees and relatives attended the event, recorded for posterity in 'Motor Industry', June 1949:

"An impressive exhibition of the Land-Rover in a variety of its many guises as handmaiden of agriculture and industry was staged in the works restaurant, and there were practical demonstrations – many of which astonished the men who built this remarkable all-purpose vehicle."

Altogether some 200 of Rover's employees gave up their Saturday afternoon to help stage the affair for colleagues and visitors.

To the casual observer, Land-Rovers leaving the production line in August 1948 had little to distinguish them from the pre-production models, but in reality many significant changes had already taken place. These differences set the pre-production models apart from all subsequent Land-Rovers, giving them a special place for ever in the hearts of all dedicated enthusiasts.

The galvanised chassis had gone for ever – a fact cleverly disguised by a thick new coat of silver paint. Integral front bumpers had gone, a separate bumper bolted to fish-plates was now standard, increasing Land-Rover length by 3 inches. Rear bodywork was made in a thinner 18 swg 'BB2', a non-corrosive marine alloy developed by Birmabright Ltd., and used extensively for both wartime landing craft and flying boats.

Maurice Wilks was familiar with the non-corrosive properties of 'BB2', and, before the war, had two small boats made of the material. 'BB2' was more suited to his original vision of the Land-Rover than Duralumin, and was conveniently produced in

CHAPTER 8 – Marketing and Modifications – Some Early Changes

Diagram from the first Workshop Manual for the Land-Rover, TP/109/A, published in December 1948

the Birmingham suburb of Quinton, not ten miles from the Solihull factory. Birmabright's chief, Mr Player (known to the Wilks family as 'Snuffles'), lived adjacent to Maurice Wilks' Kenilworth home, and was delighted to find a new peacetime use for his product.

To enable Land-Rover bodywork to align correctly with the chassis, on production models, instead of bolting the rear bin down and using wood spacers for adjustment, six upright plates were mounted on the chassis – four on the rear crossmember and two on the outriggers beneath the transom panel. The floor was also spot-welded the full length instead of being hand riveted half way, and five simple angle sections replaced the previous heavy top hat sections used for floor stiffeners. The three heavy top hat strengthening sections on the tail board were also replaced by a single simple central angle brace. Tail board hinges were repositioned to the outer edges, their retaining eyes now forming part of the capping. Corner cappings became an integral part of the hoodstick clamp, obviating the need to line up an extra set of rivet holes. Leading edges to doors were reinforced, in keeping with other edges and 'T'-handled roller slams were replaced by a more conventional internal handle and catch.

The cast aluminium sump used for P3 engines on pre-production models was replaced by a simpler steel fabrication, while cast aluminium side covers became a steel pressing, with the oil filler tube situated more conveniently at the front end. The cast aluminium bottom cover for the transfer casing also became a steel pressing. All aluminium-bronze castings – hubs, swivel housings, foot pedals, etc. – were replaced by steel, and hub 'star' driving flanges no longer had paired holes, as copied from the Jeep.

A pre-war pattern radiator with wide header tank and 19-pint capacity (referred to as a 'tropical' radiator), was fitted to pre-production Land-Rovers. However, following field trials, if the Land-Rover was to be used for stationary work for any length of time, Rover recommended an oil cooler be fitted to maintain temperature below 90°C. This could either be factory-fitted or supplied in kit form, and included a larger oil pump (from the 6-cyl P3 'Rover 75' car), an eight-bladed fan (with cowl to suit), an oil temperature gauge, and a 15 lbs/sq.in. radiator cap to replace the standard 4–5 lbs/sq.in. cap, increasing the coolant boiling point to 120°C. However, it had been discovered that under pressure test, at around 10 lbs pressure, the tropical radiator's wide header tank would start to bulge, and in consequence, it was considered no longer suitable for the Land-Rover. So for production, the tropical radiator was replaced by a more modern pressurised radiator of 17-pint capacity *"...to decrease loss of coolant under hard working conditions"*.

Before being sold off in the UK, any LHD pre-production model used as a factory demonstrator would be converted to RHD. At the same time, while the tropical radiator and front panel were off the vehicle, these would both be replaced by a standard production type.

The P3 exhaust silencer box located under the left seat area was replaced by an entirely new exhaust system suspended from a bent wire under the bulkhead outrigger. This then passed across the rear of the chassis where the silencer box was now located, and discharged behind the right, rather than left rear wheel, where it had been a tight fit. The new system meant the silencer box was less prone to mud thrown up from the wheels and less likely to foul on small hillocks. Heat shields were still not provided at this stage.

Divided or 'split rim' wheels were no longer a standard item, but optional. The simple 4-inch curved seat backs continued for around the first 150 Land-Rovers, but would soon be replaced by the more familiar 'spade' back, crudely sprung off the transom capping. These are referred to as 'bucket' seats in the first Land-Rover Parts Catalogue. Fixing holes for the earlier type of seat back remained for some considerable time. Seat bases were no longer flat, but raised towards the front edge, with much larger locating rubbers placed midway along the seat edge. Under the driver's seat, the pear-shaped fuel filler access cover and the circular fuel sender unit access plate were replaced by a large hinged panel which opened to expose the whole area above the tank. The inconvenient gap between seat base and rear body, where debris tended to accumulate, also disappeared.

Underneath, the brake fluid reservoir had moved from the handbrake mounting bracket to the engine compartment side of the bulkhead, where the now abandoned early 'push-pull' controls' bracket had once been mounted. But by Christmas it had returned to the previous location, this time with its own mounting bracket. Simple bent wire side screen steadies took on a new 'Y' shape, and the aluminium hoodstick tubes that fitted into windscreen sockets were replaced by smaller diameter galvanised steel tubes pinched at the ends – wing nuts securing them to small brackets on the windscreen frame. Vehicles left the factory with blank number plates attached to the wing and rear quarter panel, and a brass cast nameplate now appeared at the rear as well as on the grille. Unlike pre-production badges, these had a raised rim, and the 'Z' ran through all the lettering, as it had done on L03's wing badge. The new design was very soon cast in aluminium alloy.

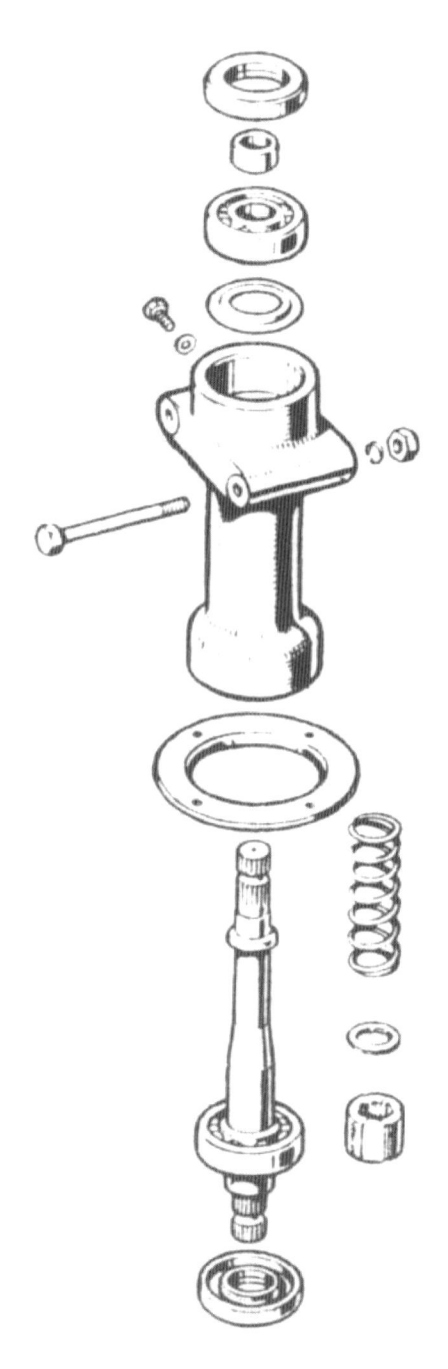

The early relay provided insufficient damping

Letter announcing free replacement of all early steering relays

CHAPTER 8 – Marketing and Modifications – Some Early Changes

C O P Y / PS.

From THE ROVER COMPANY LIMITED.   25th April 1949

LAND-ROVERS
bearing Chassis Serial Numbers
R & L 860001 - 861900 inclusive.

Standard Steering Relay Lever 230756
See Page G-26 - Land-Rover Workshop Manual.

- -

All Land-Rovers bearing a chassis number within the series 860001 to 861900 inclusive, were fitted originally with an early pattern relay unit which has a single spring-loaded Tufnol Cone. All vehicles bearing serial number 861901 onwards are fitted with the Standard Type Relay Unit which has a double damping cone. See illustrations on Page G 27 in the Workshop Manual.

The Standard Pattern Relay Unit has proved to be a more satisfactory unit than the early pattern and any tendency to wheel wobble under harsh conditions of usage has been eliminated.

The Company has decided to pass the benefit of this improved design on to all owners of vehicles concerned.

The action which is being taken is retrospective, and to this end we are arranging to despatch to you a quantity of the Standard Pattern Relay Unit, sufficient to modify all the Land-Rovers within the series affected which have been supplied through your agency.

The material is being supplied on a Free-of-Cost basis and on completion of the modification the early type Relay Lever Unit can be treated as scrap and disposed of accordingly. It is not our intention to pay the labour costs involved, but we are prepared to give consideration to any individual case which you think may justify special treatment.

On receipt of the new material, please make contact with owners and arrange conversion as soon as possible.

Please bear in mind that this change in specification will affect your spares position, and consideration should be given as early as possible to the question of obtaining appropriate quantities of spares to cover the new requirements.

Your co-operation will be appreciated.

THE ROVER COMPANY LIMITED.

A fabricated rear crossmember and bulkhead with detachable centre panel had been used on pre-production models and the first 1,500 production Land-Rovers. These were constructed on the strict understanding that no expensive tooling was to be used. In terms of labour their production was costly, but at that time Rover was just as concerned about keeping a large labour force occupied, ready for any expansion in car output. With Land-Rover production now assured for the foreseeable future, heavy pressings began to make sense, and capital investment in dies could now being justified, and rear crossmembers, bulkheads and outriggers now became pressings.

The new pressed bulkhead, introduced in December 1948, remained in service to the end of 80-inch Land-Rover production in 1953.[1] The new pressed rear crossmember lasted even longer – right to the end of 'Series One' production in 1958.

[1] *Apart from four occasions, when the die fractured and a fabricated angle iron structure clad in 'BB2' was pressed into service (known as the 'aluminium bulkhead'). This may previously have served as the Land-Rover's original steering box jig, as the earlier 'first-1500' fabricated bulkhead's transmission tunnel cover aligns with it.*

To fit the new pressed steel bulkhead it became necessary to modify wings, transmission tunnel, and seat box. With the removable centre panel now gone, the clutch became less accessible. The front floor also lost the separate steel front section where the pedal holes pass through, and new fuel pipes became necessary too. Wings on early models remained at 14 swg and can be readily identified by a cut-away section in the seam adjacent to the radiator panel where they curve downwards. New wings in thinner 16 swg – the same as the rest of the bodywork – have no cut-away as they are able to 'absorb' surplus material produced at the curve.

All these changes took place before Christmas 1948 and were the first major alterations to the Land-Rover, but many minor modifications also took place along the way. As well as the simple 4-inch curved seat backs from pre-production days found on the first 150 production Land-Rovers, clutch plates from pre-war P2 Rover cars were used in the first weeks of production. Later, this caused some embarrassment when it came to replacement time, as the different thickness of their driven plates was not initially acknowledged in any service literature. Various surplus parts from pre-production models, including bronze castings, also found their way into early production models

Factory drawing for the new pressed steel bulkhead

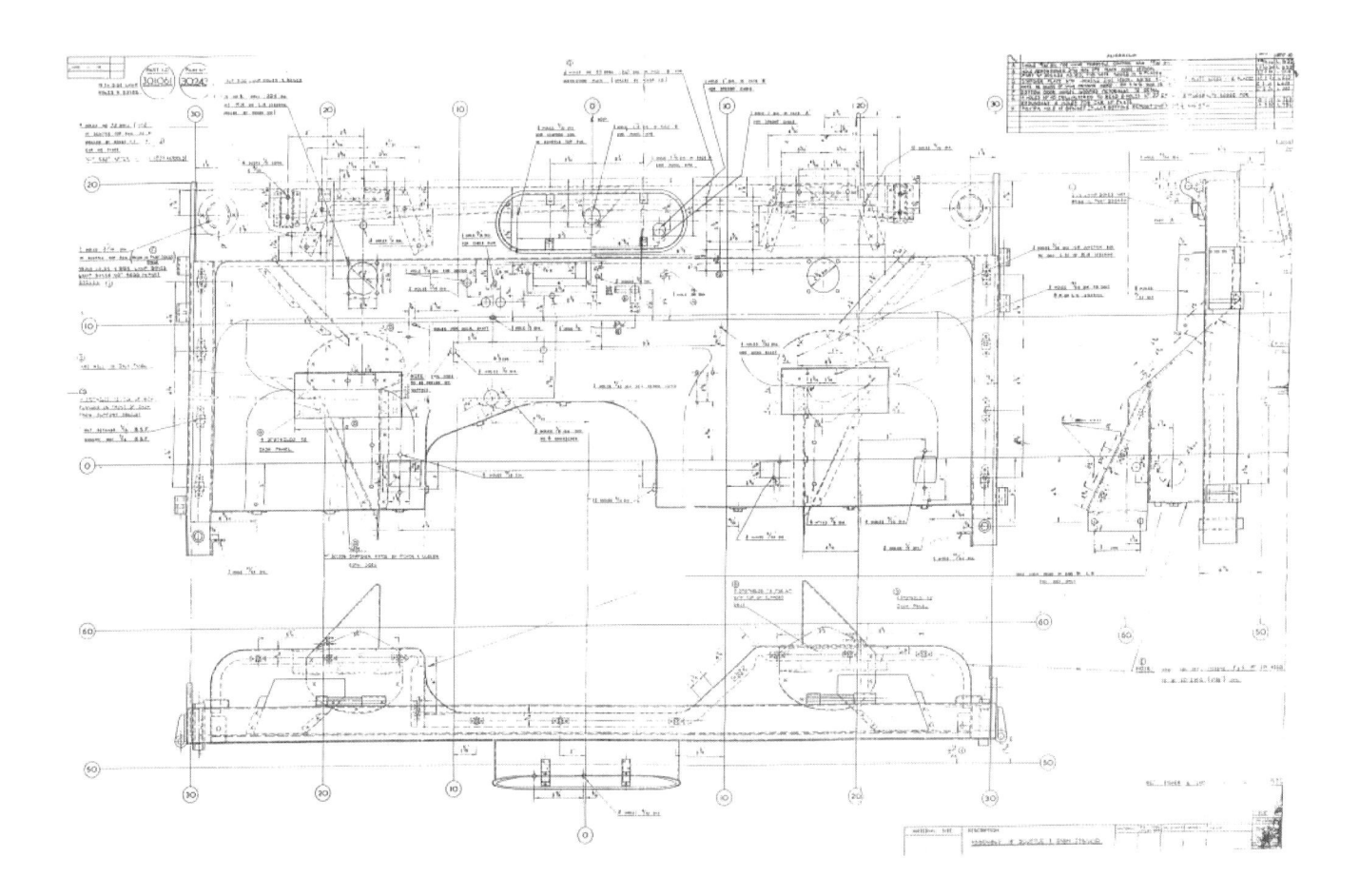

CHAPTER 8 – Marketing and Modifications – Some Early Changes

New bulkhead from the cab side

New bulkhead in situ, January 1949

117

LAND-ROVER – The Formative Years, 1947–1967

New tilt pattern uses rope cleats instead of staples to secure it

as pre-production models tried out new pattern production parts. Hardly surprising, as from mid-July into August 1948, some 13 remaining pre-production Land-Rovers were being constructed alongside production models on the new Solihull Land-Rover assembly line.

Several other mainly unrecorded changes took place in the first 12 months. Adjustable lock stops were added to the front axle in November 1948; at the beginning of December the early relay was replaced by one with two sets of damping cones; shields to prevent spring check straps from chafing the brake pipes were added in February 1949; gearbox crossmembers were boxed-in to increase strength on grounding; the unused steering relay position was blanked off; tubes lining the starting handle and PTO drive shaft holes were finished flush with the crossmember faces; and later still, to improve their strength, rear crossmembers were boxed in at the outer ends.

Rover experienced considerable difficulty in finding the correct free camber and overall strength for the road springs, partly on account of the Land-Rover's very short rear propshaft. This resulted in a number of road spring changes, at the beginning of November 1948, then in mid-November, and again in February.

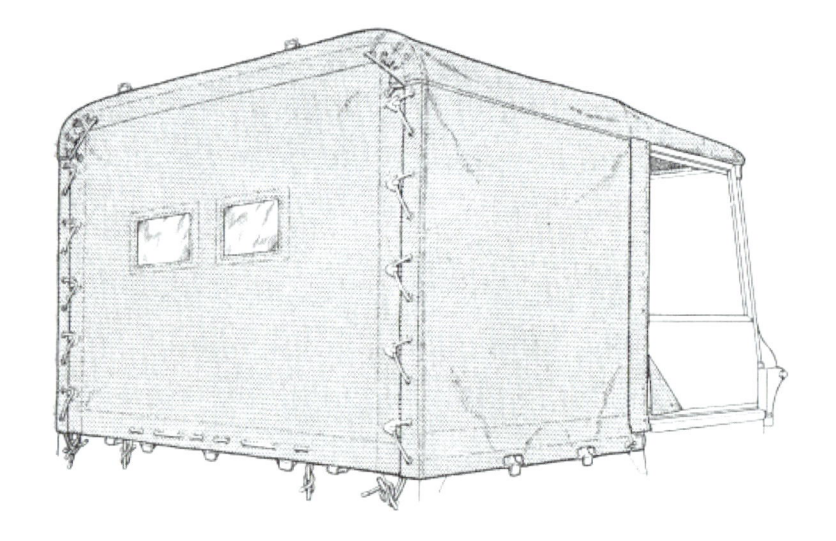

Engines planned for Rover's new P3 car had side cover plates attached by hexagonal set screws, but even before the demise of the short-lived P3 model a new block with core plugs was introduced for the Land-Rover. Initially sparking plug covers had no ventilation holes, making them waterproof, but ironically, condensation became a problem. At first a single pair of 1/16-inch holes were provided to solve the problem, but this was insufficient, and so an extra set of holes was added above these, and all were increased to 3/16-inch diameter.

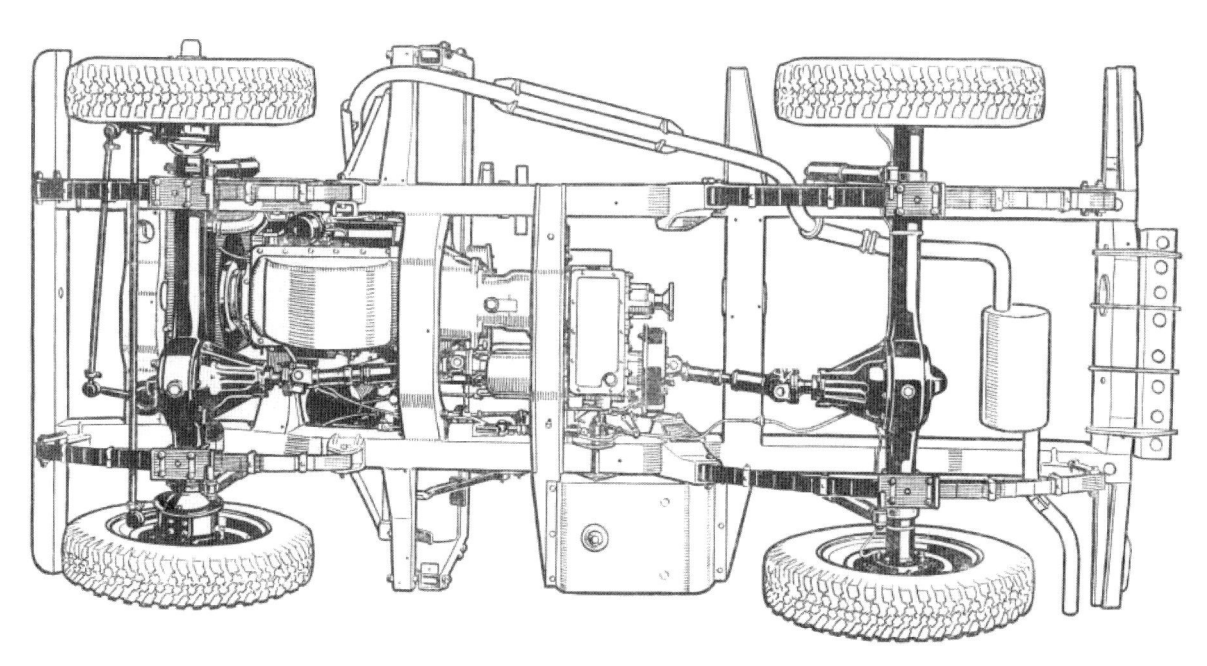

CHAPTER 8 – Marketing and Modifications – Some Early Changes

Late 1949 chassis showing pressed steel sump, production exhaust system, and detachable drawbar

Early radiator grilles had 27 squares at their widest point, but these were then reduced to 26, with the 'missing' section adjacent to the fixing screws now complete. Fan cowls had to be modified to accommodate the engine governor pulley's nut. The early 'flat' four-spoke steering wheel seen on the centre steer hybrid prototype was replaced by a two-spoke steering wheel left over from P2/P3 cars, also used on pre-production Land-Rovers. These were then superseded by a new four-spoke version that have more spring in them, but they tended not to last as long. Pinch bolts securing track rod end joint clamps were reduced in size. 'Light Green' replaced 'Silver' as the chassis colour around the 4,500th vehicle, but then changed again to the new body colour, 'Dark Green' at the 6,000th vehicle about a month later, in June 1949.

At the same time it was planned to introduce other major changes from vehicle 8666000 onwards. The chassis would lose their 'fish-plates'; "Hydrastatic" brakes would be replaced by an ordinary hydraulic system; the handbrake mechanism was to alter; and the hood pattern and method of attachment would change. However, most of these changes had to wait for the current stock of parts to be used up, and so the change was spread over several months – only the hood and colour immediately altered.

Girling's "Hydrastatic" braking system appeared to offer a number of advantages to a vehicle such as the Land-Rover, as the system was self-adjusting. This meant:

(i) a good pedal at all times – essential for heavy loads and towing;

(ii) brake shoes in constant light contact between the linings and drum – preventing the ingress of dirt;

(iii) quick drying-out after wading – something Land-Rovers do more frequently than other road vehicles.

But there were disadvantages:

(i) some owners only managed 10,000 miles out of a set of linings;

(ii) leading shoes incorporate a spring plunger and a specially scored lining that is more expensive to produce;

(iii) there is no adjusting mechanism to back-off shoes, so it was difficult to remove the drums if a rust lip had built up at the drum's edge.

In consequence, they were replaced in mid-1949 by a more conventional manually adjusted braking system.

CHAPTER 9
Land-Rovers in the Making Solihull and Tyseley

When the Land-Rover went into full production, the manufacturing techniques involved were of sufficient interest to warrant the attention not only of the motoring press, but technical publications such as 'Engineering', 'Machinery' and 'Welding'. In particular, the detailed account spread over three issues of Machinery in June/July 1949, and a later account published in 'The Autocar', May 1956, provide a very accurate description of the work undertaken. The two factories involved were Lode Lane at Solihull, where Land-Rover assembly took place, and the machine shop at Tyseley, a much older premises Rover acquired from Munitions Components Ltd., after the Great War of 1914–18.

The Solihull building was a recent acquisition, and had previously been Rover's government-financed wartime No. 2 'Shadow Factory' on some 65 acres of land. At the end of hostilities it was handed over to Rover in recognition of their war effort. When the opportunity arose, Rover's management then had the foresight to purchase 200 acres of surrounding farmland as well. All Rover's car production had been transferred there, wartime bombing having destroyed much of the old Helen Street premises at Coventry. Rover's Tyseley plant was responsible for engines, gearboxes and axles. Close-grained cast iron cylinder blocks arriving from 'Midland Motor Cylinder' or 'C & B Smith, Ltd.' (brothers Clifford and Bart), were scratch brushed, shot blasted, and then spray painted internally before the main faces were ground. A further dozen operations were then carried out at separate stations. Valve guides and seat inserts were cooled before insertion, then cylinder bores finish honed, tested and graded into two sizes – nominal –20 thou. and nominal +20 thou. – and marked accordingly. Bores were then etched before being chromed electrolytically, using the 'Listard' process, to enable them to better withstand conditions conducive to corrosion and abrasion which the Land-Rover might be likely to encounter either at home or abroad. Finally, bores were roughened to give a porous surface to provide pockets of lubrication.

Welder 0630001 at work, November 1949

CHAPTER 9 – Land-Rovers in the Making – Solihull and Tyseley

car. Gear work included differential components, and 'Maag' gear testing machines were used to check all profiles, tooth alignment, helix angles and concentricity.

Even so, many items incorporated in the Land-Rover were brought in from outside firms. These included:

AC	air cleaners, oil filters
Avon	tyres
Bendix	'Tracta' constant velocity drive joints
Borg & Beck	clutch components
Bramber	road springs
Burman Douglas	steering gear
Wm E Carey	road springs
Dunlop	tyres
Girling	shock absorbers and brake components
Hardy Spicer	universal drive joints
Lockheed	track rod joints
Lodge	sparking plugs
Lucas	electrics
Midland Motor Cylinder	cylinder blocks
Newton	clutch components
Rubery Owen	axle casings and wheel rims
Serck	radiators and fuel tanks
Silentbloc	shackle bushes
Skinners Union (SU)	petrol pumps
C & B Smith	cylinder blocks
Smiths	instruments
Solex	carburettors
John Thompson	chassis pressings, and complete chassis
Timken	bearings
Triplex	glass

When the finished components arrived, either ready assembled from Tyseley, or direct from outside firms, they became the responsibility of Rover's Quality Engineer, Paul White. This also applied to parts manufactured at Solihull, and included the finished vehicle. A great deal of trouble was taken to ensure that high standards of workmanship were maintained throughout the factory, preserving Rover's long-standing reputation for quality that eventually led to P4 'Rover 75' cars being dubbed 'The Poor Man's Rolls-Royce' in the 1950s.

As well as visual inspection, road springs were turned inside out on a powerful hydraulic press before being matched in pairs. Exhaust pipes and silencer boxes were hand-painted using a metal-based protective coating, too thick to be applied satisfactorily by spray gun. Foam rubber seat cushions had their resistance to compression tested. Hood and seat materials underwent a continuous programme of testing against rot, some pieces being half buried in a small garden for 12

Sciaky's advert for their spot-welder depicting 86-inch pre-production Land-Rover No.5, NAC 750

After completion of all machine work to cylinder heads, crankshafts, connecting rods, rockers and pistons, the engine was assembled. Particular attention was paid to crankshaft balancing, a 'Treble and Kunz' dynamic balancing machine being used for the purpose. Machining pistons involved first boring into the skirt and facing off. After that, a drawbar was inserted and held in position by a dummy gudgeon pin. This was used to pull the piston down onto a locating register entering the skirt, holding it steady while sides and ring grooves were machined.

Rover were extremely proud of the fact that they did all their own gear cutting, and emphasised that Land-Rover gearbox components were of the same specification as those used for the more powerful and prestigious six-cylinder 'Rover 75'

months, while others were placed in a malodorous cabinet full of fetid fungi and tropical growths, all at 90% humidity. Elsewhere paints, fabrics, rubber mouldings and metals were subjected to an atomised saline solution and, just to complete the torture, a slowly revolving ultraviolet light and water drip feed were incorporated in this 'chamber of horrors' to simulate burning tropical sun and monsoon rains.

Land-Rover chassis and bodies were both fabricated at Solihull. Front wings leaving the press shop passed through rollers for bending, before being placed in a special jig to form the flanges by hammering. A further jig was used to drill the fixing holes, using electric hand tools. The Land-Rover's rear body bin was constructed from simple folded sections. These were spot-welded to make two separate mirrored halves making up the wheel arches, each with just a half-width front transom panel. This gave both sides rigidity as well as convenience when manhandling for storage purposes, and also when shipping either as spares or for CKD models. Only the floor section and galvanised body cappings then had to be added for completion.

Body panels were all chemically degreased before being spot-welded by a 'Sciaky' Electric welding machine. In Sciaky's own advertisements, which featured the 1953 pre-production 86-inch Land-Rover No.5, NAC 750, they boasted of their machine that *"...1,250,000 aluminium Spot Welds are made each week in the production of the Land-Rovers. These welds must be as sturdy as the famous vehicle itself"*. Where the spot welder could not reach, hand or pop rivets were used. All body panels were then treated using the ICI 'Alcrom' process before being sprayed with a single coat of paint.

Chassis components were initially blanked from 14 swg mild steel sheet in the press shop. They were then placed into a long block with locating pegs, which separated the two sides of both longitudinal members. With the bottom edges uppermost and held by quick action toggle clamps, the underside was then tack-welded into place by two operatives working from opposite ends and separated by a protective shield that straddled the job. The resultant channel was then turned over, placed upright on another long block, and held by electromagnets in substantial side members before the top plate was similarly tack-welded into position. Each stage of construction was carried out at a separate enclosed station to protect the operatives.

Each pair of tacked longitudinal chassis members were then placed 'end to end' on a 50 foot bed above a table of rollers, above which a 'Fusarc' welder with automatic heads was centrally located. The bed would start at the extreme end of the table and then move along. As the first member passed under the heads, welding commenced.

AA Land-Rovers, April 1949

Rover's early transporter ready to roll

Rare Eezion Land-Rover, the first and longest long-wheel base?

CHAPTER 9 – Land-Rovers in the Making – Solihull and Tyseley

When the centre of the bed was reached, welding continued on the second member, while the first member was turned over, ready for the return run. As soon as the second member was completed, a high-speed reversing motor returned the bed to the start. Welding then continued on the other side of the first member, while the second member was turned over ready for welding.

This routine minimised delay in loading and enabled five pairs of longitudinal chassis members to be completed every hour, sufficient for the planned 200 vehicles a week in 1948. The moving bed with rollers was eventually replaced by a new 'Fusarc' moving welding head, which, depending on the contour of the work, could vary the rate of work between 84 and 110 in/min. After welding, longitudinal members were cleaned up with rotating wire brushes before being placed in jigs ready to receive the various brackets for springs, handbrake, etc. Further cleaning then followed, using emery discs.

Crossmembers already fabricated, along with parts such as fuel tank outriggers, body mounting plates etc., were also placed in jigs before being tack-welded into position to complete the chassis frame. Holes in the rear crossmember, together with the bumper bolt holes, were then used to support the chassis in a special open carriage mounted on the chassis assembly track. The chassis could then be rotated about its axis and locked in any position at the operative's convenience while seem welding was carried out. Altogether ten separate stations were used along the line in a manner calculated to minimise distortion to the finished job. Again, each station was separated by a heavy curtain to give a protective area for the operator.

The next step involved drilling various holes using portable power tools and jigs suspended above the track, suitably lowered into position. A special jig was also used to apply axial pressure for the 'Silentbloc' bush holes. When all these operations were completed, the chassis was again cleaned with portable hand tools before moving along the track to a spray booth. In the booth, a coat of yellow zinc chromate primer was applied and baked on at 140°F. A final coat of synthetic paint was then applied in a second booth and baked on in an infra red drying oven for nine minutes

Rover's gas turbine car, 'JET 1'

The trailer unit was used for transporting 'JET 1'

CHAPTER 9 – Land-Rovers in the Making – Solihull and Tyseley

Rover's own articulated tractor unit

(in the early 1950s, spray-painting gave way to a dipping process). The chassis was now ready to join the assembly line.

Olaf Poppe was responsible for organising the shop floor, where sub-assembly lines were strategically placed to feed the main assembly line. This consisted of two parallel tracks the entire length of the building, with a 'Start' and 'Finish' both at the same end. A transfer platform at either end enabled vehicles to return down the second track, and empty cradles to be transferred to the 'Start' as soon as a completed vehicle was removed from the 'Finish' end.

Axle assemblies, complete with springs, were first on the cradle. Then the chassis was lowered onto the suspension, shackle pins inserted, differential housings filled with oil, brake components added, and brakes bled. Next came the engine and gearbox, scuttle, complete with steering box, instruments, wiring harness etc. This was followed by the rest of the steering gear and electrics, and took the Land-Rover to the end of the first track. On the return journey, bodywork and seating were fitted, and finally, wheels added.

The completed vehicle was now ready to leave the assembly shop for testing. This was the responsibility of Alec Joyce, whose idea it was to utilise the wartime air raid shelters as a switchback circuit, where conditions were reckoned to be as severe as any likely to be encountered in service. The air raid shelters provided a series of flat-topped corrugations about 10 feet high, banked on either side by steep slopes, with just sufficient level ground between each to accommodate the Land-Rover's angle of approach and departure as it scrambled over the rows of shelters.

As well as this general test, each week one completed vehicle was removed from the assembly line and thoroughly examined for any signs of imperfection. All faults were then traced back to source, and any necessary remedial action taken immediately. As Rover's confidence in the new product increased, actual testing was eventually reduced to simply driving four times round the company's road circuit on a fault-finding exercise. (Rover's own 2.3 mile circuit was constructed at Solihull in 1954 in order to avoid the prying eyes of their competitors – all part of the normal scene at the MIRA track – when testing gas turbines cars and other prototypes.) By these various means Rover's Land-Rover product build up a reputation for total reliability, which it continued to maintain throughout the decades that followed.

Vehicles going overseas – more than 75% of factory output – had their engines sprayed externally with a lanolin solution before leaving the factory. After being driven to the docks, but before the engine was stopped, the air intake hose was removed, and a pressurised capsule of lanolin released into the carburettor. This was designed to protect the bores and valves during long periods at sea, or while the vehicle languished at the quayside in some far and distant land. Land-Rovers that were delivered to the docks by Rover's own road transporters were also similarly treated before departure.

CHAPTER 10
Identity Crisis
Tractor or Transporter?

Two pre-production Land-Rovers had been sent to the National Institute of Agricultural Engineering for extensive trials lasting nine months. Although the published report on both vehicles was generally favourable, nevertheless, two important innovations had recently taken place in the field of agriculture that would surely influence the farming community's attitude towards the Land-Rover for ever.

The Land-Rover had been specifically designed as a rival to horse, oxen and tractor, for ploughing and tilling the soil. However, Harry Ferguson had already permanently jeopardised any future the Land-Rover might have in the field of agriculture. Using a Ford 'Model T'-based tractor – the 'Eros' conversion – in 1917 Ferguson began developing a draught system for attaching ploughs directly to tractors. Ford themselves had been experimenting with tractors, and that same year went into tractor production. The following year Ford's new Fordson 'Model F' tractors began arriving in quantity from the USA, and Ferguson moved on to experimenting on this new tractor. A decade later in 1929 all Fordson tractor production ceased in the USA and was transferred to Cork in Ireland, Ferguson's homeland, where it was updated as the 'Model N'. It later transferred to Dagenham, Essex in 1933.

It was also in 1933 that Harry Ferguson decided to build his own 'Black Tractor' (now in the Science Museum, London), which then went into full production in May 1936 with the gear manufacturer, David Brown (DB), at Lockwood, Huddersfield. It was DB's first tractor venture. Powered by a Coventry Climax engine, the new Ferguson-Brown 'Type A' tractor had a price tag of £224, but still further expenditure was then required to purchase the special hydraulic lift implements. At the time, Britain's farmers could buy a Fordson to drag around their existing implements for just

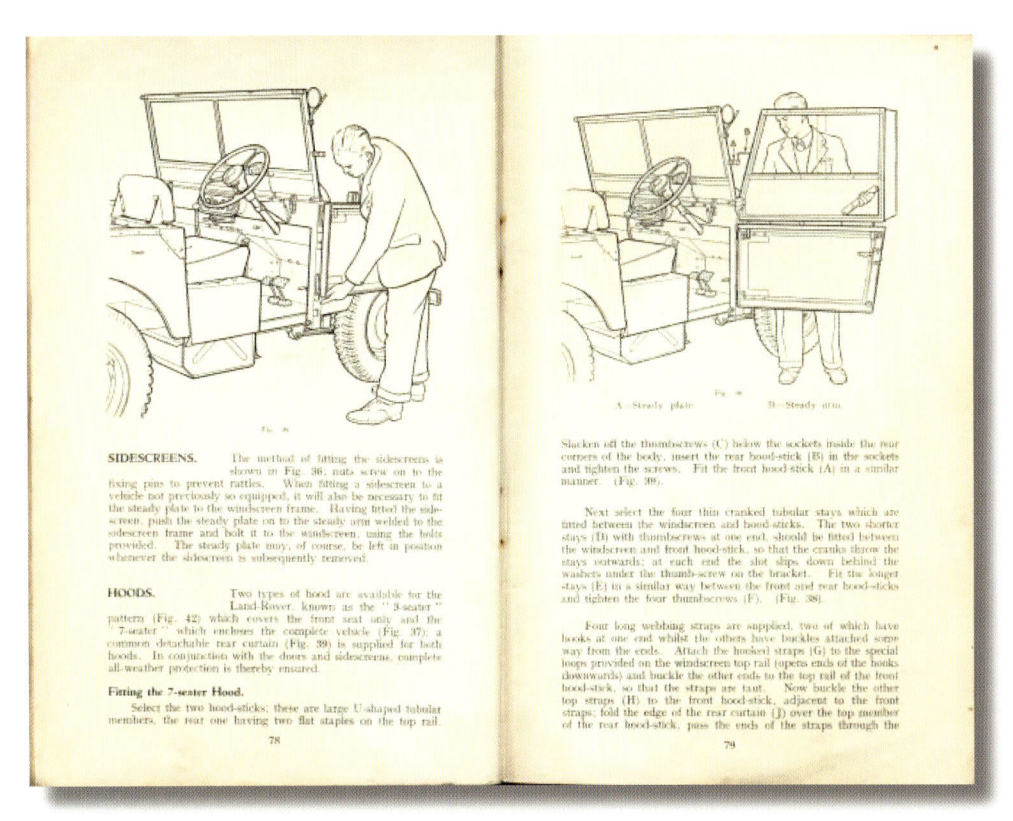

Early handbook refers to '3-seater' and '7-seater' hood causing 'jobsworth' civil servants to claim the new Land-Rover was a passenger-carrying vehicle and therefore attracted Purchase Tax

CHAPTER 10 – Identity Crisis – Tractor or Transporter?

R860101 special prepared for HM King George VI, July 1948

£155, and fewer than 2,000 'Type A' tractors were sold before David Brown began developing his own tractor in 1939, without Ferguson's approval, and the partnership dissolved.

But by October 1938 Ferguson had already turned to Ford, and on 12 June 1939 the new 'Ford-Ferguson' 9N tractor, equipped with the 'Ferguson System' of three-point linkage, hydraulic controls, and automatic draft control, was launched in the US. When production of the 9N ceased eight years later, in June 1947, over 300,000 had been sold.

Following a serious disagreement with Ford at Dagenham in Essex, concerning replacement of the ageing 'Fordson' tractor (in production since 8 October 1917), in November 1945 Harry Ferguson set up a company to design and market his own tractor. He then negotiated a manufacturing agreement with the Standard Motor Company's MD, Sir John Black (brother-in-law to the Wilks brothers) and before the end of 1946 'Little Grey Fergies' could be seen rolling out of Standard's Banner Lane works, Coventry – a good 12 months before even a pre-production Land-Rover had been completed.

The new 'Ferguson TE-20' tractor had a more powerful overhead-valve engine, the 'Continental Z120', and extra '4th' gear. Following its successful launch, Harry Ferguson severed his relations with Ford in 1947 and by the end of the year more than 50,000 TE-20s had left the Coventry works, half of them destined for export to the USA, earning Britain those much needed dollars. By1951/2 Ferguson had topped the 100,000 a year mark with 70,000 TE-20 tractors from Coventry, and a further 30,000 TO-20 tractors from the Ferguson Park Plant at Detroit, and soon he would have 50% of the British tractor market.

With the 'Ferguson System' of three-point linkage now firmly established, by 1948 it was already clear the old system of simply dragging implements behind a drawbar, which also posed a serious danger to the driver if the implement snagged, was fast becoming obsolete.

And not just in Britain and the USA, but everywhere those two countries were exporting tractors. Yet contemporary factory photographs of early Land-Rovers at work, with their integral drawbar, clearly showed this was exactly what Maurice Wilks had in mind.

The converse of this situation was also apparent. Back in 1933, in a blaze of publicity, the American tractor manufacturer, Allis-Chalmers, introduced both speed and the pneumatic tyre to the farming community with their Model 'U' tractor. It would take a little time to convince farmers they would not be continually plagued by punctures and shredded rubber, but by 1937 50% of tractors in the USA were now 'Air Tired'.

After the war, practically every tractor manufacturer in Britain and the USA had followed suit. Almost overnight, tractors shed their iron wheels, with their destructive iron cleats, for the softer comfort of pneumatic tyres, and tractors suddenly became capable of roadwork, as well as other more general duties around the farm. With tractors no longer confined to the field, was there really a need for an additional vehicle, such as a Land-Rover, for more general duties around the farm?

An important bonus of the Ferguson System for many farmers was that when fitted with a 'Link Box' attachment, full churns of milk could be easily hydraulically lifted onto a standard loading platform ready for collection by the Milk Marketing Board. There was no way you could do that easily with a Land-Rover. Against this background, could such a basic utility farm vehicle survive? Harold Hastings of 'The Motor' certainly confessed to being sceptical, as, no doubt, were many others watching Rover's fortunes at that time.

There was no simple solution to this predicament. The Ferguson System could not be readily adapted to a vehicle, such as a Land-Rover, that had a sprung suspension. Fortunately, however, Rover never had to face this dilemma, as the Ferguson System meant Land-Rovers would only rarely be used to pull a plough and till the soil, avoiding any possible impending embarrassment.

A partial acceptance of this reality became apparent when the integral drawbar was dropped towards the end of 1949 – if only for a detachable one. Certainly Rover's major buyer, the British Army, who at that time were taking 50 Land-Rovers a week – a quarter of all output – had no use for such an encumbrance, as it seriously reduced the Land-Rover's angle of departure. In consequence it was omitted from all Ministry of Supply Land-Rovers a few months ahead of civilian models.

Nevertheless, there can be little doubt about the Land-Rover's growing popularity with the farming community. But it was the Land-Rover's rugged reliability and practical capability that had become the driving force behind sales in the agricultural sector of the economy. These same characteristics had also made the Land-Rover popular as military and paramilitary scout cars, police and rescue

The King's Land-Rover had rear seats with stowage clips for the hood stick hoops

CHAPTER 10 – Identity Crisis – Tractor or Transporter?

Weed Research Organisation crop sprayer in action, 1949

A LHD version of the King's Land-Rover was later prepared for Juan Peron, President of Argentina, February 1949; Harry Smith and Spencer Wilks stand alongside

service patrol vans, missionary and medical mobiles, contractor and surveyors' site vehicles, as well as packhorse, mule, and camel, for the more adventurous users – a role for which it eventually became most famous. Estate managers, gamekeepers, park wardens, veterinary surgeons – all were finding the Land-Rover indispensable. The list was ever growing, as the Land-Rover fast became the ready-made solution to the problem.

Britain's Royal Household was also using Rover's new 'field car' (as the BBC preferred to call it, for fear of advertising), both at home and overseas. King George VI's personal Land-Rover, JYR 437, R860101, was among the earliest built, and is rumoured to still be in reserve at one of the Royal Estates. Inroads were even being made into the United States, home of Willys' ubiquitous Jeep. Wherever the task was demanding for both men and machines, the Land-Rover was sure to be there. Reliability and versatility had become the name of the game, and no matter what other shortcomings Maurice Wilks' original vision may have had, in this respect he appears to have been entirely right.

The Land-Rover's ability to be used as both a land and road vehicle meant it was an entirely new type of vehicle on Britain's roads, and it took some time for its legal status to be clarified. An initial setback came when a particularly vigilant civil servant was quick to notice the reference to '3-seater' and '7-seater' hoods in the Land-Rover's handbook, which prompted the following memo. from Spencer Wilks, dated 6 September 1949:

"We have some difficulty convincing the Inland Revenue Authority that the Land-Rover is not a passenger carrying vehicle and is, therefore, not liable to Purchase Tax.

In the Instruction Book p.88 and onwards we frequently [refer] to the three-seater and seven-seater hood. Please alter this definition A.S.A.P. and avoid any reference ... to the passenger carrying ability of the Land-Rover."

As a result of this 'error', the Chancellor of the Exchequer now intended removing the Land-Rover's commercial status in the following spring budget. Spencer Wilks took up the challenge on behalf of the Rover Company, and after some persuasive talking, was eventually able to save the day. At the meeting held on 11 July it went on record that the Rover Board *"...congratulated Mr Wilks on the successful outcome of his negotiations".*

LAND-ROVER – The Formative Years, 1947–1967

Rover's new transporter and trailer, May 1951

Loading the transporter's trailer

The Land-Rover was an entirely new type of vehicle on Britain's roads, and several years passed before the legal status of a 'Basic' model was finally sorted out in a famous test case.

In 1956 Mr C. Kidson of Wareham in Dorset was fined £3 for exceeding the 30 mph limit imposed on commercial goods vehicles on the open road. After seeking counsel, Mr Kidson decided to appeal against this judgment in the High Court. The appeal ruling, given by Lord Chief Justice Goddard, was that as four-wheel-drive vehicle, the Land-Rover fell within the definition of a 'dual-purpose vehicle' under the meaning of the Act and, therefore, was not restricted to the 30 mph speed limit imposed on ordinary goods vehicles. The Rover Company itself was delighted with this judgment, and no doubt such feelings of delight percolated down to Land-Rover users throughout the British Isles.

During the second season of production, Land-Rover output had already doubled to 16,000 vehicles, with around 350 Land-Rovers coming off the line each week by mid-1950. Even so, demand continued to outstrip supply, while at the same time combined sales of Rover's P3 and P4 cars totalled less than 4,000 units during the model changeover.

Throughout the 1950s Land-Rover sales continued to go from strength to strength, and only in 1954, when the new '86 & 107' took over from the original 80-inch wheelbase Land-Rovers, would car sales even reach 50% of Land-Rover output. The following year P4 production peaked at 13,436 units, but by this time Land-Rover sales had soared to a staggering 28,882 – the all-time record for 'Series One' models.

CHAPTER 10 – Identity Crisis – Tractor or Transporter?

The Deer Hunter. Belgian LRSOC member Claude Balteau in the Ardennes in the 1950s. His son Pierre now looks after 'Nanny' in southern France

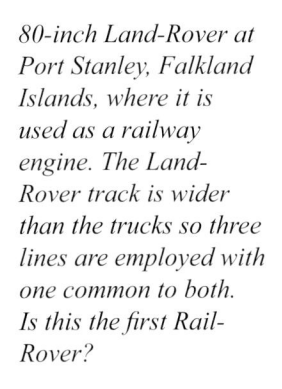

80-inch Land-Rover at Port Stanley, Falkland Islands, where it is used as a railway engine. The Land-Rover track is wider than the trucks so three lines are employed with one common to both. Is this the first Rail-Rover?

CHAPTER 11
Overseas Adventures
The Early Expeditions

The early Land-Rover was also quick to establish itself not only as a workhorse for factory and farm, but also as a reliable chariot for overseas adventures too. Sometime in 1950, the author and would-be adventurer, Barbara Toy, had a close friend living in Baghdad, who became ill. Miss Toy decided she would drive overland to see him, and planned buying, in her words, *"A cheap Jeep that'll get me there."* She quickly became disillusioned when she saw the war-weary rubbish on offer, so the brother of a friend, Bill Day, had a word with the manager at Henlys, Rover's prestigious London dealer. Not surprisingly, they had a demonstration Land-Rover on display in their Piccadilly showrooms. The next step was to persuade Miss Toy to take a look. At £540 it was certainly far more than she could afford, but with financial assistance from yet another friend, she ended up buying it. Suddenly her dream was turning into reality.

On hearing Miss Toy's plan, Henlys then promptly sent her to Rover's London depot at Seagrave Road, in Fulham, where a special cover for the rear body, that flipped up for access and also conveniently doubled as a bed, was specially made.

Barbara Toy named her Land-Rover 'Pollyanna', and their first adventure together began in Tangier, then followed the North Africa coastline through Morocco, Algeria, Tunisia, Libya, and on into Egypt. From Alexandria they set sail for Cyprus, then crossed to Syria, driving through Trans-Jordan, and on to Baghdad in Iraq. 'She seems to be a woman of remarkable courage' commented 'The Spectator', on hearing of Miss Toy's great adventure. Anyone wanting the full account of these exploits should look for a copy of her book 'A Fool on Wheels' (1955).

In the Sahara at Gebel Hauaisch

CHAPTER 11 – Overseas Adventures – The Early Expeditions

Barbara Toy and Pollyanna in 1958

A little off-road exercise

Pollyanna enters Shiraz, Iran, on her first round-the-world trip

All this had given Miss Toy a taste for the desert. But before setting off on their next adventure, Pollyanna was given station wagon bodywork by a local carpenter in Kent. Unlike Rover's own 'Tickford' Land-Rover Station Wagon conversions, the job was completed using all the existing Land-Rover bodywork. Barbara Toy chose Libya for her second adventure, where she made four advances deep into the desert with Pollyanna. This brought them into contact with a variety of desert dwellers, among them, Foreign Legionnaires, and the German War Graves' Commission *'...looking for Rommel's lost men'*. This story unfolds in *'A Fool in the Desert'* (1956).

Adventures with Pollyanna had become a way of life for Barbara. For her third adventure she shipped Pollyanna over to Kuwait, planning to drive through Saudi Arabia to Qatar and on through the British protected Trucial States (now the United Arab Emirates) to Oman. Having arrived in Kuwait, much to her surprise, Miss Toy discovered that women were not permitted to drive in Saudi Arabia. A kindly friend suggested it would be OK if she were an invited guest of the King, so she immediately wrote to ask if she could visit him. Armed with the King's invitation, she proceeded to drive Pollyanna right across the great desert of the Arabian Peninsula to Jeddah. That story is told in 'A Fool Strikes Oil' (1957).

Barbara Toy's next adventure was to be on a global scale. Now eight years old, Pollyanna was about to become the first Land-Rover to circumnavigate the world, no less. Sponsored by *'...those nice people at Rover...'*, who insisted on fitting a brand new Capstan winch to the front of Pollyanna before she set off, this latest journey would take them right across Europe to Turkey, Iran, West Pakistan, India, East Pakistan, Burma, Thailand, Cambodia, Malaya and Singapore on an overland drive to Australia, and Sydney, where 50 years earlier Barbara Toy had been born.

After travelling the breadth of Australia to Perth, Miss Toy then gave her first radio interview of the journey. Much to her surprise, over the air, the interviewer quite openly referred to Pollyanna as a 'Land-Rover', and not just a 'field car'. It was something Miss Toy knew 'Auntie', back home, would never have permitted. She was also permitted to tell her audience that Pollyanna was still running on the same set of Dunlop tyres

Barbara Toy's receipt for Pollyanna

CHAPTER 11 – Overseas Adventures – The Early Expeditions

LONDON: DEVONSHIRE HOUSE HAWLEY CRESCENT GT. WEST ROAD STREATHAM HIGH ROAD AIRPORT DEPOT HENLYS CORNER NINEWAYS PETROL STN
        PICCADILLY, W.1 CAMDEN TOWN, N.W.1 BRENTFORD STREATHAM, S.W.16 HOUNSLOW NORTH CIRCULAR RD. CAMDEN TOWN, N.W.1

COMPANY/RL/HSH

NO. 92146.

I N V O I C E

HENLYS
LIMITED

ENGLANDS LEADING MOTOR AGENTS

HENLY HOUSE, EUSTON ROAD
LONDON, N.W.1

TELEPHONE
EUSTON 4444
PRIVATE BRANCH EXCHANGE
TELEGRAMS
HENLECARS, NORWEST, LONDON
CODES
BENTLEY'S, A.B.C.

DIRECTORS
H. G. HENLY
R. G. CHANDLER
E. S. BARING-GOULD
E. H. KENNY
H. L. BUCKLEY
G. WHITE

19th December, 1950.

Miss B. Toy,
73, St. James's Street,
LONDON. S.W.1.

STOCK NO. 46490.

TO:-   ONE USED LAND ROVER Standard Truck,
          finished in Green, as seen, tried,
          and approved...........................£540. 0. 0.

          Extra Accessories and Special fittings.£ 55. 1. 9.

          Registration yo end of year .... No charge.

          Delivery charge ex. Works...............£   3. 0. 0.
                                                  ─────────────
                                                   £598. 1. 9.
          Approx. Premium - Norwich Union
               (To be adjusted later)............£ 25. 0. 0.

          Approx. Premium - Marine Risk..........£ 5. 0. 0.
                                                  ─────────────
                                                   £628. 1. 9.
BY:-   Deposit...............................£100. 0. 0.
                                                  ─────────────
(Demonstration Stock)   £528. 1. 9.
Reg. No. KYH. 628.
Chassis No. R. 06110086.
Engine No. 06110312.
    E & O E

Adventurer John Addison in Panama

Pollyanna after returning from her second round-the-world trip in 1990

The first 'Land' Rover? Dr Jeffereson's factory prepared 1904 'Indian and Colonial' model crossing the Balkans on its way to Constantinople.

Pollyanna in 1959

1950, L19 is about to cross the channel. It will be driven via Denmark to Sweden by owner E. Cadogan

fitted when they left England. Local interviews of this sort were conducted throughout her tour of Australia, which no doubt boosted Rover's export drive 'down under'.

After exploring much of the Australian outback, Miss Toy bid farewell to her mother at Sydney, and set sail, with Pollyanna, for San Francisco. From New York, they returned to England. With only a change of springs and a single puncture experienced *en route*, Pollyanna's 15 months journey had certainly proved the reliability of even a nine-year-old Land-Rover. Pollyanna had become the first Land-Rover ever to circumnavigate the globe – and perhaps also the first car to do so, who knows?

Back in London, in acknowledgement of ten years' faithful service, once again Pollyanna was put on display in Henlys' Piccadilly showroom, only this time accompanied by a large notice telling everyone of her great adventure. What more could anyone have asked of a 1950 Land-Rover? The full account of this epic adventure is told in 'Columbus was Right' (1958).

Barbara Toy had every intention of continuing her exploits with Pollyanna, but *'...those nice people in Rover's publicity department...'* had other ideas. With Pollyanna now more than ten years old they wanted their latest model to receive all publicity, and so Pollyanna was reluctantly exchanged for a brand new Series II model for still further adventures. Even so, from Barbara's point of view, the new model proved less reliable and she eventually ran out of spare rear half-shafts, managing to limp home with only the front wheels driving the car.

Some thirty years later Miss Toy re-acquired Pollyanna, with a little help from members of The Land-Rover Register, including this author. Then in 1990, at the sprightly age of 81, she decided to

CHAPTER 11 – Overseas Adventures – The Early Expeditions

drive Pollyanna, single-handed, on a second world tour. Pollyanna was, of course, a mere stripling at 40 years old.

According to Barbara, the secret of this long and happy relationship was to be found not simply in the inherent qualities possessed by the Land-Rover, but her prudent ability to avoid the mistake, so often made by the would-be adventurer, of overburdening this willing beast with every conceivable piece of gadgetry imaginable, rendering it both cumbersome and clumsy. (How oft' have stories been told of the 'miraculous recovery', which might never have happened, were it not for all that extra recovery equipment.) Miss Toy was always careful to travel light, taking only those items she really needed. Even Pollyanna's front winch was only reluctantly accepted for the global trip, at Rover's insistence, but never put to use.

A contemporary of Barbara Toy, as far as 'Land-Roving' is concerned, was the French-Canadian, Colonel M. Leblanc. A one-time pilot with the Royal Flying Corps, during the Second World War Leblanc spent time in north-east Africa with the Sudan Defence Force. Before the war, in October 1935, Italian Fascists had entered Ethiopia, taking the capital, Addis Ababa on 5 May 1936. Together with Eritrea and Italian Somaliland, this became Italian East Africa. To complete their conquest of the 'Horn of Africa', they successfully invaded British Somaliland on 4 August 1940.

On 15 January 1941 Emperor Haile Selassie returned to Abyssinia to help anti-Italian rebels, and assisted by the British Anglo-Egyptian Sudan, Colonel Leblanc's Sudan Defence Force and South African troops, the Ethiopians ejected Mussolini's Fascists. By 5 May 1941 Emperor Haile Selassie was back in the capital, Addis Ababa.

After the war, Colonel Leblanc decided to revisit the area, travelling overland by Land-Rover. That was in 1949. Like Barbara Toy, Leblanc continued to use the Land-Rover for further exploits, and in 1951 he managed to persuade Rover to let him become a sort of 'travelling salesman', taking commission on all future Land-Rover sales in pre-arranged areas that he visited.

His first expedition on behalf of the Rover Company, in early 1952, was from Algiers to Nairobi with a company Land-Rover and new P4 'Rover 75' car. However, Rover's man Roger McCahey drove the Land-Rover. Leblanc got the car. In fairness, Colonel Leblanc was later provided with a small fleet of factory-prepared Land-Rovers which he took on expedition to Africa and the Middle East between 1954 and 1959. Equipped with two of Rover's new 107 Station Wagons,

LAND-ROVER – The Formative Years, 1947–1967

Australia, 1950 the continent is circumnavigated by Land-Rover

CHAPTER 11 – Overseas Adventures – The Early Expeditions

Colonel Leblanc's four factory-prepared Land-Rovers

during these exploits his party of seven pioneered a new route across the northern Sahara from Tripoli, some 600 miles due south to the oil drilling rigs at the Robert Ray Atchan camp. The journey took two weeks to complete, during which time their Land-Rovers struggled through the most enormous sand dunes. In her book 'In Search of Sheba' Barbara Toy recalls the time she accidentally stumbled across Colonel Leblanc at Gatrun Dunes.

Later, in 1961, Colonel Leblanc returned to Sudan by Land-Rover, first travelling south across the Sahara to Chad, then east into Sudan, and on to Addis Ababa, capital of Ethiopia, a 3,500-mile journey that took some six weeks to complete. There he joined Selassie's celebrations of the 20th Anniversary of the Liberation of Ethiopia.

In 1951 an early 1.6-litre Land-Rover, privately entered by M.M. Robert and Raymond Lapalu, made quite an impact in the 'Mediterranean to Cape Town Rally'. The arduous journey lasted almost two months, from 28 December 1950 to 24 February 1951. Not only was it the only British vehicle to finish, but was outright winner of the 1,000–2,000cc class and tied first place with a Delahaye and a Jeep. The Land-Rover was not only continuing to make its mark as a reliable vehicle around the farm, but also proving its worth on exceptionally long and arduous overland journeys in places where there was very little chance of any back-up service.

Such expeditions as these were by no means the first to be undertaken by Rover vehicles. Way back in 1906, a Dr R.L. Jefferson persuaded Rover to build him a strengthened version of an already robust example of Rover's first car, 'The Indian and Colonial Model', a single-cylinder 8 horsepower car produced in 1904, which retailed at £225. This car had a three-speed gearbox and was capable of 30 mph and up to 40 miles per gallon.

In those days, no car had ever entered the Ottoman Empire, and Dr Jefferson was determined to be the first motorist to cross the Balkans and reach Constantinople (Istanbul), a journey of more than 2,000 miles, that required not only careful negotiation of the roads, but the diplomatic situation as well, as motor vehicles were still prohibited in Muslim Turkey. The journey was almost accomplished without incident, but a valve broke just outside Constantinople. Even so, Dr Jefferson was well within the Ottoman Empire. It was a remarkable achievement for one of Rovers' first cars – an Overland-Rover, if ever there was – and a taste of things to come.

CHAPTER 12
A Closer Look Into the 1950s

The evolutionary process sparked off by the hybrid prototype centre steer vehicle continued on through pre-production models and on into the production line. In these early years, hardly a week passed without some modification being introduced on the Land-Rover. Although they were often matters of only minor detail, such variation has played a major part in the enthusiasm, some 50 years later, for the early 1.6-litre Land-Rover, 41,410 of which left the factory between July 1948 and July 1951. Parts catalogues, handbooks, service bulletins and newsletters, sales catalogues, and factory records and photographs, have all played a major part in helping to determine when such modification occurred, but equally important has been the network of enthusiasts whose keen eye for detail has often drawn attention to items previously unrecorded.

The Land-Rover's identification number (VIN) was prefixed by 'L' or 'R', to denote left- or right-hand drive, and stamped on a small rectangular brass plate situated in the engine compartment above the left toe box. This corresponded with the larger number stamped on the chassis left-hand engine mounting bracket.[1] Engine, gearbox, and axles had

[1] *Smaller numbers on early chassis refer to chassis number sequence.*

The new 1950 season's model

CHAPTER 12 – A Closer Look – Into the 1950s

LHD Export model for Canada, Jan 1950; note vent panel

Tyres change from Avon to Dunlop

their own numbers, which rarely coincided with the VIN, but usually ran ahead. This was due to parts being put aside for replacement purposes. A classic example is found in the change from Girling 'Hydrastatic' brakes to standard hydraulic brakes. Workshop Manual TP/109/B, December 1949, clearly states 'Hydrastatic' brakes in use to Vehicle 8667574, but all subsequent parts catalogues put this change at Axle 8667720.

Published records do sometimes confuse the issue. For example, in early editions of the first Parts Catalogue TP/111/A, the change from 'Hydrastatic' brakes to standard hydraulic brakes is stated as occurring at 8666000, when, in theory at least, it was intended a major revision to the Land-Rover's design should take place, and that included the chassis. The revision did take place, but only in piecemeal fashion over several months, simply because many parts already in the pipeline still had to be used up. The only immediate revisions were the Land-Rover's colour change from Light Green to Deep Bronze Green, and the design of the '7-seater' hood and its method of attachment.

LAND-ROVER – The Formative Years, 1947–1967

The 1950 brochure

A further example is found in handbook T P/108/B, October 1948. This states the change from P2 car differential (4.88:1 ratio) to P3 differential (4.7: ratio) taking place at Axle 861372, a remark that persists through to TP/108/D, April 1950. But all relevant parts catalogues state this change at Axle 861320, which incidentally, coincides with the 1001st vehicle. The handbook number must therefore be based on a calculation of remaining stock, because the 1001st Land-Rover was not completed until 2 December 1948 – not October 1948, the handbook reference being published before the last 50 or so P2 differential units were put aside for replacement issue.

Numerous influences lay behind all these changes. Some came about as part of a planned programme of development in much the same way that no pre-production model 'despatched in' at the factory would continue to use mechanical parts from the American Jeep. Others, such as the detachable bumper and windscreen-mounted mirror, came about through the light of experience. Outside influences played an important part too – the first change in body colour from 'Light Green' (as used on the internal parts of Rover's wartime aircraft frames), to 'Dark' or 'Deep Bronze Green' was in response to the British Army's first major order for 1878 Land-Rovers in May 1949.

Two of the pre-production Land-Rovers had also been sent to the National Institute of Agricultural Engineering for extensive trials lasting nine months. The published report on both vehicles was generally favourable, but a number of recommendations were made, many of which were eventually adopted. But paramount among the reasons for change was customer usage. Right from the start Rover had billed the Land-Rover as *'Britain's Most Versatile Vehicle'*, and they were not about to go back on an image which they themselves had created – the Wilks brothers would have made sure of that.

When the factory reopened after the annual holiday closure in August 1949,[2] new 1950 season Land-Rovers immediately began to roll off the production line. With them came a new numbering sequence, beginning 06100001, but otherwise there

---

[2] *Rover practice was to commence a new season of vehicles immediately the factory reopened after the annual summer holiday closure.*

142

CHAPTER 12 – A Closer Look – Into the 1950s

LAND-ROVER

STANDARD EQUIPMENT SUPPLIED WITH EACH VEHICLE

Two aluminium doors with Perspex sidescreens
Full hood with rear panel
Cushions and back-rests for two front seat passengers
Spare wheel and tyre, 600 × 16
Starting handle
Towing plate for rear draw bar
Pintle hook
Socket and cable for trailer light
Hand rail

£540

OTHER ITEMS OF EXTRA EQUIPMENT
AVAILABLE IF REQUIRED AS DETAILED
IN LIST BELOW

		£ s. d.
E/2	Rear Power Take-off. Drive Section.	20 0 0
E/3	Rear Power Take-off. Pulley Unit	15 0 0
E/4	Centre Power Take-off	7 0 0
E/6a	Pulley and Fitting for E/4	2 10 0
E/6b	Pulley and Fitting for E/4 where used in conjunction with E/2	2 10 0
E/11	Rear Winch (E/2 must be specified also)	26 0 0
E/5	Engine Governor Unit	15 0 0
E/31	Oil Cooler Unit (Not supplied without E/34)	Price to be announced
E/34	15-lb. Pressure Radiator Cap. Essential with E/31	,,
E/12	Thermometer and Oil Gauge	,,
E/8	Five detachable rim wheels in place of five standard wheels	8 14 6
E/9	Extra for five 7.00″ × 16″ Dunlop Tractor Tread Tyres instead of standard 6.00″ × 16″ Tyres	10 0 0

P.T.O.

LAND-ROVER

List of extras continued

		£ s. d.
E/35	Extra for five 7.00″ × 16″ Dunlop "Fort" Tyres instead of Standard 6.00″ × 16″ Tyres	10 0 0
E/15a	Carrier on bonnet for 6.00″ × 16″ Tyres	1 0 0
E/15b	Carrier on bonnet for 7.00″ × 16″ Tyres	1 0 0
E/10	Chaff Guard	2 0 0
E/18	Ventilator for Windscreen	1 15 0
E/7	Detachable metal top covering Driver's and rear compartments	See separate leaflet
E/14	Electric Heater	7 0 0
E/23	Trafficators	3 2 6
E/28	Heavy Duty Army Type Pintle Hook	1 10 0
E/25	Cover Plates for Universal Joints	Price on application
E/27	Brockhouse 15 cwt. Trailer (For description see separate leaflet)	75 0 0

NOTES

The Engine Governor E/5 is essential if the Centre Power Take-off is specified, or if a Rear Power Take-off is specified with Pulley Unit E/3.

If both Rear and Centre Power Take-off are specified pulley and fittings E/6b must be supplied.

The prices quoted for extra equipment are valid only if such extra equipment is fitted before vehicle is delivered from Works. If ordered after delivery from Works a fitting charge will be made. All prices and specifications quoted is this catalogue of which this leaflet forms a part are subject to alteration without notice. Prices are for delivery ex Works.

No allowance can be made in respect of any item of Standard Equipment not required.

The Land-Rover is subject to the guarantee conditions contained in The Guarantee Form issued by The Rover Company Limited.

The name "Land-Rover" is a registered Trade Mark of The Rover Company Ltd.

E. O. & E. Feb./50.

Price list February 1950

was little to distinguish them from the previous season's models. But that would soon change, and by the time the Land-Rover had reached its second birthday, every major component had undergone some form of modification. Whether you view these changes as 'highly innovative', 'much-needed improvements', or simply 'crisis management', one thing is for sure – Rover was not dragging its feet.

In the autumn of 1949 Rover P3 car production came to a close, and the new P4 'Auntie' 'Rover 75' took over. In a programme of rationalisation, several Land-Rover components would now change. No part from the previous P3 car would remain on Land-Rovers if it could be exchanged for a part from the new P4 car. Such rationalisation not only lowered the cost of Land-Rovers, but more importantly, Rover's cars, which sold in far fewer numbers – just 3,563 units in the 1950 season compared to 16,000 Land-Rovers. One particular example was the clutch change from Rover's own pattern, also used on P2 and P3 cars, to a Borg & Beck clutch similar to that used on P4 cars. The old course splined clutch withdrawal mechanism was also dispensed with, in favour of a new fine splined type. All these changes were implemented by the 200th Land-Rover engine of the 1950 season. But there would be a major exception. Whereas Land-

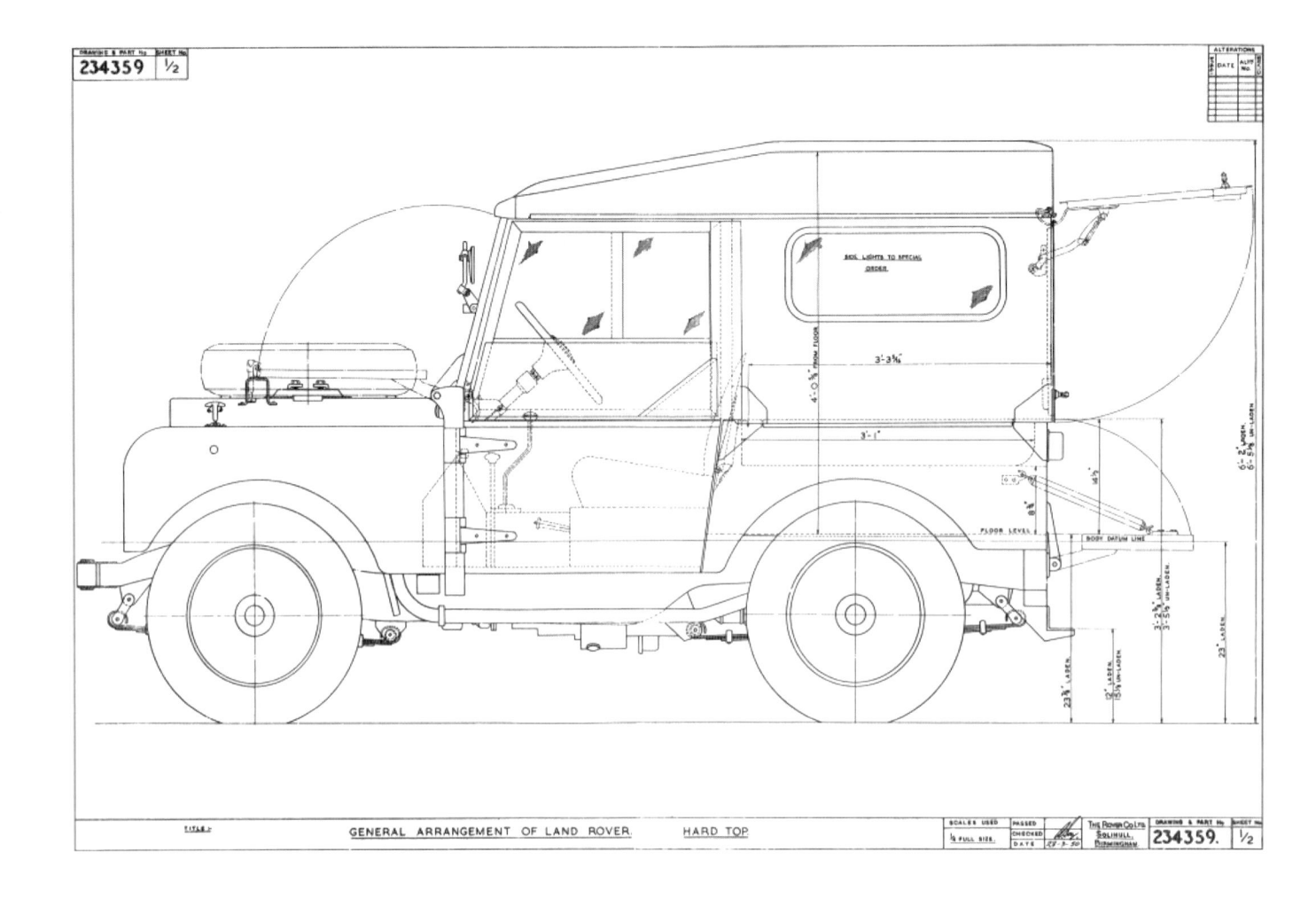

LAND-ROVER – The Formative Years, 1947–1967

Factory drawings showing new hardtop, March 1950

Rovers shared their 1.6-litre 4-cyl engine with Rover's P3 '60' car, the new P4 cars would only be using the larger 2.1-litre 6-cyl engine from the previous P3 '75' car. No 4-cyl Rover cars would be available for the next four years.

As well as changes to P4 components, in an attempt to cut costs, various measures would be introduced to economise on certain pieces of *'Rover-engineering'*, while at the same time improving the Land-Rover for normal road use. Other modifications introduced were specifically designed to overcome problems the Land-Rover had encountered along the way. For example, the switch from Girling 'Hydrastatic' brakes to standard hydraulic brakes in summer 1949.

Many such modifications were too insignificant to ever be recorded as specific to a particular Land-Rover. These included centralisation of the direction indicator switch bracket and the addition of a second mirror bracket – making windscreens no longer 'handed'. Stiffeners were added under the locker lid, which doubled as a handbook holder, and circular rubber grommets for the chassis harness replaced elaborate pressed metal covers. Door strengthening corner gusset plates were added, and drain plugs provided on swivel pin housings. Even more significant was the exchange of the heavy iron steering box housing for a light, more easily cast and machined, aluminium-alloy casing.

Rover were also out to improve certain areas of specific concern, such as dust-proofing, the transfer of gear oils, oil consumption, and wheel wobble. Early in September 1949, as the new season's models got underway, weather strips were provided on the front, rear and bottom edge of doors, and the sides and bottom of the tail board, making the Land-Rover interiors both draught- and dust-proof.

Avon 6.00 x 16 'Traction' tyres had been standard equipment on the first 10,000 Land-Rovers, with the option of 7.00 x 16 'Super Traction' for agricultural work. These had been fitted to an International Standard Rim size, the '4.50 E 16' (road wheel Part No. 217629), which is easily identified by the valve position being adjacent to a slotted section. Around mid-1949 this wheel rim was superseded by the more common 5-inch wheel rim, to accommodate the larger Dunlop 6.50 x 16 'Trakgrip T29' now being fitted to Ministry of Supply WD Land-Rovers.

CHAPTER 12 – A Closer Look – Into the 1950s

*Overleaf:
Factory drawing showing new wide front road springs, June 1950*

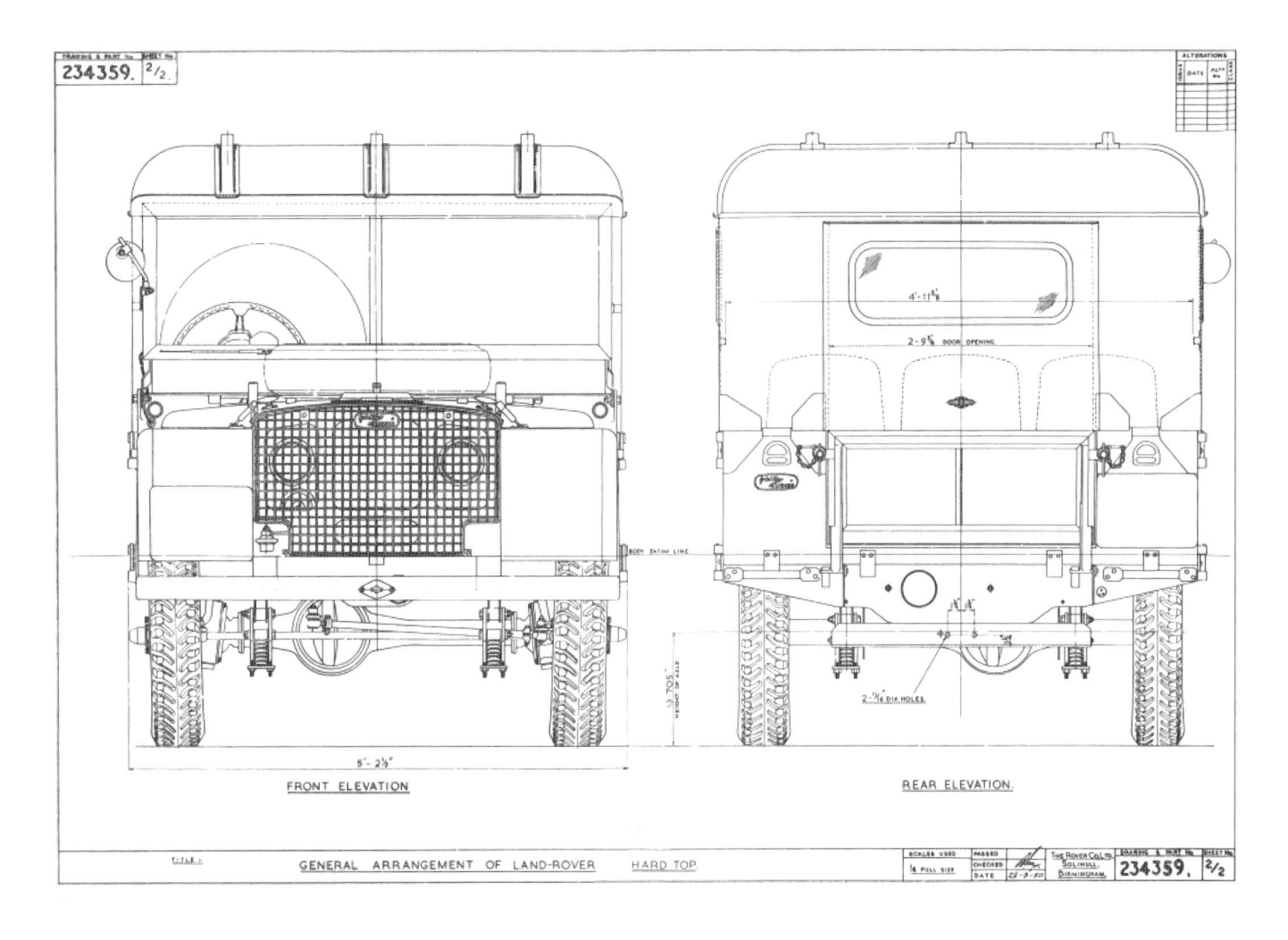

Under Ministry of Supply Contract 6/Veh/3659, dated 2 May 1949, from June 1949, Land-Rovers for army use were being delivered at the rate of 50 a week, starting with R8667261. This was a quarter of all production at the time. All WD Land-Rovers were equipped not with Avon tyres, but Dunlop's 6.50 x 16 T29 'Trakgrip' tyres. The new tread pattern was most likely a WD-approved pattern. Based on expected use and loading figures provided by the vehicle manufacturer, working out suitable tyres was the job of the tyre manufacturer.

The new 5.00 x 16 wheel rims supplied for Ministry Land-Rovers came from the 'International Wide-base Rims' category 5K, with 'Recommended' tyre sizes 6.00, 6.25, 6.40, 6.50, 6.70, and 7.10. Remaining stock of Avon 6.00 x 16 tyres and 4.50 E 16 rims continued to be used on civilian models up to chassis R0612200. The 5.00 16 rims are dated, whereas 4.50 E 16 rims are not.

By October 1949, all Avon tyres had been superseded by Dunlop's 6.00 x 16 'Trakgrip T28' tyres on civilian models. These had a less aggressive tread more suited to normal road use. Dunlop 7.00 x 16 'Trakgrip T25' became optional for agricultural work. Rover correspondingly advised tyre pressures be altered from a previous 22–24 lbs/in. to 20 lbs/in. front and 26 lbs/in. rear, for normal road and cross-country use, and from 15 lbs/in. all round to 15 lbs/in. front and 20 lbs/in. rear on exceptionally soft ground.

November saw further changes that continued the trend towards road work rather than just being an agricultural vehicle. After the 12,000th Land-Rover, the drawbar, which had been an integral part of the chassis, was dropped – though only for a detachable type – in order *'...to facilitate repair after accidental damage'*.

Most customers were pleased to see the integral drawbar go, including Rover's biggest customer – the British Army (currently taking delivery of a quarter of all Land-Rover output at the time) – as it severely reduced the Land-Rover's angle of departure. The integral drawbar was not provided on military Land-Rovers from early June 1949, but civilian models waited a little longer. At the same time, bumper 'fish-plates' moved from the chassis to the bumper itself, as bumpers changed from 'slot in' to a 'push on' type.

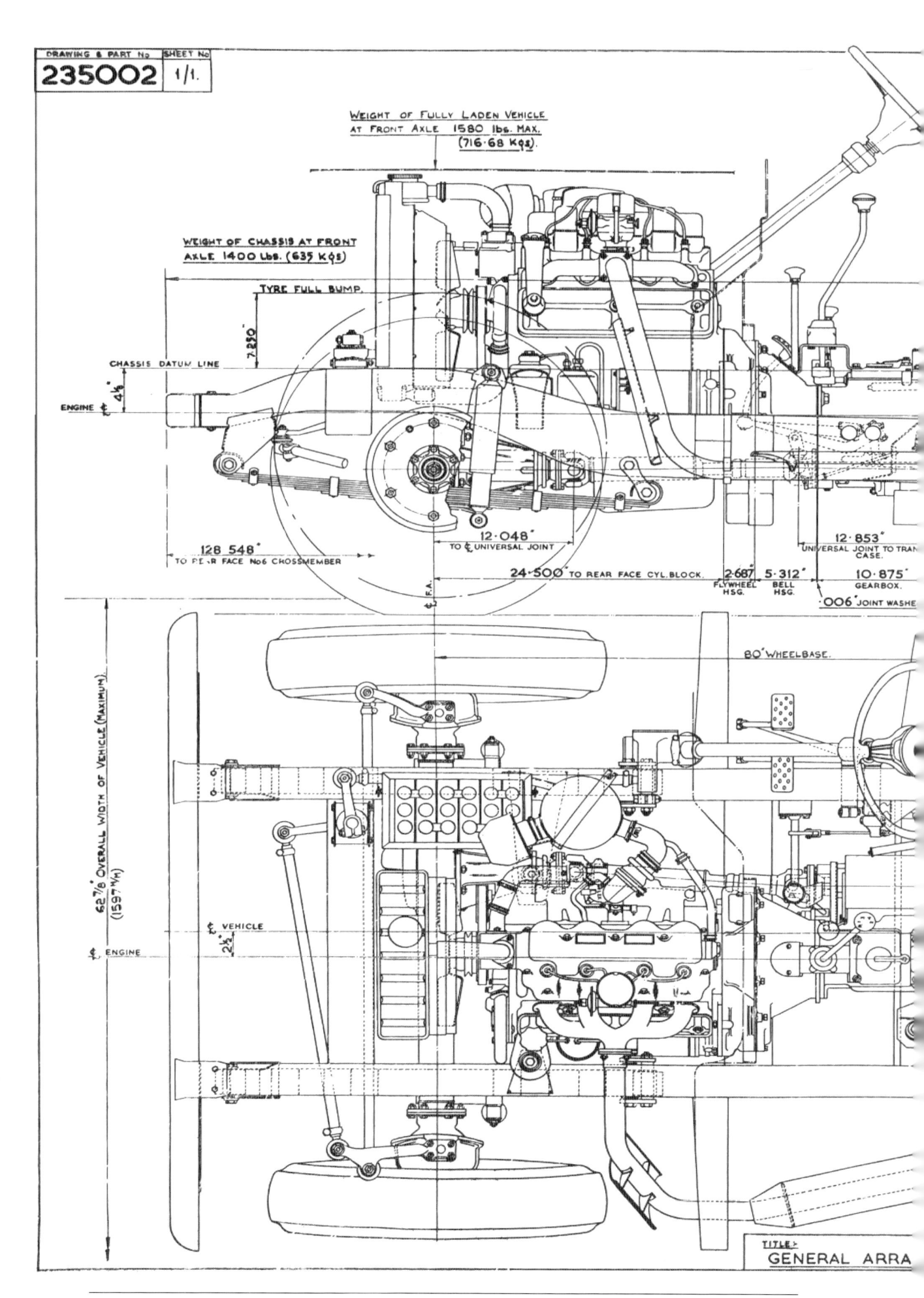

LAND-ROVER – The Formative Years, 1947–1967

CHAPTER 12 – A Closer Look – Into the 1950s

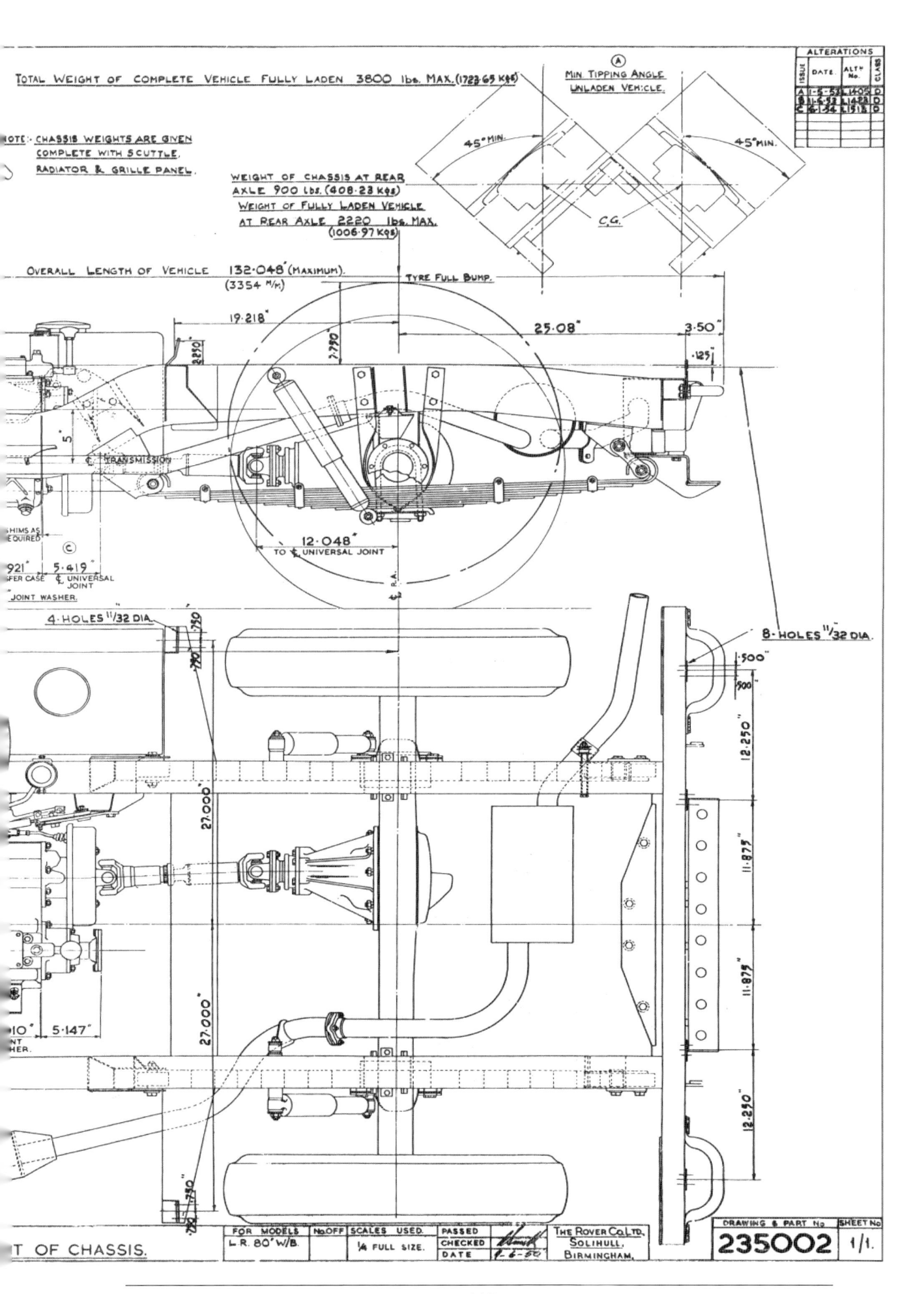

LAND-ROVER – The Formative Years, 1947–1967

Latest model rear view

November also saw the introduction of a repair kit for the wire side screen hinge – similar to that introduced in production 18 months later – and a strengthening bracket for the exhaust system, which had already been introduced on production models.

At the beginning of January 1950 a fourth production pattern hood was introduced. This replaced the 'boot-laced' rear curtain that had only recently been introduced (June 1949). Although more draught-proof than the earlier pattern, lacing it up was a laborious business, and had all the joys of a Victorian corset. The new pattern still retained the twin rear windows, but now had an envelope on either side into which tucked large side tongues on the rear curtain. Hood sticks also became arched to prevent debris and puddles settling on top and rotting the canvas. The new hood became the replacement pattern for all previous hoods and the design is still used today. The original '3-seater' hood was discontinued as stocks ran down.

April 1950 saw a third change to seat backs, the current 'spade back' being replaced by a less crude hinged set-up – affectionately termed 'shovel

Latest model with 7-inch 'Cat's Eye' headlights

148

CHAPTER 12 – A Closer Look – Into the 1950s

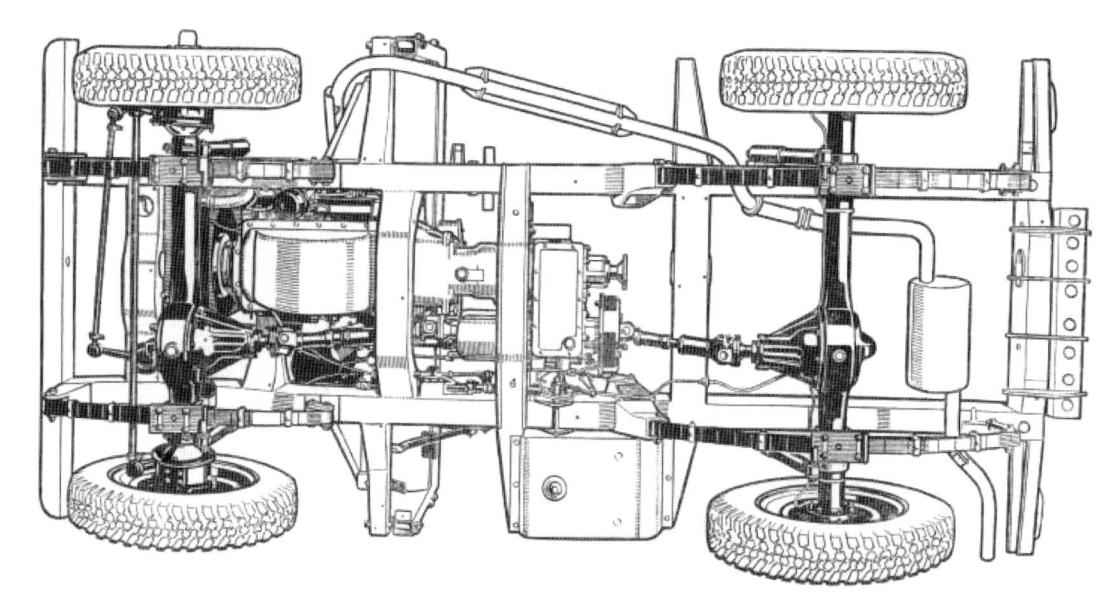

June 1950, front road spring shackles are repositioned to the rear end of the spring. Spring width is also increased from 1¾ inches to 2½ inches

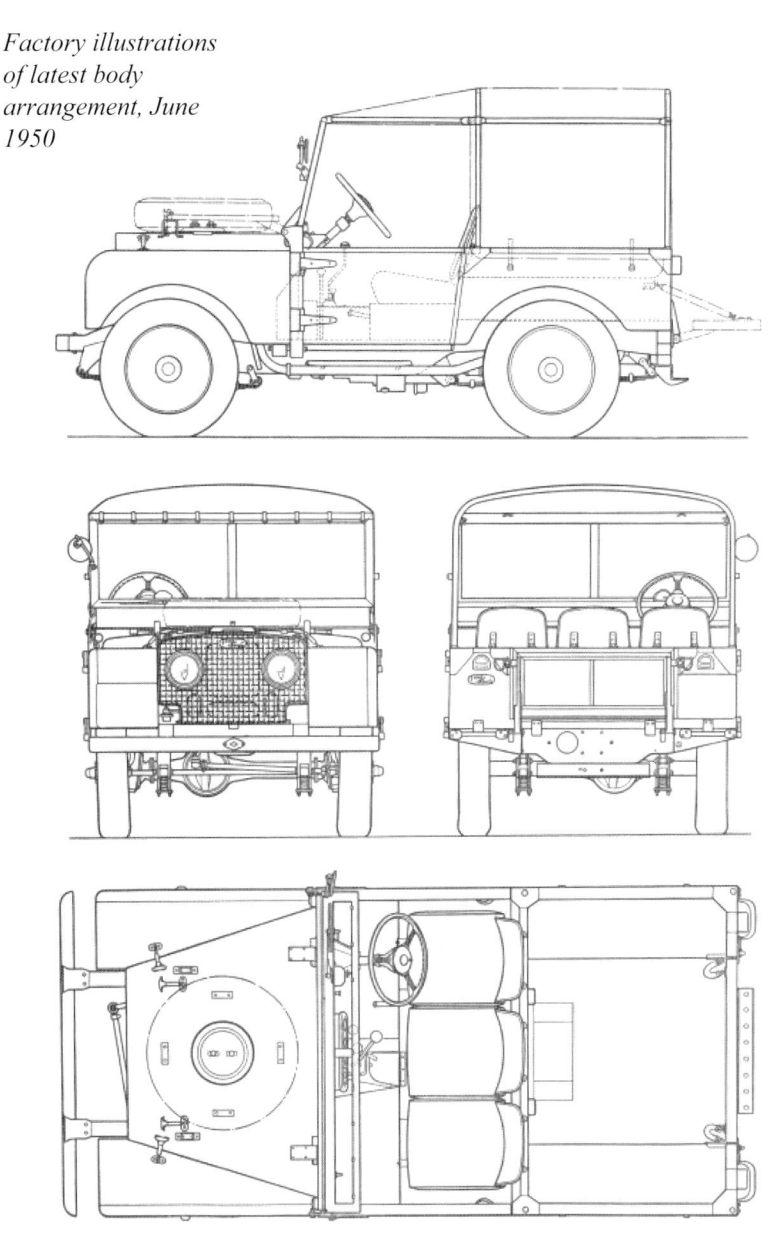

Factory illustrations of latest body arrangement, June 1950

back'. This could flip forward to give a clear surface above the transom panel either for shipping the vehicle, long loads, or simply to keep the seat bases clean and dry when the hood was removed.

May 1950 saw what was perhaps the most visually significant modification to the Land-Rover to date. The endearing round 5-inch tractor-type headlights located behind the front grille were replaced by standard round 7-inch car headlights, now referred to by enthusiasts as 'Cat's Eyes'. These were no longer behind the front grille, but peered out through two round apertures in the grille. They certainly drew a line under the Land-Rover's embryonic period as simply an agricultural machine.

The tractor type headlights had both dipped centrally, but on all UK 'Home' models, this latest arrangement had only a single filament bulb in the right side, with a double filament 'dip-left' to the left, the right headlight being extinguished altogether on dip. 'Export' models were given twin-dipping headlights to either left or right.

In an attempt to reduce serious problems of wheel wobble, an interim modification to the early pattern steering relay (which today survives only in just one known production Land-Rover in the UK, R860488, and a handful of pre-production models, L03 and L11, L14, L48) took place around September 1948, when an inch-long packer was added to further compress the spring. The early relay was superseded by an entirely new pattern relay after vehicle R861900, in January 1949. This was to be fitted 'free of charge' to all existing Land-Rovers. The new relay had no bearings, and instead of a single segmented split taper-cone, had two sets of 'Tufnol' plain split taper-cones to provide damping, and is easily identified by its four set screws holding the top and bottom covers.

The problem of wheel wobble still persisted, and in May 1950, the Land-Rover's top swivel pin bearings were replaced by phosphor bronze cones and spring-loaded seats, to help alleviate the problem, the plain top pin being replaced by a coarse spline locating inside the cone. But the problem was more deep-seated than that.

In June 1950 a highly significant modification was made to the front suspension. So far, Land-Rover front road springs had been shackled at the forward end – exactly the same on a Jeep. Neither Rover's pre-war P2 cars, or the latest P3 and P4, which had IFS and coil springs, were fitted out that

Crop Sprayer, May 1950

Brochure showing the new chassis design

CHAPTER 12 – A Closer Look – Into the 1950s

Engine compartment, July 1950

way, but the design was seen as a contributing factor to the Jeep's outstanding off-road performance. It certainly worked for the Jeep. However, the Jeep used a simple pivot arm on needle rollers as a steering relay, centrally mounted on the front axle tube, and from there two individual track rods fed directly to each wheel.

Unlike the Jeep, the Land-Rover's steering relay was not mounted centrally on the axle, but high up within the chassis frame, and also offset to left or right. From there a drag link connected it diagonally across to just one wheel – on the opposite side. A track rod then relayed steering movement from that wheel back across to the wheel closest to the relay. The Land-Rover's steering levers all lay forward of the axle, towards the shackled end of the road springs. But that's where most suspension movement takes place, and given the right conditions, the arrangement contributed to wheel wobble.

Taking an extreme example – as might be the case on unmade roads with potholes – the loading experienced by each road spring can rapidly alternate between forcing the axle tube up against the bump stop and dropping away on full extension. Under these circumstances, a rotational movement is induced about the 'fixed' rear eyes of both front road springs, causing the forward-mounted steering levers to rotate in opposite directions about the fixed rear spring-eyes.

Because the Land-Rover's steering relay cannot move with the axle, as happens on a Jeep, on extremes of suspension movement, the effective length of the connecting drag link to the front wheel may be momentarily and violently reduced by as much as half an inch. The resulting oscillations generated will then be transmitted back to the steering relay, then along the longitudinal steering tube to the steering box, and finally, back up, via the steering wheel, into the driver's hands.

Post Office van with factory hardtop

Experimental long-wheel base August 1950

CHAPTER 12 – A Closer Look – Into the 1950s

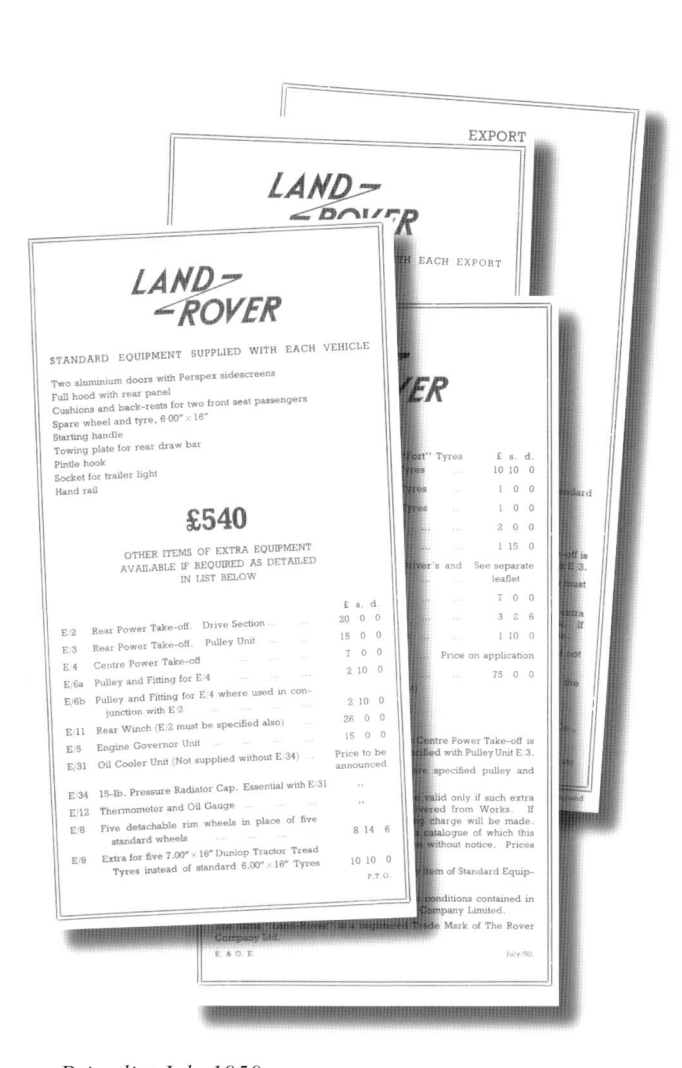

Price list July 1950

Henlys' advertisement – Rover's main agent in London

Simply reversing the front road spring's 'fixed' point to the front end of the front road spring, rather than the rear end, would effectively cure most of the problem. By doing this, the length of the Land-Rover's steering levers' arc of rotation was immediately reduced from approximately 30 in. (76 cm) to just 10 in. (25 cm), by exactly 1/3rd. Taking the example of a 3 in. (7,5 cm) total movement in suspension at the shackled ends, with spring shackles at the rear of the front springs, the steering levers rotational movement is cut from a previous possible $2^{1}/_{2}$ in. (6,3 cm) to just 1/2 in. (1,25 cm) – a reduction of 80%.

Although reversing road spring shackles to the rear of the front springs brought about a major improvement in the early Land-Rover's steering geometry, there is no evidence of acknowledgement to this in any of Rover's internal Service Bulletins or Newsletters.

At the same time, front spring width increased from $1^{3}/_{4}$ in. (45,5 mm) to $2^{1}/_{2}$ in. (63,5 mm) and, together with new shock absorbers to improve damping, and wider bump stops, stability was still further improved. The changes made to the front suspension also enabled it to support the weight of a new optional front-mounted winch, to be introduced in August 1950. The earlier rear-mounted winch could then be discontinued as the casting often sheered due to overload. Around 22,000 Land-Rovers were fitted with the original narrow front road springs and forward mounted shackles.

CHAPTER 13
Soft Seating for Hard Going
The Early Station Wagons

During the 1930s North America saw a steady increase in numbers of a new style of motor vehicle known as the station wagon. These vehicles used the rolling chassis and front end of a conventional sedan, coupled to a timber-framed utility body with uprated suspension. The 'boot' or 'trunk' was not yet part of motor car design, so station wagon bodywork enabled a car to be used for either passenger- or load-carrying on the same lines as a modern estate car. In the USA, only 4,551 station wagons were produced in 1935, but by 1941 this figure had risen to 30,000, and by 1948 had passed the 100,000 barrier, with Ford accounting for the bulk of these.

Immediately after the war in 1946 Willys-Overland jumped on the bandwagon, producing a station wagon based on their old 104-inch chassis from their unsuccessful 1941 'Americar'. Capitalising on their success with the Jeep, they called it the 'Jeep "4-63" Station Wagon'. The front end certainly resembled their new CJ-2A civilian Jeep, but apart from the side valve engine, that was about it.

Having based it on a two-wheel-drive car chassis and given it a rather unconventional transverse-leaf 'Planadyne' independent front suspension, to claim that it was a Jeep seems rather pretentious, though perhaps not as false as their earlier claim to have *'...created and perfected the jubilant Jeep'* in the first place. The only thing that made Willys' station wagon different from any other 'woody' of the period was its all-steel body. Even the wood strakes were fake – simply steel pressings painted golden brown. This trend towards less expensive metal body pressings would continue into the 1950s, although a few British estate cars, such as the Morris Minor Traveller and the 'Mini' estate, remained 'woody' into the 1970s.

With only two-wheel-drive, the Jeep Station Wagon proved a great disappointment to many potential customers. Even so, in the short 1946 season Willys managed to sell 6,533 Station Wagons, and by 1947 production had climbed to 33,214 – a record for Station Wagons. That same year Willys introduced a new 4x4 truck on the same 104-inch wheelbase. This paved the way for

The original factory photograph outside Olton Station, Solihull

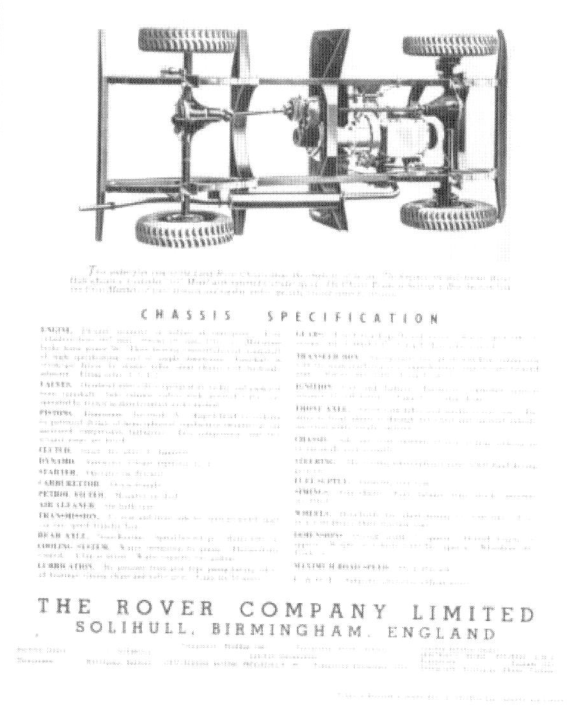

CHAPTER 13 – Soft Seating for Hard Going – The Early Station Wagons

The early Station Wagon brochure. Olton Station in background

The early Station Wagon brochure depicting pre-production model L20.

Willys to introduce 4x4 as an option two years later for the Jeep Station Wagon, in 1949. But by that time another 4x4 Station Wagon had already been launched.

The continued demise of the coachbuilt motor car after the war meant Britain's coachbuilders were only too pleased to reproduce this new-style bodywork. Even firms best known for their fast quality cars, such as AC and Alvis, jumped on the bandwagon. Rover too also saw a golden opportunity in this new expanding market, but they were not about to make the same mistake as Willys. Instead of using a car chassis, it would be entirely based on their Land-Rover, making it a genuine off-road vehicle. So on 6 June 1948, pre-production Land-Rover L20 – minus its rear body tub, windscreen and doors – was 'despatched out' to the coachbuilder 'Tickford' at Newport Pagnell, where it was given prototype Land-Rover 'Station Wagon' bodywork. Factory records show that this prototype Station Wagon went to Franco-Britanic Autos in Paris on 4 October 1948, in time for the

LAND-ROVER – The Formative Years, 1947–1967

L20 outside Tickford's offices, Newport Pagnell

Paris Motor Show (7th–17th October). Photographs of L20 taken at Tickford's premises, just after its bodywork was completed (rear lights are not yet fitted), show it clearly LHD.

Rover also wanted their new Land-Rover Station Wagon to be at the Earls Court London Show at the same time, so a second Tickford-bodied Land-Rover was built on production chassis R860071. This Land-Rover Station Wagon appeared on the Rover Co. stand alongside a Tickford prototype Rover P3 'Rover 75' drophead coupé, and featured in 'The Autocar', 22 October 1948.[1] This Station Wagon does not have the bodywork straking picked out in a 'two-tone' style as used previously for L20. Although severely accident damaged, it still survives, and is owned by Land-Rover enthusiast John Beeken, who one day hopes to restore it.

The hand of fate was not so kind to L20. After the Paris Show and Brussels, it returned home and was converted to RHD. It then went to Chas. Gibbons, Rover's dealer in Glasgow. When the road tax ran out on 31 December 1948, it was not renewed for another decade, until Christmas Eve, 1960. Was it used by Glasgow's Parks Department or on some great estate for shooting parties?

Having returned to Chas. Gibbons in 1960, it was sold for £30, but by this time the bodywork was in poor shape and doors repeatedly burst open, so the odds of passing the newly introduced MOT were remote. The new owner, Hew Alexander Sharpe, then ran it for little more than a year before taking it to Charlie Waters scrapyard in Elderslie, Renfrewshire. Apart from the factory despatch book record on L20, the only other things to survive are the original buff log book, and the original registration entry and index card issued after L20 was no longer road taxed for three years, both of which are held in Warwickshire records office.

L 20 The inside view

[1] Pictured in 'The Autocar' 5th November 1948

156

CHAPTER 13 – Soft Seating for Hard Going – The Early Station Wagons

L20 outside Tickford's offices, Newport Pagnell 3/4 rear view

Technically, the Land-Rover Station Wagon became available in December 1948, around the time production of the basic model increased from 50 to the planned 200 vehicles a week. The first batch of 70 production Station Wagons was actually completed between May and September 1949. They were given their own separate chassis sequence, which ran from 8670001 to 8670070 (basic Land-Rovers used 866... at this time). All were export models, and over 80% went directly to Rover's overseas dealers. Three, however, managed to find their way to Rover UK agents:

R8670034 to Tilleys of Brighton;

R8670038 to Sturgess of Leicester;

R8670043 to Clarke & Lambert of Eastbourne.

Surprisingly, two of these three, R8670034, and R8670038, from this first batch of 70 still survive today, the earliest being this author's Station Wagon, EPN 262, which had the strakes picked out on the coachwork as per the prototype R20. Dunsfold Land-Rovers owned R8670038 for many years before parting with it to enthusiast Andrew Ings. Keep your eyes open though, as R8670043 may still be lurking out there somewhere. A handful appear to have been shipped abroad indirectly, some being LHD vehicles going to Shell and the F.V.D.E. – both had their own shipping facilities. No further Station Wagons from this batch of 70 have ever been found, either in the UK or overseas.

In their preview published on 12 October 1948, 'The Autocar' described Rover's exciting new vehicle as *'...nearer the car of the future for the countryman that is anything which had yet been produced'*, a remark closer to the truth than anyone probably realised at the time. Not only was it a well-finished vehicle that any landowner would be proud to have on his estate, but the forerunner of the fully enclosed type of 4x4 or SUV, so popular today.

Using an expensive coachbuilt bodywork put this forward-looking vehicle not only ahead, but in some respects, a little behind the times. (See below.) The price tag of £959/1/8, included £209/1/8 Purchase Tax, compared to only £450 for a basic model (Ford's 'Anglia' listed at less than £250). This put it in the luxury class with Rover's own P3 '60' car, which used the same four-cylinder engine, and at £1080/9/6, cost only slightly more. The more powerful 'Rover 75' cost £1106/0/7. Even a 1.5-litre Jaguar cost less – £952/13/11, inclusive of Purchase Tax. Despite being first in the field with such a vehicle, there simply wasn't the sort of luxury leisure market there is today for

157

LAND-ROVER – The Formative Years, 1947–1967

First Land-Rover Station Wagon to go to a UK dealer, in Tilley's showroom at Brighton before going off to Captain Arthur Soames at Sheffield Park, Sussex – now owned by the author

such an upmarket cross-country car in post-war recovery Britain, or anywhere else for that matter.

As a 'shooting brake' the Station Wagon should have been exempt from Purchase Tax in 1948. Whitehall's civil servants, however, somehow managed to persuade Rover that the vehicle was for 'private and domestic', rather than commercial use, and Rover agreed to collect the tax. Eventually however, this was challenged, and for a short time the Station Wagon enjoyed the same legal loophole as other 'woody' estates of the period. But classed as a commercial vehicle, its speed was restricted to 30 mph on the open road – at least for the time being.

The new Land-Rover Station Wagon provided ample seating for seven people in relative comfort. Entrance to the rear passenger compartment was by way of the front passenger door and a special tipping front seat. However, when not in use as a personnel carrier, the rear seat squabs could be conveniently tilted up, or removed altogether, to give a large luggage area, accessed by means of a full-width tail board and upper rear flap, the same as used 20 years later for the Range Rover.

The prototype vehicle produced by Tickford differed from production models by having a divided windscreen and rear window. The front end, along with the bulkhead and all the running gear, were basic Land-Rover, and coloured light green. The rest of the body was light grey, with only the rubbing strakes picked out in light green, which gave the vehicle a very attractive appearance. The timber framework was not made of Ash – the usual choice of coachbuilders, because of its ability to be steam-bent, but a more durable tropical hardwood. Instead, Iroko (Chlorophora Exelsa) was used, as this is less likely to rot in humid tropical climates.

Iroko comes from the west coast of Africa and the Congo basin, and new timber has a yellow-brown appearance that darkens with age. It's often used as a teak substitute, as it has similar properties – fairly hard, strong and durable, with an open grain, and possessing natural oils that require no further preservative for outside use. The biggest difference is cost – about half that of teak. Iroko is commonly used for yacht decking, garden furniture, and science benches.

The body panels themselves used the same non-corrosive light alloy as other Land-Rovers. The colour scheme used for the prototype Station Wagon was also used for early production models, such as the author's example, R8670034. But other colour schemes were also used – light green with bodywork above the waistline light grey; light green all over. After introduction of dark green bodywork basic Land-Rovers in mid-1949, other variations crept in such as light green roof and dark green body; light green above the waistline and dark green below the waist line, and dark green all over.

As well as the one-piece windscreen and full-width rear window (35 years ahead of any basic production model), production Station Wagons also had locker boxes for tool storage at the back end.

CHAPTER 13 – Soft Seating for Hard Going – The Early Station Wagons

Ideal transport for country squires

Other standard fitments included: locking car type one-piece doors with exterior handles; wind-up windows; sliding rear windows; roof lining; door and interior panels; interior light, and rubber floor mats. Front seats were similar to those of a car, and a traditional pillar pull-strap provided assistance when entering the rear compartment from the front passenger door. Rear seat bases, like those in the front, utilised the basic Land-Rover's squab, but backs were a single padded structure at each side with a pocket between them and the front seat to hold the driver's handbook. The spare wheel was no longer an encumbrance to the floor area, but carried under a special spun light alloy cover on the bonnet. In the cab, a push-pull switch operated twin wipers, and the steering wheel remained a two-spoke P3 type, as used for very early Land-Rovers.

All 'Export' Station Wagons had a second 24-watt filament in both side and tail lamps, used as flashing indicators. These were operated by a self-cancelling switch on the steering column. 'Home' models were only produced during the 1950 season, and these had semaphore indicators mounted in their wings as standard equipment. All models carried a central hinged rear number plate bracket incorporating a single chromed 'D' stop light, which enabled the number plate to still be seen when the tail board was lowered.

The Land-Rover Station Wagon was six inches longer, and six inches wider, than the basic model. But such space and luxury came at a price, not just in cash, but also in weight. At just over 27-cwt (3,036 lbs.), it was 4-cwt heavier than a basic model. With a full complement of seven adults the gross payload was likely to exceed 36-cwt (3–4-cwt more than the maximum recommended payload of a basic model). The massively heavy tail board overhanging the rear chassis by several inches, together with the hefty timber framework of the surrounding body, meant that most of this additional weight was concentrated at the rear end of the Station Wagon. However, only standard springs were initially fitted. Not until the following season's 1950 models did the Station Wagon get the same heavy-duty rear suspension used for the 'Welder' and 'Compressor' Land-Rover models.

Although only 70 Land-Rover Station Wagons – all 'Export' models – were made during the first season 1948–49; the following season saw a substantial increase to 480 models, but this still only represented 3% of current factory output. Most went abroad, UNICEF taking over 100 in a single batch. In August 1950 the legal loophole avoiding Purchase Tax on all shooting brake cars was closed, which explains why the final batch were all 'Export' models. If this hadn't killed off sales, a final death knell would have followed when, in the first budget after the outbreak of the Korean War, the Chancellor of the Exchequer announced that from April 1951, double Purchase Tax would apply to all luxury goods. This would certainly have killed off any remaining demand in the home market. With the world economic climate as it was, the final batch of Station Wagons consisted of just 100 vehicles, 80 LHD and 20 RHD, all 'Export' models on chassis manufactured prior to October 1950.

Although Tickford were responsible for the 650 Station Wagon Land-Rovers produced, Abbey Panels of Coventry had previously produced much of Rover's prototype bodywork and special bodied vehicles, and later the 'Marauder' sports cars, based on the P4 'Rover 75'. But at this time Tickford were also involved in the construction of three prototype P3 'Rover 75' drophead coupés in

1948/49 and two P4 'Rover 75' drophead coupés and a fixed head coupé in 1950/51. Tickford also sold Rover cars from their London showroom in Upper St Martin's Lane, WC2 at that time. In 1955 the Salmons/Tickford concern at Newport Pagnell was taken over by the David Brown Organisation, and became home to the famous DB Aston Martin and Lagonda cars.

With the demise of the Station Wagon, Rover offered a combination of accessories for the basic Land-Rover as a replacement for the Station Wagon. This set of accessories consisted of an ivory-coloured hard top in the same light alloy as the rest of the bodywork, with glazed rear lid, plain glass windows and bench seats for the rear, all for an additional £50 above the basic price of a standard model. This package, was aimed solely at the export market and made a very workmanlike alternative to the Tickford Station Wagon, and served as a platform for all future Land-Rover Station Wagons. For those who could afford the luxury, however, 'Mulliner' of Birmingham could provide a traditional 'woody' estate on the Land-Rover chassis during this interim period before the introduction of the new 86-inch Station Wagon in 1954. One of these appeared in the BBC TV series 'Hadleigh' in the mid-1970s. This has since gone to the USA.

A number of prototype extended chassis Land-Rovers used the cab design from the Station Wagon and included: a pick-up truck; a prototype 6/7-seat heavy utility staff car, with reversible rear seat and map table; a hard-top van; and a most interesting, attractive four-door Station Wagon based on the original Tickford model, which Maurice Wilks took to Anglesey.

With the demise of the 80-inch Land-Rover Station Wagon, Maurice Wilks turned his attention to yet another 'shooting brake' or estate car, the 'Road Rover'. Aware of the increasing number of motor manufacturers producing estate cars and Hackney carriages,[2] he was keen for Rover to participate in this growing sector of the market. However, firms such as Rootes, who had long-term success with this type of vehicle, had based their design not on an expensive coachbuilt 'woody', but on their inexpensive Commer 'Super Van', normally priced at £350. Suitably modified with windows and rear seats, and marketed as the Hillman Minx estate, it cost only £595 when it was first introduced in 1949.

Rootes' idea of modifying a cheap van had already put Rover's Station Wagon Land-Rover at a serious financial disadvantage, and as Rover had no other utility vehicle on which to base an ordinary estate car, this was to prove a major disadvantage

[2] *7,847 New Hackney carriages were registered in 1947, and another 10,000 in 1948.*

Lodge advertisement depicting the Station Wagon

in the Road Rover's development. All Rover could do was incorporate much of the P4 'Rover 75' saloon car's running gear, along with a number of Land-Rover parts – including its four-cylinder engine – beneath a simple slab-sided body. But it just didn't work.

The first of these vehicles was finished in early 1952 and looked exactly what it was, a crude scratch-build utility vehicle. It was immediately nicknamed 'the greenhouse'. Anybody who knew anything about Rover only had to take one look to realise that in its present form it stood no chance of going into production. Nevertheless, MCW persisted with the idea, and eventually a dozen were completed before a major update of the model in the mid-1950s.[3]

[3] *It has often been suggested that the Road Rover was in some way a forerunner of the Range Rover, possibly as a consequence of one prototype Range Rover being badged 'Road Rover', but this author believes that is the sum total of any such connection. Gordon Bashford has already pointed out elsewhere, that with conventional rear-wheel-drive, there was no way the Road Rover could ever be considered a cross-country car. It was simply an austere station wagon, and as the name Road Rover implies, not an off-road vehicle. All future off-road station wagons at this time would unquestionably be based on Land-Rover running gear, and not as in the case of the Road Rover, on Rover's P4 saloon car. To have any genuine historical connection with the Range Rover, the Road Rover, would have had to have been an off-road vehicle, which it clearly was not.*

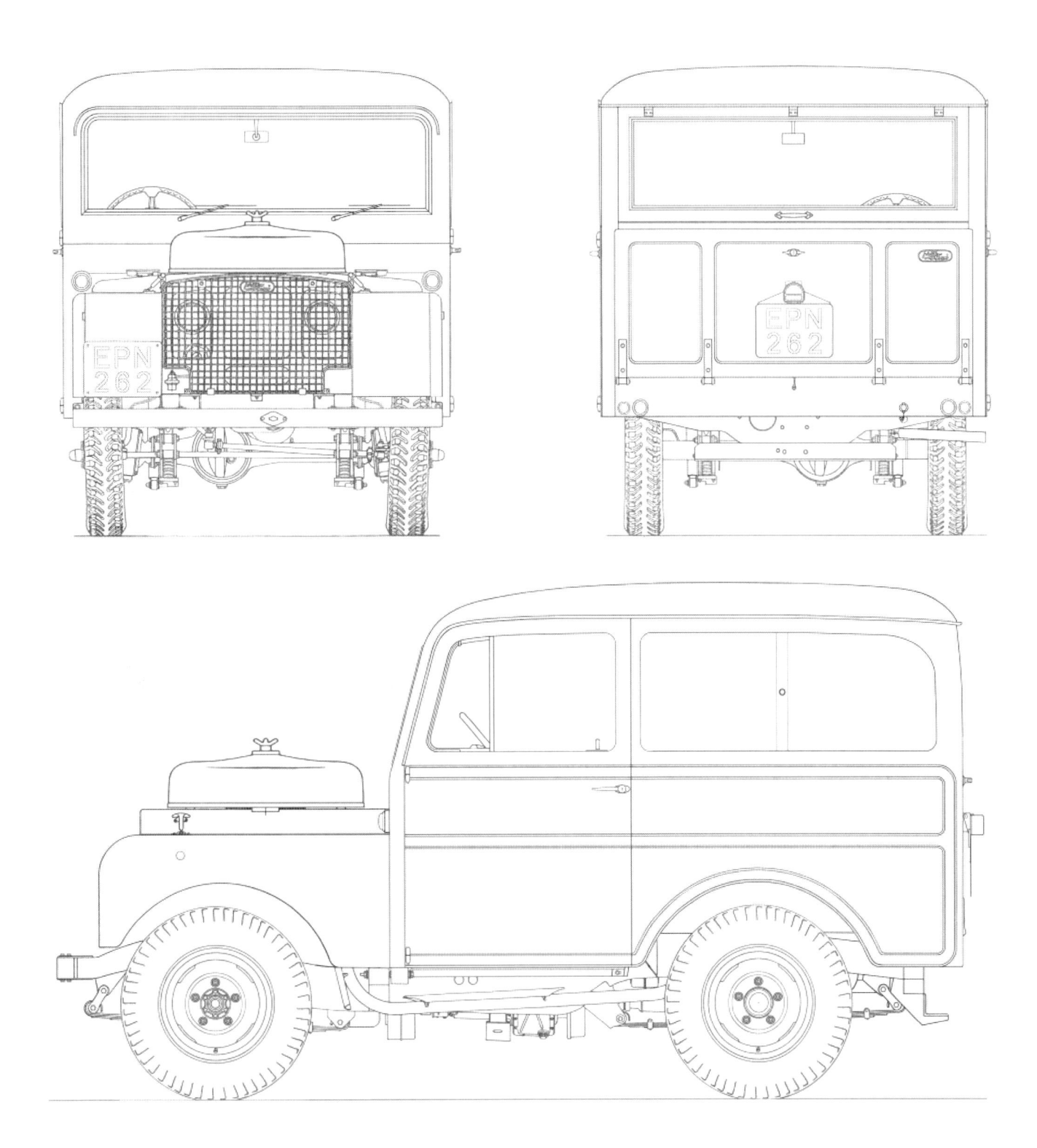

CHAPTER 13 – Soft Seating for Hard Going – The Early Station Wagons

Line drawing of the first production model
© John S Smith, 2008

The Range Rover, on the other hand, was a definite extension of the Land-Rover concept at a time when austerity was a thing of the past. Overseas competition in off-road vehicles, particularly from America and Japan, was tending towards comfort and leisure, and if Rover were to enjoy a share of this rapidly expanding market, then a totally new off-road vehicle was required. The original concept for such a fully enclosed comfortable cross-country vehicle will always remain the 80-inch Tickford-bodied Land-Rover Station Wagon, born 20 years ahead of its time, and not the later Series II Road Rover utility which was simply a two-wheel-drive affair.

CHAPTER 14
The 1951 Season
4x4 goes 4x2

The Land-Rover was now three years old. By this time Rover had already realised that not only was it here for the foreseeable future, but that most Land-Rovers would probably do many more miles on tarmac roads than they would across fields. Practically every major component had already undergone some form of modification in a conscious effort to adapt to this changing situation.

But from now on the actual pace of change would begin to slow, though its magnitude would equal anything that had taken place so far, and no one could accuse Rover of dragging their feet.

In August 1950, to coincide with the 1951 season of vehicles, a new numbering system was introduced, beginning 16100001. The prefix 'R' had already been omitted on home models since the previous February, but now there was no 'L' either. Instead, an extra digit had been placed in front of the serial number: '0' – home model; '3' – LHD 'Export'; '6' - RHD 'Export'. The third digit continued to indicate either 'Basic' model, 'Station Wagon', 'Welder', or CKD – completely knocked down (i.e. kit form), by the numbers '1', '2', '3', and '6' respectively. For example:-

16134999. 1 = 1951 Model; 6 = Land-Rover; 1 = Basic; 3 = LHD Export and 4999 = Serial Number.

The most significant change here was the complete loss of a consecutive numbering sequence for both vehicles and parts. Each of 11 model variants all had their own serial number beginning 0001. Engine, gearbox, and front axle also all had individual numbering to denote left- or right-hand model. This left only the rear axle to continue a consecutive sequence through all model types.

Early in the season gearbox and transfer box oil levels were lowered by a pint and a half as a 'cure-all' for clutch slip. Then in September 1950, ignition timing was retarded from 15 degrees to 10 degrees BTDC to cure 'pinking' (though early flywheels originally intended for the P3 'Rover 60' car had no 15 degree mark). Six months later in March 1951, the distributor contact breaker gap was opened up from 0.012 in. to 0.014–0.016 in.

The first major change came at the beginning of October 1950, when Rover dropped the 'Freewheel' device and introduced selectable 4x2. Unlike the wartime Jeep's transmission, which was a part-time affair, so far every production Land-Rover had been equipped with a full-time

CHAPTER 14 – The 1951 Season – 4x4 goes 4x2

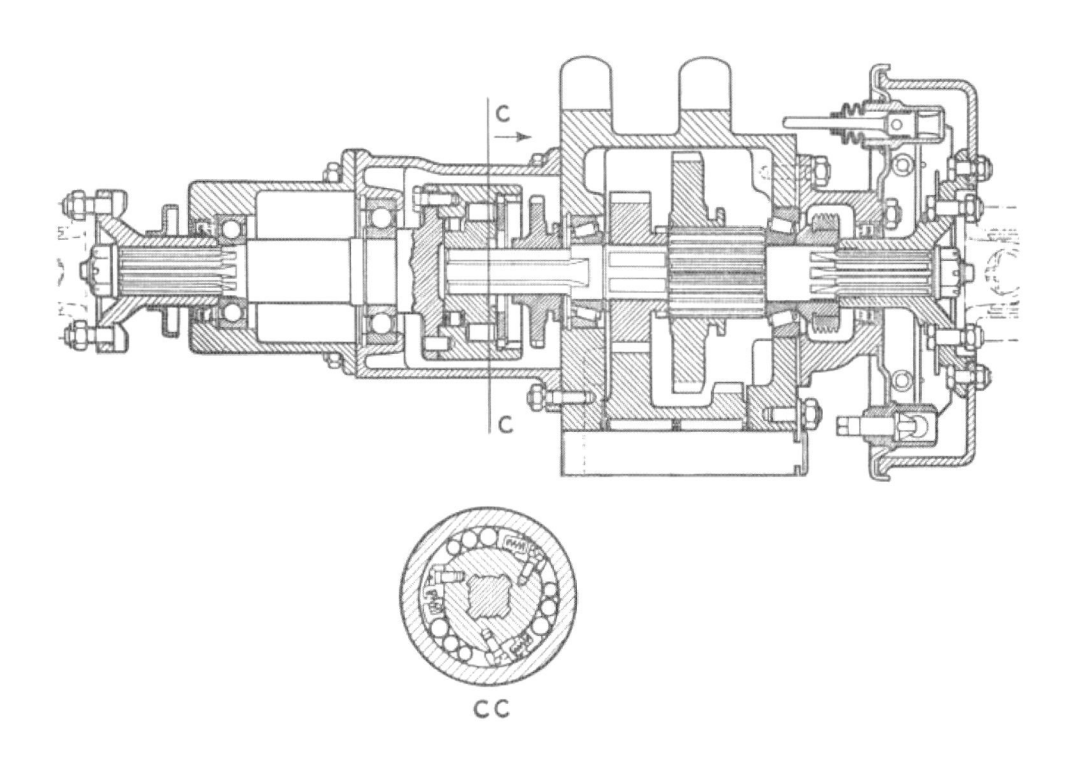

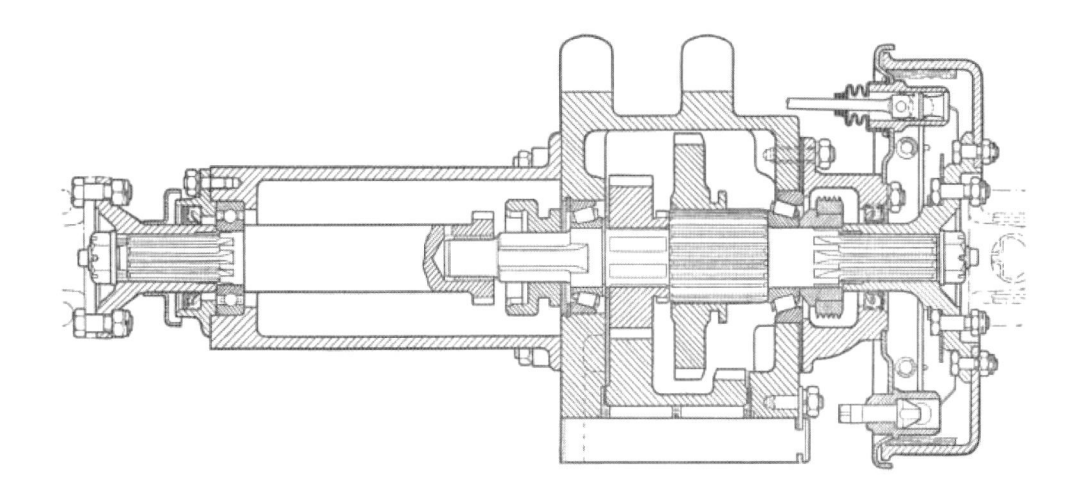

The previous 'Freewheel' device (top) is replaced by a simple selectable 4x2 front output housing (lower)

New handbook TP/131/A, October 1950 introduces selectable 4x2. Prior to this all production Land-Rovers had a full-time 4x4 transmission system.

4x4 transmission system. Two important pieces of engineering made this possible. First was the front axle's 'Tracta' drive joints. Unlike the Hardy-Spicer universal joints used on all Land-Rovers from late 1953 until the mid-1980s, the Tracta was a true constant velocity (CV) drive-joint, and had seen service in numerous military trucks in the war, including the Willys MB Jeep (but not Ford GPW Jeeps). Having a true CV drive-joint meant wheel wobble would not be generated by variable speeds in the drive shafts when cornering, as is the case with a Hardy-Spicer universal joint.

The second masterful piece of engineering was Rover's own 'Freewheel' device which had been incorporated into the Land-Rover's front output housing. The 'Freewheel' allowed the Land-Rover's front wheels to travel faster when cornering, enabling the wheel closest to the outer radius of a bend to travel slightly further in a given time period. The 'Freewheel' acted in much the same way as the central differential fitted to current Defender models, by allowing slip to occur between the front and rear drive. Without it, stresses, referred to as 'wind-up', would build up within the transmission system. These normally work their way out as tyre slip, which rapidly reduces tread life on hard surfaces such as concrete and tarmac roads.

The new model undressed, January 1951

Prototype 2.0-litre Land-Rover 07100003 on Anglesey

With the Land-Rover's increasing on-road use, the importance of a permanent 4x4 transmission diminished. The earliest 1948 pre-production Land-Rovers – possibly up to R16 – had selectable 4x2, but this was the first time it had been incorporated on a production Land-Rover. With very few Land-Rovers being asked to do the fieldwork of a tractor, the use of a less expensive transmission system also made a certain amount of economic sense.

Selecting high/low-ratio gears by means of a red-knobbed lever remained as before, but 4x4 was now automatically engaged in low ratio to prevent undue stress on the transmission. High-ratio gears, however, were now 4x2, with 4x4 selection dependent on depressing the same yellow-knobbed lever that had previously replaced the ring-pull in late 1949 for locking-up the 'Freewheel' device in the front output housing. To deselect 4x4 in high ratio, it was necessary to stop the vehicle, engage low ratio, and then immediately return to high ratio, in order to release the spring pre-load on the selector shaft, causing it to disengage 4x4. It was a ridiculous procedure that, with the exception of the 'Stage One' V8, lasted for some 35 years to the end of 'Series' production. Approximately the first 28,000 Land-Rovers had the 'Freewheel' device and permanent 4x4.

The opportunity to use an alternative simpler arrangement had been completely missed. With minimal modification, a single short standard gear lever could have been mounted on a bracket just forward of the front output housing, and used with a 'U' gate. Using the same selector shafts, it would be possible to push this single lever forward in the left groove to engage 'High 4x2' or backward to engage 'High 4x4'. From 'High 4x4', if the lever were pulled to the right, '4x4' would remain engaged, but if the lever was then moved forward, 'Low' ratio would also be engaged. In arduous conditions, such as deep mud or snow, if conditions improved, the Land-Rover could go from 'Low 4x4' into 'High 4x4', and then into 'High 4x2', without the need to stop. This would have removed the possibility of losing traction, especially when laden or towing. There would have been no need for any second yellow-knobbed lever. The fact that for 35 years this opportunity was missed almost beggars belief.

CHAPTER 14 – The 1951 Season – 4x4 goes 4x2

Later, towards the end of the season, still further changes took take place that reflected the Land-Rover's popularity for road use as a cross-country vehicle. Sidelights moved from the bulkhead (where they were less likely to be damaged by bush and scrub), down onto the front of the wings – the most vulnerable area of the vehicle. Mirrors could go from windscreen back onto wings (where they had originally been located on early pre-production models), now that they would no longer reflect the glare of a bulkhead sidelight at night. Wings themselves also became 'one-piece' before the end of the season, the outer panel being spot-welded, rather than bolted to the inner panel. In March 1951 the early 5½ in. cast Land-Rover nameplate was replaced by a larger $7^3/_{16}$ in. nameplate stamped from sheet alloy.

These changes should probably all have occurred on the following season's vehicles, but as Land-Rover output was up by more than 1,300 units they took place about a month before the end of the season.

The close of the 1951 season brought with it the end of 1.6-litre Land-Rover production, and makes a convenient point to take stock of Land-Rover output to date. By the end of July 1951, 17,362 of the current season's models had been made – the largest annual output of Land-Rovers to date. It took total production for the first three years to 41,410 units, and the Land-Rover's total currency earnings to some £5 million sterling. Of the current season's production, more than 12,000 vehicles – 75% of output – had been exported. LHD models accounted for 57% of the export figure, with less than 1% CKD (completely knocked down, ready for assembly overseas) – 78 vehicles in all. By contrast 40% of RHD 'Export' models were CKD – over 2,000 vehicles. Only Britain's traditional colonial markets, already familiar with Rover's cars, were assembling Land-Rover's locally, with Australia accounting for most of these. It was a measure mainly designed to overcome new import restrictions.

This 5½-inch cast badge was used until March 1951

The $7^3/_{16}$-inch stamped alloy badge

165

LAND-ROVER – The Formative Years, 1947–1967

2.0-litre model

Home market sales of the Basic model accounted for 24% of total output, with Rover's military contracts taking almost half of these. The remaining 1% of vehicles consisted of 20 Welders – 16 for export, with 9 of those RHD – and 100 Station Wagons, all to export specification, 80 of which were LHD. They were the last of the original Tickford-bodied model and, mechanically, all had been manufactured prior to the introduction of selectable 4x2 in October 1950.

By the turn of the decade Rover was already experimenting with over-bored P3 four-cylinder and six-cylinder engines, increasing capacity to 2.0-litres and 2.6-litres respectively. Fifty prototype 2.0-litre engines were put into Land-Rovers, the ZS1 bypass or oil filter initially being completely omitted. Some of these trial Land-Rovers were also equipped with selectable 4x2, ahead of any production model. The first of these, 07100001, was registered with Warwickshire authority as JUE 492 on 1 February 1950. The chassis for these vehicles were standard production units, and while early models have narrow front springs, later examples used the new wider springs. More than 50 prototype 2-litre engines were built, No. X 0710051 eventually going into R06, the 1948 pre-production factory Fire Tender, before it was eventually sold off.

The over-bored four-cylinder engine proved satisfactory for Land-Rover use and several of the prototypes were soon sold off. But because of its application, boring out the six-cylinder car engine was not a success, so its bores remained at 65,2 mm. Rover car engines could be expected to run for long periods at high revs. - something not generally expected of a Land-Rover – and during trials, resulted in serious scuffing due to insufficient space for coolant between the bores after they were increased in size. It was eventually decided the problem could only be overcome by

CHAPTER 14 – The 1951 Season – 4x4 goes 4x2

2.0-litre prototype engine has no oil filter, note the early square sump still in use

The gearboxes were also stamped up with an 071.... number

0710047, the author's 2.0-litre prototype awaiting restoration

Rare 'Mulliner'-bodied Station Wagon on 2.0-litre chassis owned by Scott Miller

167

August 1951, 2.0-litre brochure cover

repositioning the cylinders, and the idea of over-boring the existing P3 'six' had to be abandoned.[1]

Eighteen months later, in August 1951, Rover introduced the over-bored 2.0-litre engine into production models for 1952 season Land-Rovers.[2]

[1] *By 1953 two new 'spread-bore' blocks were in production for cars – a 4-cyl with a 77,8 mm bore (1,997cc 'Rover 60') and a 6-cyl with 73 mm bore (2,230cc short-stroke 'Rover 75' or 2.638cc long-stroke 'Rover 90').*
[2] *Because of the close proximity of bores 1 & 2 and 3 & 4, it is often referred to as the 'Siamese bore' 2-litre.*

Although bores had increased from $2^{3}/_{4}$ in. to 3 in., in all other respects the engine block, bottom end, connecting rods, gudgeon pins and bushes, and cylinder head, along with the ancillary equipment, remained pretty much as before. Exhaust valves were shortened by 1/5 in. and the carburettor choke tube, along with the jets, increased in size. The end result? An increase in torque from 80 lbs/ft at 2,000 rpm to 101 lbs/ft at only 1,500 rpm – a 26% increase, from a 25% increase in swept volume, but maximum bhp still remained around 50 at 4,000 rpm. The final product was a really 'lazy' engine, ideally suited to the type of task Land-Rovers were generally expected to perform.

CHAPTER 14 – The 1951 Season – 4x4 goes 4x2

The 'old' bodywork and grille of the last 1.6-litre models are still depicted

Brochure: The new engine

Other modifications for the 1952 season were minimal and were generally concerned with either improving vehicle performance, or again, cutting manufacturing costs. From a latter-day enthusiast's point of view, however, many of the modifications that took place after 1950 had already detracted from the original character of the early Land-Rover. Now exterior door handles, capable of ripping trouser pockets in an instant, appeared, and side screens lost their opening flap. The full-width grille was replaced by a simpler inverted 'T', which, with modification for Series II models, was used for the next 16 years, and wider bump stops appeared on the rear axle to match those on the front, introduced over a year ago for the wider road springs.

The original 'fin and tube' radiator blocks were replaced by a 'film block' pattern, and the crank case breather system ended after the 200th 'Home' model, as it was considered a contributory factor

169

to ice formation in the carburettor. (An earlier cure for this problem had been the addition of an extra section in the radiator panel.) Seat backs were cheapened, becoming quite square and flat soon after the 6,000th Land-Rover of the season. The one-piece wing, introduced at the end of the previous season, was also an economy measure and thought acceptable because of the Land-Rover's increased road use. It lasted just two years and was never used again. On the optional equipment front, a radio was made available.

Around this time, Rover became a little envious of the success John Black, brother-in-law of the Wilks brothers, was having at the Standard factory with Harry Ferguson's little grey tractor, when in 1952 Tom Barton was given the task of developing a tractor based around the Land-Rover. It had some advanced features for a tractor at that time, most noticeable being four large wheels instead of the usual two large rear and two small front wheels of the Ferguson. It had the Land-Rover's four-wheel-drive and transfer box, and a system whereby the tractor could be either raised or lowered on its axles by 10 inches in about half an hour, to give either greater crop clearance or increased stability. Two tractors are rumoured to have been made, but when one rolled over on test, the project was abandoned.

Despite the increase in output over the previous season, demand for Land-Rovers was still way ahead of supply, and prompted the company Chairman, E. Ransome Harrison, to make the following comment in the annual statement to shareholders in December 1951:

"The demand for our cars and Land-Rovers throughout the world still continues... [and] ...exceeds our capacity to satisfy it as we are limited by shortages of raw materials, particularly steel."

The new 2.0-litre model in production at this time formed the basis of all remaining 80-inch models, and the following season's Land-Rovers also remained virtually identical, with just a handful of minor changes introduced in the season. The closing years for the 80-inch model did not, however, pass without event. On 15 January 1952, the 50,000th Land-Rover emerged, Car No. 261003384, a 'Light Stone'-coloured military vehicle, registered as 11 B H 22.

Rover's four-wheel-drive 'Land-Rover' tractor undergoes field trials

CHAPTER 14 – The 1951 Season – 4x4 goes 4x2

Rear chrome swivel housing and steering levers are visible at the back, along with PTO pulley drum and the fuel tank

Track rods operate independently to each wheel, the same as on a Jeep

This view shows the front chrome swivel housing

171

The new 2.0-litre engine

By November the colour range was increased for all UK built 'Export' models, and now included 'Green', 'Beige' 'Blue' and 'Grey', and it appears the Land-Rover badge changed too, from green to black, to accommodate all the different colours. Certainly green chassis and wheels continued to be provided for green Land-Rovers. But what of the other body colours?

Practically all mechanical problems encountered along the way had now been resolved, but with Land-Rover sales continuing to exceed those of Rover's car by 2 to 1, thoughts had already turned to an entirely new range of Land-Rover models. They would, however, be strongly based on the major mechanical parts of the previous 'late 80' models. Between September 1951 and August 1953, nearly 42,000 2.0-litre Land-Rovers left the Solihull factory, taking total numbers of the 80-inch model to over 82,000 during the five-year period of its production.

When 80-inch Land-Rover production finally came to a close at the end of the 1953 season, the

Beaulieu Garage's 1953 Land-Rover being rescued from floods

A C Marvin and Son Ltd. of Beaulieu Garage, Beaulieu Village were destined to be the victims. Standing in the forecourt was their faithful 1953 short wheel based Land-Rover which normally has the noble task of towing veteran cars the firm is famous for restoring.

With our cameras laid out on another craft we followed the *Sea Truck* as it nosed itself away from the shore—when we passed the *Master Builders House* hotel Nelson must have turned in his grave to see this strange flotilla in the water, but I am also sure he looked on with interest.

CHAPTER 14 – The 1951 Season – 4x4 goes 4x2

BY APPOINTMENT TO
H.M. THE KING,
MANUFACTURERS OF
LAND ROVERS. THE
ROVER COMPANY
LIMITED

THE Rover Company Ltd., has pleasure in announcing that in future the Land-Rover will be powered by a two-litre engine constructed basically on the same efficient design and well-known principles which were incorporated in the 1·6-litre engine.

The more powerful 2-litre engine has been designed primarily to produce high torque at low R.P.M. That is, to give the Land-Rover increased "slogging" power at low engine speed, particularly for agricultural work and towing operations.

Other features of this new engine are, an increase on occasions in economy of fuel consumption due to useful working power now being obtained at low R.P.M., and, as a result of this latter characteristic, the necessity for gear changing is reduced when the Land-Rover is performing heavy duties.

COMPARATIVE SPECIFICATION

	1·6 litre	2 litre
No. of Cylinders	4	4
Bore	69·5 mm.	77·8 mm.
Stroke	105 mm.	105 mm.
Cubic capacity	1595 c.c.	1997 c.c.
H.P.	Develops 50 b.h.p. at 4,000 R.P.M.	Develops 58 b.h.p. at 4,000 R.P.M.
Torque	Max. torque 80 lb. ft. at 2,000 R.P.M.	Max. torque 101 lb. ft. at 1,500 R.P.M.
Compression ratio	6·8:1	6·7:1

Brochure: comparing the old 1.6-litre engine with the new 2.0-litre

The Land-Rover general utility vehicle is designed and built by the group of engineers, responsible for the production of "One of Britain's Fine Cars" and culminating in the introduction of the World's first Gas Turbine driven car.

The name Land-Rover is a registered trade mark of The Rover Company Limited.

Persons dealing in the Company's goods are not the agents of the Company and have no authority whatsoever to bind the Company by any expressed or implied undertaking.

THE ROVER COMPANY LIMITED
SOLIHULL :: BIRMINGHAM :: ENGLAND

Telephone: Sheldon 2461   Telegrams: Rover, Solihull

Service Depot: SOLIHULL. Telegrams: Rovrepair, Solihull. London Showrooms: DEVONSHIRE HOUSE, PICCADILLY, W.1. Telephone: Grosvenor 3252. London Service Depot: SEAGRAVE ROAD, FULHAM, S.W.6. Telephone: Fulham 1221 Telegrams: Rovrepair, Wesphone London.

Brochure back page with date

Printed in England   August 1951

Factory side elevation drawing, dated August 1951, depicting the new 2.0-litre Land-Rover

CHAPTER 14 – The 1951 Season – 4x4 goes 4x2

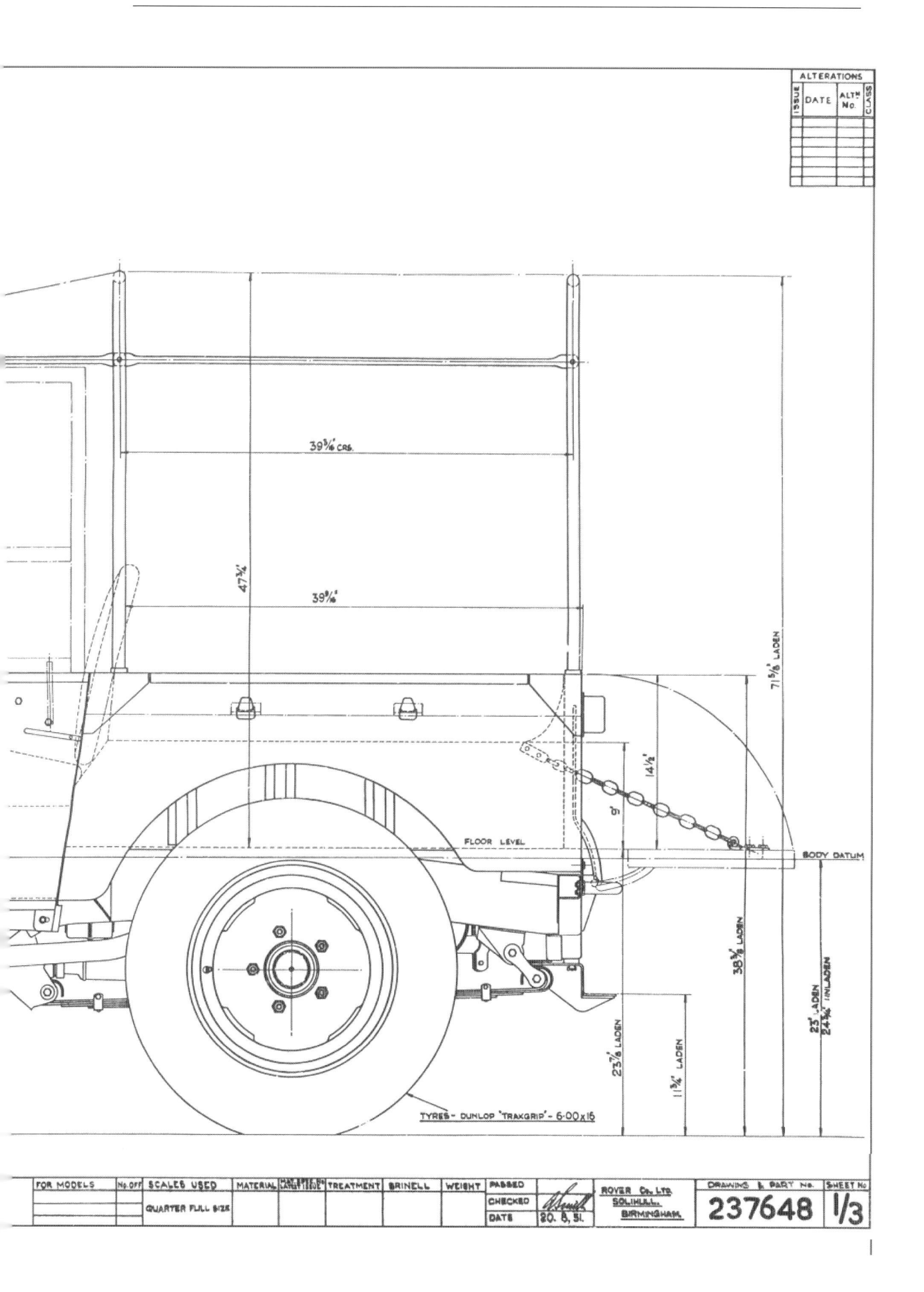

LAND-ROVER – The Formative Years, 1947–1967

Fully equipped for roadside assistance

proportion of Land-Rovers destined for the home market remained constant at 24%. RHD 'Export' models accounted for 30%, one third of which were now CKD. LHD 'Export' models remained at 46%, but more than half were CKD. They had increased from just 1% to 52% in the space of two years. It was the only really dramatic change in output figures. Some 8,800 LHD CKD models would be built in Belgium and wear the Minerva Land-Rover badge, and over 430 were also constructed in Mexico.

There was little change in the RHD market, either at home or abroad, but the proportion of RHD 'Export' models had fallen from 40% to 33%. Any actual growth in sales was confined to new export markets as the Land-Rover reputation continued to spread far and wide. Various countries outside the sterling area were now eager to have Land-Rovers assembled locally to overcome import restrictions and make savings on valuable foreign currency.

Wherever this took place the skills acquired provided a valuable back-up service for the Land-Rover, an essential ingredient in the long-term stability of the export market against foreign competition. Twenty years later in 1974, when the rest of Britain's motor industry was falling apart at the seams, Rover were still able to hold their own with the Land-Rover – the only vehicle in the vast Leyland network still able to show a profit. A major contributing factor to the loss of overseas markets by the rest of Britain's motor manufacturers, in the wake of fierce competition from the Far East, was, in part, their failure to provide any comparable service facility.

Front and rear views also dated August 1951

This plan view is a mystery; dated 10/11/48, it shows the very early 1948 rear grab handles, but an older drawing updated normally has acknowledgement in the top right corner

176

CHAPTER 14 – The 1951 Season – 4x4 goes 4x2

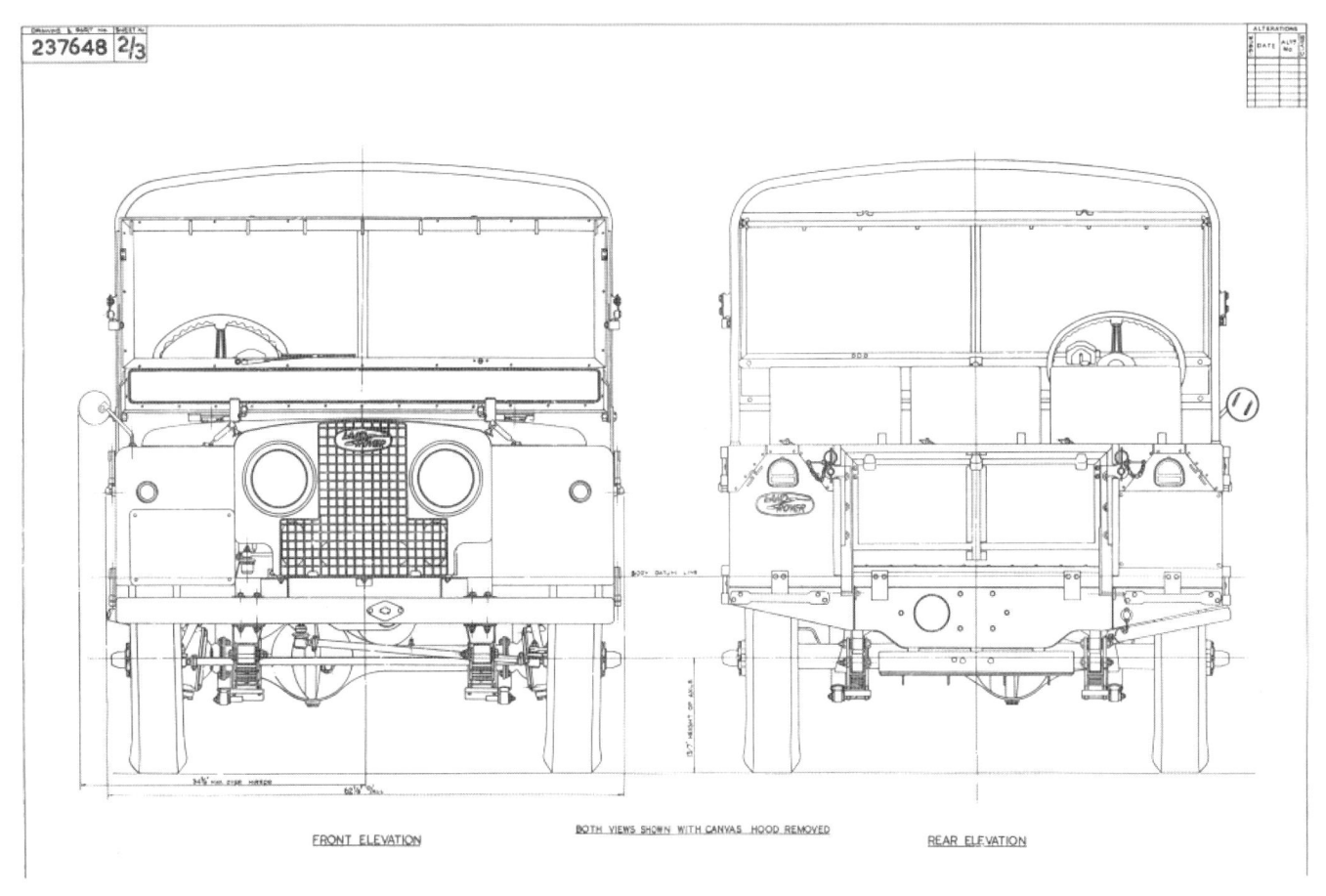

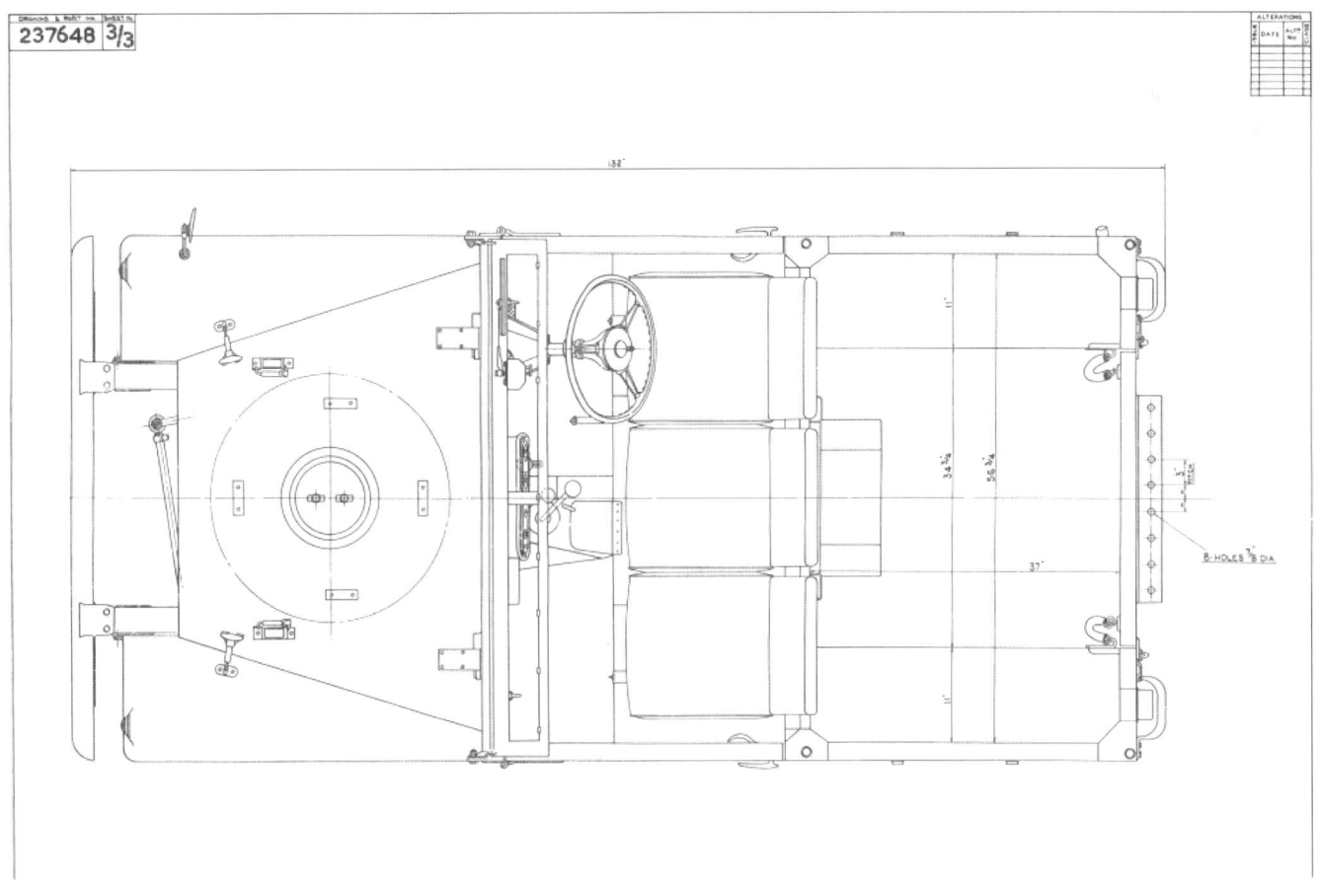

CHAPTER 15
Put On and Take Off
'Britain's Most Versatile Vehicle'

Maurice Wilks was determined that the Land-Rover should be an exceptionally versatile vehicle, and had given explicit instructions that it should be able to drive various pieces of farm machinery through optional power take-off equipment. The hybrid prototype centre steer vehicle was certainly equipped and used in this way, and the concept was further expanded with the first batch of pre-production Land-Rovers that followed in early 1948, when a whole range of specialist Land-Rovers were subsequently developed to supplement the basic model.

The first of these, L05, was equipped as a 'Welder'. It was soon followed by L06, a 'Fire Tender', then R17, a 'Dorman-Simplex Crop Sprayer'; and finally, L20, the shooting brake or 'Station Wagon', as Rover preferred to call it. This had been bodied by 'Tickford' at Newport Pagnall. A special purpose-built 'Brockhouse' trailer also became available shortly after production started, and by December 1949 a Bullows 'Compressor' had also been added to the list of special vehicles.

Even before full-scale production began, the Land-Rover was already 'Britain's Most Versatile Vehicle'. The working speed of the centre power take-off (PTO), that was easily fitted to any basic model, varied with the main gearbox ratio. This enabled stationary equipment to be driven at any one of 44 selectable speeds between 500 and 3,000 rpm, depending on whether high or low ratio was engaged in the transfer box, and the hand throttle or engine governor position. A triple pulley at the back of the PTO unit rotated anti-clockwise, with up to 20 bhp available for driving plant, such as 'milking appliances, air compressors, spraying machines, electric generators, etc.' installed in the rear body.

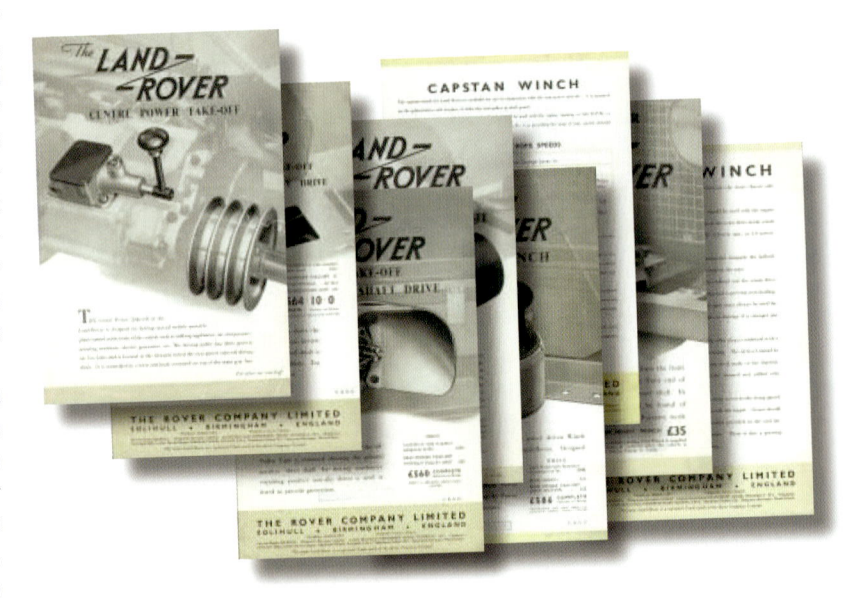

PTO sales brochures from 1949

'Eagle Comic' – "A Mechanical 'Farmer's Boy'", 30 November 1951

CHAPTER 15 – Put On and Take Off – 'Britain's Most Versatile Vehicle'

Pre-production Land-Rover L21 equipped with rear PTO

Early Welder in light green, June 1949; note Silver; painted chassis

179

LAND-ROVER – The Formative Years, 1947–1967

Advertising brochures; captions clockwise from top left.

Centre PTO with propshaft connected for rear PTO drive (11/49)

Centre PTO with triple belts fitted (11/49)

Front winch publicity (8/50)

Rear PTO and cover publicity leaflet (11/49)

Rear pulley drum (11/49)

Rear winch (1/50)

Rear winch table of rope speeds

Front winch technical information

CHAPTER 15 – Put On and Take Off – 'Britain's Most Versatile Vehicle'

Power output from the centre PTO could be relayed by a propshaft to a 5:6 reduction gearbox mounted on the rear crossmember. This unit had a 10-spline output shaft, but after the first 400 units was changed to 6-spline, in keeping with contemporary SAE (Society of Automotive Engineers) farming equipment standards. The output shaft rotated clockwise and provided up to 40 bhp at one of 44 selectable speeds between 415 and 2,500 rpm in combination with 88 possible road speeds somewhere between 3 and 44 mph.

Even with such an enormous selection, the ideal combination for farming equipment (normally powered by a tractor at the BS [British Standard] speed of 540 rpm independently of the main gearbox) could only be achieved by selecting first gear in low ratio with the engine set at 1,950 rpm – which conveniently happened to coincide with the maximum torque available.

This gave a road speed of 3.75 mph on unworn 6.00 x 16 tyres, using the original 4.88 differentials, but a road speed of 2.5 mph would have been more suitable, with 4 mph available in second gear. When the NIAE (National Institute of Agricultural Engineers) suggested this in their report, Rover pointed out that the gears in the take-off reduction box could be transposed to give a 6:5 step up, giving the BS speed of 540 rpm at 2.7 mph, but engine speed would then only be 1500 rpm, which even Rover later admitted in their March 1951 Workshop

181

Fitted with compressor

Manual TP/138/A, '...*would be too low to provide the necessary power for all but very light work.*' As it turned out, the Land-Rover was rarely asked to perform such tasks in the field so, fortunately for Rover, the matter was academic, rather than a practical issue of serious consequence.

An 8-inch diameter pulley drum was also available for mounting on the rear PTO reduction box to provide power for '... *circular saws, elevators and other belt-driven machinery*'. Again 44 speeds were available, this time between 360 – 2145 rpm. A rear-mounted Capstan, designed for a maximum line pulled off 2,500 lbs with the engine set at 600 rpm, soon followed, but was not designed to fit the first 400 PTO units with 10-spline shaft. With the transfer box set to neutral, four rope speeds were available from the main gearbox, and reversing the gears in the PTO reduction box (6:5 instead of 5:6) gave a selection of 8 rope speeds between 8 and 34.5 ft/min. A crankshaft-driven front Capstan would only have provided a single rope speed at the same engine setting.

Only this rear Capstan was considered necessary for '...*the movement of machinery and other heavy appliances in factories and grubbing out old tree roots in farm and forestry work*'. But it was not long before those familiar with the Land-Rover's ability to except overloading as a matter of course began treating the rear Capstan in a similar fashion – with dire consequences. The problem was that, without a strain gauge, there was no way of knowing when the 2,500 lbs mark had been exceeded, until either the shear pin gave out or the cast housing fractured at the mounting lugs. No amount of user instruction was able to overcome the problem, and in consequence the rear winch was dropped when stocks ran out in May 1955, after relatively few years of availability.

The simple alternative was a crankshaft-driven Capstan mounted on a thick steel plate between the bumper and the No.2 crossmember. Utilising as many parts as possible from the existing rear winch, this proved far more satisfactory and could be either

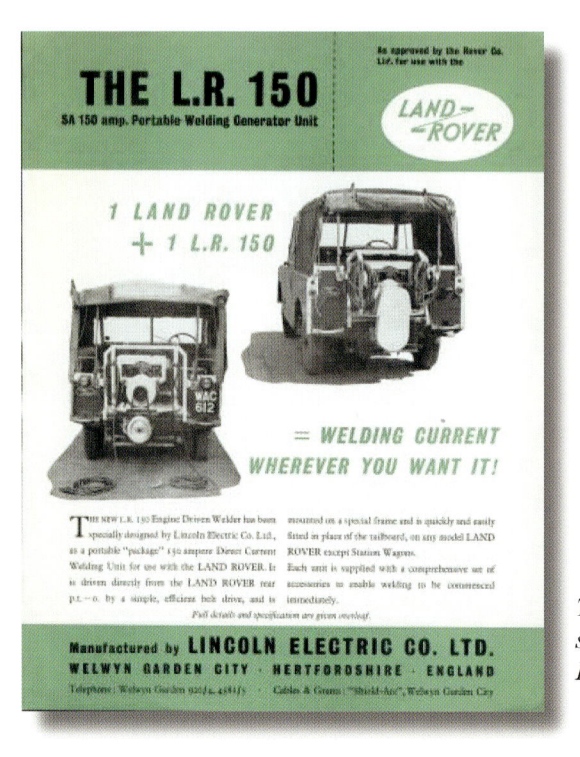

The later Welder supplied direct by Lincoln

CHAPTER 15 – Put On and Take Off – 'Britain's Most Versatile Vehicle'

Rover Service Bulletin giving engine governor's technical layout (1/49)

factory-fitted or supplied as a kit that included five special distance tubes for insertion into the No.2 crossmember to take the mounting plate bolts.[1] The new front winch was also designed to give a 2,500 lbs pull at an engine setting of 600 rpm. The worm drive ratio of 75:1 gave a single rope speed of 9.6 ft/min. Three patterns of this winch were eventually made for Rover by Aeroparts[2] of Hereford over the next ten years. The earliest model, used to 1956, can be identified by four drain grooves in the lip surrounding the bollard, while later models for '88 & 109' Land-Rovers have only two. The last type, introduced for the new Series II Land-Rover, has a flat machined on the surrounding lip, and several parts, including the shear pin, are not interchangeable.

If PTO equipment was installed it became necessary to fit an engine governor, Type 545/4, from Iso-Speedic of Coventry. This was belt-driven from the second groove on the water pump pulley – provided as original equipment up to August 1950, and optional equipment thereafter. Engine speeds between 1500 and 3000 rpm could then be set at 150 rpm intervals, by means of a hand quadrant in the cab. The Land-Rover's bulkhead was already prepared to accept this after removal of a blanking plate.

If the Land-Rover was to be used for stationary work for any length of time, it was recommended an oil cooler be fitted to maintain temperature below 90°C. This could either be factory-fitted or supplied in kit form, and included a larger oil pump (from the 6-cyl P3 'Rover 75' car), an 8-bladed fan (with cowl to suit), an oil temperature gauge, and a 15 lbs/sq.in. radiator cap to replace the standard 4–5 lbs/sq.in. cap, increasing the coolant boiling point to 120°C.

Pre-production Land-Rover L05 had been equipped as a '...mobile welding plant', by the Lincoln Electric Co. Lincoln, using their 150 amp x 30 volt 'Shield Arc Junior' electric welder. The Welder model's generator was mounted in the rear of the Land-Rover and driven by triple 'V' belts from a centre PTO, the usual centre seat being absent and part of the bodywork cut away to provide room for the belt drive. An engine governor kept a constant 3000 rpm when welding commenced, while a speed control on the inlet manifold overrode the governor when the operative was not actually welding. Lincoln carried out this conversion on a special order basis, and, in addition to arc welding, provision was also made for '...carrying Oxygen and Acetylene Gas Cylinders, nozzles and gauges for Oxy-Acetylene Welding'. This gas welding equipment was not included in the overall package, costing £825 in late 1949.

[1] *In 1953 a special optional chassis was introduced for the new 86 Land-Rover, with these distance tubes already inserted.*
[2] *Originally 'Shelton Motors', during the re-armament programme of the late 1930s, as 'Aeroparts', Peter Shelton diversified into military contracts, making various aircraft and other components for the duration. Immediately after the war Aeroparts returned to manufacturing components for the motor industry and made all Rover's optional PTO equipment for the new Land-Rover, including the original prototypes. They also installed their winches on Land-Rovers at Rover's Lode Lane premises.*

Welder, the under-bonnet view

Welder publicity leaflet (1/50)

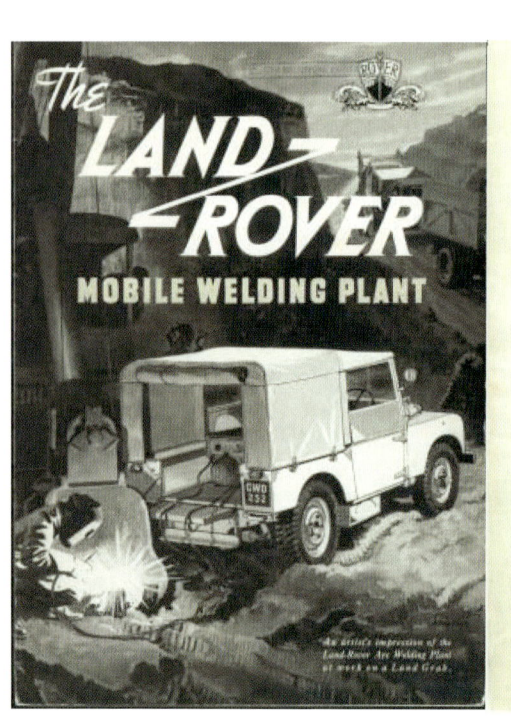

CHAPTER 15 – Put On and Take Off – 'Britain's Most Versatile Vehicle'

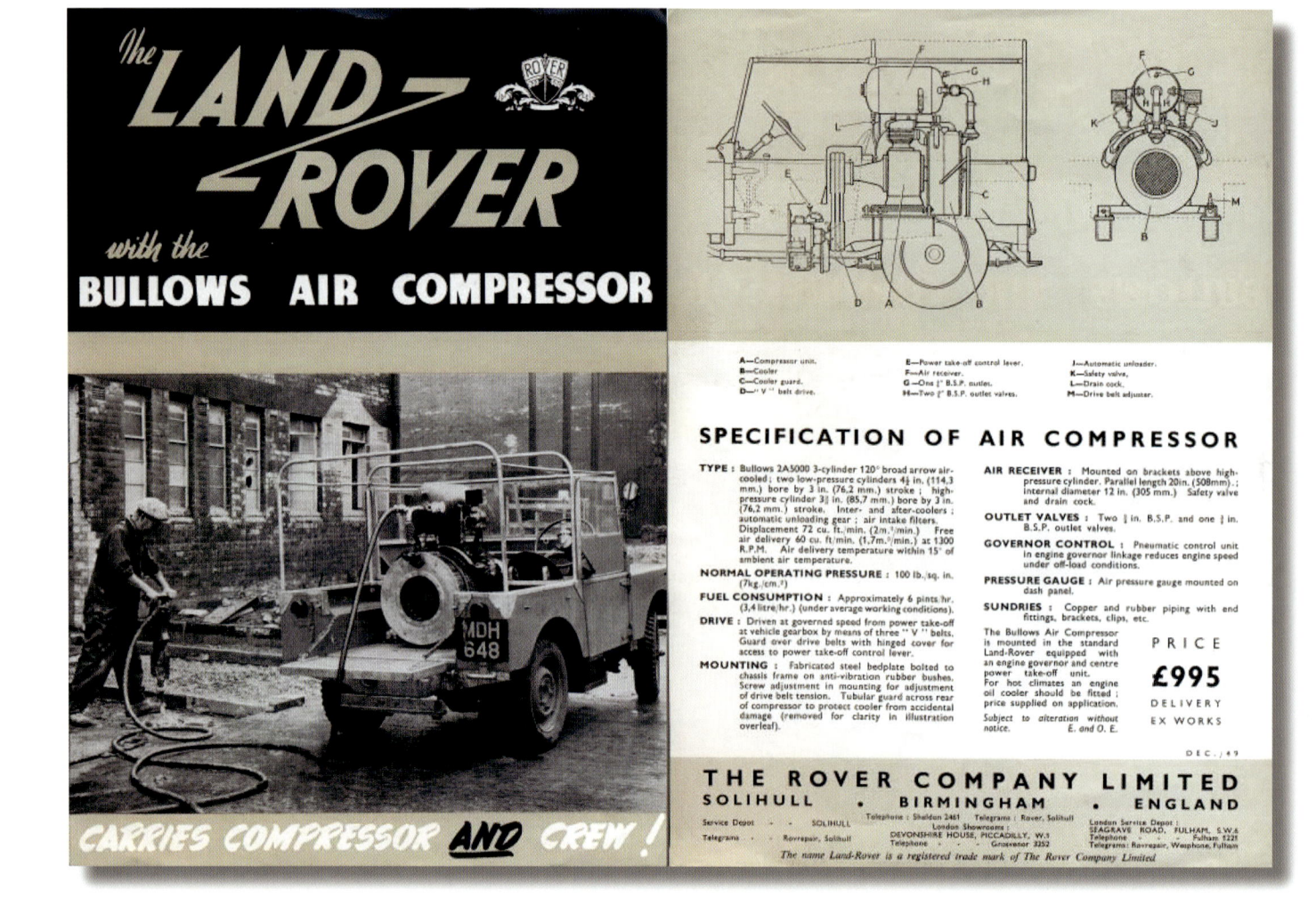

An 'Air Compressor' model, also became available towards the end of 1949, again mounted in the rear body and driven by triple 'V' belts. Rover described this option as of *'...particular interest to municipal bodies, [and] Road and Quarry engineers for operating pneumatic tools etc.'*. This conversion was done by Alfred Bullows and Son Ltd., Walsall, Staffordshire. using a two-stage three-cylinder type 2A500 air compressor with a displacement of 72 cu.ft./min. and a free air delivery of 60 cu.ft./min. at 100 lbs/sq.in. at 1300 rpm – equivalent engine speed being 1950 rpm, providing the maximum torque available. The compressor itself was mounted on a steel bed plate bolted to the chassis frame on anti-vibration mounts. For hot climates the oil cooler was also recommended and later became a standard fitment for this conversion, which had an ex-works price of £995 in late 1949.

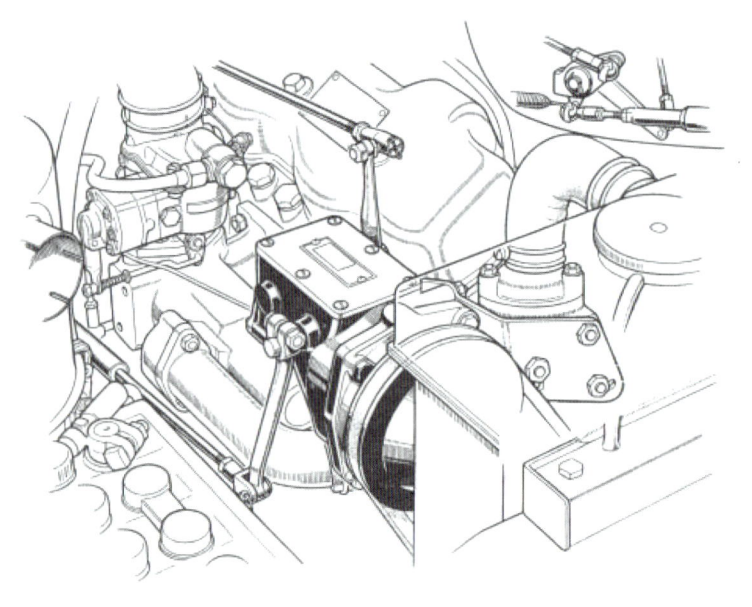

The prices of both the Welder and Compressor were somewhat prohibitive, and in terms of sales they might easily be judged failures. But in terms of Land-Rover development nothing could be further from the truth. By showing how easily the Land-Rover could be adapted to whatever purpose invention and imagination could think up for it, Rover had sown a seed which would continue to bear fruit with outside firms in conjunction with their new 'Technical Services Department' long after their own factory conversions had ended.

When Rover discontinued the Welder in the mid-1950s, Lincoln still continued to offer this conversion, along with a larger 200 amp model,

Bullow's air compressor publicity leaflet (12/49)

Compressor technical specification, showing centre PTO drive

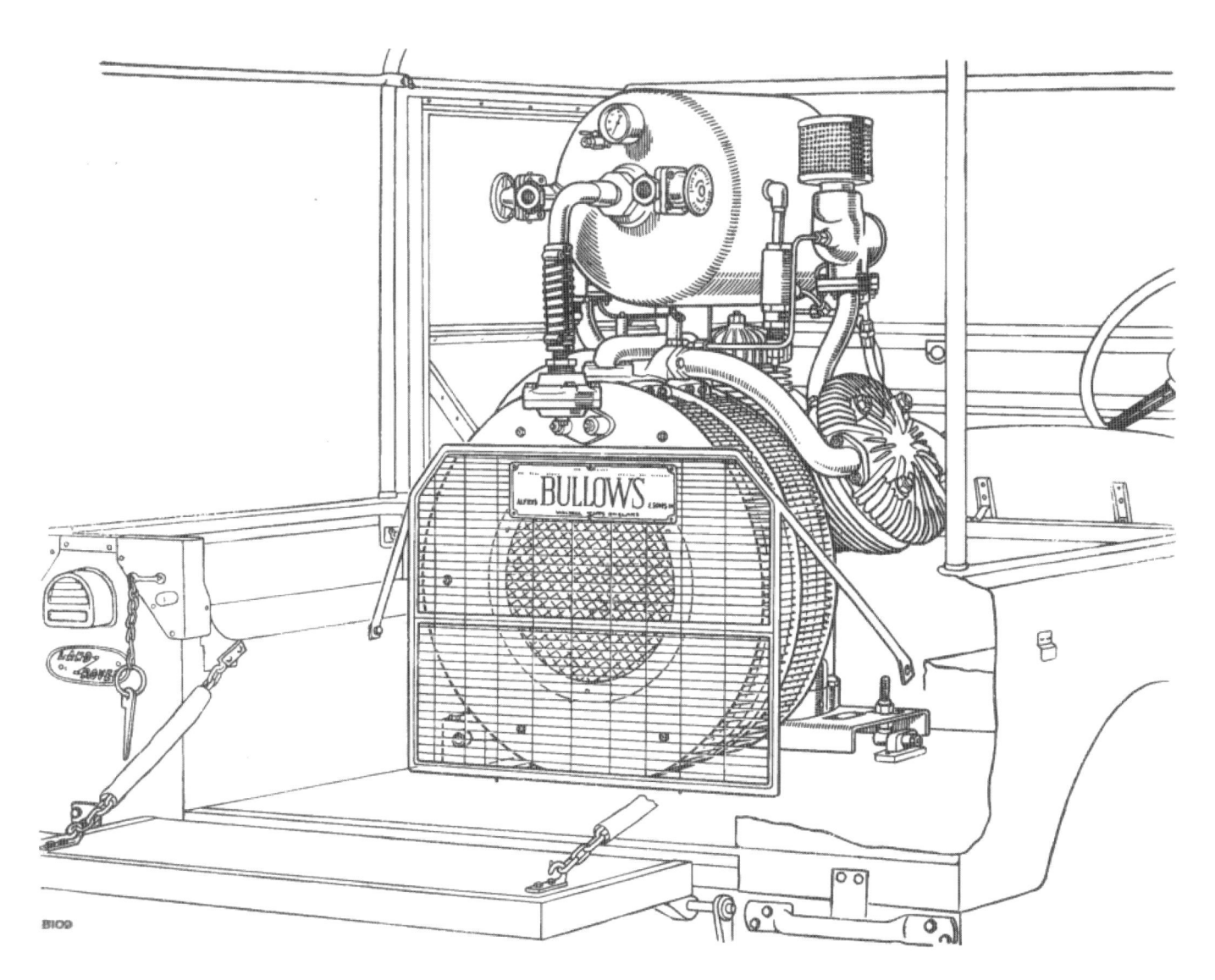

CHAPTER 15 – Put On and Take Off – 'Britain's Most Versatile Vehicle'

Line drawing of compressor mounting

Iso-speedic engine governor (left)

Compressor powered by rear PTO drive

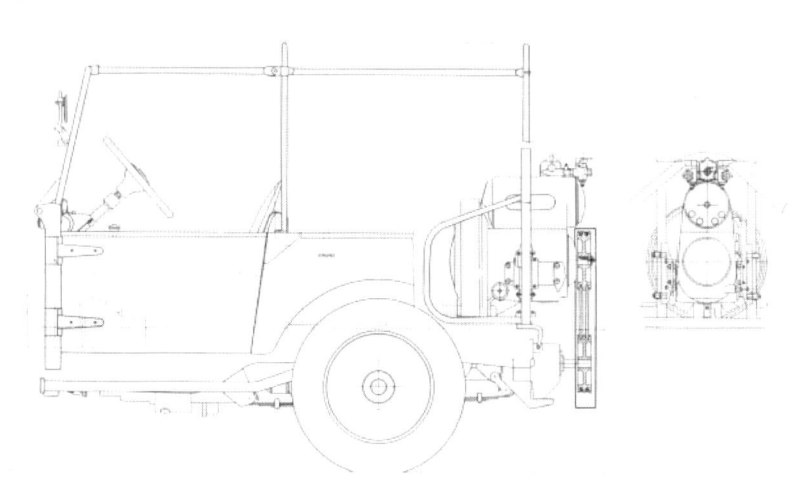

but both units were now driven by the rear PTO, with only the tail board removed. This was an interesting idea and enabled the Land-Rover to be easily returned to more basic duties, if needed.

Pegsons Ltd., Coalville, Leicestershire, offered a number of self-priming centrifugal pumps, with either high-head, or high-capacity low pressure, and a suction lift of 25 ft. which Rover also used for their 80-inch factory Fire Engines.

The pre-production Land-Rover, R17, had been equipped as a 'Dorman-Simplex Crop Sprayer' by Dorman Sprayer Co. Ltd. of Cambridge. This firm now offered an 850 gallon crop sprayer driven from the centre PTO for £107/10/-. The unit could also be self-powered at extra cost. Its working pressure of 40 lbs/sq.in. could deliver either 5, 10, 15, or 25 gallons per acre at a 5 mph or 50 gallons at 2.5 mph through a 22ft. 6in. folding spray boom, suitably mounted on an angle-iron framework, spring-loaded to prevent accidental damage from any obstruction it might come across in its wide path.

Brockhouse Engineering Ltd., of West Bromwich, a firm well known for agricultural

Early Brockhouse trailer publicity leaflet

Brockhouse trailer technical specification

implements, had specifically designed a 15-cwt trailer for use with the Land-Rover. This was first photographed behind a Land-Rover on 28 November 1948. The first entry for a Brockhouse trailer in Rover's despatch records is dated 25/4/49 (BT8-4398),[3] This was later 'despatched out' to the Ministry of Supply on 10/6/49. However, an earlier trailer exists (BT8-4260, owned by this author), confirming the story that Brockhouse initially developed the trailer without prior consultation with Rover. This annoyed Rover, and so Brockhouse initially marketed the trailer until a suitable agreement was concluded.

The early trailer sales brochure shows a prototype Brockhouse trailer behind a pre-production Land-Rover, but unlike the Land-Rover, its body was all steel. Measuring 6ft. x 3ft. 2in. x 11ft. 6in. with distinctive diagonal pressings in side and end panels, it was painted *'...green to match the Land-Rover'*. Land-Rover wheels were also used. Described as 'For the Farmer, the market Gardener, and for general use', at £75 it proved popular throughout the 1950s. A considerable number were modified by the Halesowen Engineering Co. for 'line-laying' purposes by the Civil Defence.

Among the early pre-production Land-Rovers, R06 became a Fire Engine, but a production version of this model did not appear for a further three years, in May 1952. This was almost a year after the introduction of the 2.0-litre engine, R06 itself already having been fitted with a prototype of this 2.0-litre engine, No. X0710051, before eventually leaving the factory for India.

1948 Brockhouse trailer plate

In use to 1955

In use on 'late trailers'

[3] *Serial numbers run on through all Brockhouse trailers, with no separate individual sequence for the 'BT8' Land-Rover trailers.*

CHAPTER 15 – Put On and Take Off – 'Britain's Most Versatile Vehicle'

Early Land-Rover and trailer in 'Light Green' outside Rover's office, October 1948

Rover's Fire Engine was built directly onto the basic Land-Rover using many optional parts already available, such as the centre PTO, engine governor, oil cooler, truck cab, Dunlop 7.00 x 16 tyres, bonnet spare wheel carrier, and 15 lbs radiator cap. As might be expected, bodywork, chassis, and upholstery were all red.

Using a Pegson 27H two-stage self-priming high-pressure impeller-type pump, it could deliver 200 galls/min. at 100 lb /in. pressure for a 10 ft. lift from a 40 gallon first aid tank. A choice of one or two Pyrene MFG5 Mechanical Foam Generators was available as optional extras for fitting to one or both main delivery hoses. Suction hoses were not supplied with the vehicle as their specification varied from one Fire Authority to another.

Rover described this unit as *'...particularly useful for cities and villages with narrow streets, rural areas, Forestry Service, factories, large estates, etc.'*, the Fire Engine was popular on industrial sites and small airfields, and Rover used it for their own factory Fire Service. In May 1953 the Fire Engine cost £905. The optional detachable metal cap was available for an extra £25/11/-.

Rover had moved on from describing the Land-Rover, not as 'Britain's Most Versatile Vehicle', but as *'The World's Most Versatile Vehicle'*, and although of lesser significance, it would nevertheless seem appropriate to mention those smaller items which had now become available as optional extras.

When the Land-Rover first came onto the market, anything that might conceivably be considered surplus to requirements by somebody somewhere was optional. This included passenger seats, doors, side screens and '3-seater' hood, all of which were listed as extras in TP/108/A, the very first handbook published in June 1948. By October 1948, however, such items had become standard, apart from the '3-seater' hood (a full length '7-seater' being provided as standard equipment instead), which was eventually discontinued altogether in 1950, through lack of demand.

Nearly all the items depicted in this early handbook can be identified as belonging to either production or pre-production models, but the seat backs shown, although similar to pre-production type backs are deeper and more rounded on their top edge. The cover illustration for this early handbook is based on a photograph of R01 on trial. Was these the type intended for the first 150 production models?

The Land-Rover Fire Engine

is a practical, self-contained fire-fighting appliance, particularly useful for cities and villages with narrow streets, rural areas, forestry service, factories, large estates, etc. Its powerful four-wheel drive and its compactness will take it almost anywhere—over fields, through mud, sand or scrub—and enable it to approach nearer to the fire than the larger fire engine. The same Rover 4-cylinder, 52 b.h.p. engine drives the vehicle and the Pegson 150 gallon per minute self-priming pump, which apart from supplying the twin full-sized delivery hoses, also supplies the 120 ft. first-aid hose reel from a self-contained 40-gallon tank. The front driving compartment accommodates driver and crew of two. The metal cab is an optional extra.

FIRE ENGINE SPECIFICATION

PUMP MOUNTING. Bolted to rear cross-member and draw bar.

DRIVE. The primary drive is taken from the centre power take-off output shaft, via an epicyclic step-up gearbox. This box, which has a step-up ratio of 1.678 to 1, is mounted aft of the centre chassis cross-member.

CONTROL OF ENGINE WHEN PUMPING. By engine governor. The control quadrant being mounted on the pump control panel. The governor limits the engine r.p.m. to a maximum of 2,500, which results in a maximum pump r.p.m. of 4,250 in top gear in the main box.

ENGINE OIL COOLING. By air-cooled coils mounted immediately forward of radiator matrix.

STANDARD FIRE EQUIPMENT

FIRST-AID WATER SUPPLY. Obtained from mainpump via selection valves.

FIRST-AID WATER TANK. Galvanised steel tank, capacity approx. 40 gallons, carried between wheel arches. Tank filling via hydrant connection, main pump suction or bucket filler.

FIRST-AID REEL. 120ft. of rubber hose coiled on to a drum mounted amidships. Drum assembly castings in light alloy to reduce weight. Nozzle is of ⅜ inch bore, and incorporates on-off cock.

PUMP CONTROL PANEL Situated alongside pump. Instruments and controls: Compound pressure/vacuum gauge. Pressure Gauge. Oil temperature gauge. Three parallel slide type selector valves. Engine governor control. Hydrant connection.

PUMP SPECIFICATION

PUMP CASING. Aluminium casing, incorporating a clack valve. The specially designed diffusor renders the pump casing self-cleaning. A drain plug is provided for use in frosty weather.

IMPELLER. A high-efficiency closed vane type impeller of cast-iron is fitted, capable of passing a maximum of 5/16in. solids without clogging.

IMPELLER SHAFT. Carried by two ball races and driven by a Hardy Spicer propeller shaft.

GREASE SEAL. Double end grease seal designed to give maximum sealing with minimum frictional loss.

PRIMING SYSTEM. The pump is self-priming, i.e. it carries its own priming water which provides an air seal, thus offering instantaneous priming.

SUCTION HOSE COUPLING. Standard suction round thread to British Standard Specification No. 336. This thread has three turns to the inc and carries a 3 inch suction hose.

DELIVERY HOSE COUPLING. This coupling is a Standard British instantaneous type and carries a 2½ inch delivery hose.

DISCHARGE. Twin delivery valves with large size handwheels are mounted directly on the pump body.

NOZZLES. When both delivery valves are in operation the maximum combination of nozzles which may be used is ⅝ inch and ¾ inch. If only one delivery valve is required a nozzle of a maximum of 1 inch may be used.

Specifications subject to alteration without notice.

OPTIONAL FOAM EQUIPMENT
(for petroleum and oil fires)

One or two Pyrene Mechanical Foam Generators, M.F.G.5, may be supplied as optional extras for fitting to one or both main delivery hoses.

A three-quarter rear view of the Land-Rover Fire Engine, showing the pump, control panel, and the mounting of the first-aid reel. Well illustrated in this view is the extreme compactness of the vehicle; it is this compactness which, combined with its powerful four-wheel drive, enables the Land-Rover Fire Engine to reach trouble-spots inaccessible to larger vehicles. Its speed, handiness, and good ground clearance make it particularly useful for factories and for undeveloped areas which call for a vehicle capable of operating over rough terrain.

In the new handbook, TP/109/B, published in October 1948, the cartoon character 'Calamitous Clarence'[4] makes his first appearance. Within its pages a whole new list of options also appeared under the heading 'Extra Equipment'. These included trafficators, a passenger handrail, spare wheel carrier for the bonnet, a towing plate and towing jaw with extension, combine harvester towing plate, and chaff guard. The centre and rear PTO (the later 6-spline output shaft being shown) are also mentioned for the first time in a handbook, but there is no Capstan winch as yet.

Seats, doors, hood, etc. were still listed as extra equipment, despite being supplied with each new Land-Rover. Under 'Wheels and Tyres' the Avon 7.00 x 16 'Super Traction' tyre was now listed as an alternative to the original Avon 6.00 x 16 'Traction', and also added to Avon's advertisement on the rear cover of the handbook. Where appropriate, all illustrations show the new spade-shaped seat backs, including R01 on the front cover.

In June 1949 delivery of the British Army's large order for 1878 Land-Rovers commenced. These military vehicles were all fitted with a new windscreen ventilator as standard equipment to help prevent dust being drawn in at the rear when travelling off-road with the rear curtain raised. They were also frequently fitted with rear bench seats and passenger guard rails.

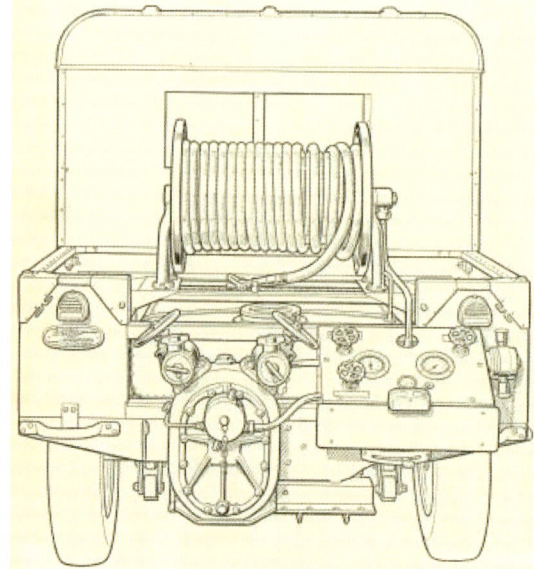

The new 2.0-litre Fire Engine with 40 gallon first aid tank

Line drawing depicting Fire Engine layout

---

[4] A name provided by this author: Clarence (from the dukedom).

CHAPTER 15 – Put On and Take Off – 'Britain's Most Versatile Vehicle'

July 1953 Advertisement

Handbook, TP/108/C, published in August 1949, has a totally new illustration on the front cover showing the current production model ascending a track across farmland. The farmhouse itself is featured in the distance, but perhaps the most amusing part is the vehicle's number plate, LRO 504, which was clearly fictitious as Herefordshire did not issue LRO registrations until January 1950. It was however, exactly right for the following handbook, published in April 1950, which featured the same cover.

A number of new items were featured in the August 1949 handbook, including a 'Clayton' interior heater to provide a little creature comfort in the cab before the onset of winter, while rear bench seats offered a little extra comfort for those travelling in the back body of an 'Export' model. Then there was the windscreen ventilator, rubber pedal pads, a special anchor bracket to enable the standard towing pintle pin still to be used when a rear PTO unit was fitted, an alternative 'military pattern' towing jaw, and the oil cooler. Three other items also appeared in the handbook for the very first time – a Brockhouse trailer, a mobile welding plant, and the Tickford-bodied Station Wagon.

In the same handbook, the original Avon 'Traction' and 'Super Traction' tyres had been replaced by new Dunlop 'Trakgrip' 6.00 x 16 'T28' and 7.00 x 16 'T25' tyres, and Avon's advertisement disappeared from the rear cover. The hood also changed and at the front edge the metal 'D' rings were replaced by a cloth strip. Rope and cleats

Clayton heater publicity leaflet (11/49)

Dorman publicity leaflet

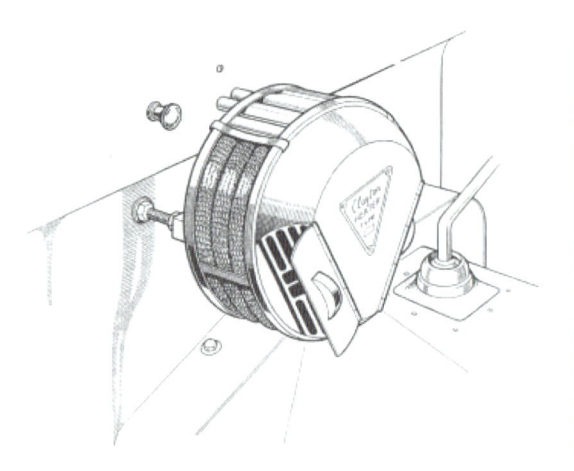

Spare wheel mounting on bonnet was an option from day 1

were also used instead of straps and staples for the side curtain. The rear curtain became integral and full width, and laced up at the sides, rather like a hiker's boot, with acrylic rear windows instead of the previous gauze mesh type.

The original sharp angles of the rear PTO shaft protector cover also changed to smoother curves, and finally, the rear view mirror appears lower on the windscreen, adjacent to the steady hinge, with small blocks for mounting Lucas semaphore trafficators now occupying the previous level.

The bench seat mentioned in the handbook was not the first rear seat to become available. J & L White of Leeds were already advertising special rear seats for the Land-Rover priced at £14/10/- the pair. Their seat back mounted directly onto the hood sticks by means of half round metal clamps. The backrests and squabs for the wheel arches were both upholstered using latex foam on a plywood base and '...covered in green leather cloth to match standard front seats'.

CHAPTER 15 – Put On and Take Off – 'Britain's Most Versatile Vehicle'

The early chaff guard

Early trafficator arrangement with 'bolt-on' control

'Calamity Clarence' appears in the 80-inch handbooks

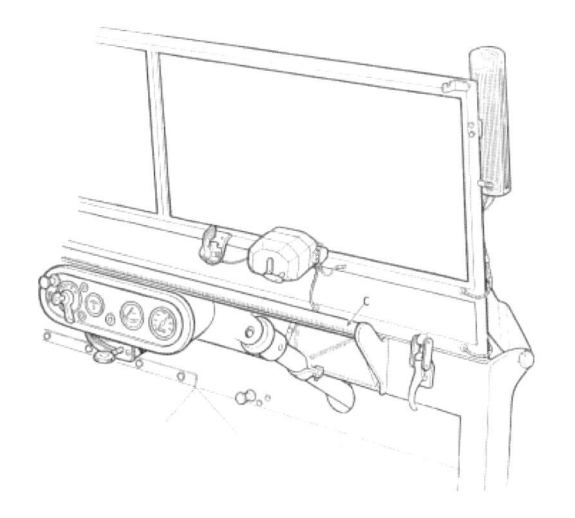

"Occasions when the owner finds himself in some difficulty."

For winter months, 'Oyler', 'the car tailor' produced a useful radiator muff for the early model. This consisted of a full width black grille cover with headlight apertures and press stud roll-up centre panel, the whole thing being secured to the grille by ten metal clips.

A fourth Land-Rover handbook, TP/108/D, was published in April 1950. It looked pretty much the same as the third, apart from the outer corners being rounded to prevent them becoming 'dog-eared'. But between the covers several new items had appeared, most notable of which was the rear Capstan winch. A further new hood design was also to be found. This had a pocket and strap on either side to retain the rear curtain in position, with new curved hood sticks designed to prevent rain water pooling on the roof top and prematurely rotting the canvas. The terms '7-seater' and '3-seater' were replaced by 'full-length' and 'driver's-hood' respectively. The illustration of the trafficator switch pointed downwards for the first time and was no longer offset, but situated midway along the windscreen rail.

A further handbook, TP/131/A (described as for 'Mid-1950 Season Onwards'), was published in October 1950 to coincide with the introduction of

Pye using the Land-Rover to advertise their 'radiotelephone'

selectable 4x2 in high ratio. The handbook describes this all-important change as from approximately the 3,075th Standard model, the 827th CKD model, the 21st Welder and 101st Station Wagon.

Rover's Service Bulletin, section Q2, 8.11.50. however, is more accurate, pinpointing the change to the 3,083rd Basic model (16100603 – 603rd 'Home' model; 16131573 – 1,573rd LHD 'Export'; 16160909 – 909th RHD 'Export'), the 101st Station Wagon, the 9th Welder, and 811th CKD model. (No more Tickford-bodied Land-Rover Station Wagons were in fact built after this time, and there was not even a replacement Station Wagon until the introduction of the 86 Station Wagon in 1954.) When totalled, this placed the change at the 4,0001st vehicle of the 1950 season, as correctly stated in the original Rover Service Bulletin, section Q1, 5.10.51, dealing with this matter.

When civilian Land-Rovers followed military models and lost their integral drawbar in the autumn of 1949, a separate towing plate and pintle became standard. Several other new items also appeared in this latest handbook. The front winch was mentioned for the very first time (the original sales leaflet is also dated October 1950), a hard top with optional tropical roof panel described as *'...robustly made from light alloy'* became available for 'Export' models (and soon appeared at home too), but reference to the '3-seater ' or 'driver's hood' had disappeared forever.

A little later, side windows in the metal hood become a further option on 'Export' models, sowing the seed for the construction of all future Land-Rover Station Wagons for the next 50 years. Side windows were not immediately available in the home market as they would attract Purchase Tax

CHAPTER 15 – Put On and Take Off – 'Britain's Most Versatile Vehicle'

Make your Land-Rover into a..... Complete UTILITY CAR

J & L • WHITE
Coach Trimmers
62a BURLEY ROAD • LEEDS • 3
TELEPHONE • 24453 • TELEGRAMS • "LEEDUM" • LEEDS • 3

Additional SEATING ACCOMMODATION FOR THE LAND ROVER

A set of specially designed bench seats and back rests are available for the 1950/51 Land Rover*

These seats, which are craftsman built throughout, have a LATEX FOAM interior, a piping in self material, and are covered in best quality P.V.C. leathercloth to completely match the original Land Rover seating.

Cleverly designed to facilitate easy removal and fitting, the seats do not require the use of clamps or screws and no alteration to the body is necessary.

The set comprises two bench seats and two back supports, the back rests clip on to the existing tubular framework and ample floor space is left between the seats which face each other when fitted.

*These seat units are only made to fit the 1950/51 Land Rovers at present

£14 10 0
PER SET
United Kingdom Only

Available at your ROVER AGENT

J & L White's seats were an early option

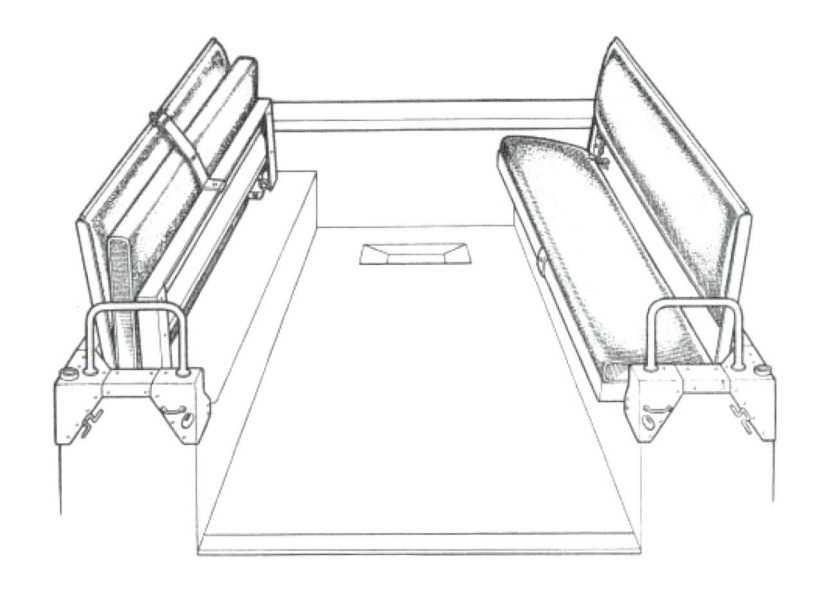

Optional rear bench seats were common on WD Land-Rovers

to the entire vehicle's price. New universal joint covers now offered protection for propeller shafts, and a combined water temperature and oil pressure gauge also featured on this latest listing. Finally, Bullows' 'Air Compressor' is also mentioned for the very first time in a handbook.

Only two further optional extras were to appear before the original 80-inch wheelbase Land-Rover went out of production. These were a light alloy truck cab (supplied as standard on the Fire Engine), with optional tropical roof panel, and a new Smith's heater with optional demister kit to replace the earlier Clayton heater unit.

By 1953 the 80-inch model had served its purpose well, acting as the platform on which to develop the ideas that really would make the Land-Rover not simply Britain's, but 'The World's Most Versatile Vehicle'. Both at home and overseas, if a vehicle was required for a less than usual task, a Land-Rover could often fulfil the role, and when the time finally came to bid farewell to the original little 80-inch model, Rover were already able to boast *'...the following government departments and agricultural and industrial organisations'* as among their valued customers.

GOVERNMENT	INDUSTRIAL AND PRIVATE
Agriculture	Building contractors
Agricultural Development	
Air force authorities	Bauxite mines
Botany departments	
Customs and Excise	Civilian airlines
Coal boards	
Colonials soil survey team	Cocoa plantations
Colonial Development Corporation	
Cotton marketing Board	Coconut plantations
Electricity supply Board	
Embassies	Dairy companies
Education	
Fisheries	Film units
Fire Brigades	
Forestry Commission	Gold mines
Game preservation	
Geological survey	Lumber companies
Highways departments	
Irrigation control	Marine engineers
Locust control	
Labour department's	Missionaries
Lighthouse authorities	
Malarial control	Oil companies
Medical services	
Military authorities	Rubber plantations
Naval authorities	
Police departments	Salvation Army
Public works	
Public health	Scouts
Post offices	
Railways	Sugar plantations
Tsetse control	
UNESCO	Tea estates
Veterinary services	
Water authorities	Welding engineers

Allman produced this portable saw bench

Allman's crop sprayer was an alternative to the Dorman

This cutter bar was an early after-market item

CHAPTER 15 – Put On and Take Off – 'Britain's Most Versatile Vehicle'

Cut Your Costs by Fitting This Cutter Bar
to your
Land Rover

Land Rover with the Mower in working position.
"Farmers' Weekly" photo.
(See other side for Transport position).

NOTE THESE POINTS:

- STANDARD 5 FOOT CUTTER BAR OF LATEST DESIGN.
- EASILY ATTACHED. NO EXTRA HOLES TO DRILL.
- CUTTER BAR DETACHED BY REMOVING 2 BOLTS AND A PIN ONLY.
- GROUND CLEARANCE NOT AFFECTED WITH CUTTER BAR DETACHED.
- HIGH, SELF-LOCKING LIFT. NO RATCHETS OR PAWLS TO WEAR.
- LIFT GEAR DOES NOT PUT ANY EXTRA WEIGHT ON THE VEHICLE'S SPRINGS.
- V BELT DRIVE TO CRANKWHEEL ENSURES SAFETY FOR KNIFE.
- TOTALLY ENCLOSED BALL BEARINGS IN CRANKWHEEL.
- ECONOMICAL AND EFFICIENT IN USE.
- THISTLE CUTTING CARRIED OUT WITH TRANSFER BOX IN HIGH GEAR.

FOR FURTHER PARTICULARS APPLY TO THE MANUFACTURERS:

WHATLEY BROS.   :   BUCKLEBURY
READING, BERKS.

CHAPTER 16
From Cattle Field to Battlefield
The Military Manoeuvre

In the early hours of 24 June 1948, the Russian Soviet administration in East Berlin cut the electricity supply to the three Western sectors. The only bridge to the West across the Elbe had already been dismantled, and all rail traffic was prevented from leaving the Western Zone. Barges navigating the Havelland Haupt-Kanal from Hamburg were also turned back. The blockade of Berlin was complete.

West Berlin had stocks of food for just 36 days, and coal for 45 days. The response of the military governor of the British sector, General Sir Brian Robertson, was to advise Prime Minister Clement Atlee of impending war with the Soviets.

That very same day two pre-production Land-Rovers were 'despatched out' to the Ministry of Supply, headed for the FVDE (Fighting Vehicle Development Establishment) at Cobham Lane, Chertsey, Surrey. One was a left-hand drive model, L29, the other was R30. This early opportunity to evaluate the Land-Rover before any production models were available soon led to an initial Ministry order for 20 production models in September 1948, under Contract No. 6/Veh/2854. On 16 December 1948 Land-Rovers R860751 – R860770 were handed over to the Army at Rover's Ministry factory at Acocks Green, the military numbers M6279781 to M6279800 ('M' standing for 'Light Reconnaissance Car') were already stencilled in white paint along the sides of each bonnet and on their tail boards. The contract stipulated that 18 were to be supplied with 6.00 x 16 tyres and two with 7.00 x 16 tyres.

Light green aircraft paint may have been acceptable around a farmyard, and possibly quite well suited to the hot and sticky climates of distant

Pre-production Land-Rover L29 sent to the Ministry of Supply for initial trials on 24 June 1948

CHAPTER 16 – From Cattle Field to Battlefield – The Military Manoeuvre

16 December 1948 the British Army takes delivery of an initial trial batch of 20 Land-Rovers from Rover's Ministry of Supply factory at Acocks Green

Ministry Land-Rovers had a contract plate instead of the standard chassis plate

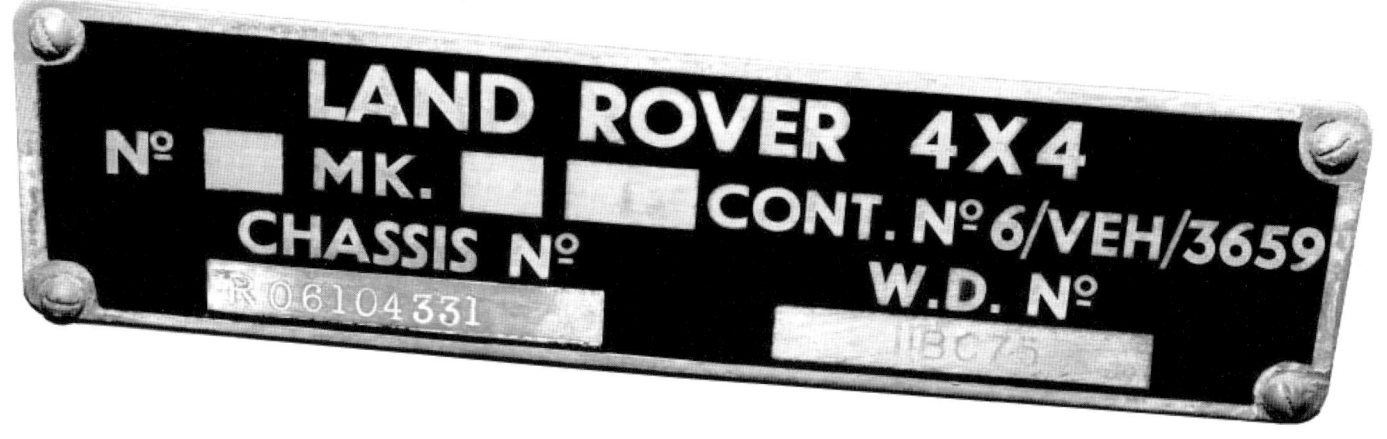

lands overseas, but for British Army vehicles serving on home territory, it was not considered suitable. All 20 Land-Rovers were therefore painted military colour No.24 (BS No. 381-1930), with 'GLOSS DEEP BRONZE GREEN', being clearly recorded in Rover's despatch book – the standard colour for all British Army vehicles serving on home territory. They were the first ever 'Dark Green' Land-Rovers. A contemporary photograph outside the Ackocks Green factory clearly shows their dark bodywork above the still 'silver' chassis.

Clearly, MCW's little farmyard vehicle had fired the imagination of the military. They not only saw its potential as a rugged reliable cross-country car, with functional simplicity in construction and maintenance, but more important, it was available NOW. The FV 1800 programme for a British jeep was still at the prototype stage, and its development costs were alarmingly high (some £16 million would eventually be written off in development costs at 1953 prices). Ordering another field car in any great quantity would require considerable diplomatic skill in negotiations with those politicians holding the purse strings. Be that as it may, within five months Rover received a further order for 1,878 Land-Rovers under Contract No. 6/Veh/3659, dated 2 May 1949, which took the total number of Ministry of Supply Land-Rovers to exactly 1,900, if the two pre-production models are also included.

Delivery commenced in June 1949 at the rate of 50 Land-Rovers a week, commencing with Land-Rover R8667261. At the time, this not only represented a quarter of Rover's entire weekly output of Land-Rovers, but also 50% of all UK Land-Rover sales. It was certainly sufficient to persuade Rover to change the colour of every Land-Rover leaving the factory to 'Gloss Deep Bronze Green'. Later Rover listed this as 'Dark Green' and then just 'Green'[1] under the same part numbers during the early years of Land-Rover production.

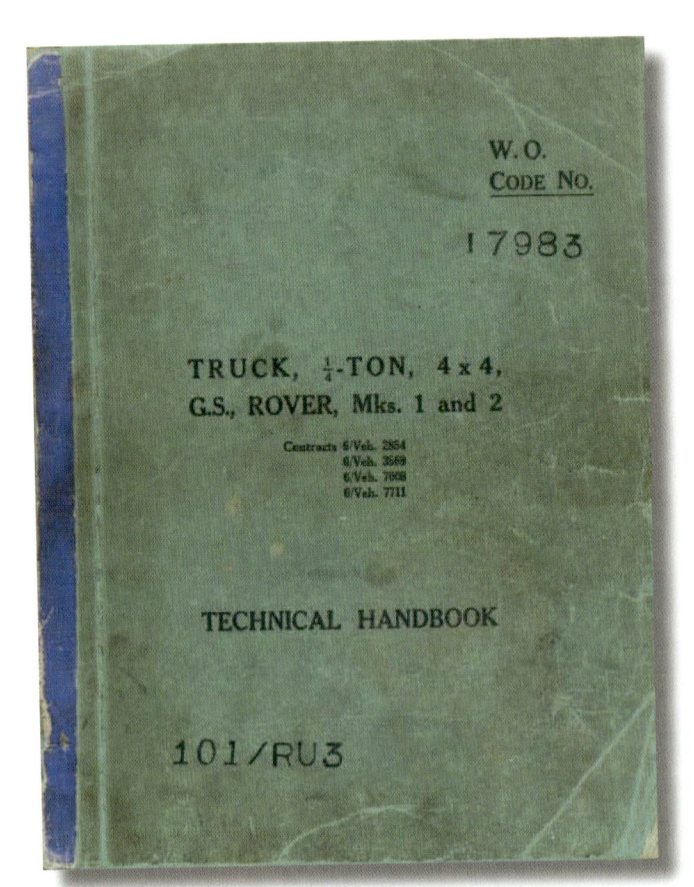

Initial handbook for WD Land-Rovers was this civilian version (War Office Code No. 17449), with update sheet giving lubricants etc. in standard military grades

Ministry workshop manual supplied for the 80-inch Land-Rovers

As well as a colour change, the integral drawbar was removed from all military Land-Rovers before delivery commenced, as it severely restricted the vehicle's angle of departure. To simplify production, in September 1949 a detachable drawbar was then introduced for civilian Land-Rovers. Using the Army's recently introduced alphanumeric markings, these latest military Land-Rovers were allocated numbers from 00 BC 01 to 18 BC 78.[2] However, before completion of full delivery, an amendment was made to Contract 6/Veh/3659 for a further 33 vehicles. What purpose did such an amendment serve?

Even before the cessation of hostilities, the FVDE had set in motion the 'Car 5-cwt. 4x4, FV 1800 Series' programme to develop a British equivalent to the ubiquitous US Jeep in an attempt to reduce further dollar debts, which were already huge as a result of the war effort. At the time, Rover, as an established manufacturer of motor cars for England's middle classes, took no active interest in the project. Eventually three prototypes were developed in 1947 by Nuffield Mechanization Ltd., under the auspices of (Sir) Alec Issigonis, using a horizontally opposed 4-cyl. L-head side valve engine. The final prototype, nicknamed 'Gutty',

---

[1] *Service Bulletin R6 (No.5137) 28/9/50, refers to 'Bronze green', possibly to differentiate from 'Connaught' dark green used for the new P4 'Rover 75' saloon car introduced in late 1949. A further dark green, 'Sage', was introduced in 1952 to coincide with modified bodywork for the P4 'Rover 75' car which brought to a close the original Cyclops model. There were never any 'Sage' green Land-Rovers, as has been mentioned elsewhere. Parts Catalogue. 1948–53 models, 7th Edition, May 1958 simply referred to dark green as 'Green'.*

[2] *The commencing letter 'A' had been reserved for RAF vehicles. Placing the numbers together gives the vehicle's serial number.*

CHAPTER 16 – From Cattle Field to Battlefield – The Military Manoeuvre

Engine bay with Rolls-Royce B40 Mk 2B engine installed

Hudson Motor's contract plate

Rolls-Royce 'B-Series' B40 Mk 2B as installed in the 81-inch Land-Rover

Beautifully restored Provost Land-Rover R06104616 built in April 1950; note the snow chain attachment lugs

would however, fail to reach the production stage, as the programme had now suddenly fallen influence to that sterling institution within Britain's motor industry, Rolls-Royce.

The years 1929 to 1931 had brought Bentley their greatest racing successes, but this was not enough to save a financial crises. Their acquisition by Rolls-Royce in 1931 brought with it Bentley's latest engine, a 6-cylinder, 4.0-litre, overhead-inlet side-exhaust (i.o.e.) job, with detachable head (cylinder heads on all previous Bentley engines were an integral part of the block) and only two valves per cylinder instead of the usual four. The new engine involved the labour of three of Britain's motor industry's top engineers – Ricardo, Weslake, and Whatmough. Ricardo was mainly responsible for the head. It was a well-designed engine and produced 10% more brake horse power from half a litre less than the old Bentley 4½-litre model, but only 50 4.0-litre cars were made before Bentley went into voluntary liquidation.

Meanwhile, across the Atlantic in America, where Rolls-Royce had been building cars at their Springfield, Massachusetts, factory until 1931, V12 engines were suddenly in vogue in all the top models. Consequently Rolls-Royce saw little immediate use for the new Bentley engine. Already the experts in V12 aero-engine design, Rolls-Royce began hastily developing their own 7.3-litre V12 car engine in 1932. Royce then died in April 1933, leaving his protégé A.G. Elliot to complete the job. Although a brilliant designer, Elliot did not have Royce's practical flare and insufficient attention was given to the future maintenance of the engine. Maintaining the free passage of oil to the hydraulic tappets, mainly through lack of owner care, would also prove something of a headache.

So by the time the new V12 'Phantom III' was announced in October 1935, Rolls-Royce engineer Jack Phillips was already experimenting with a single-cylinder version of the Bentley overhead-inlet, side-exhaust engine as a possible

LAND-ROVER – The Formative Years, 1947–1967

12 BC 05 used for HM the Queen's tour of Belfast in 1961

replacement for the now ageing 25/30 (4½-litre 'six' in the Mark V Bentley) and the new expensive and troublesome V12. Apart from the obvious attraction that most of the design work had already been done, and that the engine was also a proven unit, it also fulfilled two other important criteria - quietness and cost efficiency. Following the example of Hudson Motors, in whose engine Rolls-Royce showed the greatest of interest with the arrival of the 'Terraplane' model in 1932, it was decided to develop the engine in both 6-cyl. and 8-cyl. form, simply by adding a couple of bores to the basic design.

As a replacement for the Phantom III, the new 'eight' was tested in 'Big Bertha' in 1939, and also in an owner-driver Mark V Bentley known as 'The Scalded Cat', capable of cruising at well over 100 mph on Germany's new autobahns. The 'six' was scheduled to appear in the Bentley Mark V chassis at Olympia in 1940, but due to the outbreak of war that was not to be. The new engine was produced at a factory cost of around half that of the V12 it was to replace, with 85% of parts interchangeable between 6- and 8-cylinder engines. After the war, both Rolls-Royce and Bentley cars used the 'six', but it was not until 1950 that the 'eight' became available in a prestigious limousine for Heads of State – the Phantom IV. Only 16 were ever built.

Though not part of the original plan, W.A. Robotham, head of Rolls-Royce's Experimental Department, Derby, had not overlooked the possibility of a smaller version and according to a memo dated 24 March 1939, he suggested *'...it might be worth making a 4-cyl. 2.8-litre engine out*

CHAPTER 16 – From Cattle Field to Battlefield – The Military Manoeuvre

MILITARY LAND-ROVERS CONVERTED TO
ROLLS-ROYCE B40 2.8-LITRE ENGINE
BY HUDSON MOTORS LTD., JAN-APR 1950
CONTRACT No. 6/Veh/4679 11/1/1950

	MILITARY No.	CHASSIS No.	RR ENGINE No.
1	10 BC 71	06103860	B40 585
2	11 BC 50	06104193	B40 577
3	11 BC 65	06104265	B40 563
4	11 BC 75	06104331	B40 573
5	11 BC 77	06104333	B40 558
6	11 BC 80	06104336	B40 596
7	11 BC 85	06104396	B40 561
8	11 BC 90	06104401	B40 576
9	11 BC 96	06104446	B40 586
10	11 BC 98	06104448	B40 557
11	12 BC 00	06104450	B40 584
12	12 BC 02	06104452	B40 559
13	12 BC 03	06104453	B40 591
14	12 BC 04	06104454	B40 518
15	12 BC 05	06104455	B40 556
16	12 BC 07	06104457	B40 567
17	12 BC 08	06104458	B40 574
18	12 BC 09	06104540	B40 565
19	12 BC 10	06104541	B40 583
20	12 BC 11	06104542	B40 580
21	12 BC 12	06104543	B40 579
22	12 BC 13	06104544	B40 570
23	12 BC 14	06104545	B40 571
24	12 BC 15	06104546	B40 564
25	12 BC 16	06104547	B40 589
26	12 BC 17	06104548	B40 572
27	12 BC 19	06104550	B40 560
28	12 BC 22	06104553	B40 562
29	12 BC 23	06104608	B40 566
30	12 BC 25	06104610	B40 590
31	12 BC 27	06104612	B40 587
32	12 BC 29	06104614	B40 582
33	12 BC 33	06104618	B40 569

The 33 Ministry Land-Rovers with Rolls-Royce power plants

The 81-inch Land-Rover had its own handbook

TECHNICAL SERVICES BRANCH

LANDROVER B40 CAR 4x4

· Notes for the Information of Users ·

55/3

---

of the existing six with two cylinders omitted'. In a later memo dated 18 October 1939, he proposed using *'...the Continental car chassis 14BV'* as a test bed for the unit. Robotham planned to use this engine in a 'small' Rolls-Royce car, to be named 'Ripeletto', to be sold at £650 as a replacement for the 25/30. One Ripeletto was in fact made, chassis No. 1RT1, and plans for a truck and agricultural tractor were also under consideration using this new 'Rationalised Range' engine (11.11.39). It is interesting to note that according to Rover's despatch records, on 13 October 1948, one 'W.A. Robotham in Derby' took delivery of the pre-production Land-Rover, R13.

During the four years 1936–1939 that the Phantom III was in production, the number of cars made was only 710, with the total number of all cars, (including Bentley models), less than 1,000 a year. If Rolls-Royce's car division was to remain financially viable, not only would car sales have to be increased by cutting costs, but other uses would have to be found for their new engine. Here they were able to find a ready market in the British Army for its proposed new 'Rationalised Range' of engines.

From the military point of view, interchangeability of parts between both engines and vehicles could not only minimise the logistics of servicing and spares in the field – a major headache in itself – but even more important, would lead to a greater standardisation of fuels and oils. The huge variety of American, British, Canadian, French, and other vehicles being used during the war had caused a major logistics problem on this front. A Joint Associated Services Lubricants Panel, specially set up to deal with the matter, had so far managed to reduce the number of lubricants by two-thirds, from 361 down to 118. The concept of a 'Rationalised Range' of engines from a single top-quality manufacturer such as Rolls-Royce must have seemed like having the solution to all of their problems handed to them on one huge plate.

After the war the British Army greeted the new engine with tremendous enthusiasm and in 1946 the War Office officially confirmed the Rolls-Royce new engine suitable for military use. The Army now intended powering just about everything that moved with it, including their FV 1800 replacement for the US Jeep. Consequently, in 1948 Nuffield's engine had to immediately give way to a new Rolls-Royce B40 Mk 2A unit in a new FV 1800 pre-production model, the Wolseley 'Mudlark'. One 'Mudlark' entered service as M6279631. This placed it numerically only 150 vehicles ahead of the Army's first batch of 20 production Land-Rovers. The Army was no doubt keen to see how an 'off-the-peg jeep', such as the Land-Rover (for which the Government had borne none of the production costs), would perform up against the new 'Mudlark', particularly as full production of the FV 1800 was still a very long way off. It was a golden opportunity for Rover, and could not have come at a better time.

Not until November 1952 did the FV 1800, or Austin 'Champ', as it eventually became known, finally enter service – almost too late for the Korean War, which started in June 1950 and ended in July 1953. But by that time nearly 3,500 Land-Rovers were already on active service with HM Forces, giving them an ample opportunity to prove their worth at the battle front. Load-carrying capacity and general manoeuvrability made them far more versatile than the 'Champ', and they offered better weather protection than the Jeep. But the Land-Rover's 'Meccano'-like construction caused it to rattle a lot, making it less popular in fair weather.

After preliminary trials in various Second World War vehicles,[3] the much larger 5.6-litre, 8-cylinder Rolls-Royce 'B80' engine was installed in the Army's new FV1100 Series, 10-ton, 6x6 Leyland 'Martian' Cargo Trucks, Medium Artillery Tractors and Heavy Recovery vehicles, and eight prototype FV 1300 Series 3-ton, 6x6 Vauxhalls, which included two Field Artillery Tractors, in 1950.

The 'B80' engine's success in these vehicles soon led to its adoption in a number of new combat (CT) vehicles, such as the FV603 Alvis 'Saracen' armoured personnel carrier (APC) in 1952–72, and FV601 Alvis 'Saladin' Armoured Car, 1958–72. The updated 'B81' version was also used by Alvis in the FV620, 6x6 High Mobility Load Carrier (HMLC) 'Stalwart' from 1961–72.

The mid-range 'B60', 4.2-litre, 6-cylinder version, which Rolls-Royce also used for their cars, underwent similar trials for military use in the wartime Austin K5, 3-ton, 4x4, Truck and the American 2½-ton, 6x6 Studebaker, before going into the new FV700 Series Daimler 'Ferret' Light Scout Car, from 1952–71 and FV1600 Series 4x4 Humber 1-ton Armoured Truck from 1952.

Rover's development of the Land-Rover had been entirely independent of anything FVDE was doing, but had instead relied heavily on the American Jeep for its general layout, and the FVDE now found themselves with an up-and-running 'British Jeep' four years ahead of any FV 1800 production model. As it stood, the Land-Rover did not fit in with the Army's plan for a Rationalised Range engine. The Army did, however, decide to investigate the possibility of fitting the Rolls-Royce 'B' Series 4-cyl. 2.8-litre engine into the Land-Rover for trials in spring 1950, at the Army's Chobham proving grounds. These specially modified Land-Rovers with Rolls-Royce engines would be placed in direct competition against the current pre-production FV 1800 'British Jeep', the Wolseley 'Mudlark'.

A 'prototype' Rolls-Royce-powered Land-Rover was developed by Rover before final specifications for the project were completed by FVDE on 15 and 16 December 1949 (a year to the day that the Army had taken delivery of its first batch of 20 Land-Rovers). Some 33 Land-Rovers were about to become the very first of what eventually became a long line of Land-Rover 'military specials' extending over the next 50 years. The programme was officially set in motion on 20 December 1949. However, as Rover already had enough on their hands coping with the changeover from P3 to P4 car production and a doubling Land-Rover output (as well as gas turbine development, and Meteor and Meteorite engines at that time), they were reluctant to take on additional work. Besides, putting Rolls-Royce engines into Land-Rovers was hardly in the company's best interests.

So, at Rover's recommendation, the job went to Hudson Motors Ltd., of the Great West Road, Chiswick, in London, a company well respected by Rolls-Royce since the introduction of their 'Terraplane 8' car in 1932. After the war, with Britain's huge dollar debts and the pound sterling at a premium, under current government legislation, Hudson was no longer able to import their automobiles from the USA. A dozen or so remaining pre-war Hudson chassis, together with two post-war chassis, imported for 'experimental purposes', had already been turned into the prestigious 8-cyl. 4.2-litre 'Railton' marque, so beloved by Scotland Yard's 'Flying Squad', but now, apart from servicing cars, there was little else of real interest for Hudson Motors to do.

Under 'Instructions to Proceed', dated 11 January 1950, Contract No. 6/Veh/4679 'Modifications to Land-Rovers 4x4 (ex Contract 6/Veh/3659) to accommodate B40 engines as detailed', the Ministry of Supply were to 'issue free to the Contractor 33 each: Land-Rover Vehicles; B40 Engines and Clutches; Special Bell housings; Special Radiators; Special Air Cleaners; Modified Gearboxes and Transfer Cases; Special Front Propeller Shafts'.

This then, was the subject of the amendment to Contract 6/Veh/3659 for an additional 33 Land-Rover vehicles – replacements for those Land-Rovers taken from storage depots and now undergoing major surgery with Hudson Motors. In typical civil service fashion, the 'Men from the Ministry' were simply 'topping-up', to keep the numbers right.

---

[3] *Such as the FV11200, 10-ton, 6x4, Leyland 'Hippo' in which it continued to be used in the 1950s, the 10-ton, 6x4, Scammell 'Pioneer', and the 5-ton 4x4 Thornycroft 'Nubian', where it also continued in use throughout the 1950s in an updated FV 14000, 5-ton, 6x6, 'Nubian'*

CHAPTER 16 – From Cattle Field to Battlefield – The Military Manoeuvre

This 81-inch Land-Rover 'Saluting Vehicle' was kept at the Imperial War Museum, Duxford Aerodrome, for many years

Instructions to Hudson could not have been more explicit. Radiator assembly, engine, battery, front and rear axles, all suspension details, front and rear propeller shafts, driver's compartment footboards, and the rest of the body were all to be removed, together with any associated component. Altogether, 34 items were then detailed for modification before installation of the *'free issue'* parts. All discarded items were then to be fortwarded to Ministry of Supply stores either at Peterborough or Chilwell, with the exception of the bell housings, gearboxes, and transfer cases, which Rover were prepared to accept back (as they were supplying the replacement modified units), but Rover made no further concessions.

The *'rate of delivery'* stipulated one vehicle in January (described as the *'Pilot Model'*), another 13 in February, and the remaining 19 by 31 March 1950. Despite the detailed instructions given as to the nature of the work, January's Pilot Model *'...involved additional work in carrying out modifications in design from the details and specification of the prototype model'*. This additional work concerned the *'Bonnet, Fan, Accelerator controls, Battery cradle and other body structure items'*, together with no less than

LAND-ROVER – The Formative Years, 1947–1967

'...fifteen new drawings for additional parts required in connection with the conversion, make-up patterns, jigs, etc.' So why was none of this apparent on the aforementioned prototype? Clearly no one had taken the trouble to fit a body onto the prototype, or these modifications would have been as glaringly apparent as they had now become to Hudson Motors. (Interestingly, Rover never fitted bodywork to their second 1947 hybrid prototype Land-Rover either.)

Rover were now required to supply the following 'additional items, 33 each, ex Contract No. 6/Veh/4689: Relay Lever Hand Brake; Exhaust Manifold; Shaft for Relay'.

Because of the delay and extra work involved, Hudson were no longer able to meet the completion dates, and it was agreed that they be paid additional remuneration for the extra work. As a result, delivery of the final vehicle took place a month late, on 28 April 1950.

Although the converted vehicles remained very recognisably Land-Rovers, close inspection reveals that most of the original parts had undergone some form of modification. Chassis engine mounts and crossmembers were altered to accept the new engine, gearbox and transfer case and starter motor. Within a new larger transfer box, gear ratios were changed and their centres increased to give clearance between the front propeller shaft and the engine crankcase. Bumpers were given vertical mounting brackets to line them up with a new starting handle access hole in the No.2 crossmember, and radiator panel assemblies acquired new hand-riveted top and side panels to make room for a larger radiator and fan cowl. Bonnets were raised on buffers and dressed to accept the shoulders of the new radiator, with a hole made to accommodate the filler cap. Right-hand wings were given new panel work to accept the large cast aluminium air cleaner, and web sections were cut away on the front differential housing to clear the cast aluminium engine sump on maximum travel. The camber to the left spring was increased; new engine mounts and air cleaner cradle were fitted; front propeller shafts increased an inch in length to accommodate an increase in wheelbase (to 81-inches). New transmission tunnels were fitted and bulkheads modified to accommodate the larger bell housing and clutch (now 10 inches), with linkage all repositioned. Gearbox crossmembers were completely redesigned and underslung on the left side of the chassis to accommodate the starter motor. The SU (Skinner's Union) electric fuel pump was replaced by an AC mechanical fuel pump and the fuel sediment bowl dispensed with altogether.

In the cab, an oil pressure gauge replaced the fuel gauge, which was now remotely mounted on a bracket immediately to the right of the instrument panel. The oil warning light hole was blanked off, the mixture warning light was replaced by a new starter button, and new accelerator linkage was all inside the cab. With no spare space left under the bonnet, the battery was repositioned and placed inside the passenger seat box. A special hinged inspection cover was also added to the seatbox to give access to the gearbox dipstick.

All other modifications were concerned with moving the rear axle back an inch on the rearmost pair of spring hangers in order to maintain sufficient movement on an already extremely short propeller shaft. Shock absorber, axle check straps, and bump

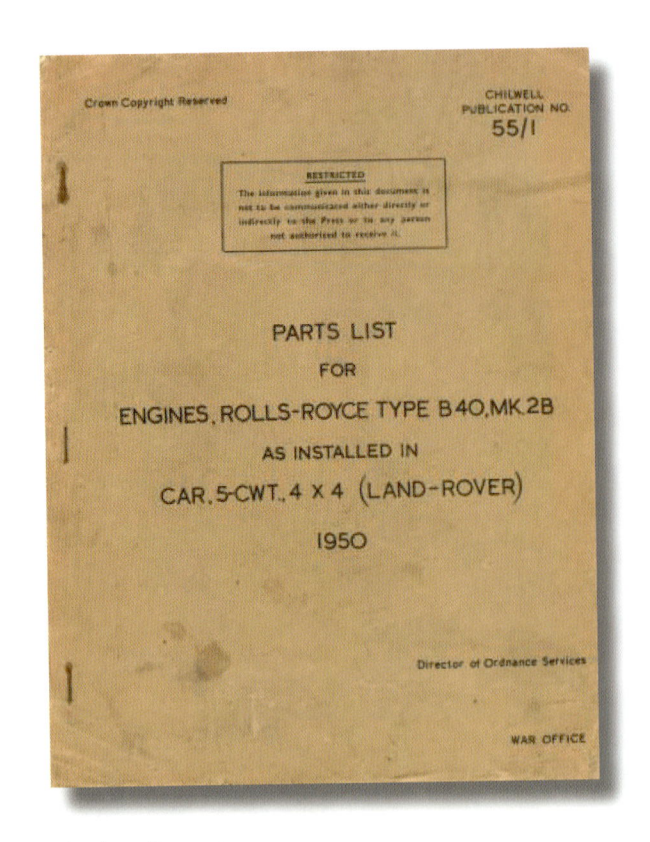

The 81-inch Land-Rover also had its own Parts List

This beautifully restored 81-inch Land-Rover is 12 BC 00 (06104450) owned by Andrew Ings

206

CHAPTER 16 – From Cattle Field to Battlefield – The Military Manoeuvre

This Prototype Military Command Car developed in May 1950 did not go into production

Prototype Military Staff Car July 1951

stops were all correspondingly moved back too. Wherever these modifications took place, cleaning up was neat, but minimal – almost as if to show what work had been done – and all paintwork was made good with a liberal coating of 'Deep Bronze Green' paint.

Taking into account the cost of (i) a basic Land-Rover, (ii) the Rolls-Royce B40 engine (around £200), (iii) other new components used, and (iv) the cost of the conversion work, each Rolls-Royce-powered Land-Rover is estimated by this author to have cost close to £1,000, compared to the current ex-works price of a basic Land-Rover to the Ministry of Supply of only £460.

Records concerning Contract No. 6/Veh/3659 for 1,878 Land-Rovers shows them all to have fallen between chassis Nos.R866 7361 – R866 7807 (1949 models); 061 00091 – 061 07434; and 061 07647 – 061 07679 (1950 models). This last group is an inclusive sequence of exactly 33 Land-Rovers – replacements for those already taken at random for modification to B40 power units. As these 33 chassis correspond to early February 1950, the timing was right for them still to be part of the original planned delivery of 50 Land-Rovers a week, which would come to an end that month.

Under Contract No. 6/Veh/3742, a total of 54 Rolls-Royce B40 engines similar to those used by the prototype FV 1800 project Wolseley 'Mudlark' were modified to specification PL 6059, becoming 'B40 Mk 2B' and designated for use in the Land-Rover. These differed from the FV 1800's B40 Mk 2A by having a belt-driven fan mounted on the water pump, instead of a crankshaft driven fan, in order to clear the Land-Rover's No.2 crossmember, thus avoiding still further chassis modification.

Many ancillary items were also different and, unlike the Mk 2A, these engines were not waterproofed. The 54 engines were numbered 518, 534, 556 to 605, 609 and 610. The first conversion, 518, may have been retained at Crewe as a pattern, then after satisfactory installation of 534 in the prototype, was later installed in 12 BC 04 (No.7).

The B40 engine removed from 12 BC 19 (No.27) turned out to be No.528, and not No.560, the recorded installation. Engine No.528 is a Mk 2A unit, but modified in almost all respects to Mk 2B specification – only the inlet manifold is slightly different – providing sound evidence of interchangeability between Rolls-Royce's 'Rationalised Range' engines. Surviving examples of these extremely reliable engines tend to have very low mileage, so it's possible No.528 may have been substituted, just for the exercise, in those long-gone days of National Service.

Nitride-hardened crankshafts, Brichrome-sleeved bores, sodium-filled exhaust valves, Stellite valve seatings and stem tips, operating in phosphor-bronze guides, all meant these Rolls-Royce 'Rationalised Range' engines would have an exceedingly long life. The Army Council's EMER EMER (Electrical and Mechanical Engineering Regulations) handbook, in fact, clearly states that *'...under no circumstances will the "B" series engines be re-worked on the line system, re-bored and re-ground irrespective of their condition when passing through a base workshop'*. After any repair the current usage was to be recorded on an 'Approval Certificate' kept in a small screw-capped canister attached to the engine.

At 2.8-litres, the B40 engine's capacity was 75% greater than the 1.6-litre unit it replaced, and, as a result, both power and torque also increased by 50% and 75% respectively. The engine weight had also correspondingly increased by about 50% from around 4-cwt to 6-cwt, vehicle overall weight increasing from 1-ton 3-cwt to 1-ton 5-cwt 2-qrs. of which 14-cwt fell to the front axle. The Rolls-Royce powered Land-Rovers had excellent performance on-road and were capable of cruising at around 80 mph – so long as there were no bends in the road – but in the rough, their excessive front end weight proved to be a disadvantage, when compared to Rover's 1.6-litre engine.

During initial trials in March 1950, when drawbar testing, the higher torque stresses produced by the Rolls-Royce engine resulted in the main gearbox layshaft front bearing collapsing at around 6,000 miles in the Land-Rover chosen for long-term testing. Later, in June 1952, at around 11,000 miles, a crack appeared in the inlet manifold in this same Land-Rover. This was put down to stress produced by the oil filter mounting, which on subsequent versions of the engine, was attached directly to the cylinder block.

The Land-Rover had served as a test-bed for the Rolls-Royce B40 engine, which the Army now proposed using for the FV 1800 project. After 20,000 miles this same Land-Rover was stripped down and in a final report drawn up on both engine condition and vehicle performance, some thirty or so problems were identified, many a direct result of the 2-cwt increase in engine weight. These included chassis fatigue, leaf spring and shock absorber failure, gearbox mounting fracture, inadequate braking, layshaft and transfer box bearing failure, excessive wear in propshaft bearings and joints. In a War Office memo dated May 1951, however, the Director of Mechanical Engineering states that such *'...defects on the Land-Rover body and chassis are no concern of these trials'*, and that the engine itself had *'...showed little sign of wear'*. The upshot was that the Rolls-Royce B40 engine was now considered suitable for use in the FV 1800 project, almost in direct competition with Rover's Land-Rover engine.

CHAPTER 16 – From Cattle Field to Battlefield – The Military Manoeuvre

RMP Provost Land-Rover 36 BD 40 (2610036) serving in Suez, 1953

10 BC 92 (R06103928) waiting to be air-lifted

Singapore – the early Land-Rover was never waterproofed

Records show that other Rolls-Royce B40 Mk 2B engines were also removed from 81-inch Land-Rovers for inspection. After 125,000 miles one particular engine was declared to have '...*negligible wear*'. Another example was stripped down by the BAOR (British Army of the Rhine) 4 Heavy Workshop in Germany, following a blown head gasket at 16,234 miles, and a further example was stripped after 25,000 miles for '...*information purposes*' only. Both were described as '...*satisfactory*' and re-entered for further service.

Rolls-Royce-powered Land-Rovers saw service with FARELF (Far East Land Forces), MELF (Middle East Land Forces), and BAOR. Ten remained in the UK, some being used in troop trials for a minimum of 25,000 miles. The Army Driving School, the MTDE (Maintenance Technical Development Establishment), and the Royal Corps of Signals 5th Training Regiment each received a Rolls-Royce-powered Land-Rover for further evaluation. The other seven, it seems, were sent off for to various units for GS (General Service) operations, where they remained in service until the late 1950s, when all but two were sold off at the Ruddington Auctions.

The remaining two were both converted into saluting vehicles, with 12 BC 05 (No.15), subsequently used in 1971 for the Queen's Tour of Northern Ireland. This Land-Rover was, until recently, kept in the Museum of Army Transport at Beverley, North Humberside. The second converted to a saluting vehicle, 11 BC 75, was, until the 1990s, housed at the Imperial War Museum at Duxford Aerodrome, and was the last B-40 powered Land-Rover to be 'sold-off'.

As far as the Army was concerned, the basic Land-Rover had already proved satisfactory and it would, in any case, have been difficult to justify the cost of the Rolls-Royce installation in quantity. Rover had proved to the Army that there were good reliable 'off the shelf' commercial vehicles available, and with a limit on funds, the Army knew such vehicles could not be ignored. As the FV 18000 (the additional fifth digit designated it a Commercial Type) the Land-Rover became the first commercial vehicle to be taken in large quantity after the war, paving the way for its eventual adoption as the 1/4-ton 'Forward Area' vehicle after final deliveries of the FV 1800 Austin 'Champ' in 1956. But the Land-Rover then in production was a far cry from the original 80-inch model that had won the hearts of the British Army, combatant and veteran of Korea.

The 33 Rolls-Royce-powered Land-Rovers were never assigned a separate 'FV' number or Mk different from any other 1.6-litre Land-Rover, but did have their own unique REME (Royal Electrical and Mechanical Engineers) code: 304010.01.904. No further Land-Rovers were ever powered by Rolls-Royce engines, which makes them something of a rarity today. Chilwell depot published a 'Parts List for Engines, Rolls-Royce type B40 2B as installed in Car 5-cwt, 4x4 (Land-Rover)', publication No. 55/1, Sept. 1950. A user handbook, entitled 'LANDROVER B.40 CAR 4x4', publication No. 55/3, was also produced by the Technical Service Branch.

Hudson Motors, not having the necessary experience, declined to undertake the *'...preservation, packing and despatch of Surplus parts removed from Land-Rovers'*. Consequently, they remained in store at Chiswick until early September 1950, when they were returned, not as originally instructed, to Peterborough and Chilwell, but back to the 'Ministry of Supply Agency, The Rover Co. Ltd., Acocks Green, Birmingham', where, under Contract No. 6/Packing/221, they were to be properly packed.

Rover were no doubt extremely pleased when the 'Truck 1/4-ton, GS, 4x4 Rover Mk 1' – the Land-Rover in standard commercial form – became firmly established with the British Army. Military forces overseas were bound to follow this example, boosting Rover's export drive still further. Initially Land-Rovers for the Royal Navy were Army vehicles passed on and re-registered (e.g. R06101394, circa September 1949, was first registered as 04 BC 25, but later re-registered 38 RN 24.)

Additional orders for Land-Rovers were placed under Contract No. 6/Veh/7008, commencing with vehicle No. 16101200, which ran over into the new Mk 2, 2.0-litre model, by which time Land-Rovers were being ordered direct for both the Air Ministry, Contract Nos. 6/Veh/5040, 6/Veh/5798, and 6/Veh/7188 (Mk 1 and 2), and the Admiralty, Contract No. 6/Veh/6818. Between December 1948 and July 1951, a total of 2,602 1.6-litre, Mk 1 Land-Rovers were delivered to the Ministry of Supply, 2,333 of which went to the Army. By 1951, the whole question of putting Rolls-Royce engines into military vehicles was under review. Only combat vehicles (CT types - 16% of all military vehicles) were to be individually tailored. Many of these continued to use either B60, B80, or the later B81 engines from Rolls-Royce's 'Rationalised Range', but the bulk of Army transport (GS and CL types) were to be on standard commercial chassis, around 50% of CL types undergoing almost no form of modification from their civilian counterparts.

Even the 'Rationalised Range' itself was becoming less rationalised. The pre-production FV 1800 vehicles had been fitted with the B40 Mk 2A engine, of which only 30 were made, and there were only 54 B40 Mk 2B units made for Land-Rovers. Early FV 1800 Austin 'Champs' fitted with B40 Mk 2A/4 engines numbered just 1,483 before the B40 Mk 5A was introduced. This was a simplified, less expensive design, and had few common parts with the earlier Mk 2A engines, and not even the head gaskets were interchangeable. Only 2,363 of the Mk 5A engines were ever manufactured by Rolls-Royce, and of the 13,750 Austin 'Champs' built at the Cofton Hackett Aero Factory, adjacent to Longbridge, between 1952 and 1955, the vast majority (9,904) were powered by B40 Mk 5A engines manufactured under licence from Rolls-Royce by Austin at Longbridge, Birmingham. These engines are easily identified by the letters UNF (unified screw threads) on the rocker cover. The largest engine in the 'Rationalised Range', the 5.6-litre B80, eventually had its bore increased from 3.5 in. to 3.7 in. to become the 6.5-litre B81, so now even pistons were no longer interchangeable.

When the Land-Rover's engine increased to 2.0-litres in 1951, as the 'Truck 1/4-ton, 4x4 GS' Rover Mk 2 FV 18001, the Land-Rover continued to be taken by all three armed services. Under Contract No. 6/Veh/7008 (originating with Mk 1 Land-Rovers), 200 Mk 2 'late 80' Land-Rovers went to the Army, followed by another 1,900 under Contract No. 6/Veh/7711. A large proportion of these – 850 in all – left the factory painted 'Light Stone'. All were 261….. models, and apart from a handful of Fire engines, were the first Land-Rovers not to be coloured green. A final four Land-Rovers (not listed in the military 'User Handbook') took the number of Mk 2 Land-Rovers to 2,104 and the total number of 80-inch Army Land-Rovers to 4,437.

Apart from Korea, these early 80-inch Land-Rovers also saw active service in three major campaigns of counter insurgency – Malaya, 1948–60; Kenya, 1952–60; and Cyprus, 1955–59. It was

CHAPTER 16 – From Cattle Field to Battlefield – The Military Manoeuvre

1949 WD Land-Rover, Contract 6/Veh/3659. R06104616, 12 BC 31, served with the Military Police, BAOR Germany. The red lugs on the wheel rims are for snow chains

1949 WD Land-Rover, Contract 6/Veh/3659. R06106231, 15 BC 49, in Army livery. The offside wing shows the Arm of Service marking and bridge plate. The nearside wing shows the Formation Sign and vehicle number

common for basic models to be modified locally by the REME to deal with the task in hand, and in Kenya, where Mau Mau tribesmen regularly attacked railway installations, REME constructed an armoured Land-Rover capable of running on the railway. Armed with a 7.62 mm light machine gun (LMG) mounted behind the cab, the four-man crew were situated behind non-splintering glass, and a large hand throttle replaced the steering wheel. Twin fuel tanks enabled it to cover long distances, and stabilisers were also added to counteract the rocking motion of the road springs, a very necessary refinement, as the vehicle was capable of speeds of up to 80 mph. A similar military version was also used at 'Suez' in 1956, and the remains of a civilian Land-Rover used on a railway were still in evidence at Port Stanley on the Falkland Islands some 30 years ago.

CHAPTER 17
Under Licence Minerva and Tempo

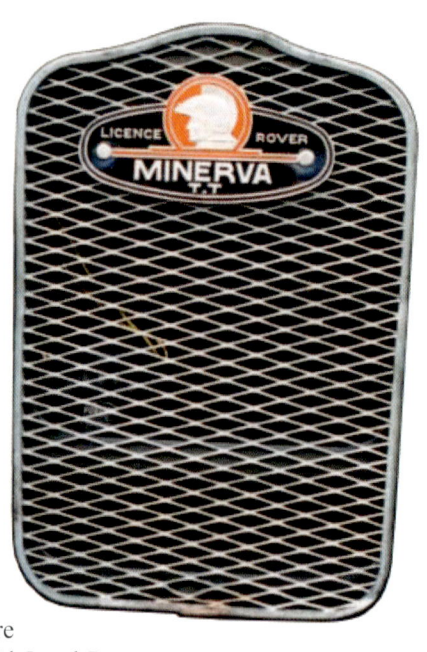

Minerva grille detail

By the time 1.6-litre Land-Rover production ended, 75% of all Land-Rovers were going overseas, a total of 12,106 vehicles in the 1951 season. Among these were 2,102 CKD (completely knocked down) models – practically all RHD – exported in kit form for assembly in some far distant corner of Britain's colonial empire – mainly Australia, where a heavy tax had been imposed on imported cars. Less than 80 CKD models were LHD. All this was about to change.

Following the introduction of the new 2.0-litre model in 1951, the number of LHD CKD models jumped to almost 2,000 in the very first season. At the same time, two independent vehicle manufacturers on the Continent were also making arrangements to build Land-Rovers under licence.

212

CHAPTER 17 – Under Licence – Minerva and Tempo

LA MINERVA MOTORS, fondée au début du siècle, a porté pendant de nombreux lustres, le renom de l'Industrie Automobile belge, à un niveau que pas mal de nations concurrentes nous envient.

Les fameuses voitures de luxe „MINERVA sans soupapes" étaient côtées parmi le high-life de l'automobilisme.

Vers 1933, la démocratisation de l'automobile rendue accessible à des couches plus modestes de la clientèle faillit porter un coup mortel à la MINERVA MOTORS. Il semblait bien à ce moment, qu'il n'y avait plus de place en Belgique pour une usine produisant des voitures de luxe. La célèbre usine de Mortsel ferma ses portes. Le nom de „MINERVA" disparut peu à peu du marché et ne restera plus que dans le souvenir nostalgique des „Minervistes" belges, amateurs de belle mécanique.

La guerre survint et les usines de Mortsel furent occupées par différentes armées. En 1945, les V1 détruisirent partiellement les locaux, et toute activité cessa. Serait-ce définitivement la fin de MINERVA?

Non. Monsieur M. van Roggen, l'actuel Président et animateur de la Société Nouvelle MINERVA, redressa magistralement la situation. Une première commande de 2.500 véhicules tout-terrain, à quatre roues motrices, fut passée par la Défense Nationale, ordre qui fut bientôt porté à près de 10.000 unités.

Avec une stupéfiante rapidité, la chaîne de montage s'organisa. En quelques mois, les premiers véhicules sortirent des usines et bientôt chaque unité comporta 63 % d'éléments belges. Non seulement l'Industrie automobile belge revivait, mais elle connaissait à nouveau un lustre de premier ordre.

A présent, chaque jour apporte un nouveau progrès.

Depuis le 1ᵉʳ octobre 1953, le véhicule utilitaire „MINERVA", fabriqué sous licence „LAND-ROVER", est vendu également à la clientèle civile. Et les voitures „ROVER", dont le renom n'est plus à faire, seront montées à Mortsel et distribuées également en Belgique par les soins de „MINERVA".

Les Usines ARMSTRONG-SIDDELEY, qui construisent la fameuse „SAPPHIRE" ont confié également aux usines „MINERVA", le montage et la distribution pour Benelux, de ses voitures. Un scooter racé et un original tri-scooter, de conception entièrement nouvelle, font également partie de la gamme de production de „MINERVA".

Bientôt d'autres voitures exclusivement „MINERVA" seront construites à Mortsel et rivaliseront par leur grande classe, avec les anciennes voitures qui firent la gloire de „MINERVA".

La Société Nouvelle „MINERVA" va de l'avant: elle n'a pas fini d'étonner ses fervents admirateurs.

LNX 403 was air-freighted to the Continent from Southend Airport

The Minerva story – in French

Like Rover, the Belgian firm Société Nouvelle Minerva SA had been manufacturing motor cars since 1904, and by 1911 was Belgium's largest car manufacturer. After the First World War, they set about making cars to rival Rolls-Royce. A decade on, when the company's founder, Sylvain de Jong, died in 1928, the technical specification of Minerva's cars had noticeably fallen behind the times, and the Wall Street Crash and Great Depression soon saw an end to their hand-made car manufacturing days. In that period General Motors and Ford installed their factories in Antwerp.

In 1935 Minerva were then taken over by the Imperia Group and continued making cars, trucks and army vehicles. In 1938 they made a last-ditch attempt to re-enter the car market, aiming at Britain, where Minerva cars had previously been well-received. To this end, two German 'Adler' cars were re-bodied by Imperia and badged 'Minerva'. Both were front-wheel-drive, and to this author's knowledge, used J.A. Gregoire's 'Tracta' constant velocity drive joints, which, after Second World War, would be used in all 80-inch Land-Rovers.

LAND-ROVER – The Formative Years, 1947–1967

Minerva in full battle dress

Unfortunately for Minerva, their factory was destroyed by USAAF bombing in the last months of the war in 1945. But this was still not enough to prevent them attempting to get back into car manufacturing, and they soon began assembling British 'Standard Vanguard' cars under licence. Then in early 1951, Belgium's army, the Defense Nationale, let it be known it was on the prowl for a lightweight 4x4 to replace their ageing wartime Jeeps. In 1951 the Belgian Gendarmerie had already ordered their own Land-Rovers from the Solihull factory, and following a failed attempt to make a deal with Fiat, Minerva's President, Mr van Roggen, made an approach to the Rover Company, with the idea of part-manufacturing Land-Rovers under licence.

On 21 June 1951 Minerva's negotiations with the Rover Co. commenced. Mr van Roggen's next step was to solicit an initial order for 2,500

Minerva in service livery

214

CHAPTER 17 – Under Licence – Minerva and Tempo

LNX 406 undergoing trials at Brasschaat Camp

"vehicules tout-terrain, a quatre roues motrices" from Belgium's Défense Nationale, an order he hoped to increase to 10,000. A new Land-Rover, 16135179, built in April 1951, and registered LNX 406 on 26 July 1951, was sent over to Belgium for the Défense Nationale and put on trial at the Brasschaat Camp. (LNX 406 later returned to the UK, going to Rover's Inverness dealer, MacRae & Dick, on 18 February 1952.)

An agreement was reached, and in October 1951 Rover received an initial order for 2,500 left-hand drive CKD models. It would not be long before Land-Rovers were being assembled under licence in Minerva's factory at their Mortsel premises, just outside the beautiful Flemish town of Antwerp. The premises had previously been used by the German ERLA to repair damaged and crashed Luftwaffe Messerschmitt Bf 109s during the Second World War. Minerva also made use of the nearby former REME workshops in Fort V before the former factory buildings were repaired.

To aid post-war recovery, in their 'Technical Specifications for a National Jeep', the Belgian Government insisted on 60% of the vehicle being of Belgian manufacture. Knowing this, in his negotiations, van Roggen managed to persuaded Rover to allow many parts to be made in Belgium, and so the Land-Rover CKD kits supplied were consequently minus all bodywork, seating, roofing, electrical components, exhaust pipework, tyres, radiator grilles and badges, as well as a myriad of smaller parts. Even chassis frames were eventually constructed locally. Unlike Solihull's Land-Rovers, the Minerva rear crossmember was fabricated instead of using a pressing, and had no PTO hole, although later civilian models had this included.

Minerva gave the official date for production as 1 October 1951. The first batch of CKD Land-Rovers was 'despatched out' from Rover's factory on 12 September 1951, and all 2,500 were delivered within the next 12 months, averaging roughly 50 a week. These were all 2663… series models from Rover's 1952 season Land-Rover output, and were equipped with the new 'Siamese' bore 2-litre engine, currently being installed in all production Land-Rovers at Solihull. By the end of the 1952 season (July 1952), a total of 1895 CKD kits had reached Antwerp for construction into Minerva 'tout terrain' vehicles.

Belgium's Défense Nationale consisted not only of the Army, but also the Navy and Air Force, and soon all three services were taking Minerva Land-Rovers in varying quantities. Engine, gearbox, and general transmission components for these vehicles, all came from Solihull, but over 63% of the Minerva Land-Rover was said to be made in Belgium, right down to the tyres from Englebert. Their major distinction from Land-Rovers built in England, was an all-steel body with distinctive angular front wings, the lack of any form of tail board, and a new-style grille made from expanded steel sheet that sported a distinctive nameplate portraying the head of 'Minerva', Roman goddess of wisdom.

There are three main badge variants. The early military Minerva 'T T' (Tout Terrain) badge does not have the Land-Rover oval within it. In 1953 a new badge incorporating Rover's oval badge was

'Tout Terrain' badge is quite rare

The 86-inch Minerva Badge

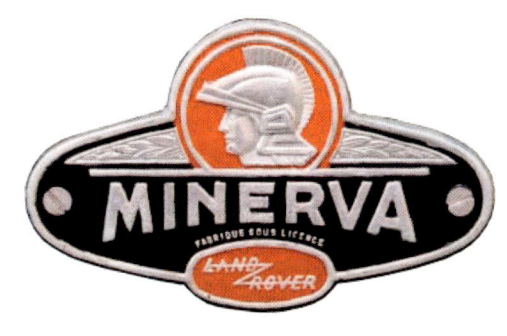

June 1956 brochure for the civilian Minerva

introduced. This has a black border around the head. For the 86-inch Minerva, this same badge had a red border around the head. Late Station Wagons reverted to the standard Land-Rover oval, carrying a "sub badge" with either 'Fabriqué par MINERVA sous Licence' or 'Importé par MINERVA Société Nouvelle'.

Only two seats were provided in the 80-inch Minerva, a toolbox being installed in the centre position. They also used a shortened exhaust pipe which discharged just forward of the left rear wheel. A 6-volt battery was installed under the bonnet where Land-Rovers have a 12-volt battery, with a second 6-volt battery housed in the tool box compartment under the driver's seat – an arrangement Rover themselves would later use for diesel Land-Rovers.

There was a price to pay for using steel bodywork. At 1,370 kg a Minerva Land-Rover was almost 4-cwt heavier than its Solihull counterpart. Nevertheless, personal experience with these vehicles suggests they are no slug. A particularly interesting feature is the curvature of the rear curtain, which is reminiscent of the earliest 3-seater rear curtain used for the original pre-production Land-Rovers of 1948.

During the 1953 season a further 5,964 LHD CKD Land-Rovers went to Antwerp. This took the total number of 80-inch CKD models received to 7,859. Strangely, almost 2,000 of these did not leave Rover's Solihull works until after Rover's new 86-inch Land-Rover was in full production, the final batch of 80-inch LHD CKD Land-Rovers being 'despatched out' to Antwerp on 11 January 1954. In January 1954 a further 946 sequential chassis numbers were allocated to Minerva for use on Belgian-produced chassis, but again these were for 1953 80-inch models, taking the grand total of 80-inch Minerva Land-Rovers to 8,805.

It is known that the Rover Company was involved in litigation with Minerva, who were suing for damages to the tune of £25,000 for breach of contract, over Rover continuing to supply 1953 80-inch CKD models during the six months after the model had in fact been out of production at the Solihull works. This deception may not have initially been obvious in Antwerp, but from Minerva's point of view, it happened at a critical time, as from 1 October 1953, Minerva attempted to break into the civilian market. The Minerva Land-Rover was, however, still based on the outdated 80-inch Land-Rover model. In late 1954,

CHAPTER 17 – Under Licence – Minerva and Tempo

Technical spec sheet for the Minerva

Minerva outside a pub in East Kent

Spencer Wilks and George Farmer negotiated an out of court settlement. This resulted in 270 86-inch models being delivered in January/February 1955, and a further 630 '1956' 86-inch models between November 1955 and October 1956, all at a discounted price (see below).

Unlike the military Minerva, the civilian model maintained such Solihull features as three front seats, the tail board, and a PTO hole in the rear cross-member. Alternative options were a full-tilt, steel cab, seven seats, steel full-length hard top, winch, and PTO equipment – in fact, practically everything offered by Solihull – but few sold before production of the 80-inch model came to an end.

Thirty years later the Belgian authorities were still taking Minerva Land-Rovers, partly disassembled, from the original stockpile. Around 1000 were still 'on the shelf' in 1980, and spares were still being supplied from the UK by K A S (Kingsdown Agricultural Services) at Ditton, near Maidstone

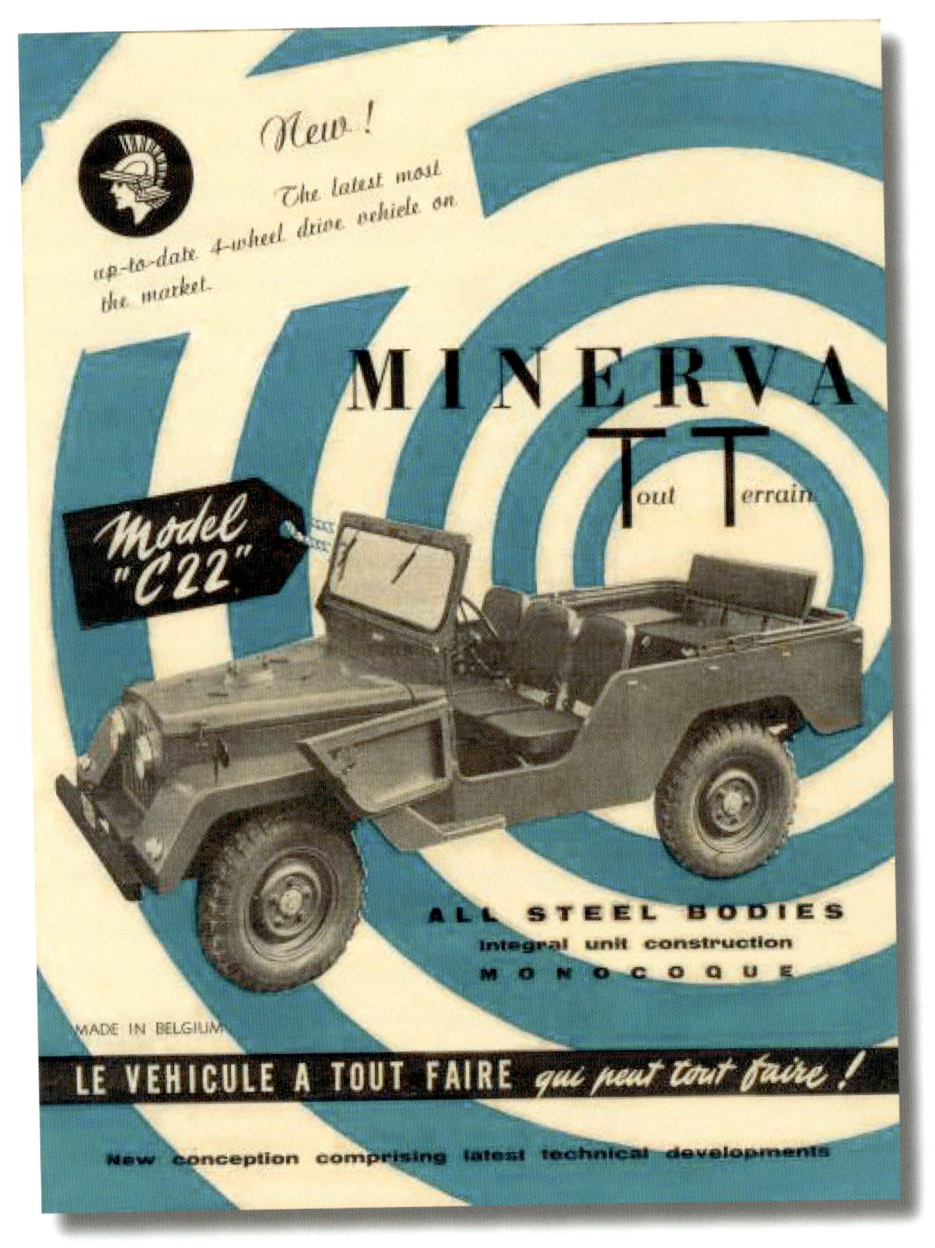

1955 Minerva C22 brochure

in Kent. Items such as Tractor joints, half-shafts, brake shoes, wheel cylinders, steering worms and nuts, etc., were still being shipped over to Belgium by the hundred. This author became involved in a consultative role concerning the dimensions of the transmission brake shoes. Although these had been correctly specified, an error in the workshop manuals had given the Belgian authorities cause for concern. In 1985, over 2,500 Minerva Land-Rovers were still in service.

As well as the standard military Minerva Land-Rover used by the Défense Nationale for the Army, Navy, Air Force, and later the Gendarmerie, other military variations of the model were also produced by ABL (Armée Belge/Belgish Leger – the Belgian Army) workshops. These included:

(i) GS and MP (Military Police) versions;
(ii) an ambulance with 1.3 meter extension overhang at the rear to accommodate stretchers;
(iii) Blindé (Armoured) paratroop/commando assault vehicle, armed with three FN NAG 7.62 mm LMGs (light machine guns), two above the passenger section and the third in the rear body – two small semi-circular aero-screens with inch-thick bullet-proof glass replaced the standard windscreen;
(iv) Blindé Airfield Defence with twin Browning 0.30 MMGs (medium machine guns);
(v) Milan, a standard 80-inch rebuilt by ABL in the Arsenal of Rocourt
(vi) a Radio Wagon.

In addition ABL also rebuilt standard models into dual control Driving School vehicles. It is interesting to note, that although the Belgian Gendarmerie used Minerva Land-Rovers – a batch being transferred over to the Gendarmerie in the

CHAPTER 17 – Under Licence – Minerva and Tempo

Military Minerva engines were always painted red

Spare wheel and Jerry can were carried at the back

1960s – preference appears to have been given to the Solihull Land-Rover over the home-built model.

Civilian 80-inch Minerva's included tilt, steel truck-cab, and steel hardtop models. In 1954 plans were made to introduce two civilian 86-inch Minerva models – a basic tilt/hard top version, and a Station Wagon. A new sales brochure was produced and between February and September 1954 another 200 CKD Land-Rovers left Solihull bound for Antwerp. A further 270 were delivered in early 1955, and another 630 between November 1955 and October 1956, taking the total of 86-inch Minerva Land-Rovers to 1,100. Adding the 7,859 80-inch models takes the total of LHD CKD Land-Rovers exported to Antwerp to 8,959. Together with the 946 locally produced chassis, this gives the grand total of Minerva Land-Rovers assembled in Belgium by Société Nouvelle Minerva SA to 9,905.

Building on experience gained sourcing and fabricating parts, in 1954 Minerva decided to manufacture their own 'Tout-Terrain' the M 20, and civilian C 20, on an 80-inch wheelbase, using a 2.6-litre Continental engine. Although the M 20 bore a close resemblance to the CJ3A post-war Jeep, built under licence in Haren by SABCA (Société Anonyme Belge de Construction Aéronautique), currently in service with the ABL, it was cleverly different from the CJ3A.

Semi-unitary construction was used to enable the body and rear end of the M20 to be rolled away from the engine sub-frame, leaving the front axle, engine, and gearbox as a single unit for servicing purposes – a concept based on the lines of the British Army's contemporary Austin 'Champ', then in service with British troops serving in Western Europe. The M20 had half-door access for driver and passenger, much on the lines of the CJ3A, but removable solid, rather than canvas, doors that could be hinged from the bulkhead to close this gap.

The Tout-Terrain was updated in 1955, as the 'M22' and 'C22', on an 86-inch wheelbase, but with the addition of automatic diff-locks and optional Austrian two-cylinder, two-stroke, 40 bhp, 'Jenbach' diesel engine – the JW 35 – which, in some respects, put it at least two years ahead of the Land-Rover. Despite its excellent qualities, the Tout-Terrain failed to make any real impact and apart from a handful of prototypes, few, if any, were produced. They are certainly much rarer than the Land-Rover version. Sadly, the Société Nouvelle Minerva SA went into liquidation in 1958.

During the early 1990s, all remaining Défense National Minerva Land-Rovers were finally released by the Belgian Army, along with their spares. For a time they could be seen lying derelict in scrap yards, and could be bought individually, in roadworthy condition, direct, for around £1,700. All were soon snapped up. A dealer in ex-WD parts in Antwerp took most of the spares, but many did go to major UK dealers of 'Series I' parts, such as John Craddock.

Among these spares were fully reconditioned engines, all painted bright red. In Belgium they could be bought for a few hundred pounds, but by the time they reached the UK the price had doubled. A year or two later they were about the same price as a complete Minerva direct from the Army.

CHAPTER 17 – Under Licence – Minerva and Tempo

The 86-inch Tempo Land-Rover

Tempo badge, reminiscent of a 1930s radio microphone

THE 'TEMPO' LAND-ROVER

From the end of the Second World War until May 1955, the German Federal Republic (West Germany) remained under Allied occupation. This meant they had no need for military vehicles. After the Soviet blockade of Berlin in 1948, 'cold war' tensions between East and West Germany were at their peak.

The West German border police, the BGS ('Bundesgrenzschutz') had a requirement for 250 lightweight all-wheel-drive vehicles to patrol the east-west borders of this then divided country. No longer permitted to build any form of military vehicle, they would have to import such a vehicle from elsewhere.

Following Belgium's example, in 1952 the Hamburg-Harburg firm of Herbert Vidal, who had been responsible for the 'Tempo' command car before the war, saw a good opportunity to build Land-Rovers under licence to fulfil this role. Like the Belgian vehicle, their Tempo Land-Rover would utilise many locally made parts, including all bodywork, and they would be specifically designed to fulfil BGS requirements.

An agreement was reached with Rover in early 1953 with delivery commencing to Hamburg-Harburg in April 1953. It is not clear how many 80-inch Tempo Land-Rovers may have been produced (possibly 100, but it may be as high as 178). They all came from the 1953 season's Land-Rover production, which ended in August. Their first batch of 80-inch chassis are believed to have been made by Minerva in Mortsel, Antwerp.

Herbert Vidal continued producing Tempo Land-Rovers in 1954, but these later vehicles, designated 'Tempo 041' were on an 86-inch wheelbase, the same as their Solihull counterpart. Compared to the Minerva, the number of Tempo Land-Rovers made was negligible – only 150 86-inch models were produced. Both models were used by the BGS, the West German border police.

221

LAND-ROVER – The Formative Years, 1947–1967

Extremely rare 80-inch Tempo Land-Rover

Like the Minerva, all bodywork was produced locally (apart from the bulkhead and bonnet), along with seating, roof, etc. They also had their own very distinctive grille badge which looks a bit like something from a 1930s Buck Rogers film – a radio microphone perhaps? Twin fuel tanks were provided at the rear and useful locker-boxes were installed within the front wings. A further locker box was attached on top of the bonnet, the spare wheel being attached at the rear in typical Jeep fashion. A negative earth electrical system was also used.

In 1956 a new West German 'Federal Army' was formed, the 'Bundeswehr', and with typical national pride, immediately looked to West German firms for a new military field car. After trials with prototypes from Auto Union, Goliath, and Porsche, the vehicle chosen was the 'Munga' from Auto Union, but under the DKW label.

In 1958/9 two 'Series II' Tempo Land-Rovers were built but the 'Bundeswehr' were not interested, and Herbert Vidal was forced to cease production.

Around 100 of the original Tempo Land-Rovers were transferred over to the 'Bundeswehr' where they remained in service until the mid-1960s. Vidal & Son did, however, continue as Land-Rover distributors from their Tempo-Werk GmbH in Hamburg.

CHAPTER 17 – Under Licence – Minerva and Tempo

The Tempo has no tail board access

THE 'SANTANA' LAND-ROVER

From 1952 CKD left-hand drive Land-Rovers were also assembled locally in Spain, but entirely from parts shipped out from Solihull. These vehicles were used by the Spanish armed forces. In 1955 negotiations began to take place with the newly-formed 'Metalurgica de Santa Ana' (MSA) of Madrid, concerning the possible manufacture of Land-Rovers under licence. Agreement was reached in 1956, but by this time Rover already had plans for a major update of the current model, and after careful consideration, it was decided that 'Santana' should not manufacture Land-Rovers until the advent of the new Series II model in 1958. This would ensure that all capital expenditure on the project at the new Linares factory, in the province of Jaen, would be put to the latest technology, rather than a vehicle Solihull would already have phased out by the time the MSA were ready to go into production. It was also in Rover's interest not to be seen producing outdated models, no matter where they were made. Minerva and Tempo Land-Rovers used 60% locally manufactured parts. Santana increased this proportion to 75%, with initial options of 2¼-litre petrol, or 2.0-litre diesel engines, the 2¼-litre diesel being introduced in 1962. Over the next ten years Santana steadily increased the number of locally manufactured parts used, until 1967, by which time their Land-Rover was 100% Spanish. Santana continued making 'Series' Land-Rovers until 1983.

CHAPTER 18
Bigger and Better More New Models

Avon Traction Mileage tyres were now standard equipment on 86-inch Land-Rovers

As early as 21 December 1948, the company Chairman, E. Ransome Harrison, felt able to announce to Rover's shareholders, that Land-Rovers would be *'...very much more than an additional source of production'*. The Land-Rover was officially now no longer a 'stop-gap' model and every opportunity could be taken to further its development. The original 80-inch wheelbase models continued in production for five years and their success became the firm basis on which bigger and better Land-Rovers would be developed as part of Rover's long-term future strategy.

Compared to the Jeep, the Land-Rover's lower centre of gravity, brought about by a combination of heavy chassis, light alloy body, and slightly wider track, gave it greater stability for cross-country work. The resultant 30° angle of safe operation was well beyond the nerve of most users, and is a major reason for the Land-Rover's continued popularity in competitive events even today, despite the ever increasing number of potential alternatives now available.

From the very start, however, there were those who would have preferred the Land-Rover to have had a greater carrying capacity, including the British Army. By the early 1950s various lengthened prototypes were already being considered. These included: a coachbuilt four-door station wagon, very much on the lines of the 'Tickford'-bodied Land-Rover Station Wagon already in production;

86-inch prototype stuck in the dunes near Newborough Warren, Anglesey

'I distinctly remember you saying "it'll go anywhere and do anything"' (note the one-piece wing inners and no front vent)

CHAPTER 18 – Bigger and Better – More New Models

THE 86in. WHEELBASE LAND-ROVER GIVES 25% MORE CAPACITY

The above illustration shows graphically just what the 6-inch extension in the Land-Rover wheelbase means. The rear load-carrying section is extended by 9 inches, giving a 25% increase in carrying capacity and more space for bulky loads. In addition, riding and road-holding qualities—always outstanding—are now even better.

Rover's publicity illustrating the new 86 model's 25% increase in load space

At Vancouver International Airport a Land-Rover Fire Engine stands by as an airliner starts its engines

an enclosed van; a military command car; a pick-up truck; a front-wheel-drive 'lo-loader'; and an articulated tractor unit.

All of these were considerably longer than the existing basic model and would most certainly have adversely affected the Land-Rover's general cross-country performance. Some form of compromise was needed, and was eventually reached when nine new prototypes on an 86-inch wheelbase were developed. They were given chassis numbers in the range P86/1–9. The first, P86/1, was road-registered on 1 June 1952. One was taken to Anglesey by Maurice Wilks in order to evaluate its performance, but was 'lost' at sea with the help of an encroaching tide. Just like the original centre steer Land-Rover and the second prototype of 1947, these were hybrid vehicles, cobbled together from a mixture of, in this case, 80-inch Land-Rover components and some scratch-built parts for the proposed 86-inch Land-Rover. Three examples are known to survive and all have modified 80-inch Land-Rover bulkheads. The rear body on one has much higher sides - the same as would later appear on the 107-inch Pick-up Truck.

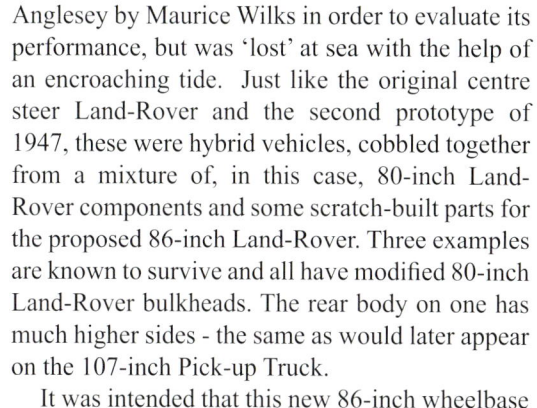

It was intended that this new 86-inch wheelbase should be the basis for all basic models for the foreseeable future, and by June 1952 a new jig had been completed for chassis construction. The final drawing for the model (No. 242736) was checked by Rover's General Manager, A.B. Smith, on 26 January 1953. Sixteen pre-production models were then completed between 19 February and mid-July. The first of these was road-registered in February, followed by three more in March: No.3, NAC 747 on 13 March; No.4, NAC 749 (which eventually became the first of a new breed of Station Wagons); and No.5, NAC 750, on 18 March. The last two were both used exclusively for publicity purposes, NAC 749 appearing in the new sales brochure for

LAND-ROVER – The Formative Years, 1947–1967

The new brochure for the 86 model

New Zealand advert in 'New Commonwealth', May 1954

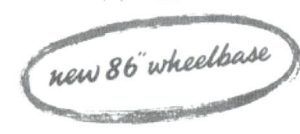

the Station Wagon, while NAC 750[1] appears in the first sales brochure for the basic model, and the company's first 'Land-Rover in Action' publicity booklet, as well as the leaflet on 'Agricultural Terms' and a full-page colour advertisement *'No Road - Except for Land-Rover'* which appeared in Country Life. Two other pre-production 86-inch models, Nos. 7 and 11, went to Royal estates. Just like the original 1948 pre-production Land-Rovers, all these 86-inch pre-production Land-Rovers have a number of specific features not found on any of the production vehicles.

In July 1953 the factory began full-scale production of the new 86-inch models, and the first production model, chassis No. 47100017 was completed on 3 September 1953. It was to have been chassis No. 46100001, and this appears in the first editions of the Parts Catalogue, TP155/A, dated July 1953, as previously '6' had stood for a production Land-Rover and '7' for a pilot run.[2] But someone decided, intentionally or otherwise, to continue with the existing 471… numbering sequence of the 86-inch pre-production models.

[1] *Rover kept this vehicle almost three years until December 1955, before it went to the Wilks brothers' brother-in-law, Sir John Black, on his retirement as MD of Standard-Triumph. It remained at his north Wales estate until 1961. Before its temporary acquisition by this author in 1987, it resided at Tyn-Y-Gonel, just a mile away from Red Wharf Bay.*

[2] *1950 prototype 2.0-litre model was serialised 071, '7' representing a prototype, 1952 production models becoming 261 series. The 86-inch prototypes became 471 series, with production models listed as 461 in the first edition Parts Catalogue. However, someone decided to keep 471 for production models too, so any numerical distinction was lost.*

226

CHAPTER 18 – Bigger and Better – More New Models

LAND-ROVER
(86" WHEELBASE)
PRICE, BASIC VEHICLE, £570 0s. 0d.

THE FOLLOWING ITEMS OF EQUIPMENT ARE SUPPLIED WITH EACH BASIC VEHICLE

Two aluminium doors with metal framed perspex sliding windows
Full hood with rear panel
Cushions and back-rests for two front seat passengers and driver
Spare wheel and tyre
Driving mirror
Starting handle, jack, wheelbrace and toolkit
Towing plate for rear draw bar
Pintle hook
Ventilators beneath windscreen glass
Windscreen wiper

OTHER ITEMS OF EXTRA EQUIPMENT AVAILABLE IF REQUIRED AS DETAILED IN LIST BELOW

When ordering, please state specification No. and full description of each item

Spec. No.	Description	£ s. d.
E.61	Rear Power Take-off Unit. Drive Section	27 0 0
E.3	Rear Pulley Unit, for use with E.61 (see note)	17 0 0
E.83	Centre Power Take-off	8 0 0
E.6a	Pulley and Fittings for use with E.83 (see note)	2 12 6
E.6b	Pulley and Fittings for use with E.83 when Rear Power Take-off is also fitted (see note)	2 12 6
E.17	Front Capstan Winch (see note)	40 0 0
E.11	Rear Capstan Winch for use with E.61 (see note)	29 0 0
E.62	Engine Speed Governor	15 15 0
E.8	Five Detachable Rim Road Wheels instead of Five Standard Road Wheels	10 0 0
E.10	Chaff Guard	2 6 6
E.25	Universal Joint Covers	1 3 0
E 28	Heavy-Duty Pintle Hook for Towing	1 13 0
E 29	Rubber Pads for Clutch aud Brake Pedals	8 6
E.63	Metal Top Roof without Side Windows	37 10 0
E.76	Truck type Cab for Driving Compartment (see note)	25 11 0
E.65	Combined Water Thermometer and Oil Pressure Gauge	6 16 0
E.71	Trafficators	2 15 0

P.T.O.

List of Extras continued.

Specification No.		£ s. d.
E.75	Rear Seats (see note)	13 3 0
E.79	Interior Heater and Blanking Cap E.42	8 15 0
E.80	Demisting Equipment (see note)	2 15 0
E.91	Windscreen Wiper for Passenger's Side	4 0 0
E.92	Hand Throttle Control	15 0
E.93	Spare Wheel Carrier on Bonnet	1 3 0
E.94	Trailer Lead Plug and Socket,	1 7 6
E.72	Extra Driving Mirror	15 0
E.101	Flyscreens for Dash Ventilators	17 6
E.67	Dunlop 6.00" × 16" T.28 "Trakgrip"	No extra charge
E.47	Dunlop 6.50" × 16" T.29a. "Super Trakgrip"	5 12 11
E.9	Dunlop 7.00" × 16" T.25 "Tractor Pattern"	17 14 6
E.35	Dunlop 7.00" × 16" "Fort"	17 14 6
E.98	Dunlop 7.00" × 16" T.29a "Super Trakgrip"	17 14 6

NOTES

E.3, E.6a, E.6b — When any of these units are ordered it is essential that an Engine Speed Governor E.62 is supplied also.

E.11, E.17 — When either of these units are ordered a Hand Throttle Control E.92 must also be fitted unless Engine Speed Governor E.62 has been specified.

E.75 — If 7.00 section tyres are to be fitted a Spare Wheel Carrier on Bonnet E.93 must also be supplied.

E.76 — When this unit is ordered it is essential that a Spare Wheel Carrier on Bonnet E.93 is supplied also.

E.80 — This extra cannot be used unless Heater E.79 is fitted.

The price quoted for Centre Power Take-Off does not include any alterations to the body which may have to be made before the Centre Power Take-Off can be put into use. If any alterations are made by The Rover Company Ltd. an extra charge will be made

The prices quoted for extra equipment are valid only if such extra equipment is fitted before the vehicle leaves the works. If ordered after delivery from works a fitting charge will be made. All prices and specifications quoted in this catalogue, of which this leaflet forms a part, are subject to alterations without notice. Prices are for delivery ex Works.

No allowance can be made in respect of any item of Basic Equipment not required.

The Land-Rover is subject to the guarantee conditions contained in the Guarantee Form issued by The Rover Company Ltd. The name Land-Rover is a Registered Trade Mark of The Rover Company Ltd.

Persons dealing in the Company's goods are not the agents of the Company and have no authority whatsoever to bind the Company by any expressed or implied undertaking.

The Land-Rover can be supplied as a mobile Welding Plant or as a Fire Engine.
Prices and particulars on application.

E. & O. E.   Printed in England   October, 1953

October 1953 Price list for the new 86 model

The new 86-inch model was considered by many to be far better suited to the tasks Land-Rovers were currently being asked to perform. Any mechanical weakness in the early vehicles had already been sorted out by the time engine capacity increased to 2.0-litres, a couple of years earlier. Now with the 86-inch wheelbase and the promise of even bigger Land-Rovers with still greater carrying capacity than the 86 model, just a matter of weeks away, customers were at last satisfied, even if the basic model did weigh 180 lbs more than its old 80-inch counterpart. There was no doubting the Land-Rover had moved on from Maurice Wilks' original vision of the 'Basic' model as purely an agricultural workhorse, laudable though this may have been at the time.

Many mechanical components from the 2.0-litre 80-inch model had been kept, and even the chassis frame was similar, if 9 inches longer. Every extra inch of body length went into the cargo area to enable Rover to claim a full 25% increase in carrying capacity in their sales literature. The rear axle had moved back 6 inches, but there was little change to the Land-Rover's overall appearance. To the casual observer at least, there was probably more to distinguish the first and last 80-inch models, with their different colours, grille and headlights, hood and door handles, than a late 2.0-litre 80-inch and the new 86 model.

The engine, ancillary equipment, gearbox, transfer box, differentials, rear half-shafts, front axle casings, swivel housings, steering relay, horn, grille, bumper, radiator and front panel, fuel pump, windscreen wipers, steering wheel, braking system, and wheels, all remained the same. On the body, rear 'D' lights, sidelights and headlights, were also the same, along with the standard colour, 'Bronze Green', for both body and chassis – at least for the time being – but practically everything else had changed.

Front wings reverted back to the early pattern with detachable outer panel, as used on the 1.6-litre model up to mid-1951. At the same time vulnerable wing front panels became a separate item for the very first time, to aid repair after accidental damage. New parallel-sided doors had a recessed door handle, and the front panel to the rear body became upright. The spare wheel still fitted in the rear body, but the awkward recess had gone, something the National Institute of Agricultural Engineering (NIAE) complained about on the pre-production models they tested several years earlier. Stronger galvanised steel top hat section strengthening ribs were used to support the load area instead of the previous simple 'Birmabright' angles, and vertical galvanised cappings were also added to the rear body corners. To cope with the increase in length, the number of rope hooks increased from two to three along the sides, while underneath a new exhaust system also became necessary, connected to a new manifold with offset connection.

In the cab, the new bulkhead had a full-width parcel shelf, with rolled top edge, to replace the previous grab rail. The centre section housed a large rectangular instrument panel with a large, car-size, speedometer paired to a matching new single

Special 'Hire Purchase' arrangements were introduced to help farmers purchase a new Land-Rover

1954 AA 'Highland Patrol'

This advertisement appeared in Country Life in June 1954; it depicts 86-inch pre-production Land-Rover No.5

CHAPTER 18 – Bigger and Better – More New Models

Chassis layout of latest 86-inch model

housing for the fuel gauge, ammeter and headlamp main beam warning light. Above the parcel shelf ventilators became a standard fitment, operated by a single lever on each side. Foot pedals were less upright and protruded through an entirely different toe-box arrangement, constructed from separate panels spot-welded together, instead of a massive single pressing, which previously resulted in the press die fracturing on an annual basis.

The new steering box was no longer mounted on the bulkhead, where previously metal fatigue dogged the mounting panel with any prolonged off-road use (all 'late 80' and military Land-Rovers were fitted with a special strengthening plate in an attempt to overcome the problem). Instead it was mounted on a strong rigid leg that bolted directly to the chassis.

Apart from the extra length, the most noticeable changes to the chassis were 'S'-shaped outriggers supporting the bulkhead, specifically designed to accommodate a repositioned brake master cylinder, now situated on the outside of the main frame for easier servicing. To give extra support to the tail board access, an additional central mounting plate was added to the rear crossmember, while underneath, the rear suspension had been uprated

HM Queen Elizabeth II and HRH the Duke of Edinburgh on tour

with 2½-inch wide springs all round, with new shock absorbers and bump stops to suit. The old deep fuel tank of the 80-inch model, which could foul obstacles off-road, was replaced by a longer shallower fuel tank that no longer required a heavy steel undershield.

From an engineering point of view, the most significant change was to be found in the Land-Rover's front axle. Here, the original 'Tracta' constant velocity drive joints had been replaced by a Hardy Spicer universal coupling of the type commonly found on propeller shafts. Gregoire's 'Tracta' joint was a far superior piece of engineering, but expensive to produce. The Hardy Spicer 'Hooke' joints, although not a true constant velocity joint, had the advantage of being mass-produced in their thousands for motor vehicles everywhere, with the consequence that service replacement parts were readily obtainable anywhere in the world. Their replacement was a fairly straightforward business involving only the joint itself, and not the complete drive shaft, as with the 'Tracta' joint. However, it is very rare for a properly lubricated 'Tracta' joint to give any sort of trouble even after 50 years of constant use.

Dunlop 'Trakgrip' T28 tyres had been standard equipment on 80-inch Land-Rovers for the past four years. These had a uni-direction tread well suited for general off-road use. But with the recognition that Land-Rovers were very much an on-road vehicle, at least as far as current use was concerned, the new 86-inch Land-Rover was provided with Avon Traction Mileage tyres. These were a non-directional tyre, so not only could they be moved around the vehicle to compensate tread wear, but they were also always facing the right direction when a spare was pressed into service. They were, however, a compromise: their off-road performance was not as good as the Dunlop Trakgrip tyre, but they were much better as a road tyre, and Avon were not slow to make full use of Rover's adoption of these tyres for Land-Rovers in contemporary advertisments.

Optional extras for the new 86 model included: flyscreens for the now standard ventilators; hand throttle, previously a standard fitment; a 35 mph speed limiter governor; and heavy-duty springs and shock absorbers – standard items on the Welder and Fire Engine – that were also available at the start of 86-inch production. But there was no longer any mention of either a Station Wagon or a Bullows compressor, not for the moment at least.

Perhaps the most surprising feature of the new model was its price. In September 1948 when the very first production models started to appear in Rover agents' showrooms, the Land-Rover listed

CHAPTER 18 – Bigger and Better – More New Models

New 86-inch 'Royal' Land-Rover

The interior was fully trimmed

The colour of the saluting vehicles was not always black

231

LAND-ROVER – The Formative Years, 1947–1967

New Land-Rover destined for the Post Office

Civil Defence Corps, Cumberland Division, operating at Great Dunfell, in the Lake District

A letter from Rover's Home Sales Manager, explaining to a customer that there is a 6-month waiting list for new Land-Rovers

CHAPTER 18 – Bigger and Better – More New Models

TELEPHONE
SHELDON 2461
2613

LONDON SHOWROOM
DEVONSHIRE HOUSE
PICCADILLY LONDON W1
TELEPHONE
GROSVENOR 3252
3253

BY APPOINTMENT TO THE LATE KING GEORGE VI
MANUFACTURERS OF LAND ROVERS

THE ROVER CO. LTD.

METEOR WORKS
SOLIHULL
BIRMINGHAM
ENGLAND

TELEGRAMS
ROVER SOLIHULL

LONDON SERVICE DEPOT
SEAGRAVE ROAD
FULHAM LONDON SW6

TELEPHONE
FULHAM 1221

ALL COMMUNICATIONS TO BE ADDRESSED TO THE COMPANY AND NOT TO INDIVIDUALS

REF. 2/EJ/MC   11th June 1954.

John Elliott Esq.,
Audley Park Secondary Modern School,
for Boys,
TORQUAY,
Devon.

Dear Sir,

   We thank you for your enquiry and have pleasure in enclosing herewith particulars of the Land Rover models.

   We have taken the liberty of asking our representatives Messrs. South Devon Garages Ltd., 5 Market Street, Torquay, to communicate with you as they will be pleased to give you any further information you require and probably some indication as to the delivery date in the event of an order being placed.

   Owing to our export commitments and Ministry requirements, we cannot promise delivery of further orders for approximately six months.

            Yours faithfully,
            THE ROVER COMPANY LTD.,

            Home Sales Manager

LAND-ROVER – The Formative Years, 1947–1967

Rover's own 86-inch Fire Engine

These Land-Rovers were converted by Dewar's Garage (India) Private Ltd. for daylight film projection in backward areas of India. They have 3 kw power units and 16 mm cinema equipment. The screen fits across the front of the canvas shroud.

CHAPTER 18 – Bigger and Better – More New Models

The 86 Station Wagon brochure, September 1953

at £450. A couple of months later, on 1 November, this increased to £540, when doors, seats, etc. all became part of the package. Then with the introduction of the 2.0-litre engine in September 1951 there was a further increase to £598. Now, with the introduction of 'Bigger and Better' 86-inch models, the price was actually reduced, to just £570.

Rover planned to increase output of the new model by 10,000 units over the previous 2.0-litre 80-inch model, and to encourage sales a special brochure was prepared, entitled:

'A LAND-ROVER for your Farm'
AGRICULTURAL TERMS

This offered Hire Purchase on *'...special Agricultural Terms'* as a means of acquiring an new Land-Rover 'By special arrangement with United Dominions Trust Limited', of Eastcheap in London. A down payment of *'...less than £125 in cash...'*, was required with *'...the remainder being spread over at twelve, eighteen, or twenty-four monthly payments'*.

Without records of the total number of Hire Purchase agreements under this scheme it is not possible to judge their impact on total sales, but sales certainly soared to record levels, showing clearly that the Land-Rover's current price represented excellent value for money. The new 86-inch model was so successful that despite a huge increase in productive capacity, output fell far short of demand, and it was not long before Mr Jackson, the Home Sales Manager, was obliged to send every potential customer a letter of explanation stating that:

Owing to our export commitment, and Ministry requirements, we cannot promise delivery of further orders for approximately six months.

The new model certainly had plenty of publicity. Britain's new young Queen, together with her husband, Prince Philip, Duke of Edinburgh, began their Royal Tour on 23 November 1953, just a few months after the Coronation. The whole world's eyes were upon them. After pausing for a brief stop in Canada and Bermuda, they flew to Jamaica where the liner 'Gothic' awaited. The tour could

235

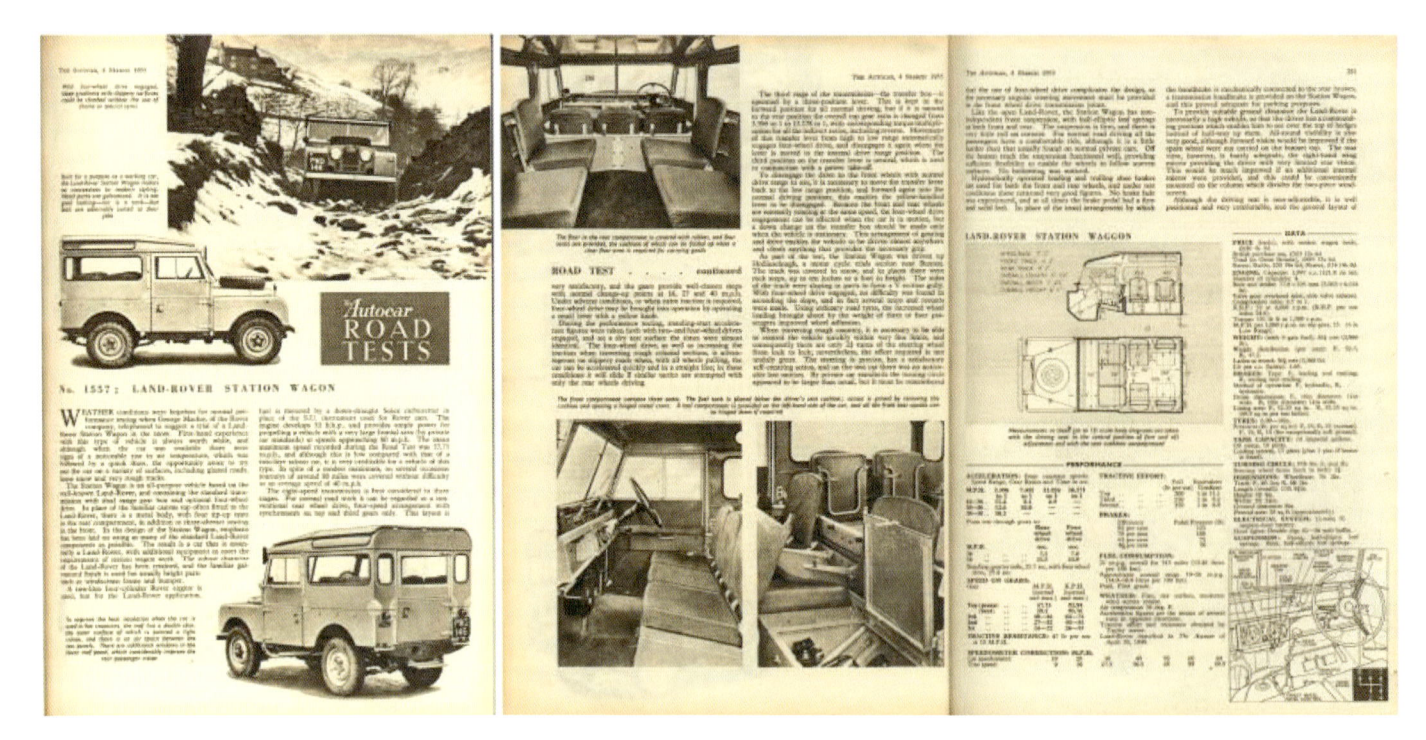

LAND-ROVER – The Formative Years, 1947–1967

The Station Wagon road test in 'The Autocar', 4 March 1955

not have been better timed to provide maximum publicity for Rover's latest Land-Rover, particularly overseas. The various High Commissioners for British territories overseas had all received new 86-inch Land-Rovers specially prepared for such an occasion, and the Queen and Prince Philip first used the new model in Jamaica, and then continued to do so throughout their tour.

The quality and finish to these 'Royal' vehicles was to the highest standard. Bodywork and leather upholstery were all black, along with the parts normally galvanised, apart from the bumper and grille, which were chrome-plated. These Land-Rover's were also given a front apron panel and valances below the door, well ahead of any other production model, and side screens had unique car-type quarter lights. Access to the high-sided rear compartment was by means of a folding step and lower door, similar to that of the new 86-inch Land-Rover Station Wagon soon to be introduced.

Further publicity for the new model was forthcoming when, on 30 November 1954, warlord and ex-Prime Minister, Sir Winston Churchill, was presented with a new Land-Rover for his 80th birthday. One of the Royal vehicles also received further publicity when it was again used in 1956

August 1954, the Station Wagon is equipped with flashing indicators using a twin filament bulb in side lights, and the brake light filament in the rear light

236

CHAPTER 18 – Bigger and Better – More New Models

The Station Wagon was initially equipped with semaphore trafficators

Station Wagon badge

Station Wagon price list, September 1953

LAND-ROVER
4-WHEEL DRIVE STATION WAGON

STANDARD EQUIPMENT SUPPLIED WITH EACH VEHICLE

Two side doors with Perspex sidescreens; rear door; cushions and backrests for two front seat passengers; backrests and folding seats for four passengers in rear compartment; spare wheel and tyre, 6.00″ × 16″; starting handle; driving mirror; direction indicators.

PRICE	£630	0 0
PURCHASE TAX	£263	12 6
TOTAL	£893	12 6

Subject to price and purchase tax current at time of delivery.

S.505　　　　　　　　　　　　　　　　　　　SEPT., 1953

LAND-ROVER – The Formative Years, 1947–1967

Rover made a number of useful adaptations for expeditionary and other roles

This Australian Scoop Aero Crop Sprayer has to be one of the most bizarre adaptations of the 107

for the Queen's 20-day, 2,000-mile tour of Nigeria. In March 1983 an original 86-inch 'Royal' Land-Rover was brought out of mothballs in Australia and used by Prince Charles and the late Lady Diana not long after their wedding. A few years later, in 1986, it was used again by the Queen and Prince Philip. Despite this 'Royal' vehicle's 33 years, it still looked immaculate, the only apparent update being a set of flashing indicators. At the same time, back home, desperate efforts were being made to 'Keep Land-Rover British', and this author had the dubious pleasure of driving his own 1948 pre-production model, L11, up to London to lead the huge, and temporarily successful, deputation to No.10 Downing Street.

Arabian American Oil Company 107

CHAPTER 18 – Bigger and Better – More New Models

Rover's Ecole Mobile complete with Brockhouse trailer

This 107 has a special coachbuilt body for use by the Post Office Engineering Department

LAND-ROVER – The Formative Years, 1947–1967

Aware of the need for a Land-Rover of even greater carrying capacity than the new 86 model, Rover made preparations for the introduction of an even longer Land-Rover, as any further extension of the existing basic model would have compromised its off-road capability. Earlier prototypes for a longer pick-up truck go back to 1950, but the current prototype was completed towards the end of 1952. When the 86 model was first introduced however, Rover had sufficient work on their hands just coping with current Land-Rover orders, military contracts, and the introduction of two new cars, the 'Rover 60' and 'Rover 90'. An immediate addition to the existing Land-Rover range at that time would simply extend the existing waiting list and jeopardise customer goodwill.

When it did finally arrived – 47200001 was completed on 14 October 1953 – Rover described the new 107-inch wheelbase Land-Rover as a more conventional 'pick-up' truck, but able to take *'...you and your load through where others fail'*. It was available with either Light Grey bodywork and blue wheels and chassis, similar to the Station Wagon, or RAF Blue bodywork and grey wheels, a choice also extended to the 86 Station Wagon. The first 1,150 107 chassis frames had a much simplified rear crossmember, with no provision for rear PTO equipment, but it was soon replaced by the standard back end once it was realised this was a misjudgement of user requirement. It was around this time that distance tubes for mounting the front winch were inserted into the No.2 crossmember as a standard fitment on the 107 'pick-up' truck.

Continuing Rovers now well-established practice of rationalisation, the new 107 model incorporated as many parts as possible from the existing 86 models, but an entirely new chassis frame was necessary, along with several other parts. These included: uprated suspension; larger tyres; longer rear propshaft; new exhaust system; and a new rear body. Although there was no increase in vehicle width, the rear body length was a full 6ft and had a depth of over 20 inches – extremely generous proportions when compared with the 3ft. 9in. length and 14 in. depth of a basic model. The optional truck cab of the basic model was a standard fitment and, together with the locking doors, gave the vehicle at a much higher level of security. There was no standard full-length hard top for the model, just hood sticks and a hood or a tonneau cover, both available as optional extras.

The Pick-up Truck front view showing the high sides

Pick-up Truck had a very useful cargo area

CHAPTER 18 – Bigger and Better – More New Models

Pick-up Truck brochure introducing the new 107 model

However, Rover occasionally fitted, to special order, a metal top behind the cab, using modified panels from the 86 hard top.

The 'Pick-up Truck' listed at £635 when introduced, and was available with 'De Luxe' trim for an additional £20. This utilised various parts later shared with the 86 Station Wagon, but the one-piece seat back in checker patterned vyanide was not shared elsewhere at this time. Most of the options for the 86 model applied, and in addition, a spare wheel cover in blue was offered.

With the demise of the 80-inch 'Tickford' Station Wagon in 1950, Maurice Wilks was concerned that Rover should still have some sort of civilised vehicle suitable for use by the countryman, on the lines of a conventional shooting brake or estate car. The first efforts in this direction resulted in a rather slab-sided affair constructed in early 1952 and nicknamed 'The Greenhouse'. The official description was 'Road Rover' and, as the name suggests, it was based on the P4 'Rover 75' car, with only a handful of Land-Rover components. The Road Rover was a long way off production at this stage, and it soon became apparent that a new Land-Rover Station Wagon would be needed if Rover were to make any impact in this rapidly expanding sector of the British car market. The Road Rover was nothing to do with Land-Rovers, and Spen King has since confirmed that 'Four-wheel-drive was never part of the equation', and that 'The Road Rover was simply an experiment that never made it into production'.

By September 1953, as the 86 model reached volume production levels, it was decided to reintroduce the Land-Rover Station Wagon. This time it would not be a coachbuilt vehicle, but on

Rare 1954 coachbuilt 107 Station Wagon at Anglesey

Bodywork was not unlike Rover's earlier Tickford Station Wagon

lines similar to the existing hard top option with side windows and rear seats – previously offered only to overseas buyers as an inexpensive alternative after the demise of the original 'Tickford'-bodied 86 Station Wagon. This time the job would be done properly. Fixed side windows ran the full length of the rear body with quarter lights at the rear and alpine lights in the roof. A tropical roof panel, roof ventilators, and an interior light were also added. The normal tail board and rear-opening lid were replaced by a proper two-piece door, the lower part of which was actually a converted right-hand door. The top glazed section could then be easily removed for additional ventilation or carrying long loads. Also at the rear a folding step replaced the usual agricultural drawbar, and all doors and windows could be properly locked.

Inside, the Land-Rover Station Wagon was extremely civilised compared to a basic model, with scuttle and doors all trimmed in blue along with the front floor. In the rear a rubber mat was provided, and the four individual rear seats could be tipped up to provide ample room for bulky loads. Outside, semaphore direction indicators were mounted on the windscreen pillar as standard equipment, and the spare wheel was mounted on the bonnet. Extras included a radio, and a Smith's recirculating heater for both front and rear passenger compartments.

Listed at £630 + £263/12/6 Purchase Tax, £893/12/6 in all, it was substantially dearer than a basic model, but the new method of construction still made it £120 or 16% cheaper than the original 1948 'Tickford'-built model. The colour of the new Station Wagon was not the usual Land-Rover

CHAPTER 18 – Bigger and Better – More New Models

LAND-ROVER PICK-UP TRUCK
(107" WHEELBASE)

PRICE, BASIC VEHICLE, £635 0s. 0d.

THE FOLLOWING ITEMS OF EQUIPMENT ARE SUPPLIED WITH EACH BASIC VEHICLE

Truck type drivers cab.
Two aluminium doors with metal framed perspex sliding windows
Cushions and back-rests for two front seat passengers and driver
Spare wheel and tyre 7.00" × 16"
Driving mirror
Starting handle, jack, wheelbrace and toolkit
Towing plate for rear draw bar
Pintle hook
Ventilators beneath windscreen glass
Windscreen wiper
Door locks

✱

PRICE, "DE-LUXE TRIM" VEHICLE, £655 0s. 0d.

THE FOLLOWING ITEMS ARE SUPPLIED WITH EACH "DE-LUXE TRIM" VEHICLE
as for "Basic Vehicle" in addition to:

Roof headlining of plastic covered felt
Leather cloth casings fitted to rear of cab, doors and dashboard parcel shelves
Door pockets
Padded waistlines and arm rests
Floor carpet of plastic covered felt
One piece seat squab
Squab and seat cushions upholstered in plastic woven fabric
Roof lamp with switch combined

✱

OTHER ITEMS OF EXTRA EQUIPMENT AVAILABLE IF REQUIRED AS DETAILED IN LIST BELOW

Please state specification No. and full description of each item when ordering

Specification No.		£	s.	d.
E.184	Rear Power Take-off Unit. Drive Section	31	10	0
E.3	Rear Pulley Unit, for use with E.184 (see note)	17	0	0
E.83	Centre Power Take-off	8	0	0
E.6a	Pulley and Fittings for use with E.83 (see note)	2	12	6
E.6b	Pulley and Fittings for use with E.83 when Rear Power Take-off is also fitted (see note)	2	12	6

S.507   P.T.O.

List of Extras continued.

Specification No.		£	s.	d.
E.185	Front Capstan Winch (see note)	40	0	0
E.62	Engine Speed Governor (see note)	15	15	0
E.74	Oil Cooler Equipment (see note)	25	15	6
E.10	Chaff Guard	2	6	6
E.25	Universal Joint Covers	1	3	0
E.28	Heavy-Duty Pintle Hook for Towing	1	13	0
E.29	Rubber Pads for Clutch and Brake Pedals		8	6
E.175	Hood, Hoodsticks and Tie Bars. Without Side Windows	21	0	0
E.176	Body Cover Sheet	5	0	0
E.65	Combined Water Thermometer and Oil Pressure Gauge	6	16	0
E.71	Trafficators	2	15	0
E.79	Heater, (only)	8	15	0
E.80	Demisting Equipment (see note)	2	15	0
E.91	Windscreen Wiper for Passenger's Side	4	0	0
E.92	Hand Throttle Control		15	0
E.94	Trailer Socket, Plug and Lead	1	7	6
E.182	Spare Wheel Cover	1	7	6
E.72	Extra Driving Mirror		15	0
E.101	Flyscreens for Dash Ventilators		17	6
E.98	Dunlop 7.00" × 16" T.29a "Super Trakgrip" Tyre		No extra charge	
E.9	Dunlop 7.00" × 16" T.25 "Tractor Pattern" Tyre		No extra charge	

✱

NOTES

E.3 ⎱
E.6a ⎬ When any of these units are ordered it is essential that an Engine Speed Governor E.62 is supplied also.
E.6b ⎰

E.185   A Hand Throttle Control E.92 must be fitted with this unit unless Engine Speed Governor E.62 is fitted or ordered.

E.62   A Hand Throttle Control E.92 must **NOT** be fitted with this unit.

E.74   An Oil Temperature Gauge is supplied with this extra and the following standard parts are replaced: Oil Pump Assembly, Radiator Block (incorporating a special high pressure Radiator Cap), Fan and Oil Sump.

E.80   This extra cannot be used unless Heater E.79 is fitted.

The prices quoted for extra equipment are valid only if such extra equipment is fitted before the vehicle leaves the works. If ordered after delivery from works a fitting charge will be made. All prices and specifications quoted in this catalogue, of which this leaflet forms a part, are subject to alterations without notice. Prices are for delivery ex Works.

No allowance can be made in respect of any item of Basic Equipment not required.

The Land-Rover is subject to the guarantee conditions contained in the Guarantee Form issued by The Rover Company Ltd. The name Land-Rover is a Registered Trade Mark of The Rover Company Ltd.

Persons dealing in the Company's goods are not the agents of the Company and have no authority whatsoever to bind the Company by any expressed or implied undertaking.

B. & O. E.   *Printed in England*   March, 1954

---

107 price list, March 1954

green but 'Light Grey', the same as the '107' Pick-up Truck. This colour has a slightly pinkish hue provided by a *'...trace of Turkey Red Oxide'* in the mix. The chassis, wheel rims and interior were all in contrasting 'RAF Blue'. The new colour scheme certainly providing a refreshing departure from the traditional military bronze green. Very soon 86 Station Wagons also became available in 'RAF Blue' too.

Apart from colour, there is no obvious distinction in Rover's despatch records to identify the new 86 Station Wagon from any other 86 model. The first 'grey' 'Home' model listed is 47102179, completed on 9 April 1954 and 'despatched out' to Rover's 'Experimental Department.' It was closely followed by 47102180, 47102187 (which went to Rover's Publicity Department), 47102194, 47102195 and 47102916. Three of these 'grey' Land-Rovers – 47102179, 47102194 and 47102195 – have been confirmed as Station Wagons today. This all ties in nicely with there being no reference to any Station Wagon in any sales catalogues, technical publications, or parts catalogues, prior to this date.

By comparison the Welder, priced at £915, and Fire Engine, priced at £905, were both available from the beginning of the 1954 Season. Both were fairly straightforward additions to the range, as they used the same equipment left over from the previous season's 80-inch models. The new Station Wagon model was a more complicated affair, needing several specialist parts, and so had to wait for the 107 'Pick-up Truck' to be introduced first. This delayed its introduction until the following spring, which was half way through the new season.

CHAPTER 19
A Sweeter 2.0-Litre The Mid-1950s

On 28 September 1949 Rover launched their new P4 'Rover 75'. This was the car designed to take them into the second half of the 20th Century and was powered by their existing 2,103cc 6-cyl. engine, as used in their previous P3 car. By 1950 Rover were already experimenting with over-board versions of their P3 F-head i.o.e. (inlet-over-exhaust) engines, used in both cars and Land-Rovers since 1948. The company tried increasing capacity of the 'four' from 1,595cc to 1,997cc, and the 'six' from 2,103cc to 2,638cc.

By now autobahns were already in use in mainland Europe, and although touring the Continent may have been restricted to the rich and famous, any new car of quality would be expected to be capable of running for long periods at high revs. Under test, however, over-boring their P3 car engine produced a significant side effect – scuffing of the bores – when driven for long periods at high revs. Rover therefore decided that the P4 car would have to make do with the 6-cyl. engine's existing 2.1-litre capacity, at least for the time being.

The Land-Rover, on the other hand, had only ever used the 4-cyl. engine and, as a workhorse, was unlikely to be subjected to prolonged high rev. use. After experimenting with a batch of 50 prototype 2.0-litre engines installed into Land-Rovers in early 1950 – the 071… Series – to prove the point (07100001 was registered as JUE 492 by Warwickshire authority on 1/2/1950), the over-board 4-cyl. engine was officially introduced into all new Land-Rovers in the late summer of 1951. Today, these 2.0-litre Land-Rovers are usually referred to as the 'late 80'.

Work then immediately began on redesigning both P3 engines in order to overcome the problem

The latest brochure for the 86 and 107 models

CHAPTER 19 – A Sweeter 2.0-Litre – The Mid-1950s

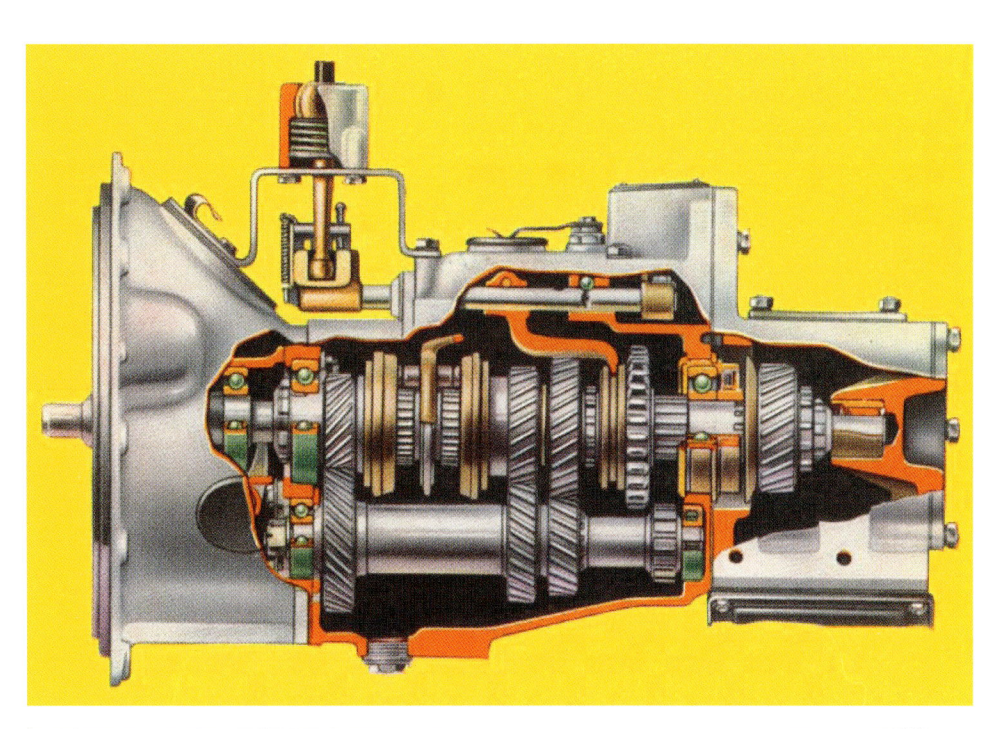

Cross-section of the latest gearbox

The new 'spread-bore' 2.0-litre engine

of scuffing. The resulting new 'spread-bore' (SB) 2.0-litre 4-cyl. version of the engine was not tested in the Land-Rover, as the previous 2.0-litre engine had been, but instead was put into the P4 car and prototype Road Rovers in 1952. Test results proved satisfactory, and by mid-1953 two new 'SB' versions of the engine were in production, a 2.6-litre 'six' for use in a new P4 saloon car, the 'Rover 90', and a 2.0-litre version for use in Rover's first four-cylinder version of the P4 car, the 'Rover 60'. It did not immediately go into the recently launched 86 and 107 Land-Rovers. For the time being, the original P4 'Rover 75' continued as before, but was eventually given a 2.2-litre short stroke version of the new 'six' in 1954.

After the first 2,000 4-cyl. units in the new 'Rover 60' proved satisfactory, the 'SB' engine was installed in the new '86 & 107' Land-Rovers in August 1954, continuing Rover's policy of not introducing an entirely new model and engine all at the same time. The 'Rover 60' saloon car was given an aluminium cylinder head with integral manifold and SU carburettor, producing 60 bhp at 4000 rpm. The Land-Rover, on the other hand, kept the same iron cylinder head and Solex carburettor which had been in use since 1948, and produced only 52 bhp at 4000 rpm. In most other respects these engines were identical.

When asked why the iron cylinder head had been retained in the Land-Rover, Maurice Wilks' own comment was that it not only kept costs down, but even more important, as *'...there was no way of telling what liquids might be used as coolant in distant parts...'*, iron would be less likely to corrode than aluminium. His point was proved much closer to home when, in the UK, calcium chloride-based antifreezes of the time, introduced into the coolant system, began eating away alloy components.

Maurice Wilks also believed the advantages of light alloy were exaggerated, the only significant gain being a saving in weight (its higher thermal conductivity also enables it to disperse heat more rapidly). An iron head was also less likely to distort from overheating – probably the deciding factor as far as the Land-Rover was concerned. As for the Solex carburettor, wartime service had shown it able to cope in situations where the carburettor was far from horizontal. The Solex carburettor was therefore preferred for all off-road use, as under extreme conditions, the concern was that the piston in an SU carburettor might jam on the side of the suction chamber and result in 'engine screaming'.

To coincide with the introduction of the 1955 model, a new parts catalogue, TP/155/B, dealing with the new engine, was published in August 1954. The general specification of this latest version of Rover's F-head engine remained pretty much as before, but it had undergone a number of modifications. As well as more evenly spaced bores to provide better cooling, bores were no longer chromed, as the hard surface had caused a certain amount of difficulty when re-boring. A new crankshaft and improved rear main bearing and oil seal were also used, together with a new oil pump, increasing pressure from 35–50 lbs/sq.in. to 55–65 lbs/sq.in.

The previous ZS1 disposable external bypass oil filter was replaced by a new full-flow paper element system, better able to remove abrasive particles from oil before it reached the bearings, now that all oil circulating around the engine was being filtered. With bores no longer chromed, this was particularly important, and did not happen with the old bypass system.

The previous shrouded 'inboard' Lucas M418G-type G76 starter motor was also replaced by a later, simpler design that required a new flywheel and housing. The pre-cleaner on the AC 'Sphinx' air cleaner was also dropped. Other modifications included new seals on the gearbox selector shafts, and 'pork-pie' rear lights in place of the 'D' lights, to conform with new Lighting Regulations introduced from 1 October 1954.

In 1955 a number of mid-season modifications were introduced. Special distance tubes were inserted in the rear crossmember to take a ball hitch or towing pintle direct, or lower down on a new standard drop plate that replaced the agricultural drawbar – now optional. On Station Wagons, semaphore direction indicators gave way to flashing indicators, using an ingenious system whereby a panel switch, fed from the brake lights, operated the brake lights normally when in the 'off' position. As soon as this switch was turned 'left' or 'right', the brake light circuit would be interrupted on that side, and fed instead to the flasher unit, causing that brake light to flash. On the front wing a new Lucas 488 twin-filament light unit also flashed. Although a little confusing to other road users, this system remains legal today on any vehicle first registered before 1 January 1965, but it did rather make a nonsense of the three-pin trailer plug then in use on the Land-Rover.

The Land-Rover Fire Engine was also updated with a new 'KSB' pump, replacing the original 'Pegson' unit, to conform with the new BSS336/1954 regulations in force. The original 'Bullows' compressor, which had previously disappeared along with the 80-inch Land-Rover in 1953, now suddenly reappeared under 'Miscellaneous Extras' in this latest edition of the Parts Catalogue, but not quite as before. Instead, the unit was now installed towards the rear of the Land-Rover and driven by a rear-mounted, rather than a centre-mounted, PTO unit. This arrangement was also extended to the 'Lincoln' Welder. By mounting such equipment in this way, it was no longer necessary to alter the Land-Rover's bodywork, enabling the vehicle to be returned to normal duties if this equipment was removed. From April 1956 Rover also offered to fit, at the factory, auxiliary charging units suitable for two-way radio systems, to any model from 1948 on.

In 1954 the Oxford and Cambridge Trans-African Expedition used two new 86-inch Station Wagons for a four-month trek from London to Cape Town and back, a distance of some 20,000 miles. A year later in 1955 two similar Station Wagons were again used for the Oxford and Cambridge Far Eastern Expedition, an overland journey to Singapore – and back – covering a distance of some 32,000 miles. Certainly a good road test for both the 86 Station Wagon and the new engine.[1] In 1955 the Station Wagon also became the subject of a very favourable Road Test published in 'The Autocar' on 4 March 1955. Described as *'...an outstanding car that can be driven almost anywhere'* with *'...commendable average speeds*

---

[1] *For a gripping first-hand account of this journey see 'First Overland' by Tim Slessor, published by George Harrap, 1957. Republished in 2005 by Signal Books at £12.99.*

CHAPTER 19 – A Sweeter 2.0-Litre – The Mid-1950s

The 86-inch Fire Engine

Fire Engine side view

Fire Engine rear view

LAND-ROVER – The Formative Years, 1947–1967

The Oxcam team alongside their two 86 Station Wagons and kit

on normal roads' and *'...a first-rate machine of which the engineers of The Rover Company may be proud'*. It seemed clearly able to fulfil the role of the proposed Road Rover without the need for any further additional development, factory space, or special tooling.

Nevertheless, the idea of the Road Rover was not yet abandoned and the programme would soon be updated, with all future thoughts on the model confined to the more elegant Series 2 prototypes, in a bid to enter the rapidly expanding estate car market in which Rover had yet to compete. The Series 2 prototype Road Rovers looked far more like something out of Ford's rather than Rover's stable. Early examples continued with the 2.0-litre engine, but later examples used a new prototype $2\frac{1}{4}$-litre 'Series II' Land-Rover engine, along with a mixture of a 3.0-litre car and other Land-Rover components, all clad in the usual light alloy bodywork. Designed with an eye to the North American and Australian markets, by British standards these were large vehicles. After the successful introduction of the Series II Land-Rover Station Wagon on a 'long' chassis in November 1958, the Road Rover project was postponed indefinitely in April 1959.

In the mid-1950s there was certainly no shortage of ideas on the Land-Rover front at the Solihull factory. In August 1954, Rover registered a prototype '10-seater' Station Wagon model, followed by the first Forward Control model, a prototype '12-seater' minibus, which had two extra small seats situated in the rear so as to exempt it from Purchase Tax. This vehicle's bodywork, built by Saunders Roe, was in GRP (fibreglass). It was eventually sold to Marples Ridgeway and Partners on 12 December 1955. That was also the same day that the Wilks' brother-in-law, Sir John Black, registered an 86-inch pre-production Land-Rover, No.5, NAC 750, in his name, having acquired it from Rover after his enforced retirement as MD at Standard-Triumph. Ernest Marples MP, the then Minister for Transport, had the Saunders Roe Forward Control Land-Rover delivered to Switzerland in time for Christmas, where he apparently used it to take his new bride on honeymoon. As the first Forward Control prototype, Rover retained the right to re-acquire the vehicle at any time.

On 7 November 1955 the first 10-seater Station Wagon on the 107 chassis rolled off the production line. It was a right-hand-drive 'Export' model and, a few days later, headed for Puzey & Payne, Rover's main agent in Salisbury, Southern Rhodesia (now Zimbabwe). A month later on 14 December 1955 the first 'Home' model was completed, and on 29 December was delivered to Henlys' showroom in Piccadilly, Rover's main agent in London, just in time for the New Year.

CHAPTER 19 – A Sweeter 2.0-Litre – The Mid-1950s

Land-Rovers at Kathmandu

The route taken by the Oxford and Cambridge Far Eastern Expedition

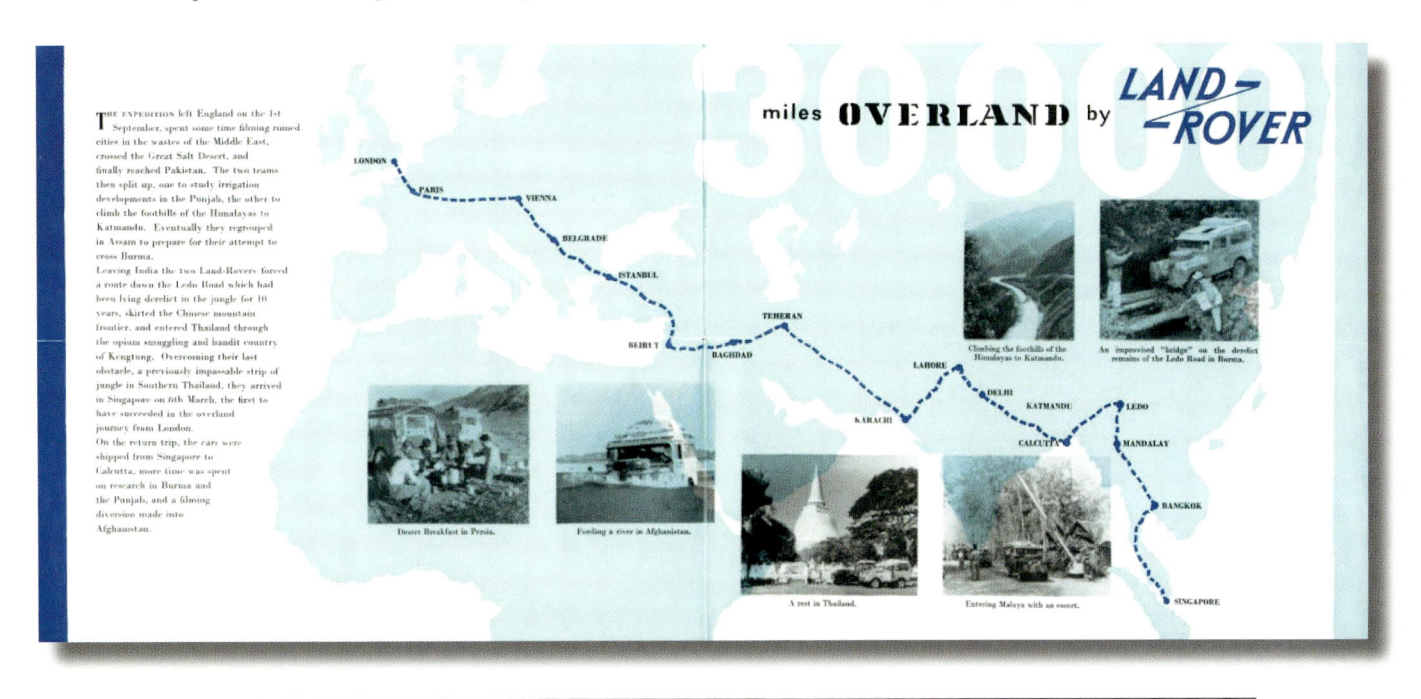

The 10-seater Station Wagon was a much more complicated adaptation than the 86-inch Station Wagon had been. It required modifications to the standard 107-inch chassis frame, the suspension points, exhaust and steering relay lever, rear axle casing, front road springs and bottom plates, shock absorbers, and wing top panels, and had a new stronger steel radiator mounting panel which then became standard on '88 & 109' models. The chassis was also given a simple box section rear crossmember, as the centre compartment's floor section blocked the way for any rear PTO driveshaft. To prevent body roll, spring hangers were positioned outside the chassis rails. The rear body of the 107 model was also extensively redesigned to take the extra doors and transverse seating. Other items peculiar to the model included: one-piece back rest; centre trim and mat; rear side panels, and roof (no full-length hard top was generally available for either the 107 or the later 109 'Series I' Land-Rovers, which had only been marketed as 'Pick-up Trucks').

Several items were able to be taken from the 86 Station Wagon with little or no modification, while other parts were already available as optional extra extras for the 107 Pick-up Truck. These included: the rear door top and step; glazing and ventilators; floor mats; some of the interior trim; tropical roof panel; and optional full-width seat backs and rear seats. The new centre compartment transverse seating had been cleverly designed to fold down into a double bed, with a little assistance from the front seat squabs, and the overall colour scheme was again Light Grey or RAF Blue.

LAND-ROVER – The Formative Years, 1947–1967

The Land-Rover 'bus' chassis during development

An extensive road test of the 10-seater carried out by 'The Motor' on 19 July 1956 concluded that *'Most buyers of the Land-Rover Station Wagon probably do not choose it – there is nothing else available which will do so much in such difficult conditions, so they buy it almost inevitably'*. At the time, this statement was an accurate description of the situation, for there was little about its 'Meccano'-like appearance – so much part of the vehicle's appeal today – to commend it to the styling of the 1950s, just an ability to cope with the job in hand. Not until the advent of the Series II model in 1958 did the 10-seater really find the same level of sophistication existing in the 86 model. It listed at £790 plus £397/7/- Purchase Tax, a total of £1186/7/- in the home market, and sales were promising.

By the mid-1950s, there was no question that the Land-Rover had moved even further away from the agricultural machine Maurice Wilks originally envisaged.

With new models such as the 10-seater Station Wagon, it was clear the role of agriculture was no longer dominant. In acknowledgement of this fact the agricultural drawbar which had been supplied as standard equipment with every new Land-Rover since 1948 was finally dropped in January 1955.

The Land-Rover's PTO system was, for most agricultural purposes, outmoded from the outset, as the only means of de-clutching the drive in the likelihood of mobile apparatus becoming fouled also stopped the vehicle dead in its tracks, making entanglement almost a certainty, instead of pulling now stationary apparatus, clear.

529 OP undergoig road tests in the snow

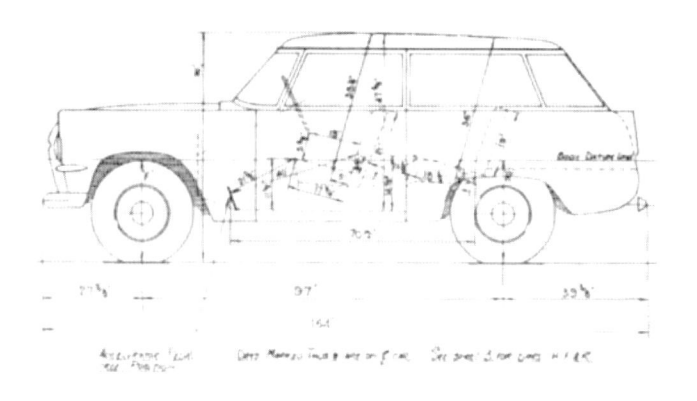

Dimensional details of the Road Rover, February 1957

250

CHAPTER 19 – A Sweeter 2.0-Litre – The Mid-1950s

The Minister of Transport, Earnest Marples, about to set off with his new bride

The Land-Rover 'bus' in GRP

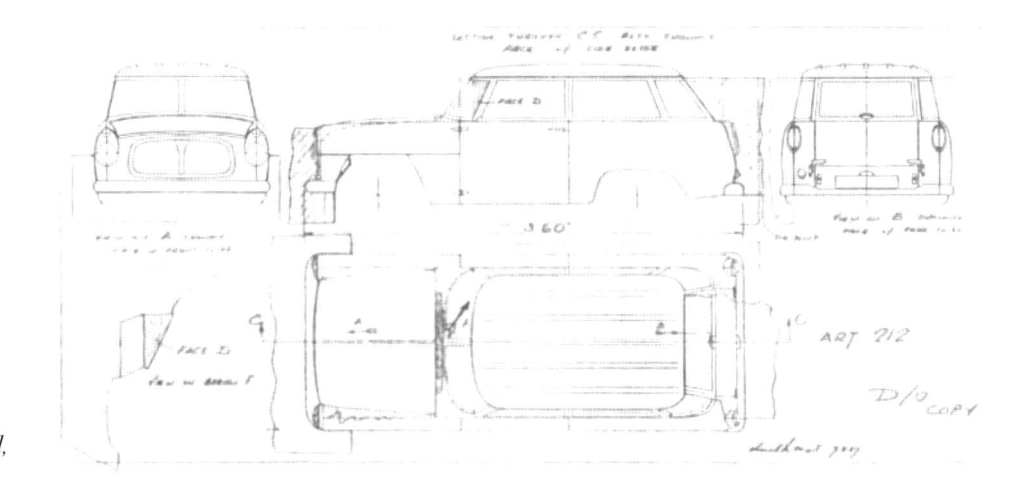

Last drawing of the Road Rover before the project was abandoned, February 1957

251

LAND-ROVER – The Formative Years, 1947–1967

86" WHEELBASE STATION WAGON

7 Seater version of the famous 4 wheel drive Land Rover

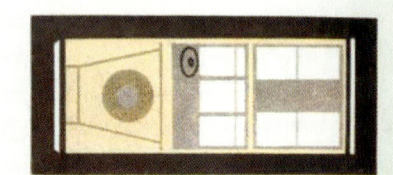

As an alternative passenger or goods carrier the Land-Rover 86 in. Station Wagon has great appeal in territories where tough conditions are likely to be met. It will, for instance, travel smoothly and comfortably on made-up roads, deal easily with untended tracks, or with four-wheel drive engaged, take to the rough with a facility achieved by no other make of vehicle.

As a passenger carrier the Station Wagon is a seven seater. Accommodation is provided in the front compartment for three people, while four fold-up seats are fitted in the body, these being easily accessible through a wide door at the rear. With the seats folded, excellent floor space is available for the transport of goods and equipment of every kind.

Toughly built and having a generous ground clearance, the Land-Rover 86 in. wheelbase Station Wagon is ever ready for day to day duty or high adventure in the inaccessible places of the world.

The Canadian Cockshutt Plough company had solved this problem in 1947 by the introduction of the live PTO, using two clutches and a two-stage pedal, the first movement disengaging only the PTO drive, allowing the tractor to pull any mechanical apparatus clear. By the early 1950s this arrangement was commonplace throughout North America and was now rapidly finding its way into British agricultural equipment. On top of this, more and more tractors were being provided with a two-speed transfer box to improve road performance. Both these developments were rapidly moving the Land-Rover ever further from being a possible motive power source around the farm. Fortunately, however, even from the beginning, the Land-Rover was never dependent on this idea for sales.

By the mid-1950s the Land-Rover had certainly proved itself to be the 'go-anywhere' and 'do anything' vehicle Rover made it out to be, and as the range of models expanded, government departments just about everywhere were taking the vehicle. Already more than a dozen and a half nations were now using Land-Rovers for their armed forces, and half as many again had them as police vehicles. The Land-Rover's role as military and paramilitary field car and patrol vehicle had seen an enormous expansion, particularly at home, where 40% of sales were to the Ministry of Supply. References to agriculture in the latest sales literature for 1956 had now become conspicuous by their absence, compared to the publicity given the new models when they were first introduced in 1953.

This Brochure shows the latest 86 Station Wagon

The latest AA Patrol Land-Rover, April 1955

252

CHAPTER 19 – A Sweeter 2.0-Litre – The Mid-1950s

Experimental Station Wagon, July 1955

The interior seating could be converted into a useful bed

Keeping up the 'Go Anywhere' image with this latest Land-Rover

This colourful 107 Station Wagon brochure would put the new model on many a wish list

Wide doors give excellent access to the back seat which will comfortably accommodate three people.

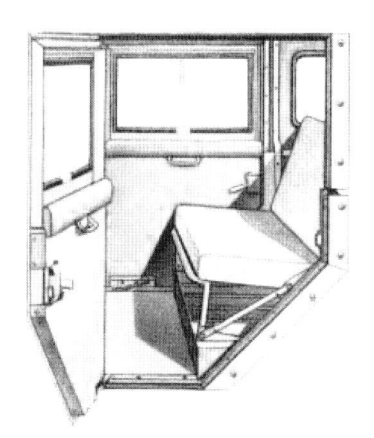

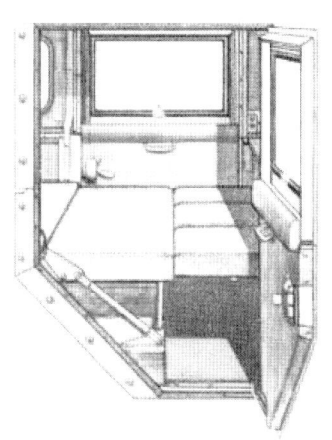

With the rear seat squab folded backward a bed can be made by redisposing the cushions and squab of the front seat.

Additional seats mounted on the rear wheel boxes will carry four passengers, two on each side.

LAND-ROVER LONG STATION WAGON

253

LAND-ROVER – The Formative Years, 1947–1967

The annual 'open day' for Rover's workers and their families to celebrate the success of the Land-Rover took place on a Saturday afternoon

In the 1953–54 season when new '86 & 107' Land-Rovers were first introduced, Land-Rover sales rose from 18,570 to 20,135. With a new wider range of models to choose from, the following season's sales then rose to an all-time high for 'Series I' Land-Rovers of 28,882. The extra 8,000 vehicles sold was the equivalent of total Land-Rover output for the first year of production,1948–49. This increase in output was made possible by the acquisition of two additional premises at Perry Barr in 1952, and then Percy Road in 1954. The 1955–56 season was almost as good at 28,365, and took total sales of Land-Rovers from 1948 to 157,036.

While the range of models had expanded, prices for the first two seasons of '86 & 107' models were held constant. But in mid-1955, when the vehicle numbering system changed, the price of a 'Basic' model was increased from £570 to £585, and the 'Pick-up Truck' from £635 to £655. Twelve months later in July 1956, further price increases came with the introduction of the '88 & 109' models for the later part of the season, a Basic model now costing £615, and the Pick-up Truck £690. The 7-seater Station Wagon increased from £893 to £1,029 over the same three-year period.

TWD 713, was the '10-seater' used for The Motor road test

The 10-seat road test published in The Motor, 18 July 1956

CHAPTER 19 – A Sweeter 2.0-Litre – The Mid-1950s

The Motor Road Test No. 18/56

Make: Rover **Type:** Land Rover "107" Station Wagon de Luxe
Makers: The Rover Co. Ltd., Solihull, Birmingham.

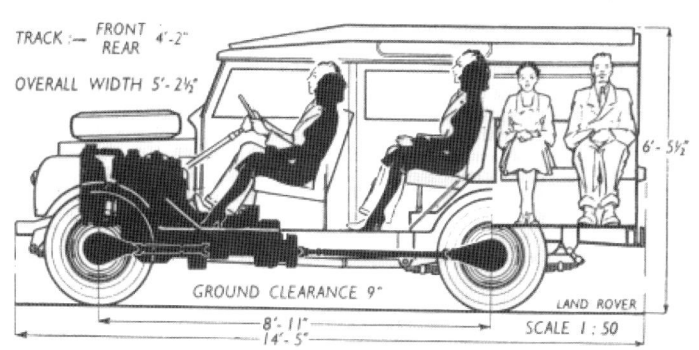

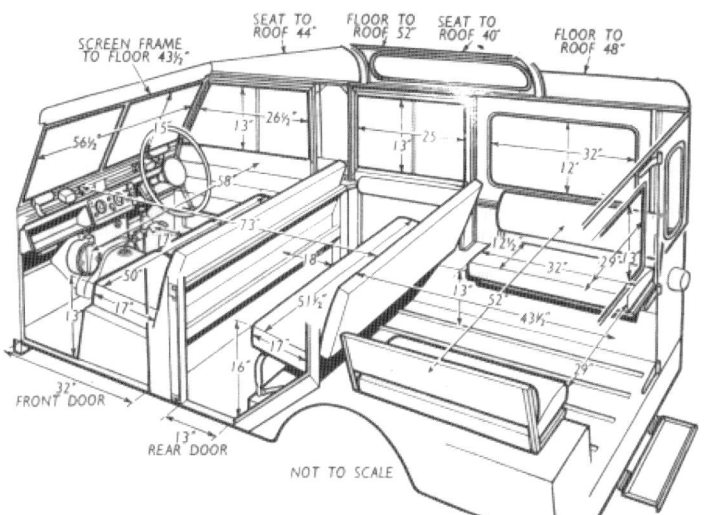

Test Data

CONDITIONS. Mild, showery weather with gusty wind (dry for brake test). Temperature 59-62°F., barometer 30.0 in. Hg. Smooth tarred road surface. Standard-grade pump fuel.

INSTRUMENTS

Speedometer at 30 m.p.h.	4% slow
Speedometer at 60 m.p.h.	2% slow
Distance recorder	3% slow

MAXIMUM SPEEDS

Flying Quarter Mile
- Mean of four opposite runs .. 58.1 m.p.h.
- Best time equals .. 60.4 m.p.h.

"Maximile" Speed (Timed ¼-mile after one mile accelerating from rest)
- Mean of four opposite runs .. 57.2 m.p.h.
- Best time equals .. 58.8 m.p.h.

Speed in gears
- Maximum speed in 3rd gear .. 51 m.p.h.
- Maximum speed in 2nd gear .. 37 m.p.h.
- Maximum speed in low top gear .. 31 m.p.h.
- Maximum speed in low 3rd gear .. 22 m.p.h.

FUEL CONSUMPTION

- 26½ m.p.g. at constant 30 m.p.h.
- 23 m.p.g. at constant 40 m.p.h.
- 19½ m.p.g. at constant 50 m.p.h.
- Overall consumption for 998 miles, 55 gallons = 18.2 m.p.g. (15.5 litres/100 km.)
- Fuel tank capacity 10 gallons.

ACCELERATION TIMES Through Gears

0-30 m.p.h.	7.8 sec.
0-40 m.p.h.	14.7 sec.
0-50 m.p.h.	28.9 sec.
Standing Quarter Mile	26.2 sec.

ACCELERATION TIMES on Two Upper Ratios

	Top	3rd
10-30 m.p.h.	12.7 sec.	8.2 sec.
20-40 m.p.h.	15.7 sec.	11.9 sec.
30-50 m.p.h.	24.7 sec.	—

WEIGHT

- Unladen kerb weight .. 30¾ cwt.
- Front/rear weight distribution .. 51½/48½
- Weight laden as tested .. 34¼ cwt.

HILL CLIMBING (At steady speeds)

- Max. gradient on top gear .. 1 in 12.7 (Tapley 175 lb./ton)
- Max. gradient on 3rd gear .. 1 in 8.7 (Tapley 255 lb./ton)
- Max. gradient on 2nd gear .. 1 in 6.7 (Tapley 330 lb./ton)

BRAKES at 30 m.p.h.

- 0.93g retardation (=32½ ft. stopping distance) with 140 lb. pedal pressure
- 0.67g retardation (=45 ft. stopping distance) with 100 lb. pedal pressure
- 0.32g retardation (=94 ft. stopping distance) with 50 lb. pedal pressure
- 0.06g retardation (=500 ft. stopping distance) with 25 lb. pedal pressure

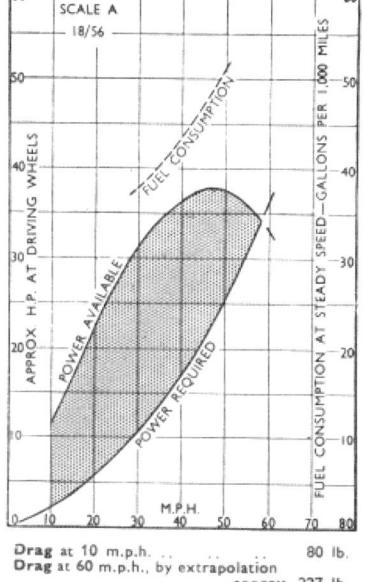

Drag at 10 m.p.h. .. 80 lb.
Drag at 60 m.p.h., by extrapolation approx. 227 lb.
Specific Fuel Consumption when cruising at 80% of maximum speed (i.e. 46.5 m.p.h.) on level road, based on power delivered to rear wheels .. 0.80 pints/b.h.p./hr.

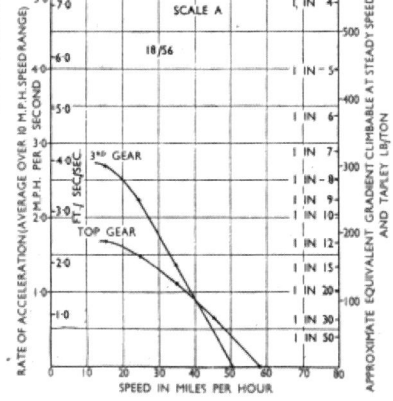

Maintenance

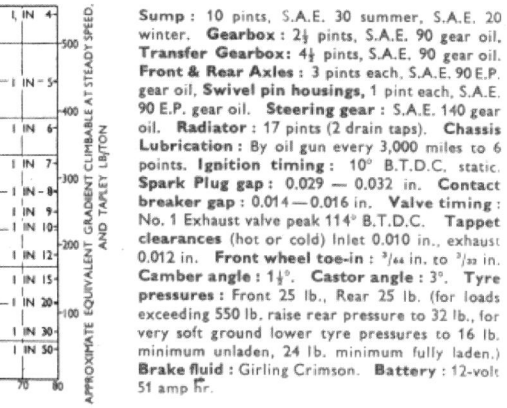

Sump: 10 pints, S.A.E. 30 summer, S.A.E. 20 winter. **Gearbox:** 2½ pints, S.A.E. 90 gear oil. **Transfer Gearbox:** 4½ pints, S.A.E. 90 gear oil. **Front & Rear Axles:** 3 pints each, S.A.E. 90 E.P. gear oil, **Swivel pin housings,** 1 pint each, S.A.E. 90 E.P. gear oil. **Steering gear:** S.A.E. 140 gear oil. **Radiator:** 17 pints (2 drain taps). **Chassis Lubrication:** By oil gun every 3,000 miles to 6 points. **Ignition timing:** 10° B.T.D.C. static. **Spark Plug gap:** 0.029 – 0.032 in. **Contact breaker gap:** 0.014–0.016 in. **Valve timing:** No. 1 Exhaust valve peak 114° B.T.D.C. **Tappet clearances** (hot or cold) Inlet 0.010 in., exhaust 0.012 in. **Front wheel toe-in:** 3/64 in. to 3/32 in. **Camber angle:** 1½°. **Castor angle:** 3°. **Tyre pressures:** Front 25 lb., Rear 25 lb. (for loads exceeding 550 lb. raise rear pressure to 32 lb., for very soft ground lower tyre pressures to 16 lb. minimum unladen, 24 lb. minimum fully laden.) **Brake fluid:** Girling Crimson. **Battery:** 12-volt 51 amp hr.

Ref. B/20/56

CHAPTER 20
Forward Area Vehicle MoS Land-Rovers

Throughout the 1950s, the Ministry of Supply continued to place contracts for Land-Rovers – quite an achievement on Rover's part when you consider that the Army was taking its own 'Truck, 1/4-ton, Cargo, Austin Mk 1, FV 1801' 'Champ' by the thousand at this time, nearly 14,000 of these vehicles going into service between 1952 and 1955. When Champ production ceased, the Land-Rover received the final accolade in 1956, when it was officially adopted as the Army's standard 1/4-ton Forward Area vehicle.

From the Army's point of view, the Land-Rover was a well tried and successful vehicle with no associated development costs, whereas some £16 million (1953 prices) of taxpayers' money had to be written off on the Austin Champ, which even so, could hardly be described as an unqualified success – the problems associated with the back axle were in fact never overcome. It is hardly surprisingly that the matter raised a few questions in Parliament.

Designated 'Truck, 1/4-ton, GS, 4x4, Rover Mk 3.', under Contract No. 6/Veh/16223, dated 26 May 1954, a total of 2,600 86-inch Land-Rovers soon entered military service. This was followed by another 1,500 under Contract No. 6 Veh/18599, dated 22 January 1955. Each of these 86-inch Land-Rovers cost the Ministry of Supply £550, apart from the last 450, delivered after July 1955, which cost £650 each. The next order, under Contract No. 6 Veh/20244, dated 3 October 1955, was for another 1,000 costing £570 each and was followed by a final 2,000 under Contract No. 6 Veh/22633, dated 24 April 1956, but only 1,500 were 86-inch models, the remainder being 'Mk5' 88-inch models so, excluding these, altogether, 6,600 86-inch Land Rovers entered service with the British Army.

Various military adaptations were made to the 'Mk3' model. A Special Air Services (SAS) version was specially prepared to War Office requirements with reinforced uprated suspension, Vicker's twin 'K' forward mounted LMGs, a Browning Mk2 0.30 caliber MG armament in the rear, and a 0.303 Bren at the side. The later Mk5 vehicle was fitted with a Browning Mk2 0.30 MG on the bulkhead instead of the Vickers twin 'K'. The spare wheel on these vehicles was slotted, almost horizontally, forward of the radiator between two Jerry cans stowed in front of the wings. These vehicles were designed as rapid raiders in NW Europe. Desert versions

The initial conversion was carried out by REME

A bird's eye view of the general layout

'Truck, 1/4-ton, GS, 4x4, Rover, Mk 3', 86-inch Land-Rover fully equipped for 'line laying'

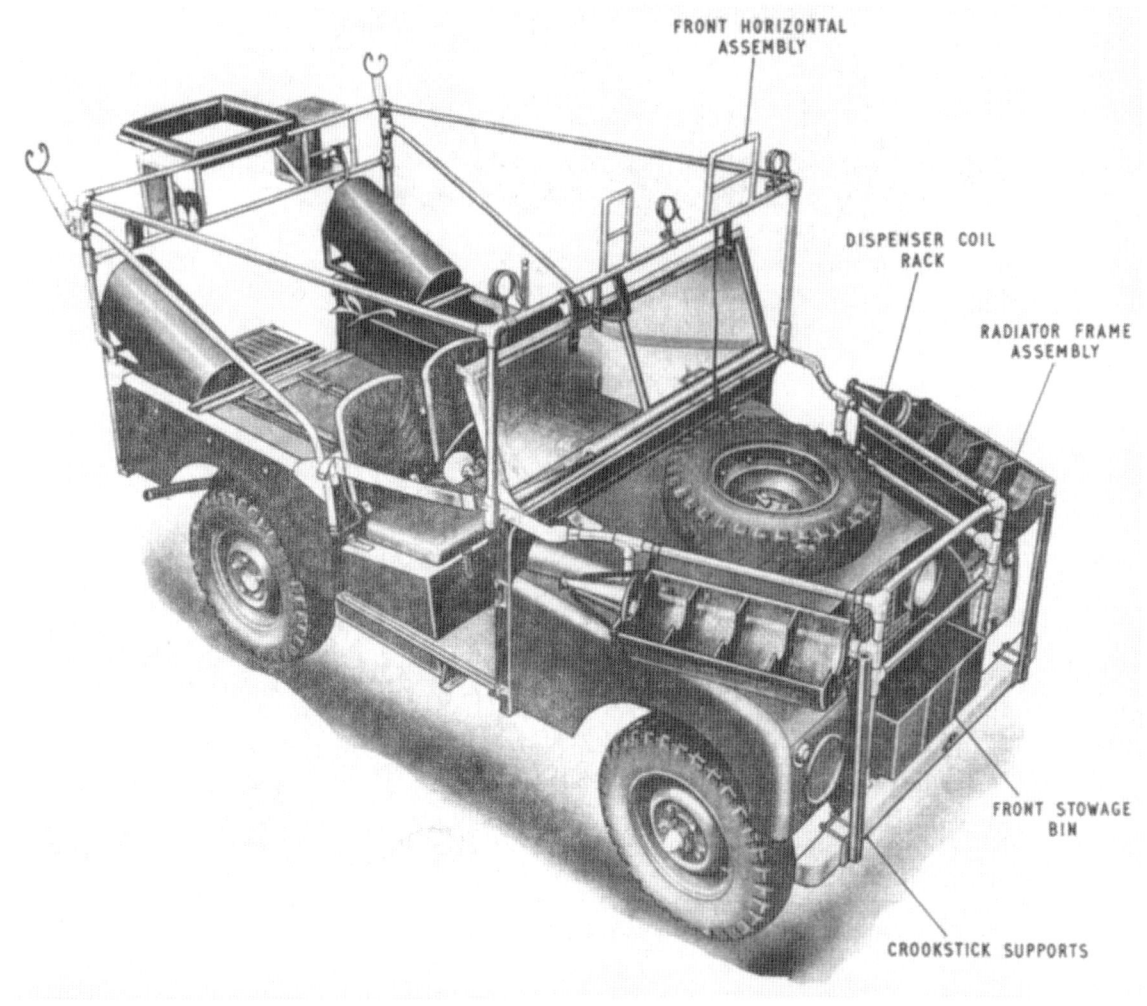

CHAPTER 20 – Forward Area Vehicle – MoS Land-Rovers

FRONT HORIZONTAL ASSEMBLY

DISPENSER COIL RACK

RADIATOR FRAME ASSEMBLY

FRONT STOWAGE BIN

CROOKSTICK SUPPORTS

LAND-ROVER – The Formative Years, 1947–1967

Truck, 1/4-ton, 4x4, SAS, Rover, Mk 3, FV18006' is the military title for this 86-inch Land-Rover

had the addition of a sun compass mounted on the bulkhead and were the forerunners of the later 'Pink Panther' Land-Rovers. Weighing nearly 2-ton 2-cwt, these vehicles were well over 3/4-ton heavier than a basic 86 model. For many years the original 86 prototype for these vehicles lay derelict behind the SAS workshops at Hereford.

Although the Royal Artillery only began using Land-Rovers for 'line laying' in 1959, the prototype for these vehicles had been based on the MK3 86 model specifically converted by the Royal Electrical and Mechanical Engineers (REME). All subsequent conversions were by means of a special kit supplied, one per gun battery, but they were only suitable for '86 & 88' 'Series I' Land-Rovers. The suspension on these vehicles was also specially uprated, and when in action, line was dispensed from two racks situated on the bonnet, with a special tubular frame replacing the hood sticks, to enable a line to be raised up to 21 ft. in order to clear crossroads, railways, etc. Equipment such as shovels, pick axe and sledge-hammer were all carried in one of the stowage bins mounted above the wheel arch, while smaller items such as telephone batteries, tape, nails, etc. were carried in a small bin mounted in front of the bumper. The personal kit of the three-man crew was all carried in a trailer normally left at base when line laying was in progress – hardly surprising as a good crew was said to be able to lay line at speeds of up to 30 mph under favourable conditions.

A particularly interesting military adaptation of the 86-inch Land-Rover came from Captain F.W. Miller of the Royal Australian Electrical and Mechanical Engineers (RAEME). While serving in Malaya, he devised a cable bridge capable of supporting an 86-inch Land-Rover, its two-man crew, and even a trailer, across a 200 ft. gap, using special flanges bolted to the wheel hubs. The Miller Bridge was not only light, easily transported, cheap to produce, and easily replaced, but was also able to withstand a bombing raid with little or no consequence. The British Royal Engineers and REME needed little convincing of the worth of such a bridge.

The Parts List is only intended for 86 and 88 models

The latest Handbook covers all Military Land-Rovers from 1948 to 1958

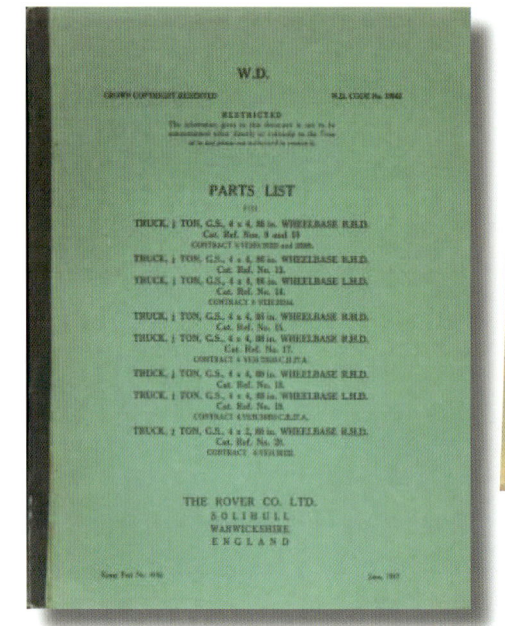

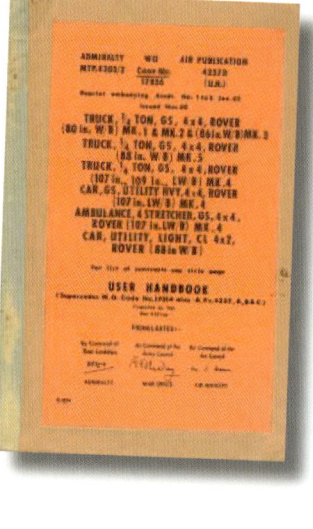

258

CHAPTER 20 – Forward Area Vehicle – MoS Land-Rovers

Truck, 1/4-ton, GS, 4x4, Rover, Mk 3', 86-inch Land-Rover and trailer try out the Miller bridge

'You're still supposed to look where you're going'

It gave 'off-road' an entirely new meaning

259

LAND-ROVER – The Formative Years, 1947–1967

The 107 10-seater Station Wagons were also used by the Army soon after their introduction, a total of 20 being ordered under Contract No. 6/Veh/19981. As 'Car, GS, Utility, Heavy, 4x4, Rover Mk4', they were used as signals vehicles by the War Office. Fully equipped, the vehicle carried a five-man crew and a comprehensive kit consisting of: a No.19 wireless set; signals batteries; a folding map table; four carbines; pick and shovel; machete; petrol and water in Jerry cans; a gallon can of oil; a fire extinguisher; first aid and tool kit; snow chains; tow rope; a camouflage net; and blackout blinds. Lifting rings were attached to the front bumper mounting points, while at the rear, a towing jaw was attached to the back crossmember, midway between a two-part rear bumper equipped with a pair of lashing hooks.

One other fully enclosed 107 model was also tried by the military. This was a less elaborate Station Wagon, based on a standard 107 chassis and seating six people beneath a hard top made up from a Station Wagon roof and side panels, minus tropical roof panel and vents. The gap left between the side screens and side panel, normally filled by a second set of doors, consisted of a small side panel with fixed window. It could well be the only example of a 107 truck with a full-length hard top.

The RAF used the 107 to develop an 'Ambulance, 4-stretcher, GS, 4x4, Rover Mk4', with special insulated bodywork by 'Bonallack', and primarily intended for the RAF Mountain Rescue Service. These vehicles were 12 inches wider, 11 inches higher, and 6 inches longer than the 10-seater Station Wagon. At the rear they had full-width double doors with a folding step. Unladen, the vehicle weighed 1-ton 14-cwt. The RAF also used other 107-inch models fully equipped for Fire and Crash Rescue duties at airfields.

When it came to really unusual conversions, the military by no means held the prerogative on this front. J.A. Cuthbertson Limited of Biggar, Scotland, developed a four-track drive caterpillar system for the 86-inch Land-Rover. It was certainly unique, and consisted of a special frame with twin bogies at each corner onto which the 86-inch Land-Rover, fitted with chain wheels in place of road wheels, was lowered. Special endless tracks were then fitted over each chain wheel and pair of bogies, to give four-track drive, power steering being provided for the front bogies. Sitting on top of this special frame gave the vehicle enormous ground clearance and the Army showed considerable interest in this conversion for bomb disposal purposes.

With the introduction of the new 88-inch wheelbase on 6 June 1956, any new 'regular' Land-Rovers supplied to the Ministry of Supply were then designated 'Rover Mk 5'. Taken in two batches, the first under Contract No. 6 Veh/22633, dated 28 April 1956, had been for 2,000 'Mk 3' 86 models, at a final cost of £570 each, but as delivery did not finish until 10 July 1956, the last 500 were to be 'Mk 5' 88 models. A further 100 'Mk 5' Land-Rovers were ordered under Contract No. 6 Veh/24950, dated 9 May 1957 at £620 each. The latest diesel-powered Land-Rovers were also taken by the Royal Navy. Otherwise models remained unchanged, with one particular exception.

RAF Provost Land-Rover

Typical sight at an RAF Airfield in the 1950s

Armoured 107 in Malaya

260

CHAPTER 20 – Forward Area Vehicle – MoS Land-Rovers

Twenty new 107 Station Wagons entered service as 'Car, GS, Utility, Heavy, 4x4, Rover, Mk 4, FV18004'

This 'Truck, 1/4-ton, 4x4, Ambulance, Special, Rover Mk 4, FV 18005' with 2-stretcher bodywork by Bonallack & Sons, Ltd., Basildon, Essex was used by the RAF Mountain Rescue service

LAND-ROVER – The Formative Years, 1947–1967

The Ministry of Supply's final order for 'Series I' models, under Contract No. 6/Veh/26222, dated 1 November 1957, was for a batch of 655 Land-Rovers designated 'Car, Utility, Light, CL, 4x2, Rover'. Their military numbers commenced 01 CE 89 and ended with 08 CE 63.

These otherwise standard 88-inch Land-Rovers had been specially fitted with a plain front axle tube, blanked at both ends. The stub axles had oil throwers fitted in the swivel housings to ensure continued lubrication of the swivel pins. On the transfer box, a conical cover replaced the output housing, and the 'red'- and 'yellow'-knobbed controls were omitted, as it was necessary for these vehicles to remain permanently in high ratio if damage to the rear differential was to be avoided. Twenty of these particular vehicles are recorded as being Station Wagons. All had a nominal weight advantage of 255 lbs (115.66 kg) over the 4x4 Land-Rovers.

Although they cost the Army only £520 each, £100 less than a standard model, the Land-Rover had already been designated a 'Forward Area' vehicle in 1956. These 4x2 Land-Rovers had nothing to do with that role. Their purpose must therefore be seen in terms of the number of vehicles to be allocated to the Army's 'CL' class (standard commercial chassis not normally provided with all-wheel-drive) which were to total 50% of all Army transport. When selecting vehicles for this class, the Land-Rover was well suited in terms of spares stocked, technical expertise, longevity, reliability, etc. but there was the military's own 'Catch 22' – a 4x4 Land-Rover (its standard commercial form) did not conform to CL type. Rover were, no doubt, only too pleased to oblige with a 'modified' 4x2 Land-Rover if it overcame the logistics problem and increased military sales. Rover even considered selling such a vehicle on the commercial market until they realised it would be far too expensive to compete against the existing light trucks in the 15-cwt class from firms such as Ford and Morris.

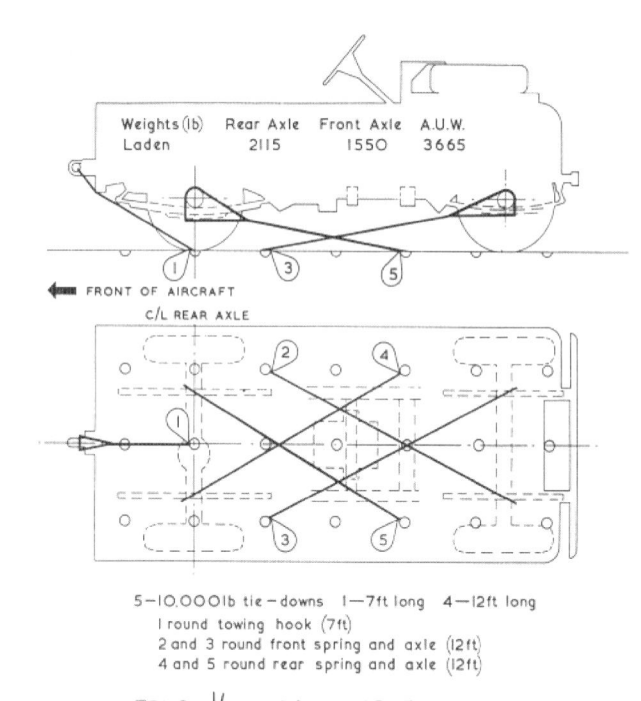

Army transport vehicles in the 'CL' class were not generally required to go off-road, but the problem with this arrangement, as far as the 4x2 Land-Rover was concerned, was that military

107 RAF Aircraft Crash Rescue Land-Rover

Lashing instructions for Rover Mk 3 and Mk 5 for air transportation

262

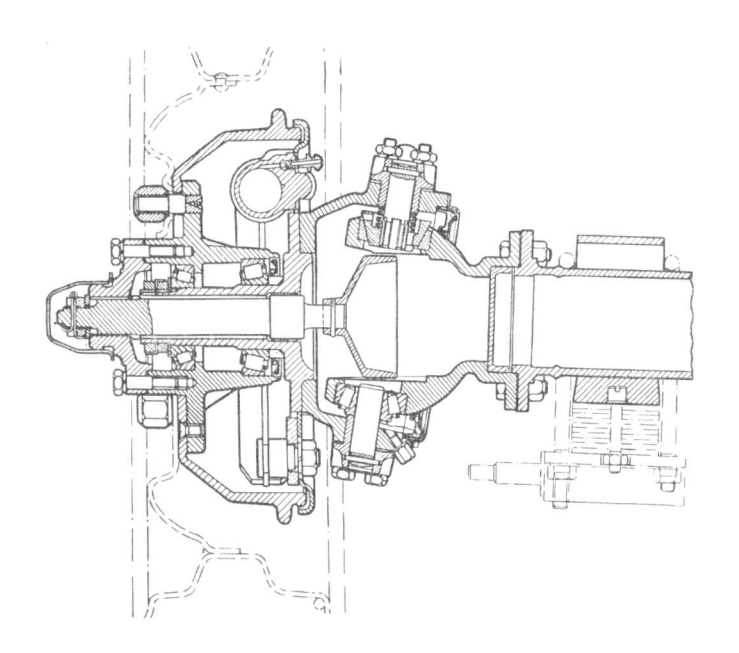

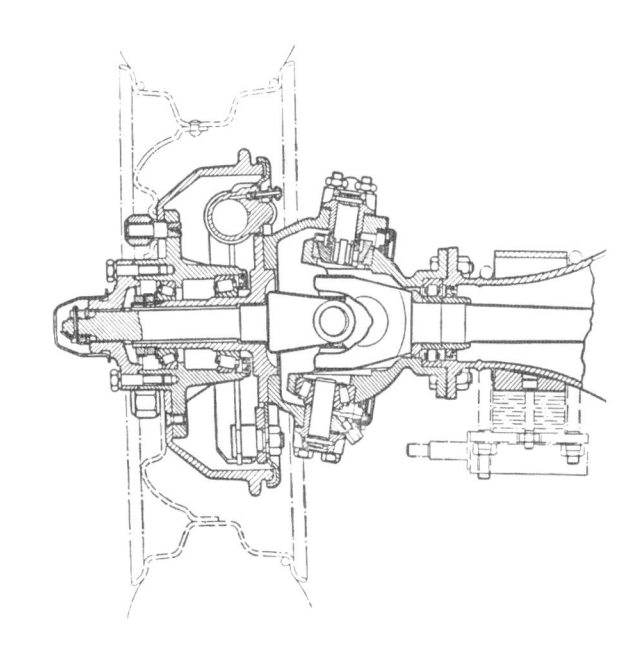

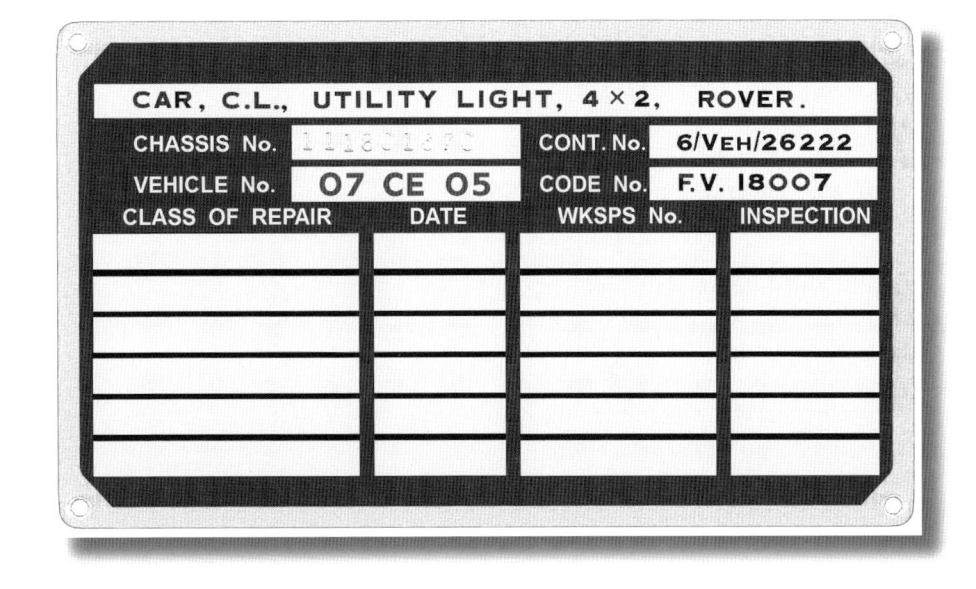

CHAPTER 20 – Forward Area Vehicle – MoS Land-Rovers

Front axle cross-section of the 4x2 Land-Rover

Front axle cross-section showing drive shaft in the standard 4x4 Land-Rover

Military plate supplied with the 4x2 Land-Rover

personnel already familiar with Army Land-Rovers expected the same off-road performance as any other Land-Rover. When these vehicles failed to oblige, it caused a certain amount of 'red-faced' frustration on the part of whoever happened to be in the 'hot' seat at the time. The error of the decision to put Land-Rovers in the CL class was eventually realised, but not before a further batch of 275 early Series II models under Contract No. 6/Veh/27756 were also supplied, equipped this way. Most were soon withdrawn from Army service and given lighter duties with other Ministry departments, before eventually being sold off, often in very good condition.

Certain 109 'Series I' Land-Rovers serving in the Far East were given armour plating for crew protection. These were designated 'Car, Armoured, Patrol, 4x4', and had headlights fitted in the wings, some ten years ahead of any other production model. Short Brothers & Harland Ltd., of Queens Island, Belfast, later produced the 'Shorland Armoured Car' based on the Series II chassis, with Rover's approval. Following the example of the Royal Artillery, the Civil Defence Corps' 'Field Cable Party' also used 'Series I' Land-Rovers for 'line laying', together with a Brockhouse trailer, specially equipped with a tubular frame to carry ladders and other equipment.

CHAPTER 21
A Change of Heart
The Diesel Option

From the beginning of June 1956, apart from the recently introduced 10-seater Station Wagon, all Land-Rover models had their front axle moved forward two inches, to give either an 88-inch or 109-inch wheelbase. However, there was no overall increase in the total vehicle length. The new terms 'Regular' and 'Long' were also officially introduced to describe the new alternatives in wheelbase. At the same time a revised numbering system was introduced for all models, no longer stamped on the left rear spring hanger, but on the right-hand front one.

Because these changes in wheelbase occurred mid-way through year, the new prefix for '88 & 109' models was followed by whatever serial number continued after the last '86 & 107' model rolled off the line. The first 'Home' 88 Land-Rover, built on 6 June 1956, was chassis 111604808.

The events leading up to these changes in wheelbase were the consequence of more general changes that had been taking place in industry, commerce, and agriculture over the past 25 years. In 1897 Germany gave birth to the first of Dr Rudolf Diesel's compression-ignition engines. Twenty-five years later in 1923 Benz then went into production with the world's first diesel engine tractor, the 3 HP twin-cylinder Benz-Sending S7. By 1926 they had a competitor, the Deutz MTZ 222, and very soon Fahr and Ritscher tractors were also using Deutz diesel engines.

Back in Britain in 1929, Mercedes-Benz began a new trend when they won the Dewar Trophy for the successful installation of their six-cylinder, 6.5-litre, high-speed diesel engine into a 'Karrier' six-wheeled bus chassis. This was the first diesel engine-powered commercial road vehicle in Britain, and it then went into service with Sheffield Corporation. A year later in 1930 Mercedes-Benz entered a single-cylinder four-stroke diesel tractor – the OE model – in the World Tractor trials held in England. The following year at the Royal Show in Warwick, Garrett of Leiston, Suffolk, won a Royal Agricultural Society of England (RASE) award when they entered a tractor powered by a British 4-cyl. four-stroke Aveling and Porter diesel engine. Garrett had broken new ground in Britain at a time when multi-cylinder high-speed diesel engines were still unheard of outside of Europe, and the RASE had been quick to recognise its potential.

Throughout the 1930s high-speed diesel engines rapidly began to gain popularity as a power source for buses and lorries, and in Germany their reliability was such that by the mid-1930s they were being used in military vehicles (MAN) and aircraft (Junker), including the Zeppelin airships (Mercedes-Benz). Although these engines were far too large for smaller road vehicles, it was not long before Mercedes produced a lightweight 2.5-litre 4-cyl. diesel engine for use in Daimler-Benz passenger cars and taxicabs.

Turner's diesel engine

Turner's advert in 'The Autocar', September 1955

CHAPTER 21 – A Change of Heart – The Diesel Option

25 SEPTEMBER 1955 — *The Autocar*

TURNER DIESEL

LIGHTWEIGHT TWO STROKE SUPERCHARGED ENGINES

45·5 M.P.G FITTED IN A 6 SEATER FAMILY SALOON UNDER OFFICIALLY OBSERVED R·A·C TEST

For the Greatest Economy

Whether used for transport or industrial purposes, these new Turner Diesel 2-stroke supercharged engines offer remarkable economies in fuel costs. Light, compact and with a low weight-to-power ratio (only 8 lb. to 1 h.p. on 3-cylinder models), they run smoothly and silently, and have an exceptionally long life of service with minimum maintenance. The engines are ideally suitable for light commercial and passenger vehicles, taxis, jeeps, and a wide range of industrial and marine uses. **Enquiries regarding Land-Rover conversions are particularly invited.** We invite you to write for fully illustrated literature on these sensational new engines.

"OPERATION ENTERPRISE" — 20-page illustrated brochure on the Turner-Diesel trans-African reliability trial — available free on request.

TURNER MANUFACTURING CO. LTD., VILLIERS STREET, WOLVERHAMPTON

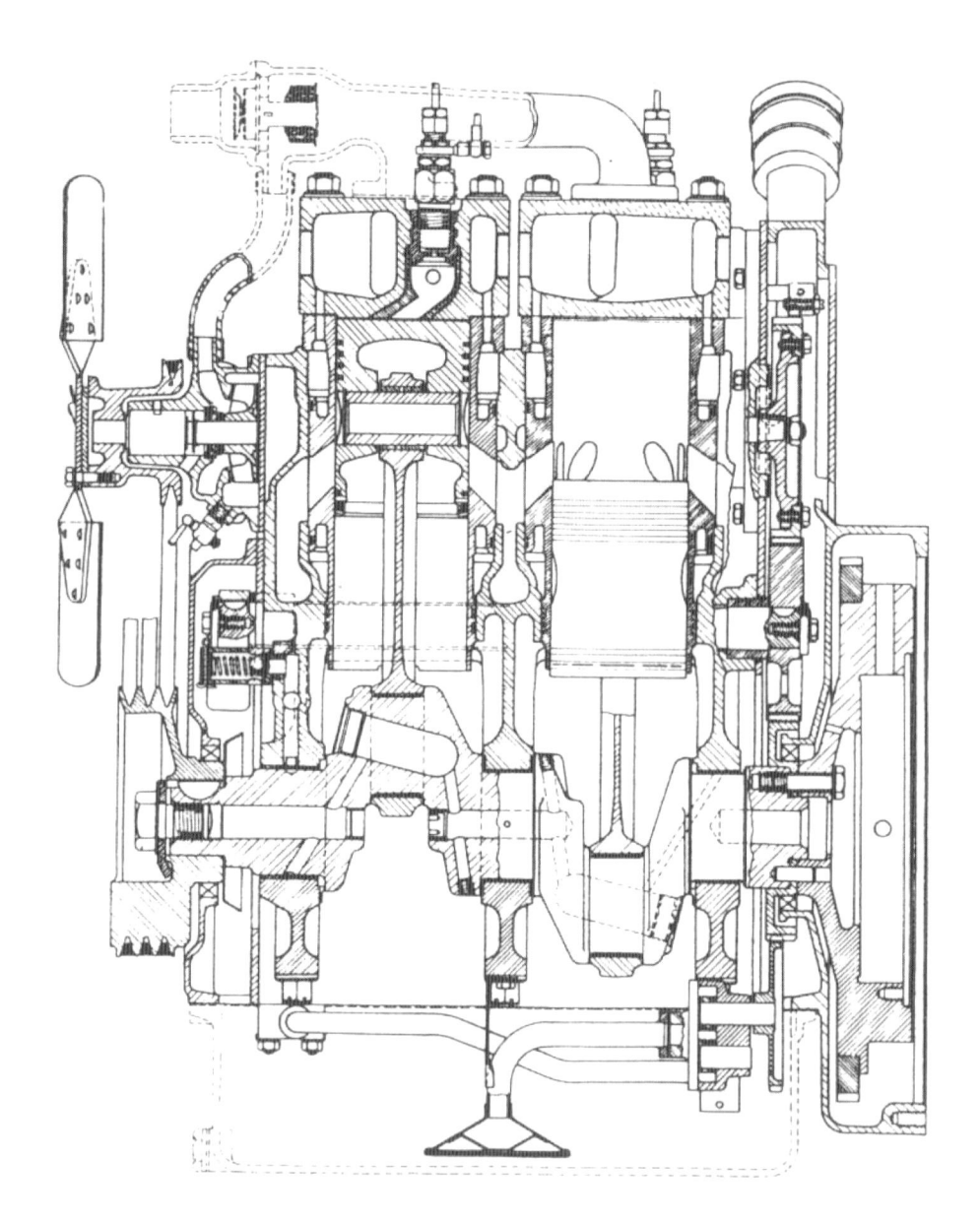

Turner engine cross-section

Back in Britain, in 1932 F. Perkins Ltd., of Eastfield, Peterborough, began manufacturing diesel engines, and following Mercedes example, soon produced a range of lightweight four-cylinder high-speed diesel engines. Named 'Vixen', 'Fox', 'Wolf', and 'Leopard', these engines ranged from 2.2-litres up to 4.0-litres. All could be used in relatively light vehicles, and for test purposes the 2.42-litre Wolf was installed in a Studebaker Saloon car. It proved capable of up to 38 mpg, had a top speed of 64.75 mph, and could reach 60 mph in 40 seconds. The 6-cyl. petrol engine it replaced only gave around 18 mpg, although the top speed and acceleration were considerably better.

Around 1940, Perkins announced two new models using their new 'Aeroflow' cylinder head. These were the 'P6', a 4.73-litre engine developing 85 bhp at 2600 revs per minute, and the smaller 'P4', a 3.1-litre engine developing 56 bhp at 2600 rpm, which at only 406 lbs (895 kg) – less than 4-cwt – was Britain's lightest four-cylinder diesel yet.

Soon after the Second World War, these two engines found their way into a number of tractors, including the Fordson E27N 'Major' (P6–1948), the Massey-Harris 744D (P6–1951), and Nuffield's 'Universal Four' (P4–1951). The trend, however, was by no means universal. Throughout North America, where both petrol and 'distillate' remained cheaper than diesel fuel, there was little incentive to adopt the diesel engine into agriculture before the advent of the 'giant' tractors of the early 1960s.

In Britain most tractors still continued to run on petrol or TVO well into the mid-1950s, but the writing was on the wall. The low-speed single-

CHAPTER 21 – A Change of Heart – The Diesel Option

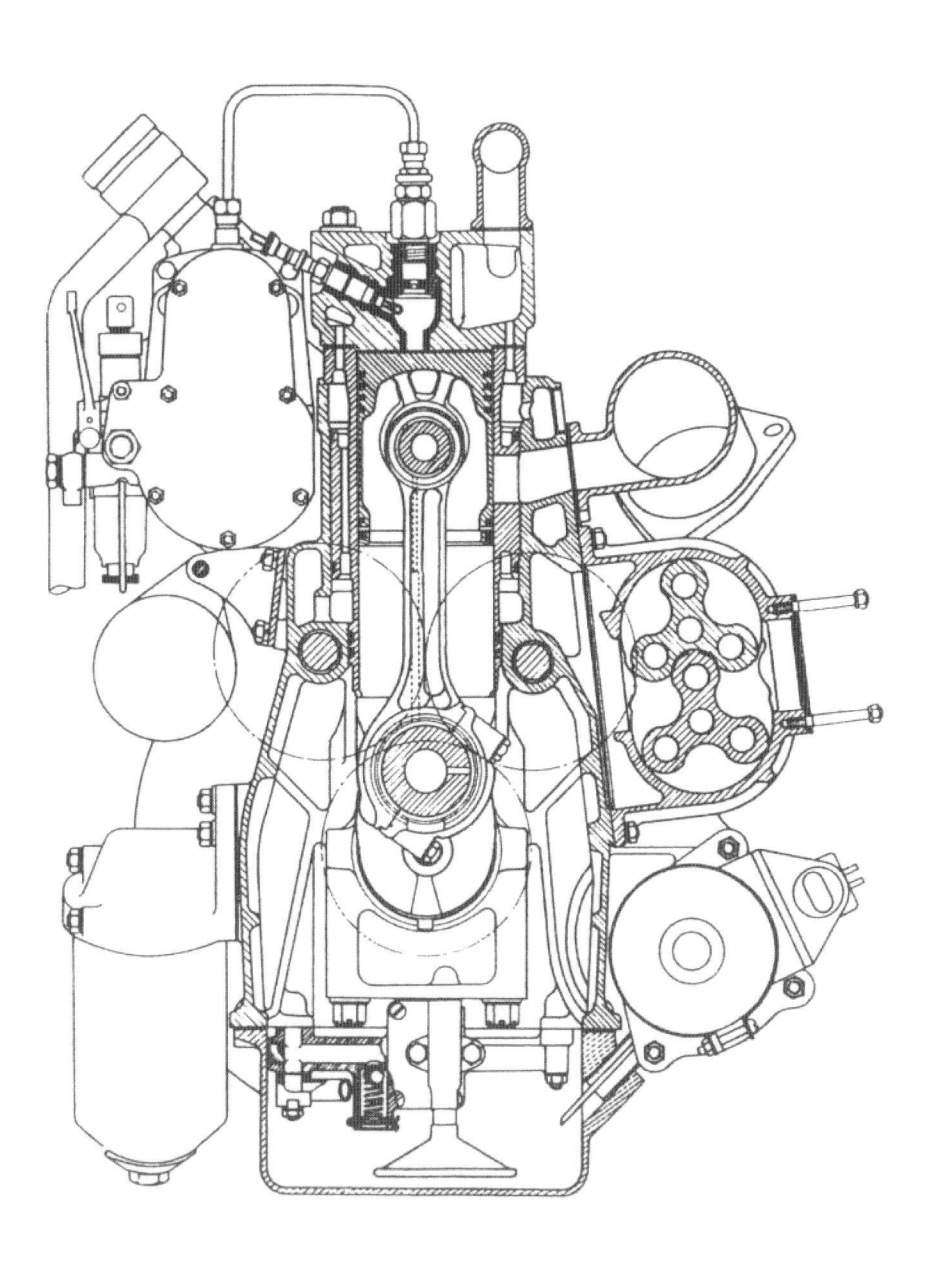

The supercharger can be clearly seen

cylinder 'Field-Marshal' apart, in 1949 David Brown became the first major British tractor manufacturer to use his own diesel engine in the 'Cropmaster' model. Also at the Royal Show that year was a less well known concern, the Turner Manufacturing Co. Ltd., of Villiers Street, Wolverhampton. Their first tractor, the 'Yeoman of England', was powered by a V4 diesel designed by the outstanding engineer, Freeman Saunders. Selling at £669 in 1950, Turner's 'Yeoman' was unfortunately overpriced in a very competitive market, and brought the company little commercial success.

In 1953 Turner went into production with two small aluminium alloy supercharged diesel engines, the L40 and L60. Weighing only 340 lbs (154 kg) and 450 lbs (204 kg), they were marketed as ideally suited for light commercial and passenger vehicles, taxis, jeeps, etc. Using a 'Rootes' type supercharger, the L40 produced 40 bhp from a 2.0-litre, two-cylinder, blown two-stroke engine, and had a torque of a 75 lbs/ft at 1800 rpm.

In terms of performance, it did not compare favourably with Rover's own 2.0-litre petrol engine currently in use in the Land-Rover. But as far as economy goes, that was another story. Turner's diesel could return 34 mpg, and with agricultural diesel costing only 1/3d (6.25p) a gallon, the cost per 100 miles (3 gallons) was only 3/9d (18.75p), compared to five gallons of petrol at 4/2d (21p), totalling £1/0/10d (£1.04p). For use on the public highway, DERV (Diesel Engine Road Vehicles) fuel cost about the same as petrol, with 100 miles costing about 12/6d (62.5p), so there was still a considerable saving to be made.

The larger L60 was a light compact 3.0-litre, three-cylinder, blown two-stroke engine with a power/weight ratio of 8 lbs per horse power. Overall power output was equivalent to that of the 2.0-litre Land-Rover engine and Turner installed it in their prototype 1½-ton 4x4 truck, which they hoped to sell to the British Army, but it never went into production. The running gear used was probably all 107 Land-Rover, and apart from the fibreglass front end, the rest of the vehicle had an uncanny resemblance to a Series II Land-Rover.

There was nothing particularly new about supercharged two-stroke diesel engines and firms such as Junker, Jung and Michel in Germany, Bolinders in Sweden, and Petter and Climax in Britain had all produced such engines in the 1930s. Nor were Turner's engines new designs, but based on Austrian 'Jenbach' diesel engines made by the Jenbacher Werke at Graz, the L40 being based on the Jenbach JW35 as used for the 1955 Belgian Minerva C22 *'Tout-Terrain'* vehicle. Production ceased in 1958.

In 1955, in an attempt to gain maximum publicity for their diesel engine, Turner embarked on a 10,000 mile 'Trans-African' reliability trial, known as *'Operation Enterprise'*. Using Rover's recently introduced 107 Land-Rover fitted with their diesel engine, they bravely set off from their Wolverhampton works and headed across the great Sahara desert to Nairobi in Kenya, then part of British East Africa. A free 20-page illustrated booklet covering the event was made available and stated clearly *'...that inquiries regarding Land-Rover conversions are particularly invited'*.

Turner's diesel was by no means the only such Land-Rover diesel conversion. Other Land-Rovers are known to have been fitted with Perkins diesel engines, a number of which were exported to Czechoslovakia. To Rover, all this was a clear indication that diesel engines could no longer be ignored. Turner also enterprisingly offered a mechanical drum winch for fitting behind the front bumper of the Land-Rover as an alternative to Rover's own 'Aeroparts' mechanical Capstan winch.

By 1956 Britain's tractor population had doubled from 200,000 in 1946 to around the 400,000 mark, and represented an eightfold increase over the immediate pre-war level. Farmers had become increasingly aware of the contribution mechanisation could make to their output and all major tractor manufacturers had been obliged to offer diesel engines by 1954, including Standard (1951), though apparently much against the wishes of Harry Ferguson. High-speed diesel engines needed far less maintenance than petrol engines, and having no 'spark' made for easier starting after a night out in Britain's damp climate. Diesels were also cheaper to run and had more torque at low revs. Now that their initial costs had begun to fall, they presented a serious challenge to the petrol engine in the field of agriculture, commerce, and industry.

Aware of this challenge, Rover were keen to market a diesel-powered Land-Rover before Austin, or anybody else, stepped into the field car market at home to jeopardise the Land-Rover's coveted position of being not only Britain's most versatile vehicle, but also its most exported commercial vehicle. After the resignation of Sir John Black as Chairman of Standard-Triumph in January 1954, formal discussions took place between Rover and Standard-Triumph over the possibility of a merger between the two firms.

Despite the success of Harry Ferguson's little grey tractor, the car side of the business was not doing too well, and they were now *'...on the search for a partner'*. Taking advantage of their car's non-unitary construction, as an added incentive in 1954, Standard introduced their own 2.1-litre diesel engine, as used in the Ferguson tractor, into their Series II 'Vanguard' car, making it Britain's first diesel-powered production car, but less than 2,000 would be sold. In August 1954, Britain also got its first diesel taxicab, when BMC introduced the 2.2-litre Morris 'Commander' diesel engine into London's famous 'black cab', the Austin FX3D taxi.

The idea of diesel power for the Land-Rover certainly appealed to Rover, and an amalgamation with Standard-Triumph began to look promising. However, Standard's Alan Dick wanted an equal partnership for the much weaker Standard-Triumph concern. Maurice Wilks would hear nothing of such an arrangement, and talks came abruptly to an end. As it turned out, this was just as well, for Rover's engineers were soon to discover that Standard's diesel engine would not have entirely suited the Land-Rover. Had the merger gone ahead, there would no doubt have been considerable pressure to make use of it.

A further complication was also lurking in the background. Unbeknown to Rover, Harry Ferguson had apparently already made up his mind to merge his tractor business with Massey-Harris as early as 1953, with the result that Standard's tractor production now had only two more years to run. For Rover it had all been a lucky escape.

With the breakdown in these talks, Rover immediately began working on their own diesel engine in consultation with Jack Pitchford of Ricardo Consulting Engineers, Shoreham, in

CHAPTER 21 – A Change of Heart – The Diesel Option

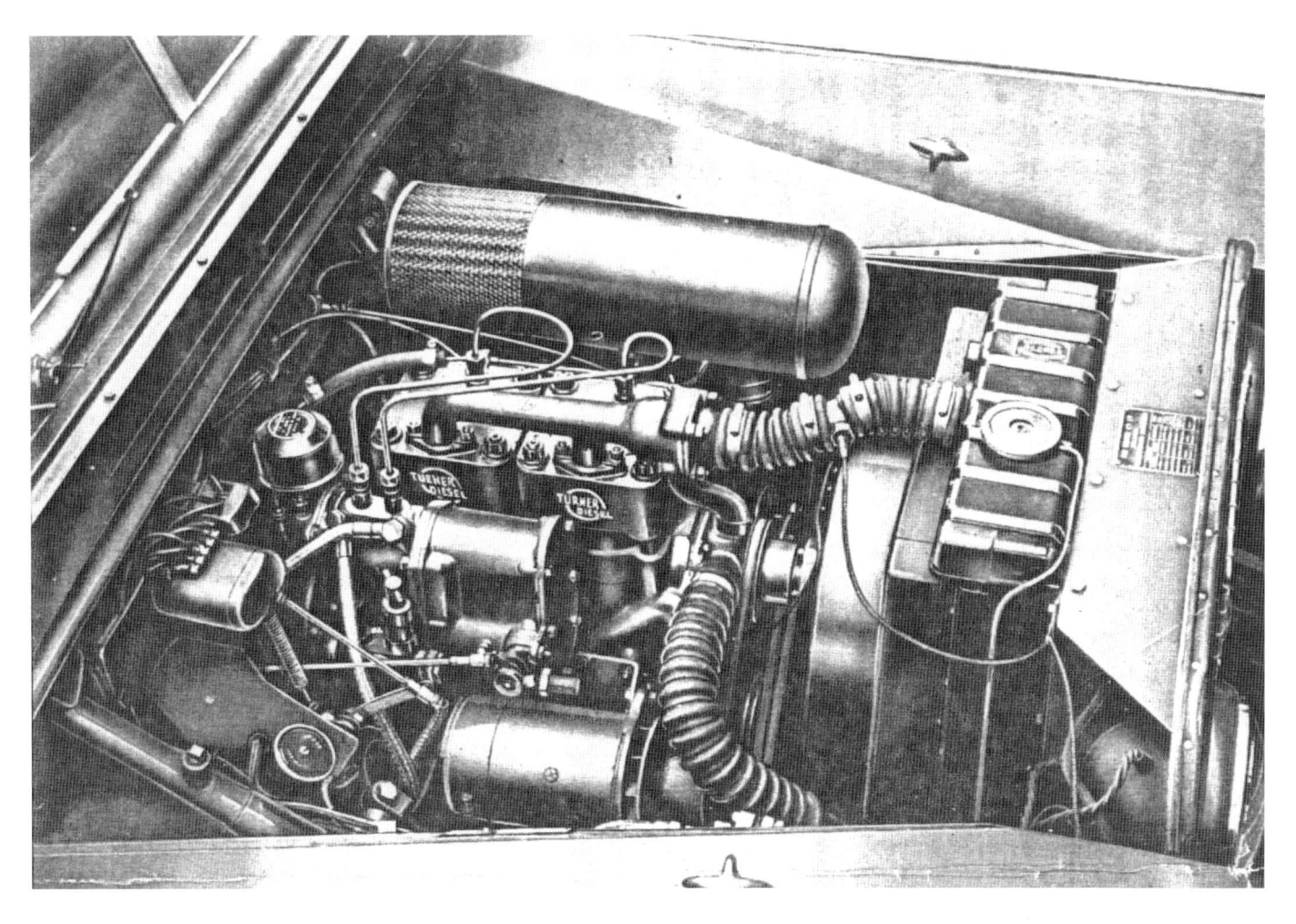

The final installation

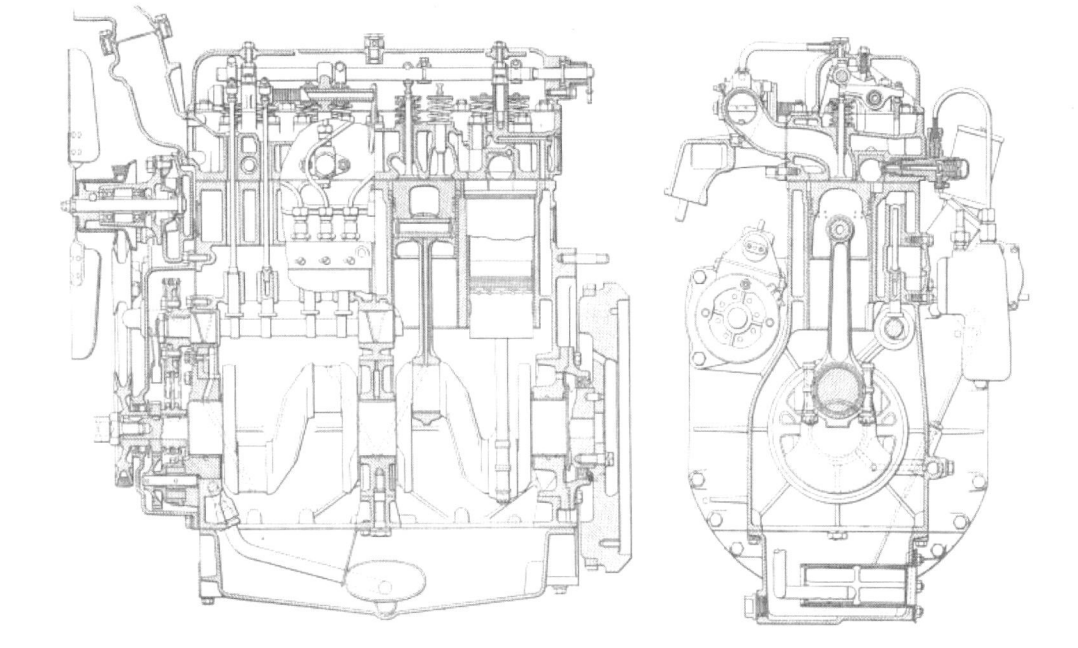

Standard Diesel 2092cc 3 3/16" bore, 4" stroke (80.96 mm x 101.6 mm) light tractor engine – also used in Standard's Vanguard Estate Car and 12-cwt Van and PU Utility from 1954

The inside story

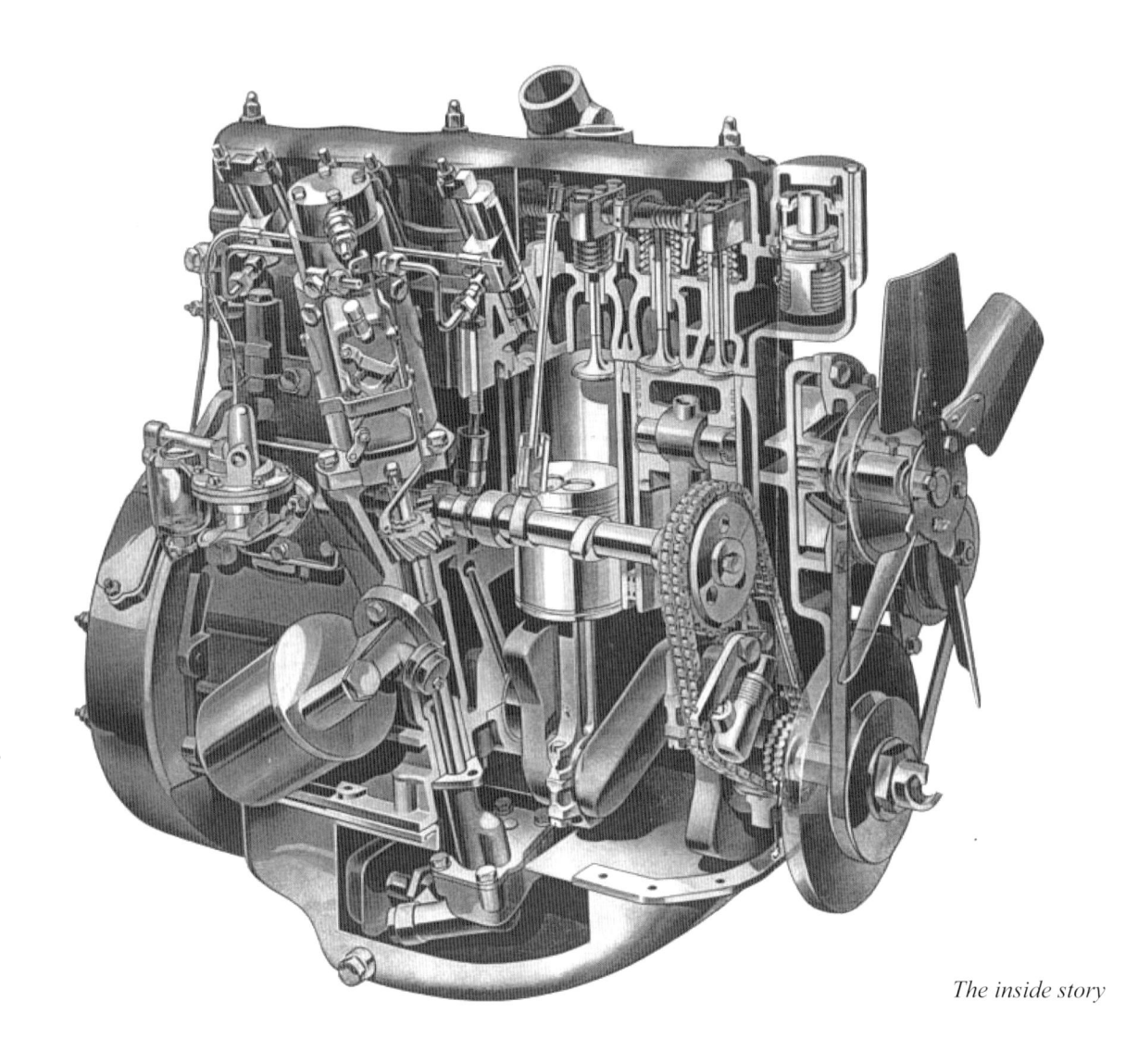

Sussex. Pitchford was already a personal friend of Maurice Wilks and their children spent happy times together on Anglesey. A 'Mark V' version of a Ricardo 'Comet' combustion head was to be used on the new engine in preference to direct injection on such a small engine. The new head had a separate pre-combustion chamber leading to the main combustion area through a narrow passage, a design originally invented by Herbert Ackroyd-Stuart in 1890. As early as 1930 Harry Ralph Ricardo had first introduced 'swirl' into Ackroyd-Stuart's pre-combustion chamber in the first of his 'Comet' heads.

By 1956 Rover's diesel engine was sufficiently advanced to warrant an increase in wheelbase for all existing Land-Rover models except the 10-seater Station Wagon, in order to give the current models sufficient clearance in the engine bay. The initial trial batch of 300 Rover diesel engines finished up as 293 diesel-powered Land-Rovers, commencing with serial number 116600001. The first of these was completed on 13 January 1956, but 116600005 was not built until nearly a year later on 12 December 1956. Only one pre-production 109 diesel model was ever built, car No. 126600001, completed on 28 August 1956. There appears little reference to these particular 1956 models in any literature outside the factory.

Although fairly robust, the engine had some less than common features such as the CAV Rotary distributor pump instead of the more usual 'in-line' type, and teething troubles even included simply starting the engine. It is on record that number 116600003 of the pre-production batch (registered as UAC 331 on 14 April 1956) went to Ricardo at Shoreham in an attempt to solve this particular problem. The very early diesel Land-Rovers distinguish themselves by having a manually operated mechanism, instead of a solenoid, to pre-engage the starter motor. Between January and September 1957 a further 298 88 diesel Land-Rovers and 153 109 diesel Land-Rovers were built, taking the total for the 1957 season to just 451.

Compared to Perkins now ageing 'P' series 'Aeroflow' head, Rover's engine unfortunately suffered serious diesel 'knock', ironically,

CHAPTER 21 – A Change of Heart – The Diesel Option

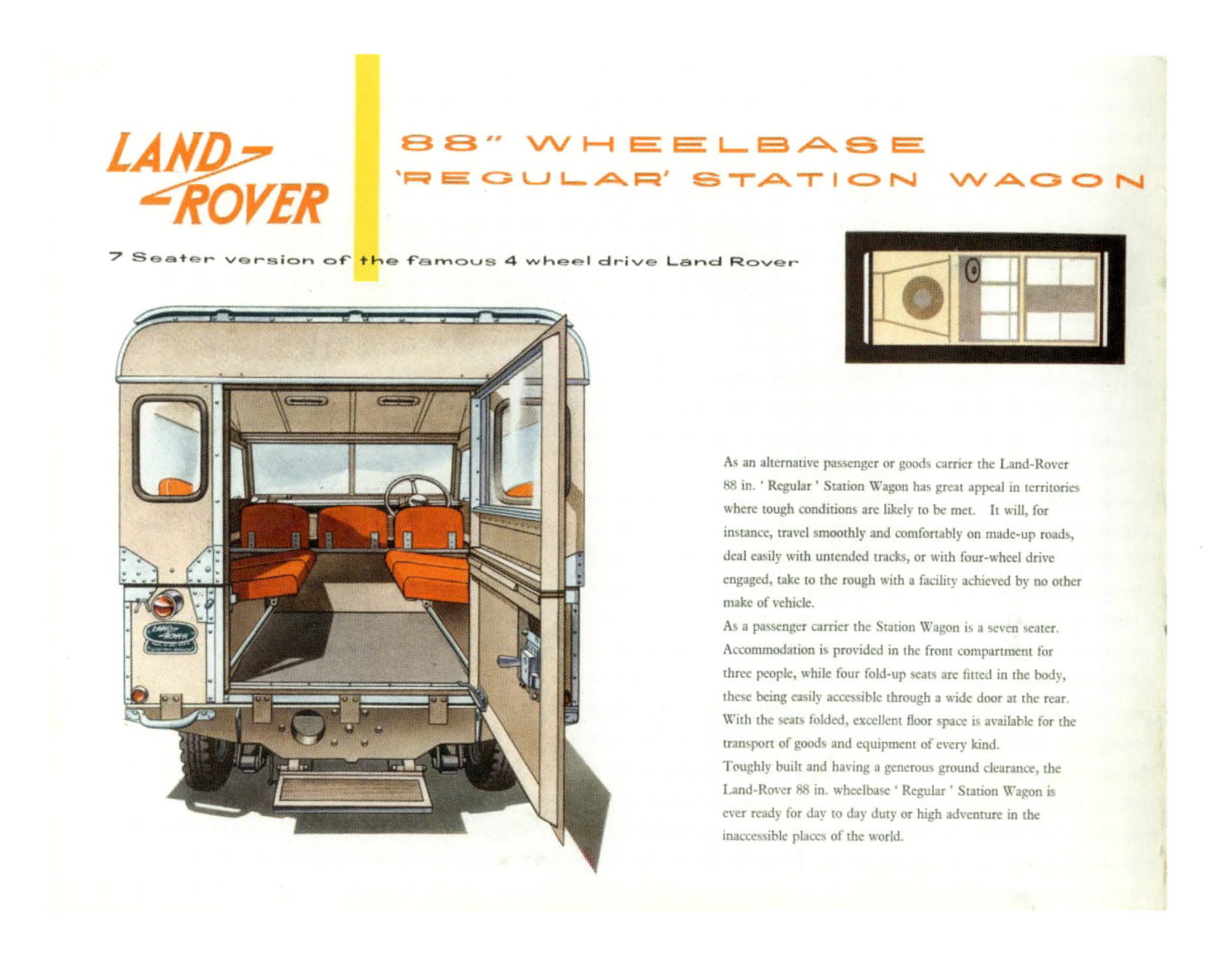

LAND-ROVER | 88" WHEELBASE 'REGULAR' STATION WAGON

7 Seater version of the famous 4 wheel drive Land Rover

As an alternative passenger or goods carrier the Land-Rover 88 in. 'Regular' Station Wagon has great appeal in territories where tough conditions are likely to be met. It will, for instance, travel smoothly and comfortably on made-up roads, deal easily with untended tracks, or with four-wheel drive engaged, take to the rough with a facility achieved by no other make of vehicle.

As a passenger carrier the Station Wagon is a seven seater. Accommodation is provided in the front compartment for three people, while four fold-up seats are fitted in the body, these being easily accessible through a wide door at the rear. With the seats folded, excellent floor space is available for the transport of goods and equipment of every kind.

Toughly built and having a generous ground clearance, the Land-Rover 88 in. wheelbase 'Regular' Station Wagon is ever ready for day to day duty or high adventure in the inaccessible places of the world.

The 88 Station Wagon was now available with diesel power

something the Mark V 'Comet' head was designed to overcome. This, together with the occasional failure of the bottom end, made the new engine seemingly unpopular. In retrospect it is easy to argue that up-dating an already existing manufacturer's proven design would have been a far better proposition in terms of both R & D costing and limited volume production. But for a prestigious company such as Rover, whose design department developed the world's first gas turbine car – the 150 mph 'Jet 1' in 1950 – and were now in the throws of producing their first purpose-built gas turbine car – the four-wheel-drive 'T3' – such an idea would have seemed unthinkable.

When announced in June 1957, the diesel option listed at £715 for a 'Regular' model and £790 for a 'Long' model – £100 more than the petrol equivalent. In terms of power output, the 2.0-litre diesel engine was certainly a success, developing 52 bhp at 3500 rpm with a maximum torque of 82 lbs/ft at 2000 rpm. This compared quite favourably with the 52 bhp at 4000 rpm and torque of 101 lbs/ft at 1500 rpm, produced by the current 2.0-litre

petrol engine. The performance of the two engines was sufficiently similar to warrant no new parts being fitted in the existing transmission beyond the clutch housing, but the diesel engine added an extra 1-cwt (50 kg) to overall weight and the front suspension had to be uprated accordingly, ingeniously done by giving the 88 diesel the front springs of the 109 petrol model, and the 109 diesel the driver's side front spring of a 109 petrol on the passenger's side, the driver's side receiving an uprated spring – the only new spring actually required. Even so, Rover were still able to claim a 50% increase in mpg for the model.

The diesel engine option represented a significant change in the philosophy of Land-Rover development and from now on Land-Rovers would grow much further away from Rover's cars. Other necessary modifications to accommodate the diesel engine included: front spring hangers forward 2 inches; radiator block forward 1 inch, with deeper fan cowl and longer hoses; front wheel arches forward 1 inch in the wings; and an extra 1 inch in bonnet length. There was also a new re-

Diesel model in livery colour at the Commercial Motor Show

Rover's diesel used two 6-volt batteries in series

circulating ball-type steering box, similar to that used in Rover cars, adjustable for wear, with horn push no longer in the steering wheel's centre, but mounted on a bracket attached to the column. The dip-switch was now foot-operated.

Why, you may wonder, did the 10-seater Station Wagon remain on the 107-inch chassis? As a personnel carrier, it was likely to be used more on-road than off-road, and under such conditions as a full load, needed the extra performance offered by the petrol engine, if it was to maintain any sort of reputation at all. As it was, it could barely reach 60 mph unladen in the most favourable conditions, and Rover therefore had little alternative but to stick to the petrol engine. Having made this decision, there was no immediate need to increase its wheelbase, and it now became a convenient way to use existing stock of chassis and any front end parts left over from the previous models.

CHAPTER 21 – A Change of Heart – The Diesel Option

COUNTRY LIFE—ROYAL SHOW SUPPLEMENT—JUNE 27, 1957

The news you've been waiting for...

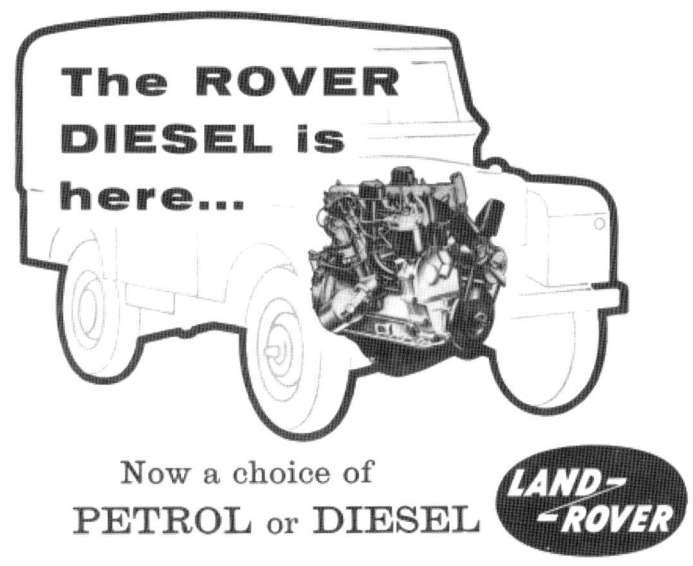

The ROVER DIESEL is here...

Now a choice of PETROL or DIESEL LAND-ROVER

Years of research and rigorous testing have resulted in a Diesel engine as robust and reliable as the Land-Rover itself. An alternative to the famous Petrol engine, this Rover-designed, Rover-built Diesel combines tremendous thrust and pulling power both on and off the road with all the economy of diesel operation. Petrol or Diesel, this is the ideal vehicle for fetching, carrying and towing around the farm or factory. Furthermore, when fitted with centre or rear power take-off, the Land-Rover provides mobile or stationary power capable of operating all kinds of machinery.
Regular Land-Rover: Petrol £515; Diesel £715
Long Land-Rover: Petrol £590; Diesel £790

Petrol or Diesel, there's <u>no</u> substitute for the 4-Wheel Drive LAND-ROVER

See the LAND-ROVERS at the 'Royal'
STAND No. 312

THE ROVER COMPANY LTD., SOLIHULL · WARWICKSHIRE AND DEVONSHIRE HOUSE · PICCADILLY · LONDON

'County Life' advertisement, June 1957

ROVER DIESEL ENGINE ...

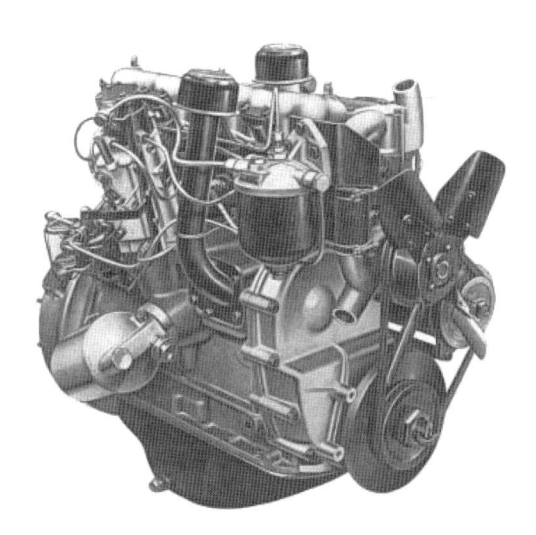

... POWERFUL, ROBUST, ECONOMICAL

Rover's new 2.0-litre diesel

CHAPTER 22
End of the Beginning
The Close of an Era

In June 1956, with the exception of the '10-seater' Station Wagon, all current production of '86 & 107' wheelbase Land-Rovers had been superseded by the new 88 'Regular' and 109 'Long' models in readiness to accept Rover's new diesel engine. Even so, these new models had less than a two-year production run.

Throughout the 1950s Land-Rovers remained Rover's main source of income and activity. In the aftermath of the Suez crisis in 1956, when petrol rationing was reintroduced for a brief period, Rover's car sales fell from an all-time record of 14,855 to only 8,607, but Land-Rover sales took only a slight dip from 28,365 to 25,775, clear indication of where customer loyalty lay. In response, January 1957 saw Rover set up a much-needed 'Technical Sales Department' to deal with customer enquiries regarding specialist applications and other equipment.

Despite what would later be referred to as 'Series I' Land-Rover production coming to a final end, the late 1950s still saw a significant number of modifications and new optional extras for these models.

Land-Rovers destined for Canada were given 'one-piece' door seals. Previously all Station Wagons were either Light Grey or RAF Blue, now Bronze Green became an option, with a spare wheel cover in matching green too. Upholstery in a pretty blue checker pattern was also introduced, and a rear heater, to be used in conjunction with the front heater also became available for both the '7-seater' and '10-seater' Station Wagon.

From October 1956 all 109 models and 107 10-seater Station Wagons were given reinforced rear axles, then a couple of months later, in December 1956, higher-rate roads springs were also introduced for these models. The potential increase in load-carrying capacity of all 'Long' models had a downside, and soon the rear differential became the most frequently replaced item. This was not because of any inherent fault in the unit – it was simply the weakest link in the drive chain.

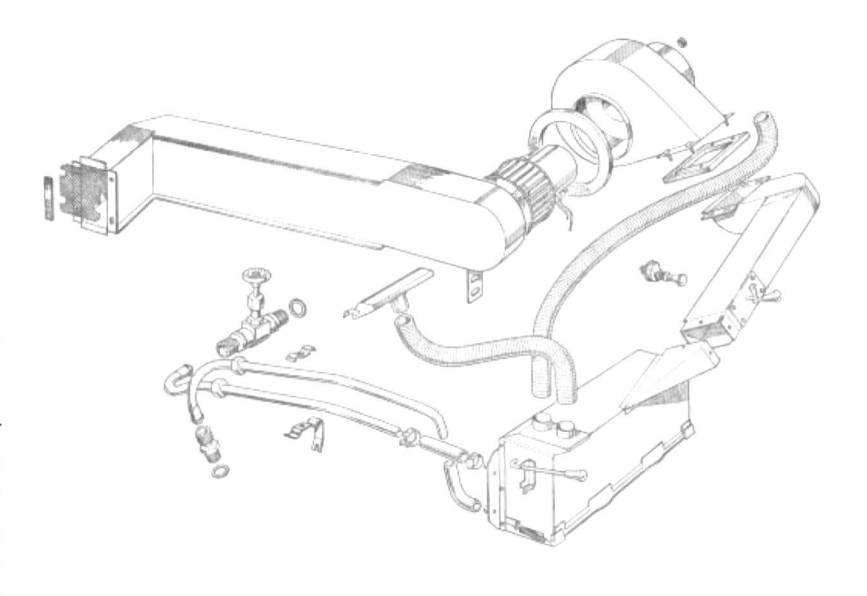

The free-wheeling hub is an accessory which will be of great interest to Land-Rover owners. When fitted on the front wheels these hubs make it possible to stop the rotation of the front transmission.

Apart from saving wear and tear on the front transmission, the removal of rolling resistance on the front wheels results in quieter running with a considerable increase in m.p.g. and tyre life.

Produced in this country especially for the Land-Rover by the Barton Motor Company, Hyde Park Corner, Plymouth, they are easily fitted and the makers claim that the cost of £25 per set is soon recovered by the reduction in operating costs.

LHD heater unit intended for the North American market

'Freewheel' hubs are introduced

Rover produce their first 'Land-Rover In Action' brochure

CHAPTER 22 – End of the Beginning – The Close of an Era

1948 Land-Rover R860405 in LROC trials in the 1960s

Beihan, February 1958

To overcome this problem, a new fully floating axle was introduced in April 1957 that used less expensive and more easily replaceable separate half-shafts as the weak link. This modification was not considered necessary for the 88 'Regular' model, but nevertheless was offered as a factory option. The final modification introduced before 'Series I' production came to a close was a new slightly longer handbrake lever, which would carry over into 'Series II' models, soon to be introduced.

There were quite a number of new 'optional extras' that only appeared in the final 12 months of 'Series I' production. These included: May 1957, a fully floating rear axle conversion kit for earlier 'Long' and 'Regular' models; June 1957, a swivel housing gaiter kit that could be fitted retrospectively to any Land-Rover; March 1958, an optional exterior sun visor and mud flaps (there was no 'Land-Rover' logo on these); towing and lifting rings; and an elaborate fresh air heater for LHD petrol models, which had the heater/blower unit in the engine bay above the toe-box, supplying fresh air from a long rectangular duct via an aperture in the wing. This unit was mainly intended for the North American market as an alternative to the current Smith's recirculating heater.

The first 'Freewheel' front hubs also appeared around this time from the Barton Motor Co. Hyde Park Corner, Plymouth. Barton's hubs received Rover's official approval in 1959 and were soon taken over by Mayflower Automotive Products Ltd., Hamilton Works, Tavistock, Devon, then several years later by Fairey Winches Ltd., of Whitchurch Road, Tavistock, Devon, though 'MAP' still remained on the cast housings.

'Freewheel' hubs would have been no use to 1948–51 Land-Rovers with constant four-wheel-drive (unless, of course, the 'Freewheel' unit's rollers, roller shoes and springs are removed to

The last 'Series I' model to be made by Rover was a 107 10-seater Station Wagon.

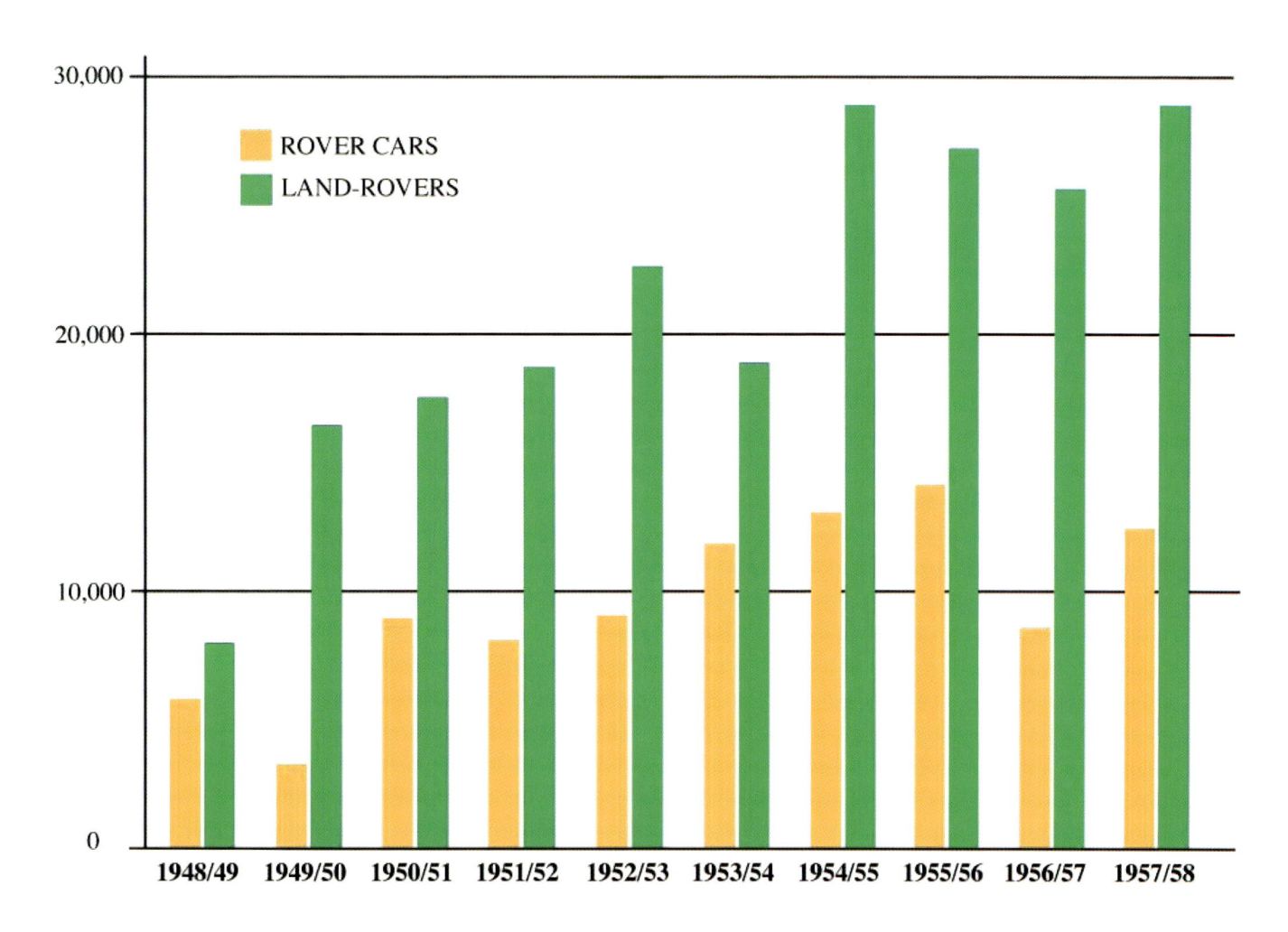

CHAPTER 22 – End of the Beginning – The Close of an Era

CAR AND LAND-ROVER PRODUCTION, 1948-1958

© John S Smith 2009

1948–58 production chart

give 4x2 in high ratio). But now that front drive could be disengaged at the transfer box, with a pair of 'Freewheel' hubs attached, the front differential, drive shafts, and associated universal joints need no longer rotate in thick EP 90 oil. In cooler climates, such as Britain, this offered the promise of a measurable increase in fuel economy when undertaking normal road work, particularly in winter.

Just for the record, although still available, from mid-1955 the Land-Rover's 'Brockhouse' trailer was no longer made by Brockhouse 'in house', but farmed out to another manufacturer and updated with various modifications, including a new pattern casting for the pull-pin housing. Conspicuous by its absence from the list of options, however, was Bullow's compressor unit.

The last 88 'Series I' Petrol Land-Rover to be despatched into the factory on 24 March 1958 was a RHD 'Export' model destined for Auckland, New Zealand, while the last 88 Diesel LHD 'Export' model, was 'despatched in' on 20 March 1958 and went to Kepaco, Guatamala.

The last 109 Petrol 'Series I' Pick-up Truck was a RHD 'Export' model 'despatched in' on 12 March 1958 and headed for Johannesburg, South Africa. The last 109 Diesel Pick-up Truck was a 'Home' model, 'despatched in' on 7 March 1958, it went to R.H. Collier, Birmingham.

The very last 'Series I' Land-Rover to be produced at Solihull was a 10-seater Station Wagon, LHD 'Export' model. 'Despatched in' at the factory on 28 November 1958 – it went to Shell Petroleum in Turkey.

If the calculations are correct, the number of 'Series I' models produced over the ten-year period 1948–58 (excluding all prototypes apart from the 071... series, but including CKD models not actually assembled at the factory), totals 201,501 Land-Rovers.

LAND-ROVER – The Formative Years, 1947–1967

The rear mounted 'Welder' unit

When H. Howe Graham retired as Chairman of Rover in 1957, Spencer Wilks took up the position. His younger brother Maurice, whose idea the Land-Rover had been, remained as joint MD, only now with George Farmer rather than brother Spencer. This opened a new era in Rover's history, generally referred to as 'The Wilks Partnership'. The Land-Rover itself was about to undergo a major rethink in time for the vehicle's 10th anniversary, to be held in April 1958.

At the same time, two new Rover cars were again being developed simultaneously, the 'P5', to tide them over into the 1960s, and the 'P6', which would still be around in the mid-1970s. It was almost a repeat history of the transition from 'P2' to 'P4', through 'P3', that had taken place in the late 1940s. Gas turbine work was also reaching a high degree of refinement in the 'T4' project, and it looked as if a production model might even be ready by the mid-1960s. The gas turbine engine was certainly sufficiently advanced for the Rover-BRM car '00' to take 7th place in the 24-hour 'Le

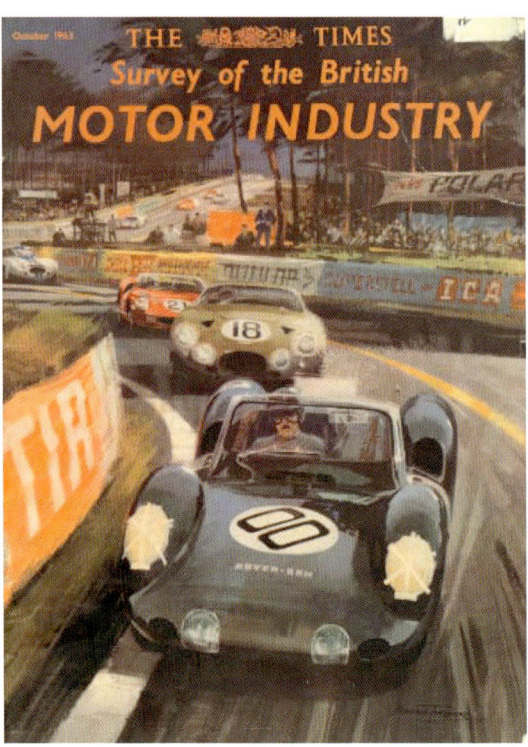

Rover-BRM gas turbine Le Mans car

278

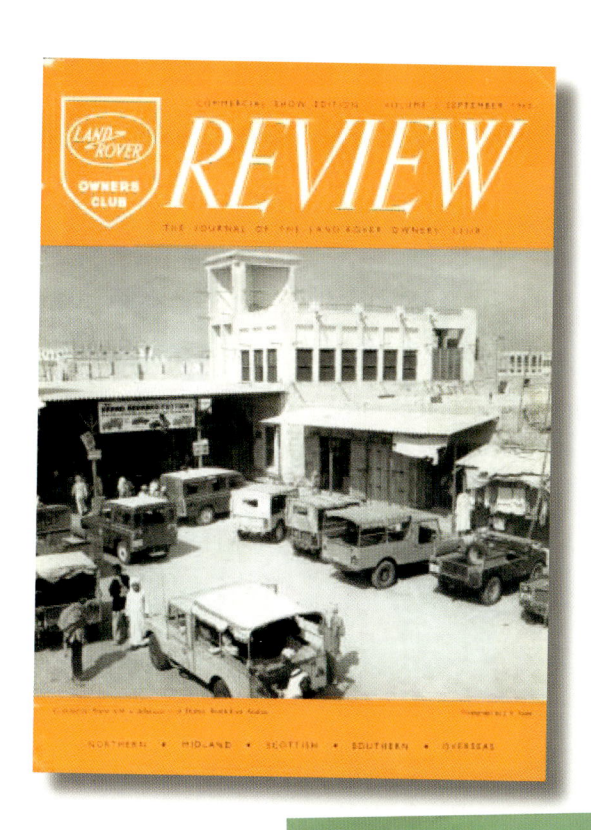

CHAPTER 22 – End of the Beginning – The Close of an Era

'Review' magazine, journal of the LROC

By the early 1960s Series II models were taking prominence

The Lincoln brochure

Welder technical data

279

Mans' as an 'unofficial' entry in 1963. These were certainly exciting times at Rover, the like of which would never be seen again.

Under the guidance and sponsorship of the parent factory, a 'Land-Rover Owners' Club Ltd.' (LROC) was set up in 1955, with the object of providing 'Support and maintenance of country sport and promotion of Land-Rover events throughout the World'.[1] The first National Rally, hosted by the LROC in 1955, took place at the factory and Fenny Compton. Northern, Midland, Southern, and Scottish branches were set up in the UK, and the club's first magazine, 'Review' – an 8-page newspaper-style publication – appeared in September 1957, timed roughly to coincide with the launch of Rover's 2.0-litre diesel engine. But by this time 'Series I' models had only another six months to run, and Rover's prime intention was to use the new owners' club and 'Review' as a means of maintaining brand loyalty at a fairly critical time.

At the very moment Rover planned to introduce their new 'Series II' Land-Rover, Austin's new 'Gypsy' was already lurking in the wings, just a stone's throw away at Longbridge. In a pre-emptive attempt to upstage Rover's new 'Series II' models, the Gypsy would be launched in February 1958, two months ahead of the new Land-Rover. Rover was therefore particularly keen to maintain and preserve their existing advantage, not simply at home and overseas, but in the coveted military market too, where further inroads were now being made. So far, 'jeep' had remained the generic term describing light cross-country cars, and it was felt important that the name 'Land-Rover' should in no way meet with a similar fate, becoming synonymous with any old 4x4. In their publicity that year, Rover were therefore quick to point out that *'When better Land-Rovers are made, the Rover Company will make them.'*

[1] As stated in 'Who's Who in the Motor & Commercial Vehicle Industries' 1965.

Britain's 'Workhorse of the World' was fast entering a growing leisure market at this time, not only in outdoor pursuits, such as boating, climbing, and equestrian activities, where the vehicle was an aid to the sport, but also in competitive trials, exploratory expeditions, and safaris, where the vehicle was central to the activity. Whether a Land-Rover remained a brand name specific to Rover's vehicle, or simply became a type of vehicle in the mind of the market would be critical in determining any future competitor's survival, and subsequently Land-Rover's own fate.

The leading article in the first edition of the 'Review' magazine invited members of the club to 'TEST YOUR LAND-ROVER AT SOLIHULL'. To many a would-be off-roader, such an invitation must have seemed like a dream come true in the same way that an opportunity to drive your vehicle around the present Solihull 'Jungle Track' might seem today. To this end, every Land-Rover club member was *'...urged to regard this as a tremendous recruiting opportunity, with incentives to each sector to obtain a maximum number of new members in time for the event'*. As well as the usual 'trials' there was also a Concours D'élégance: *'Awards will go for the state of preservation, pride of ownership, and all the aspects of Land-Rover owning that distinguish this from the ownership of an ordinary vehicle'*.

Such brand loyalty would continue to be encouraged for the next decade, but then quite suddenly the Leyland organisation, Rover's new owner, became increasingly embarrassed by the age of vehicles turning up at such sponsored events. Ten years earlier it was understandable that 'Series I' models dominated the scene, but when in the 1970s little had changed, they could not see how this helped to sell new Land-Rovers. Clearly the message this gave out to any newcomer visiting these sporting events, was that he should go and find a Land-Rover of at least ten years' standing, and preferably near to twenty, if he was to take

Southern Land-Rover Club badge

Rover Owners Association badge

CHAPTER 22 – End of the Beginning – The Close of an Era

A Series II version produced by Roadless Traction was approved by Rover in 1961

Forestry Commission trials in Hampshire; the Land-Rover is fitted with 10.00 x 28 tractor-type wheels

the whole business seriously. The very last thing he should be doing was going round to the local dealer and ordering a brand new one.

The old Rover Company had never taken this too seriously, as it meant good publicity for the vehicle as a whole, and besides, it sold plenty of spares. But with the virtual collapse of the new parent organisation, British Leyland, in 1974, when the government took a 95% shareholding, such things were all too much. Whitehall's minions were far more concerned with trying to salvage what had already sunk to the bottom rather than making sure all those hopefully still afloat would weather the storm. Besides, what knowledge did they have of the part played by such sporting events and the people involved in their organisation – farmers, traders, dealers, and country folk, for many of whom the Land-Rover was a constant companion in their everyday working life, and the very reason why they were so closely attached to these vehicles.

By 1959, the 'Review' had become a proper monochrome 'glossy' of around 20 pages and would continue in production for a further decade. The magazine was always full of exciting adventures and expeditions involving Land-Rovers in faraway

End of the road – the 1957 production line would soon be superseded by Series II models

places. Volume 10, No.1, January 1967, however, was the last edition to invite membership of the Land-Rover Owners' Club. In the merger with Leyland in March 1967, the Rover Company's loss of independence was to coincide with the demise of the LROC. Instead, a new 'Rover Owners' Association' (ROA) was to take over, the inaugural meeting taking place on 8 April 1967. There would, however, be little bonding between Land-Rover owners and Rover car owners, reflecting a complete lack of understanding, on the part of Rover's current management, of the real world situation.

By this time there was a total of eight area organisations for Land-Rover owners – Scottish - Northern - Midland - South Eastern - South Western - Overseas - South Africa - Australian – and it was clearly hoped they would all become foster children of this new parent organisation. The 'Review' itself continued for a while, but was eventually replaced by the BLMC magazine 'High Road' in 1969, which as the title suggests, had little to do with Land-Rovers.

The ROA itself continued for a while with a simple newsletter, but there was nothing to take the place of the old 'Review' for the Land-Rover man. Instead, the real enthusiast now had to rely on the various independent newsletters being produced by an ever-growing number of Land-Rover clubs, both at home and overseas, for up-to-the-minute information on events and so forth, but there was generally little of real adventure within their pages.

With increasing foreign competition, particularly from the Far East, Rover's Viking ship would certainly sail through choppy waters. Although the Land-Rover continued to make a profit, none of it was to be made available to Rover's management, and in the hot summer of 1978 the sponsoring organisation, the 'Rovers Owners' Association', which had been based at the Lode Lane 'Meteor Works' at Solihull was forced to give way to a new independent 'Association of Rover Clubs'. How that was supposed to help Leyland out of its crisis is anybody's guess.

Certainly history has recorded the British as a nation of adventurers, ill content to be bound by their island shores. With the Second World War behind them, it was as if they were catching up on time as they rushed off to all corners of the world. If their means of overland transportation was not the camel, horse, or simply shanks's pony, it was

CHAPTER 22 – End of the Beginning – The Close of an Era

1958 Central Brazil still offered a serious challenge

The long wheelbase Land-Rover was a popular load carrier for expeditions

invariably the Land-Rover. As a consequence of this almost frenzied activity, the Land-Rover soon became a familiar sight in almost every country in the world. It needed no one to boast of its outstanding rugged reliability. The simple fact that the Land-Rover was there was proof enough.

But by the 1960s the adventurous were facing a different problem – they were running out of room. In 1956 the Australian, Len Beadel, pioneered the first access road across central Australia and the infamous Gibson Desert in a Land-Rover. 'The Gunbarrel Highway', as it became known, was officially opened two years later on Saturday, 15 November 1958.

The one great journey not completed by the end of the 1950s was that from Alaska to Cape Horn, the greatest obstacle being the impenetrable jungle and swampland of the Darien Peninsular on the southern side of the Panama Canal. There can be few areas of the world more inhospitable to a creature such as man. Finally on 18 May 1960 even this seemingly insurmountable barrier tumbled when Richard Bevir and his Australian companion/mechanic Terence Whitfield, crossed the Darien Gap in a new 'Series II' Land-Rover. It was to be the first north-south crossing of the great American continent, from Fairbanks in Alaska to Tierra del Fuego on the southern tip of Chile. One of the world's last land barriers had at last fallen to the appropriately named Land-Rover. What better foundation could the Solihull firm have to assure the company's long-term future?

CHAPTER 23
Into the Sixties
The New Series II

The original 80-inch Land-Rover of 1948, and even the later 'Series I' models of the mid-1950s, had all been conceived in a period of post-war austerity, reflected in the vehicle's simple functional design over the past decade. Times had changed though, and Britain's Conservative government now felt able to tell the population of Britain 'You've never had it so good' in the run-up to the general election of 1959. The period of 'Wilks' Partnership' had already begun, and the two brothers were particularly concerned at the growing level of competition in the field car market, especially overseas.

India, Ceylon, and Ghana had all received their independence in the last ten years, and another twenty Commonwealth nations would also receive theirs within the next ten. Within five years Britain would make a first abortive attempt to join the European Economic Community. All this would mean that Rover, along with the rest of Britain's motor industry, could no longer expect the same preferential treatment they had received from the Commonwealth countries in the immediate post-war years.

The merger of Nuffield with Austin in 1952 left Britain's motor industry dominated by the 'Big Five'. Maurice Wilks now felt that Rover's problem was that as an independent company, they were now 'too big to be small, and too small to be big'. This made the threat from Willys-Overland, with its huge distribution network, seem very real indeed. Willys had already updated their Jeep as the CJ-5 (M38A) in 1952, replacing the now ageing 2.2-litre L-head side valve engine with their more powerful 2.3-litre inlet-over-exhaust F-head 'Hurricane' engine, to give a useful power increase from 54 to 72bhp.

In April 1953, Willys-Overland was taken over by the industrialist Henry J. Kaiser, and renamed Willys Motors Inc. Now, not only would the Jeep be built in the USA and Canada (Ford), but also, under licence, in Europe (Hotchkiss in

The Series II 10-seater

CHAPTER 23 – Into the Sixties – The New Series II

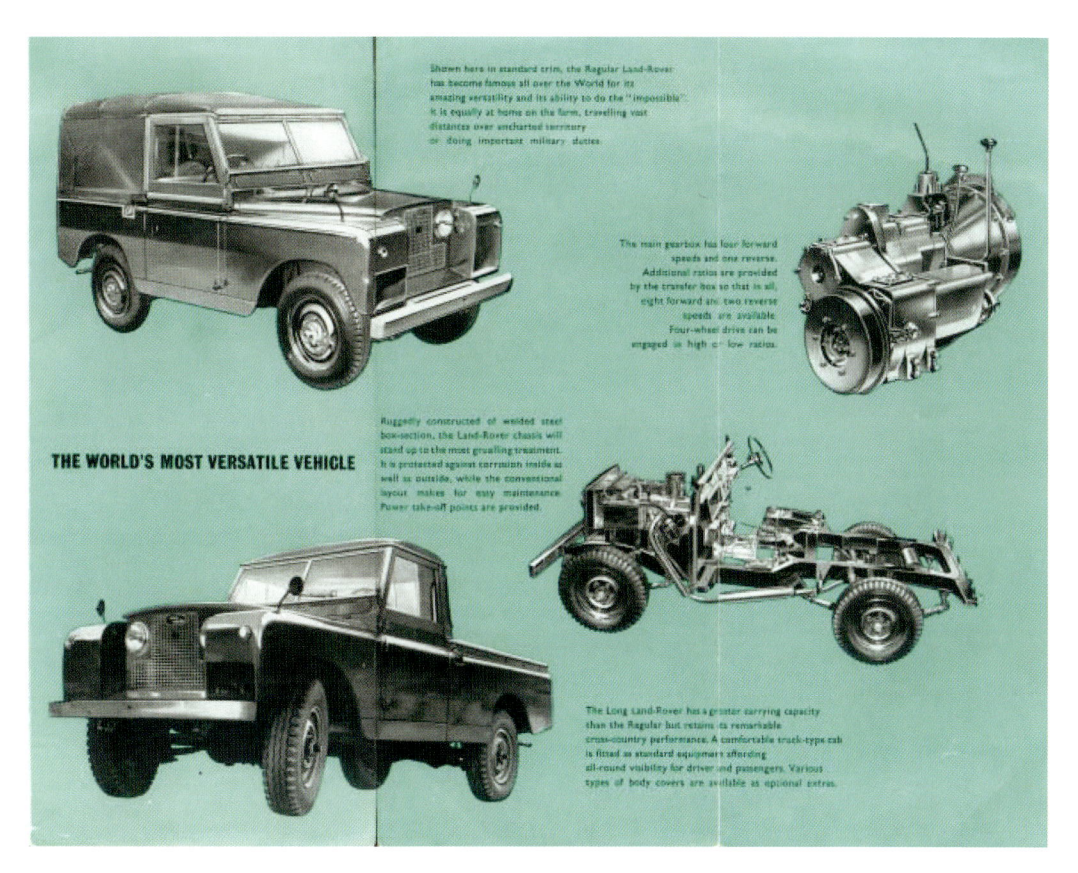

The new Series II brochure

Rover's press release pack announcing the new Series II Land-Rover

Land-Rover chassis specially adapted to take the Jeep body; the Land-Rover's engine, transmission and suspension will still be used

The cab of the Land-Rover/Willys Jeep

France; Kaiser-Frazer in the Netherlands; VIASA in Spain), the Indian sub-continent (Mahindra in India), the Far East (Mitsubishi in Japan), and South America (Kaiser in Argentina). Within a decade the name 'Willys' would be gone for ever when, in March 1963, the company became the 'Kaiser Jeep Corporation', and finally, from 1970, the 'Jeep Corp.'

Rover's concern over the expansion of Jeep production facilities during the 1950s was such that, soon after the launch of their new Series II Land-Rover, the following announcement appeared in the 'Daily Telegraph', 12 June 1958:

LAND ROVER AND JEEP MAY LINK
By Our Motoring Correspondent

Production and distribution of the two four-wheel-drive cars, the American Jeep and the British Land Rover, may be linked, an announcement by the Rover Co. of Birmingham, hinted yesterday.

"The Rover Company," said the statement, "have commenced discussions with Willys Motors Incorporated to see if there are mutual advantages in an association between these two companies in certain fields of production and distribution of four-wheeled drive vehicles. It is too early at the present time to say if any results are likely from these discussions."

Rover severed their relationship with their north American distributor, Rootes Motors and set up the Rover Motor Company of North America.

At the same time Rover decided to set about building a Land-Rover/Willys prototype using the entire transmission and rolling chassis from their new $2^{1}/_{4}$-litre 'Regular' model, but with the wheelbase shortened from 88 to 83 inches to accommodate the wheel arches of the CJ-5 Jeep's pressed steel body. It was the complete antithesis of their hybrid prototype Land-Rover of 1947.

Where all this was supposed to lead, nobody quite knows, for although discussions did take place between the Rover Co. and Willys Motors Incorporated, for better or worse, nothing seems to have materialised from them.

A short time later, in the early 1960s, the Jeep really did come almost too close for comfort. It was bad enough that Jeeps were already being manufactured in Europe and supplied to the Dutch, French and Spanish military, but when Joe Bamford of JCB fame started to examine the possibility of manufacturing Jeeps under licence in Britain too, as a complement to his existing range of JCB excavating equipment for the construction industry, it must have sent shivers down Rover's spine. Bamford imported around a dozen Jeeps for evaluation purposes, but fortunately for Rover, he concluded that JCB already had sufficient work on their hands without extending their concern into new areas.

By this time not only had Mitsubishi, Nissan, and Toyota penetrated the Far East, but they were now conquering Britain's traditional markets in the Middle East, Africa, and Australia with their cross-country cars. In Europe around a dozen

Jeep chassis with body removed

CHAPTER 23 – Into the Sixties – The New Series II

LAND-ROVER – The Formative Years, 1947–1967

manufacturers had also been making an effort to break into the field car market too, although Alfa Romeo, Auto Union, and Fiat seemed to be the only ones enjoying any real measure of success. Still closer to home was Austin at Longbridge, who just a year or two earlier had tried to persuade Tom Barton and Jack Pogmore to leave Rover's Land-Rover and help develop a new British 4x4, the Austin 'Gypsy'.

This was the background surrounding a major revision of the Land-Rover, and was all part of Rover's celebrations for the vehicle's first decade of success. Based on the late 'Series I' model, then still in production, pre-production models for the new Series II Land-Rover first appeared at the Commercial Motor show in October 1957. The original semi-floating rear axle was retained on the 'Regular' model, and both axles sat well inside the new bodywork, but they were abandoned on the first production models that appeared in February 1958. The 'Long' model followed in March, and Maurice Wilks personally announced both vehicles on 15 April 1958 as part of the official 10th Anniversary celebrations. The following day a press release headed 'TWO NEW LAND-ROVERS' gave full details.

The Series II 'Regular' model was certainly a far cry from the models of 1948, but mechanically remained remarkably similar to the later 'Series I' model it replaced. The engine was still the same 2.0-litre petrol or diesel unit, along with most of the transmission. The main distinction from any previous model was the bodywork, which had been totally restyled by David Bache, who had only recently finished work on the P5 Rover car, a new 3.0-litre Coupé to be announced in the autumn.

Bache did an excellent job and the end result was equally as pleasing considering the difference in these two vehicles. There will, of course, always be those diehards who argue that the real functional appeal of the Land-Rover was lost from that day on, and that its smooth new look would now compromise it as a genuine workhorse. But left to them we would probably still be waiting for the

The Land-Rover chassis can be clearly seen under the Jeep bodywork

Recognisably Jeep, but unrecognisably Land-Rover

Was this a 'Wolf' in Jeep's clothing?

A British-made Jeep may have had its appeal

CHAPTER 23 – Into the Sixties – The New Series II

Regular with canvas hood removed

Regular with truck cab (optional extra)

Regular hard-top (optional extra)

Regular hard-top with side windows for export (optional extra)

Land-Rover Regular Station Wagon

Land-Rover Regular Fire Engine

The large capacity body of the Long Land-Rover

Long with three-quarter length hood (optional extra)

Long three-quarter length hood with side windows for export (optional extra)

Long with full-length canvas hood (optional extra)

Land-Rover Long Station Wagon

Land-Rover Long Fire Engine

Series II – the full range

four-wheeled cart. What really mattered was that the Land-Rover still remained a rugged reliable working vehicle, which is more than can be said of the majority of 4x4s by the 1980s.

Rover explained the new style: 'To achieve a smoother and more pleasing appearance, the wings had been given a small curve which was carried along the waistline for the length of the vehicle'. This gave a simple unity to the whole structure. Above the new waistline, such bodywork as there was now tapered towards the roofline, and final touches included valances below the doors, a front apron, and deeper bumper. The door and side screen frames were no longer galvanised, but completely skinned in light alloy and painted, again giving the vehicle a more uniform appearance. Fully floating axles, now standard on all models, were marginally wider, increasing track by a mere $1\frac{1}{2}$ inches, but it was sufficient to reduce the turning circle by 3 ft. on a 'Regular' model, and 5 ft. on a 'Long' model and lower the centre of gravity, sufficient to increase the safe angle of tilt from 30° to 45°.

Inside the cab little had changed, apart from the pendant brake and clutch pedals hanging down inside the toe box instead of coming upwards, and ventilation was controlled by two screw in/out hand-wheels on the dash. Upholstery was in the same grey leather cloth and the fuel tank also remained under the driver's seat, but the filter cap was now remote and conveniently situated externally adjacent to the driver's door. Other new features included a single lever catch for the bonnet and new tail board catches.

It may be recalled that when the 86 model was being developed back in 1952/3 certain prototypes were fitted with a deeper rear body, but it just did not look right and was eventually only used on the 107 model. This time the deeper body was also being used for the 'Regular' model too, but with the new bodywork it now looked perfectly satisfactory, a credit to David Bache. The dimensions of the 'Regular' model changed very little, but the increase in overall weight of 160 lbs, coupled with a slightly larger frontal area, reduced the power

LAND-ROVER – The Formative Years, 1947–1967

Dubai – 1960 new Series II models mix with earlier Land-Rovers

to weight ratio, and in consequence, the vehicle's overall road performance was also reduced.

The new-look 'Long' model was given exactly the same styling treatment as the 'Regular' Land-Rover. This included a redesigned cab for the standard model, with new curved roof and quarter lights, together with a 'de luxe' bonnet with a rolled edge to match the body line. The driver's seat was also adjustable now, and 'one-piece' doors were avaiable for the Canadian market.

Mechanically, however, the 'Long' Land-Rover was very different. It had a new $2\frac{1}{4}$-litre overhead valve petrol engine, specially designed for the Series II Land-Rover, but in keeping with past policy, it was not introduced immediately with the Series II models when they came out on the 'Regular' chassis a month earlier. The new engine developed 77 bhp at a 4250 rpm with a maximum torque of a 124 lbs/ft at 2500 rpm, which represented an increase of 48% in bhp and 22% in torque over the old 2.0-litre engine. Harry Weslake can be credited for the improvement in performance, as he was apparently responsible for the new cylinder head design.

The rest of the engine was based on an 'over square' bore to allow the use of large valves in the head to maintain adequate breathing. Unlike the recently introduced 2.0-litre diesel engine, wet liners were not used, and the bottom end was also more robust to ensure longevity under the most arduous conditions. Roller cam followers were used to reduce wear of the cam lobes, the first item generally to show signs of wear after prolonged use of the previous 1.6-litre and 2.0-litre F-head engines. Under the bonnet, the traditional Skinner's Union electric fuel pump, which always managed to provide fuel to the float chamber under the most arduous conditions, was no longer in evidence, having been replaced by a new camshaft-activated 'AC' mechanical lift pump, that had seen service in the diesel model since 1956.

Rover capitalised on their milestone with this advertisement

It made their customers happy too

CHAPTER 23 – Into the Sixties – The New Series II

The 250,000th Land-Rover

250,000 LAND-ROVERS prove...

...there is no substitute for EXPERIENCE

250,000 Land-Rovers ago, the Rover Company — long famous for fine cars — sold their first Land-Rover. The intervening 11 years have proved that the owner was not gambling. Since then there have been developments and improvements, but today's Land-Rover confirms the basic rightness of the original Rover-engineered design.

The Land-Rover has proved itself in 157 world markets. Police and Armed Forces, farmers, forestry and fire authorities, oil companies, contractors, construction engineers and explorers — these are the regular users whose loyalty shows that

...there's no substitute for the 4-wheel drive

LAND-ROVER Petrol or Diesel

THE ROVER COMPANY LTD SOLIHULL WARWICKSHIRE also DEVONSHIRE HOUSE PICCADILLY LONDON

250,000 LAND-ROVERS

WING PARK FARM,
WING,
LEIGHTON BUZZARD, BEDS.
December 7th, 1959.

The Rover Company Limited.

Dear Sirs,

I was interested in your advertisement in the 'Daily Mail' today, Monday 7th December.

When you first started making Land-Rovers I had a friend in Twickenham who rang up and said that at last he had a vehicle which I as a farmer could not use too roughly. (My car was always getting knocked about on the farm).

He made me buy same, which I think was the third Land-Rover to come on to the market in England. Since then I have never been without a Land-Rover, particularly since you have made it capable of being used as a car — quite comfortable and warm, it makes me really happy !

I remember my neighbours used to laugh when I first used to drive round my farm and said that they would never be seen driving about in a box like that ; but after a very little time they had all got Land-Rovers themselves.

Once again I say well done for manufacturing such a versatile vehicle.

Yours truly,

VICTOR J. NORTH.

LAND-ROVER – The Formative Years, 1947–1967

Princess Margaret in the RAF's latest 'Saluting' model

From the previous colour range only 'Bronze Green', 'Light Grey' 'Poppy Red' and 'Beige' (although the latter was later replaced by 'Sand') remained, and there was a revival of 'Light Green', which was a close match to the original 1948 colour. The old 'RAF Blue' was replaced with 'Marine Blue', and an additional 'Dark Grey' was also available. With the exception of 'self colour' for 'Bronze Green' and 'Poppy Red' Land-Rovers, all wheels were now painted 'Off-White'.

The biggest surprise, however, was the vehicle's price. The 'Regular' model listed at £640, an increase of only £10 over the 'Series I' model it replaced, while the 'Long' model, with its new engine, was slightly more at £730, compared to £708. The diesel option was an extra £90 – £10 less than before – which meant the 'Regular' diesel was in fact no more expensive than its 'Series I' counterpart. Initially there were no Series II Station Wagons, petrol or diesel, but 'Series I' 107 10-seater Station Wagon models remained available as before.

By June 1958, the new $2\frac{1}{4}$-litre engine had found its way into all Series II petrol models, including a new Station Wagon on a 'Regular' chassis, which appeared a little later in August. This had been a fairly straightforward development, requiring only the addition of a hard top with sliding windows this time, alpine and quarter lights, a tropical roof panel, a new one-piece rear door specially let into the roof for additional head clearance, rear seats, and a rear step. The 'Long' model was, however, a much more complicated affair, and the 'Series I' 107 10-seater soldiered on to fill this gap. Only the 'Rover 60' car and 107 Station Wagon now retained Rover's four-cylinder F-head engine.

When the last 'Series I' 107 10-seater Station Wagon finally rolled of the production line on 28 November 1958, headed for Shell Petroleum Co. Turkey, it marked the end of an era. The original four-cylinder F-head engine, which had faithfully served the Land-Rover so well for over a decade, would now be confined to the last 1,500 or so 'Rover 60' cars, before being discontinued for ever. That same month, the new Series II Station Wagon on the 'Long' chassis was announced to the world and immediately replaced the former model.

The new Station Wagon on the 'Long' chassis had completely lost the 'Meccano' appearance of the previous model, now that it had the same smooth clean lines as all other Series II Land-Rovers. But it needed many new or modified parts not found elsewhere. Even the chassis had to be specially modified to take the centre compartment and pillars supporting the second pair of one-piece side doors. Between these pillars the transverse panel had gone, with just a grab rail remaining to support the front seat backs. The rear body, specially modified from the 'Long' model, utilised the same glazed side panels as the 'Regular' Station Wagon, but a lengthened roof and tropical panel were needed, which would be shared later with a full-length hard top for the long model.

Initially, the number of seats provided in the Series II 'Long' Station Wagon was still ten, and the central transverse seating continued to provide a useful bed, but three years later in early 1962 a 12-seater version also became available. This was primarily intended for 'Home' consumption, as Rover had found a nice little loophole in the law, which they made clear in their sales literature: *'...the twelve-seater Land-Rover is not subject to United Kingdom Purchase Tax and represents outstanding value for money'.* In the UK, a vehicle with 12 seats or more was not classed as a passenger car, but a bus, and as such was a commercial vehicle and not subject to the tax. To buy a 10-seater Station Wagon, including Purchase Tax, cost £1,293, while

CHAPTER 23 – Into the Sixties – The New Series II

New Series II Land-Rovers entering service get a bigger bumper

Desert Patrol

293

LAND-ROVER – The Formative Years, 1947–1967

Latest 'Land-Rover In Action' brochure

the new 12-seater version weighed in at only £950. It was a significant saving indeed.

Increasing the seating capacity involved a simple modification, the length of the rear-most wheel arch seats along the side being increased in length to accommodate three passengers, and the transverse 'bed' seat giving way to three individual folding seats. There was certainly nothing 'Vorsprung Durch Technik' about the 'Long' Station Wagon, just good old solid, simple and reliable British engineering. More frequently referred to as the 10- or 12-seater 'Safari', today many enthusiasts of the marque consider these Series II and IIA Station Wagons to be the Land-Rover at its very best.

At the time the original 10-seater Station Wagon first appeared, Rover was already able to boast a range of nine vehicles in seven colours with 76 optional extras for specialised duties. The 'Regular' Land-Rover was available as either: a basic model with canvas hood; a truck with cab; a hard top with optional windows for export; a Station Wagon; and a Fire Engine, specially converted by Carmichael of Worcester. 'Long' models were available as: a pick-up truck with cab and an optional three-quarter-length canvas tilt with windows for export; a full-length canvas tilt; a Station Wagon; and a Fire Engine, similar to the regular model, but with additional seating in the form of an extra transverse bench seat similar to that already offered as an optional item.

Sales of Series II models continued to top 28,000 per year, a figure regularly achieved since the introduction of the late 2.0-litre engine in 1955. Careful planning and an increase in the number of CKD models saw output increase to over 35,000 by 1961. This was by no means the end of the current expansion programme. When production of the P4 'Auntie' Rovers finally came to an end in 1964, a new factory on the northern boundary took car production out of the main Solihull building, allowing still further expansion of output, long overdue, to 45,000 Land-Rovers a year.

The latest 'Special Vehicles' range

294

CHAPTER 23 – Into the Sixties – The New Series II

MULTIPLICATION!

The Land-Rover demonstrates quite perfectly the Darwinian theory of natural selection which suggests that the best adapted forms are the ones which survive. And how the Land-Rover adapts! The eighteen examples above, photographed during a recent demonstration at Solihull, in fact represent only a tiny percentage of the total number of special purpose Land-Rovers available.
Right. And this is how it was done!

1. A rotating hydraulic platform by Simon Engineering with a maximum height of 25 feet.
2. A Dixon Bate articulated 88 inch Land-Rover with fifth wheel coupling and vacuum brakes, towing a special personnel carrier.
3. An Edgehill high level conveyor and aircraft loader mounted on a 109 inch Land-Rover.
4. A Station Wagon based mobile cinema with a generator for supplying its own power.
5. Shorland Armoured Car.
6. A Forward Control mounted engine compressor unit.
7. A 109 inch Station Wagon fitted with Mayflower recovery winch and free-wheeling hubs.
8. A 109 inch Land-Rover with a Broom & Wade under-floor rotary compressor, and an hydraulically operated drum winch.
9 & 10. Two ambulance conversions by Invercarron and Pilchers respectively.
11. A Dormobile Station Wagon caravan conversion.
12. An H.C.B. Angus Forward Control Fire Tender conversion fitted with Aeon rubber springs.
13. A McConnell rear-driven mobile saw bench and a centre-mounted forestry winch.
14. A 109 inch Land-Rover fitted with a straight-bladed snow plough, an engine heater, an hydraulic pump and welding generator.
15. An Evers & Wall field sprayer with folding booms.
16. A light vehicle recovery unit by Harvey Frost.
17. A Carmichael 109 inch Fire Tender with hollow rubber springs.
18. An 88 inch Station Wagon with air conditioning and Bostrom suspension seats.

CHAPTER 24
IIA and Beyond
Widening and Deepening the Range

The new Series II Land-Rover had a production run of only three and a half years before it was superseded by the new updated Series IIA model in September 1961. Land-Rover output was now at its highest level – more than 35,000 units a year. In all, around 100,000 Series II were produced, roughly the same as post-'54 'Series I' Land-Rovers, but that had taken five years to accomplish.

These were certainly eventful years at Solihull, and were responsible for much of the success the Land-Rover would enjoy while the rest of Britain's motor industry began its slow and almost inevitable decline the following decade. In the ten years leading up to the Series II model, Rover had developed their cross-country car into a product of unrivalled versatility. The formative years of the Land-Rover were clearly over, and there now seemed no limit to the vehicle's future potential.

Right from the start, overseas sales dominated factory output, many vehicles now being constructed overseas from CKD parts or completed using additional parts made locally under licence.

Early Series IIA brochure

CHAPTER 24 – IIA and Beyond – Widening and Deepening the Range

IIA Station Wagon

109 chassis layout

This trend was about to continue with renewed vigour. The Spanish armed forces had been using 'Series I' Land-Rovers for only a short time before their own Spanish-built 'Santana' Series II model began to appear from the MSA factory at Linares, Jaen, in 1959. These were generally similar to the Solihull range of models, but in addition they also produced their own 'topless' 109 Station Wagon for use by the Spanish armed forces. Their civilian Station Wagon models also differed from their Solihull counterparts by not having the rear door let into the roofline, and in this respect remained similar to 'Series I' models. Santana severed its relationship with Land-Rover in 1983.

Land-Rovers used by the Australian Army were also constructed locally, mainly from CKD parts, but had specially modified front wings and sometimes a shortened rear end. Although the Australians had been using 'Series I' models for some years (27,000 were shipped over in the first ten years), it was not until 1959 that the Land-Rover was officially adopted by their Army. Since the early 1950s, the Swiss Army had used a small number of 'Series I' Land-Rovers. In 1960 they decided to officially adopt the Land-Rover with their first large consignment of 240 Series II 'Regular' models. By 1965, they had taken, in total, 2,200 Land-Rovers.

LAND-ROVER – The Formative Years, 1947–1967

A new '12-seater' is introduced to the range

At home, the British armed forces continued to take Land-Rovers as their most numerous transport, the 'Regular' Series II models becoming the 'Mk8' and the 'Long' model the 'Mk7', but these vehicles were no longer the basic commercial vehicle of 'Series I' days. All military Land-Rovers were now specialist vehicles with bumperettes, easily detachable headlight units and, on 'Regular' models, a special grille protected an oil cooler unit installed immediately in front of the coolant radiator. Military models also had their suspension uprated, with extra long shackles used on 'Long' models. Those converted into ambulances had special extra large bodywork and anti-roll bars fitted to compensate for weight transference when cornering. Ambulances and Air Crash Rescue vehicles used by the RAF also had an additional full-width guard above their bumper.

'Series I' Land-Rovers were never equipped at the factory as FFW (Fitted For Wireless) or later, FFR (Fitted For Radio) vehicles, as this role was generally undertaken by the Austin 'Champ', specially fitted with a 24-volt electrical system and supplied as either GS or FFW models. A number of Land-Rovers were however, converted by the REME as and when necessary, but with the introduction of the Series II model, FFR vehicles became available direct from the factory using a 24-volt, 40-amp rectified AC electrical system, with facilities for charging radio batteries.

Specialist conversions for the SAS and various other roles continued to expand, taking military Land-Rovers even further away from their civilian counterparts. Such specialisation would, however, soon take the Land-Rover full circle in its development with the advent of the 'Airportable' lightweight model in 1965 – a purpose-built military Land-Rover which had little visual resemblance to any model then in production.

The origin of the Lightweight Land-Rover goes back to when the Army first discovered that the new Series II models, being slightly wider than any previous Land-Rover, could apparently no longer be fitted two abreast in the Army's latest transport, the Blackburn 'Beverley C1'. The Beverley was the first British aircraft specifically designed for dropping heavy equipment through removable rear loading doors, and the largest aircraft in service

CHAPTER 24 – IIA and Beyond – Widening and Deepening the Range

NEW ROVER 2¼-LITRE DIESEL ENGINE FOR THE LAND-ROVER

In the first edition of the Review in September 1957 (it was then an 8-page, single-colour, newspaper-style, publication) the Rover 2-Litre diesel engine was introduced to members. During these last four years many thousands of Land-Rovers equipped with the 2-Litre diesel engine have been giving service in all conditions throughout the world. This unit has now been replaced by a 2¼-Litre diesel engine, which, with its additional ¼-litre capacity and improvements made to component parts, develops 62 b.h.p.—an increase in power of more than 20%.

Rover engineers have used the same basic design of the 2-Litre unit with the result that the 2¼-Litre diesel engine is in every way as robust as its predecessor. With the new engine fitted, the governed maximum speed of the Regular Land-Rover is increased from 52½ m.p.h. to 60 m.p.h.; Long vehicles, due to the larger diameter tyres fitted, now have a governed top speed of 66 m.p.h.

Fuel consumption has not appreciably changed except, of course, when the higher speeds and loads are used, and up to 28 m.p.g. can be expected.

Many advanced features have been incorporated in the new diesel engine. To ensure the highest possible degree of air utilisation the Ricardo Comet V type combustion chambers include a Rover provisional patent which was conceived for the 2-Litre engine and has been further developed for the 2¼-Litre unit. This takes the form of "pimples" which improve the heat transfer between the chamber surface and the gas, and assist the mixing of air and fuel, thus reducing the delay period and permitting a more retarded timing without loss of efficiency. These "pimples" also facilitate starting at very low temperatures: in tests conducted by Rover engineers quick starts have been obtained with ambient temperatures as low as minus 30°C. Normal cold starting is, naturally, improved and is almost instantaneous when assisted by glow plugs operated by the ignition switch.

To allow the engine to run satisfactorily up to 4,000 r.p.m. full load, the C.A.V. fuel distributor pump is now fitted with a speed-sensitive automatic advance which covers a range of 10° crankshaft operation. The crankshaft itself is of increased stiffness with bigger diameter crankpins and increased fillet radii. After intensive research a new rear oil seal has been developed for the engine. The rear oil seal on the Land-Rover is always put to a severe test as it must be able to function properly under arduous conditions and on steep slopes.

A heavier flywheel, giving 8% increase in inertia, has been fitted and the sump has been constructed with a stiffer flange. Integral cylinder bores are used as exhaustive tests have shown that these have increased life over wet liners in this particular application. The cooling capacity has been increased with a larger radiator and larger fan. The pistons now have a V trough in the crown.

COMPARISON OF 2-LITRE DIESEL ENGINE AND NEW 2¼-LITRE DIESEL ENGINE

	2-LITRE DIESEL ENGINE	2¼-LITRE DIESEL ENGINE
CYLINDERS	4, Wet cast iron liners	4, Integral with block
CYLINDER HEAD	Detachable carrying all valve gear	Detachable carrying all valve gear
COMBUSTION CHAMBERS	Ricardo Comet V	Ricardo Comet V plus Rover provisional patent
VALVES	Overhead	Overhead
CRANKSHAFT	Forged steel, 3 copper-lead bearings	Forged steel, 3 copper-lead bearings
CAMSHAFT	Forged steel, 4 white metal bearings	Forged steel, 4 white metal bearings
PISTONS	Aluminium alloy, Ricardo Comet recess cast in crown	Aluminium alloy, Rover V trough cast in crown
CAPACITY	2,052 c.c.	2,286 c.c.
BORE AND STROKE	3⅜" × 3½" (85.7 mm. × 88.9 mm.)	3 9/16" × 3½" (90.475 mm. × 88.9 mm.)
MAXIMUM B.H.P.	51.2 at 3,500 r.p.m.	62 at 4,000 r.p.m.
MAXIMUM TORQUE	87 lb./ft. at 2,000 r.p.m.	103 lb./ft. at 1,800 r.p.m.
COMPRESSION RATIO	19.5 : 1	23.0 : 1

Comparing old with new

with the RAF. Altogether 47 entered service between March 1956 and May 1958. They were used to run a regular weekly supplies service to British troops in Aden, deliver helicopters to Cyprus, and fly supplies to British forces in the Yemen (1957), and Kuwait and Kenya (1961). The Army was certainly annoyed by the problem, and it has since been disclosed that had there been any real alternative to the Land-Rover, they would probably have bought it.

Rover were quick to recognise the importance of satisfying any military requirement, and on 19 December 1958, Jack Pogmore, Rover's Assistant Chief Engineer (Land-Rover), sent an inter-office memo to Robert Boyle and Gordon Bashford, requesting a meeting the following Tuesday at 10am in Jack Pogmore's office. The purpose of this meeting was to determine what action should be taken to initiate the development of a special lightweight 4x4 vehicle, which they code-named the 'L4 Project'. A brief was drawn up and circulated to those concerned on 5 January 1959. Tom Barton became the official Project Engineer, with Michael Broadwood as his Assistant.

This new lightweight model was to be completely different from any existing Land-Rover and would have a wheelbase of only 79 inches, a width of 60 inches, and weight of only 2,000 lbs. Some form of chassis-less construction, with independent front suspension and five-speed gearbox (no transfer box) was envisaged, and the 'angle of approach' was to fulfil NATO requirements.

The lightweight 4x4 was seen as an attractive possibility and in 1961 a more detailed study of the project was undertaken, but by this time Austin already had the 'Se7en' (Mini) developed into a lightweight field car – the 'Moke' (donkey) – and the following year the 'Twini-Moke', a twin-engined four-wheel-drive version had also appeared. Were Rover already too late?

With a wheelbase of only 79 inches – an inch less than the original 80-inch Land-Rovers – and a width of just 60 inches, it seemed like a step back to the original Land-Rover concept of 1948. Weighing in at only 2,000 lbs, it would be 600 lbs lighter than any 80-inch Land-Rover, and to achieve this, some form of chassis-less construction would have to be used. It *'...should not be ugly'* but resemble *'Something on the lines of a DKW at the rear, with perhaps some resemblance to the Land-Rover at the front...'*. It was also to have a flat cost of £242.

By 21 March 1961, 1/4-scale drawings of the layout of the very first 'lightweight' Land-Rover were completed, and the body scheme followed a few weeks later on 17 April 1961. These drawings, officially numbered as D700/1 and D700/2, fortunately still survive to this day.

Surprisingly, at the start, the lightweight 4x4 had not been planned as a military vehicle, and even as late as December 1962, was viewed as some form of competitor to Germany's DKW 'Geländewagen' (marketed as the Auto-Union MUNGA) and Austria's Steyr-Puch 'Haflinger'. As such, it was stated, it *'...would have to be priced fairly low if we are to enlarge our 4x4 market – probably in the region of £550 U.K. Basic and Retail'*.

Such things as *'...extremely rapid removal of the engine - gearbox - transfer box assembly'* were all part of the programme. Gone were the usual Land-Rover leaf springs at the front end – the L4 would have IFS (independent front suspension). The initial power plant envisaged was a 3-cyl. ohc design of only 1.5-litres (a 2.0-ltre OHC engine *'...was generally considered to be too big for the vehicle.'* The front-wheel-drive unit was to be integral within the sump, with power transmitted through a five-speed gearbox, and no transfer box, but contemporary drawings do, however, show a 'Low Ratio Gearbox'.

Eventually the new lightweight Land-Rover's military potential would be taken into consideration. The L4's 'angle of approach' now needed to fulfil NATO requirements of 45°, and detail drawings show it as 60°. Provision also had to be made for *'...a rear PTO; towing devices; hood and doors; flashers; front Capstan winch; space for additional instruments; rear seats (double); lifting and towing rings; oil cooler; engine governor; hand throttle; second wiper; F.A. heater; 12v and 24v AC systems; twin dynamo schemes; and Army suppression requirements'*.

With all extras, fuel, oil and coolant, a spare wheel, two-man crew and 700 lbs payload, gross weight was estimated to be around 3,250 lbs. Based on this figure, the tyre manufacturer's recommendation was for 5.50 x 16 tyres on $4^{1}/_{2}$ J x 16 rims, or for flotation purposes, 7.00 x 16 tyres on 5.50F x 16 rims. Both sizes could be accommodated in the existing design, but the latter would have left very little running clearance.

It was intended the lightweight Land-Rover should use as many parts from the new P6 car, the 4-cyl. Rover 2000, an extremely advanced car at the time which had been given the go-ahead for production in Autumn 1960 and would be launched on the buying public three years later in October 1963.

By December 1962 it's clear that Rover's management had become increasingly aware of the growth potential of the 4x4 market as a whole, and in a memo sent from Rover's MD, William Martin-Hurst, to those involved, he states that:

'...since the lightweight vehicle cannot be considered in isolation this note deals with 4x4 development as a whole' and that *'...it is clear the*

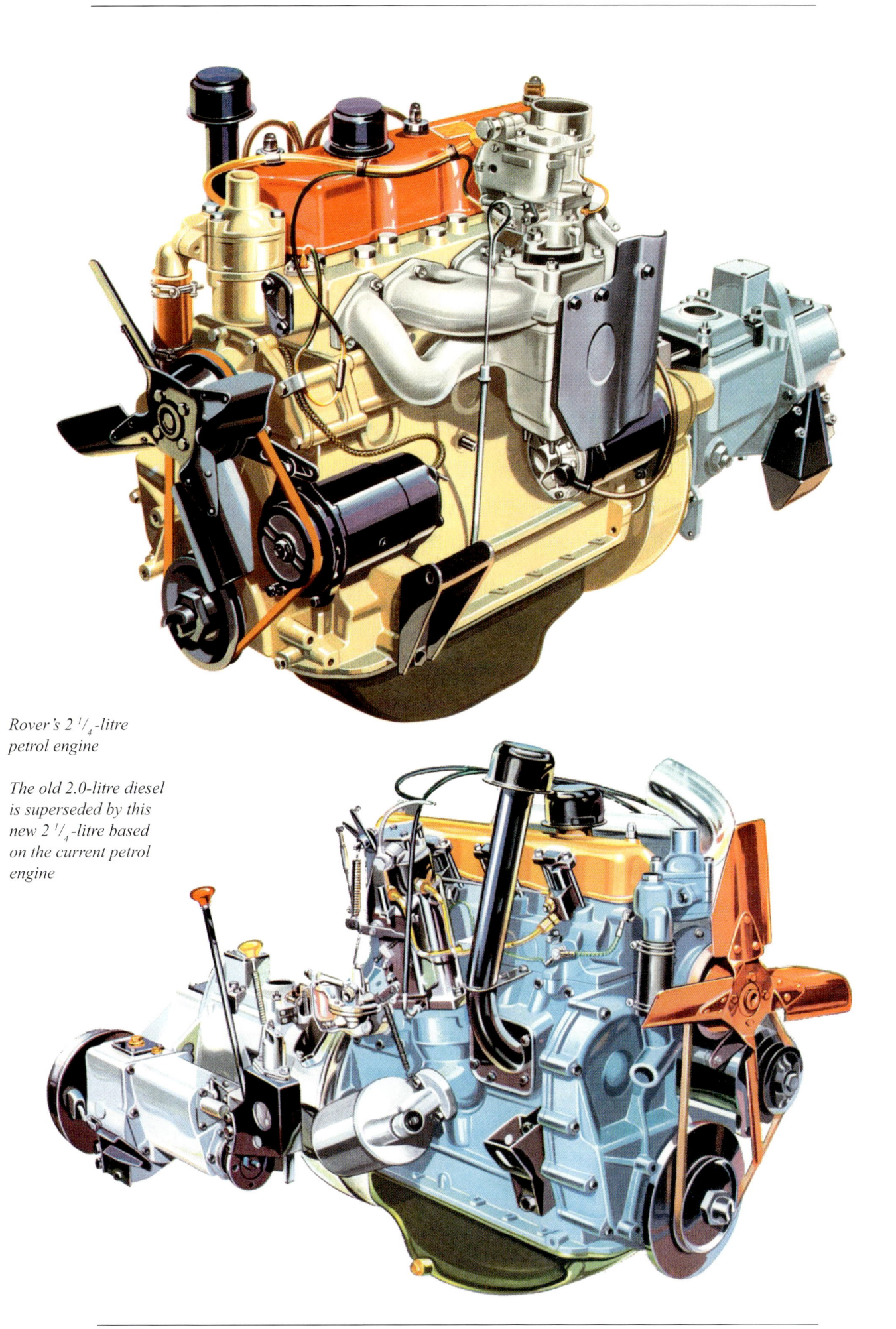

CHAPTER 24 – IIA and Beyond – Widening and Deepening the Range

Rover's 2 ¼-litre petrol engine

The old 2.0-litre diesel is superseded by this new 2 ¼-litre based on the current petrol engine

world market for 4x4s is growing... Our range of vehicles has to enable us to maintain or increase our share of the market and, if possible, to stimulate its growth'.

The L4 Project would soon be seen as just one of a whole range of future possibilities for the Land-Rover, for both civilian and military use, and altogether eight projects had been put up for serious consideration under the following two headings:

a/ Widening the range by introducing:
- i) A 'Stark', 'Pioneer' or stripped 88" or 109" Land-Rover;
- ii) 4x2 version of the Land-Rover;
- iii) Forward Control versions of the 88" and 109" Land-Rover;
- iv) A Low-Loader version of the 109";
- v). A 30-cwt Normal Control.

b/ Deepening the range by introducing:
- i) Heavy 4x4s (over 10,000 lbs GVW);
- ii) A lightweight 4x4;
- iii) Amphibious or Air Cushioned Vehicles.

The comment was made that 'Willys experience does not suggest that there is a very strong case for introducing 4x2 or further forward control versions of our existing range (which is fairly wide)'.

The Forward Control prototype developed in 1960 had only recently been launched as a production model at this time, but it was already believed that such vehicles were in direct competition with light commercial vehicles from both car and truck manufacturers, that could provide the same payload and load space for about two thirds of the cost, coupled with greater economy in operation. To their cost, Rover were all too soon proved right with the existing forward control model. A heavy 4x4 was also rejected, as this would clearly have involved entering an entirely new ball game.

Based on replies to a questionnaire given to distributors, the idea of the stripped version of the Land-Rover was initially rejected as it was believed that customers would go elsewhere if they wanted something more basic, but the important proviso – *'...unless we should receive a military development contract'* – was, however, added. In point of fact the first prototype 'Stark' Land-Rover was already under development, an 'Air portable' model of 1-tonne capacity, based on the existing 109 chassis (the APGP Scheme A, FV18501). It is said to have amphibious capabilities, the chassis being filled with foam. Altogether 26 of these were built for military trials.

109-inch IIA Forward Control

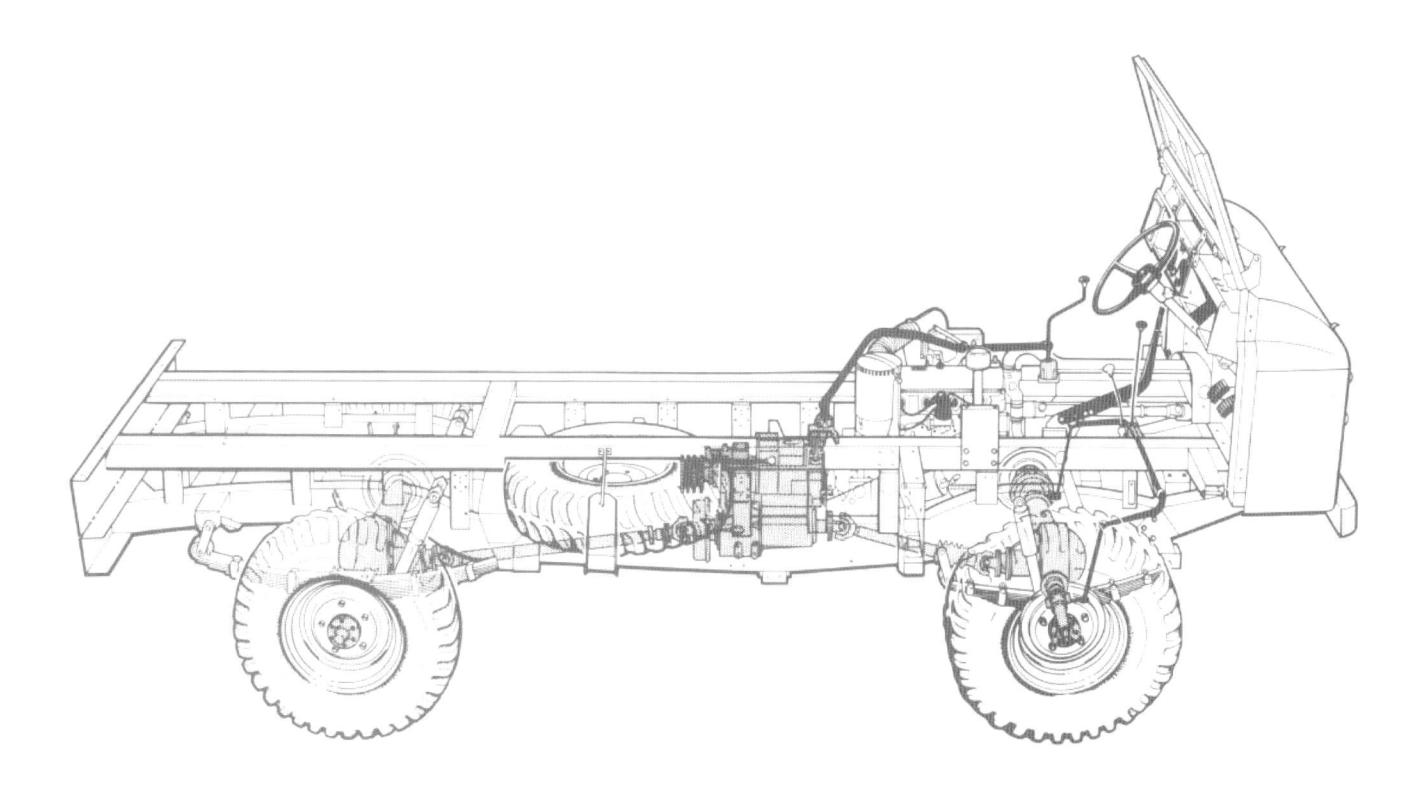

CHAPTER 24 – IIA and Beyond – Widening and Deepening the Range

The new Forward Control Land-Rover layout

IIA Forward Control model in Portugal

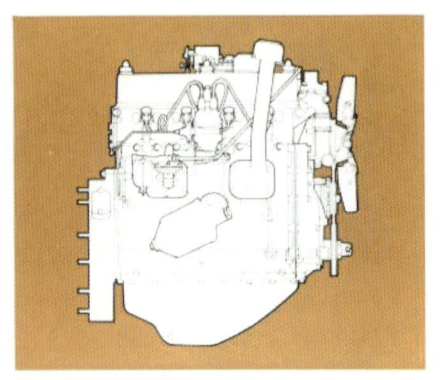

LAND-ROVER – The Formative Years, 1947–1967

2¼ LITRE PETROL ENGINE
Designed to meet the exceptional demands of the versatile Land-Rover under all conditions, this four-cylinder unit is both tough and reliable. Its flexibility makes it suitable for both road and cross-country use.

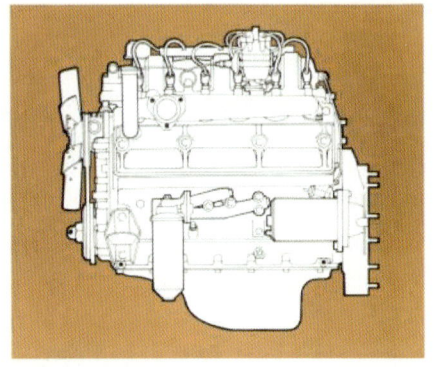

2.6 LITRE PETROL ENGINE
The six-cylinder petrol engine is offered as an added alternative on Long and Forward Control Land-Rovers.
Its greater power output and smoothness at high operating speeds make it particularly suitable for personnel carriers and all kinds of duties where a high proportion of road work is called for.

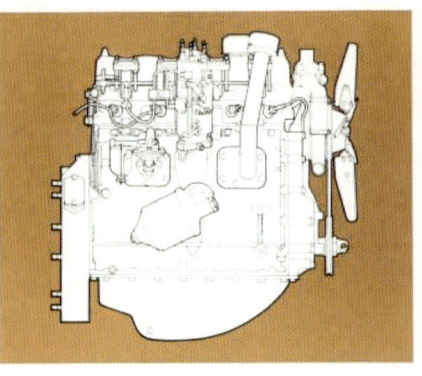

2¼ LITRE DIESEL ENGINE
Available as an alternative to the petrol engine, to which its power and speed range are closely matched, the rugged diesel engine contributes further to the economy and efficiency of the Land-Rover in conditions favouring diesel operation, or where prolonged stationary power take-off projects are envisaged.

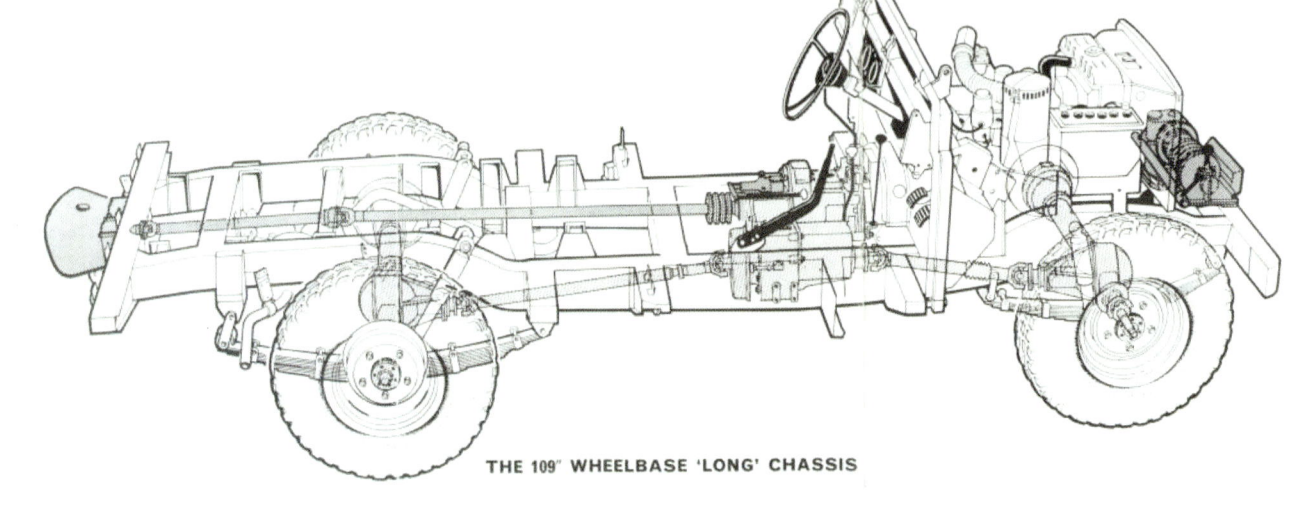

THE 109" WHEELBASE 'LONG' CHASSIS

The 'Stark' Land-Rover, then under development, had been specifically designed to overcome the air transportation problem, the idea being that this vehicle not only had a good payload capacity, but could also be stacked three-high in a transport aircraft. In addition, as part of a flotation kit, a propeller could be fitted on the rear propshaft, and four airbags then be inflated from the exhaust. The initial response from the military was encouraging.

A further 97-inch wheelbase vehicle with exoskeletal body to provide inherent flotation, was also under consideration (the APGP 'Scheme B', FV18601). But suddenly the request came for a military vehicle capable of being airlifted not only by transport aircraft, but also by the Army's new Westland 'Wessex' helicopter. It also had to be capable of being airdropped too. Clearly the goal posts had moved.

While a 'lightweight' and forward control Land-Rover were foremost in the minds of those responsible for Land-Rover development, by the early 1960s, a number of other developments on the Land-Rover front were also taking place.

By 1960 NATO was looking towards the idea of a multi-fuel engine capable of running not just on either petrol or diesel, but on vegetable-based fuels too. Here Rover's concern was that they should not be faced with a similar situation to that of the early 1950s, when they found another manufacturer's engine being installed in their Land-Rover for military evaluation purposes – even if it was Rolls-Royce – and so they decided to develop their own multi-fuel engine by modifying their own diesel engine's cylinder head.

One of the alterations was the inclusion of a series of 2 mm-high spikes adjacent to the throat of the Comet Mk 5 swirl chamber. This soon proved a major key to improving the diesel engine's performance and enabled Rover to introduce a new improved diesel engine based on their existing petrol $2^{1}/_{4}$-litre engine as early as September 1961, heralding the Series IIA Land-Rover, and replacing the somewhat troublesome 2.0-litre diesel engine that had been in production since 1956.

Just as the concept of a 'Rationalised Range' Rolls-Royce engine in every army vehicle never came to pass because existing commercial units

The current engine options

1/4-scale drawing showing general layout of L4 Project

1/4-scale drawing of L4 Project showing unitary construction

304

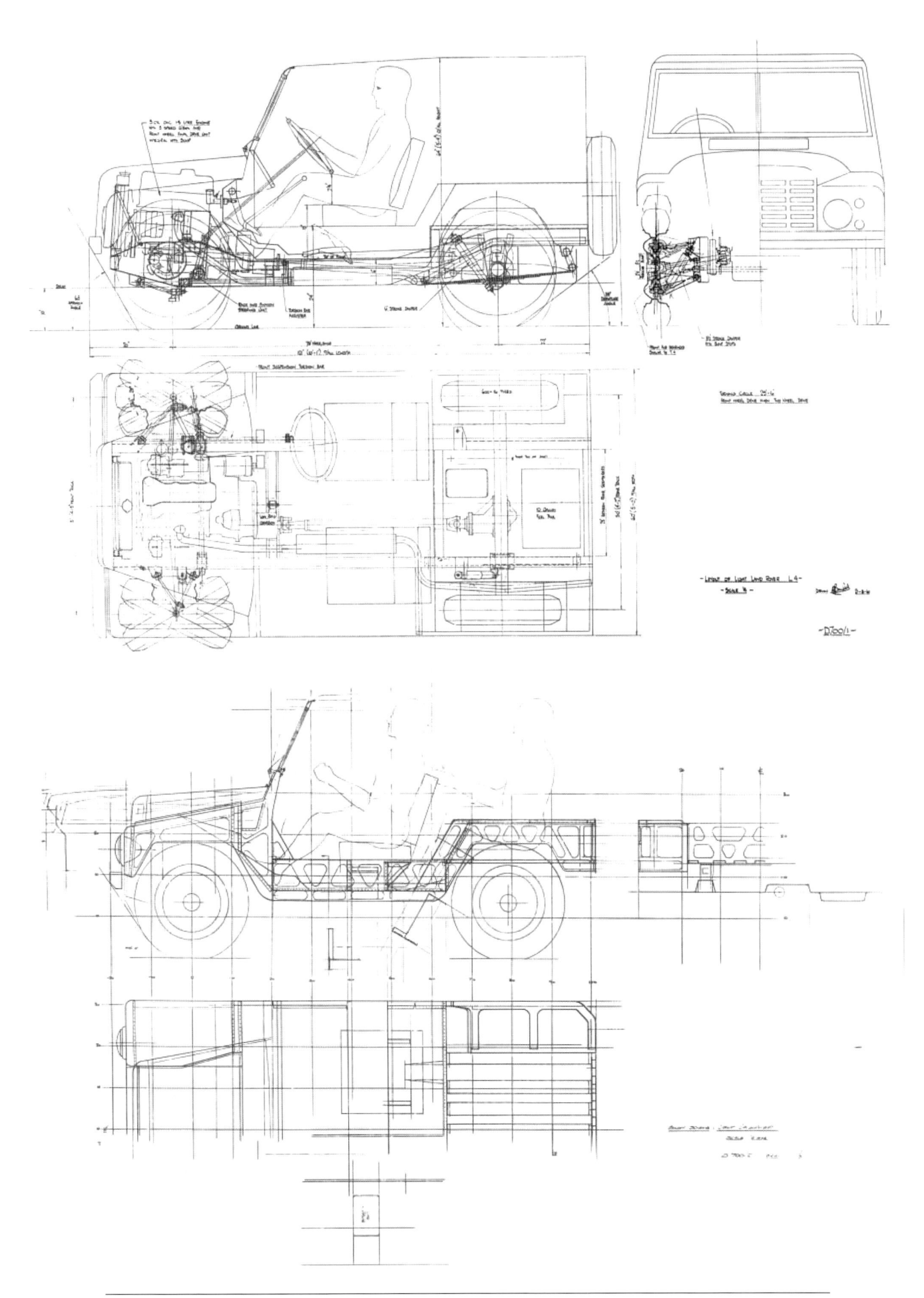

CHAPTER 24 – IIA and Beyond – Widening and Deepening the Range

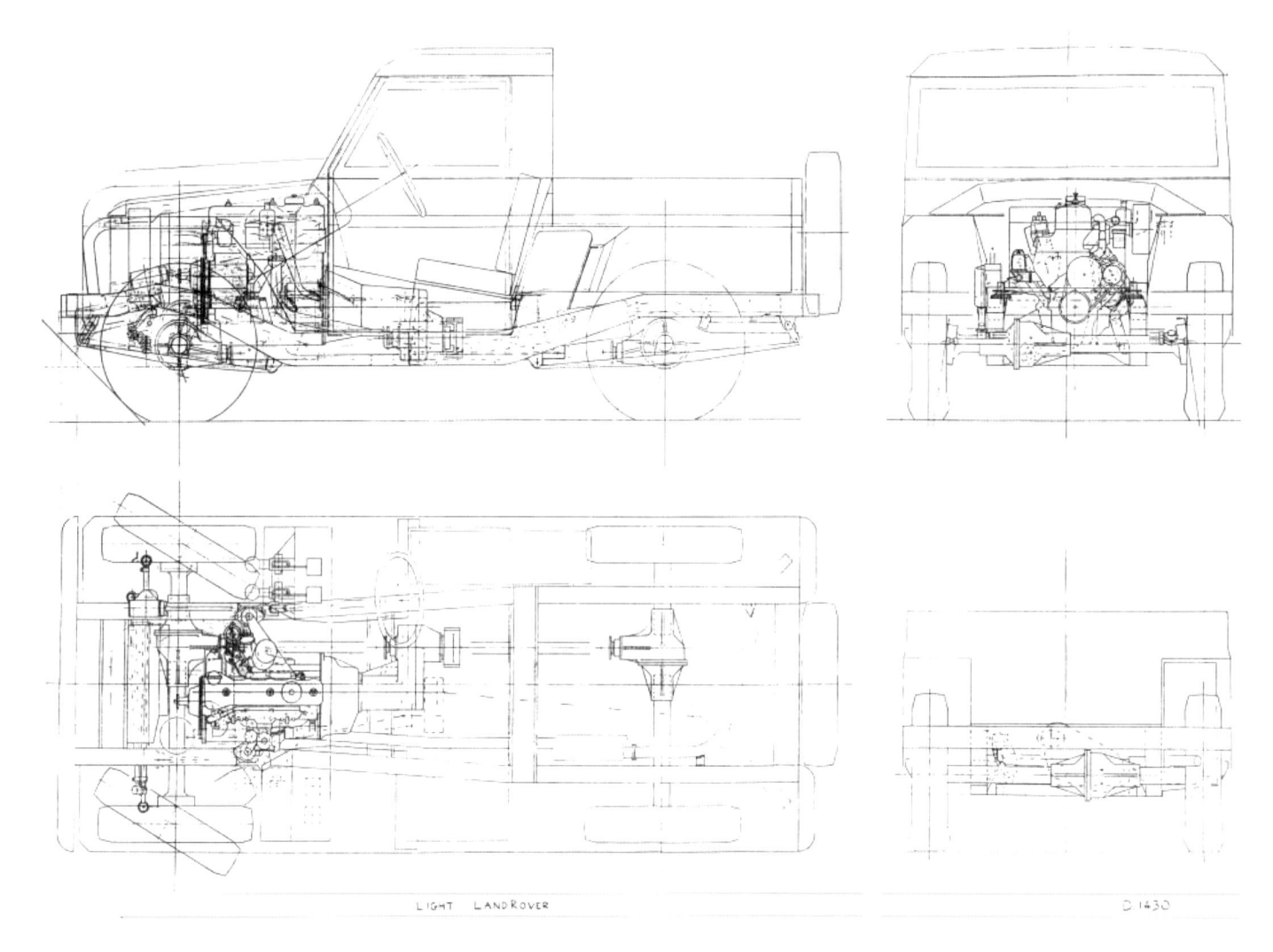

General layout of 91-inch lightweight based on conventional Land-Rover

were already doing an excellent job at a fraction of the cost, so too was the multi-fuel engine to meet a similar fate. There were a good many problems to overcome with such an engine, and no doubt Rover were glad to see the back of it, but at least some of its technology had now been put to good use.

At the same time as Rover's new $2\frac{1}{4}$-litre diesel engine went into production, certain changes were also made to the petrol models. The Solex carburettor, which had been in service since 1948 in one form or another, was replaced by a new Zenith model. By this time practically all ties with the original 'Series I' models had been broken, and it was decided that from now on, for service identification purposes, all major mechanical changes in the Land-Rover would be identified by a letter suffix to the model, which is why the latest models became known as 'Series IIA'. No other suffix letter was ever attached to the Series II Land-Rover, apart from the 110-inch Forward Control model which became the 'IIB'. This system of identification continued for the next 18 years until October 1979.

Another project to reach the prototype stage in 1962 was a huge 129-inch truck with 35-cwt load capacity, intended for trials by the Belgian Army. This would be powered by either Rover's 2.6-litre six-cylinder 'F-head' engine used for the P4 car, or a five-bearing 2.5-litre Rover prototype diesel with CAV turbocharger and intercooler. Road springs were mounted above the axles to give sufficient clearance for its large 11.00 x 16 tyres. A number of rear body styles were used, some with drop sides, while others had rigid sides. Altogether five were built.

As well as two '88' Forward Control prototypes, two '2-tonne', 120-inch Forward Control prototypes were also built. The first was intended for trial as a medium load platform for military use. At the Army's request, this had a 5.8-litre 6-cylinder Perkins diesel engine. Later, painted 'yellow' and used as a works recovery and general hack, it was nicknamed 'Buttercup'. The other '2-tonne' built in 1963, had only a front driven axle, with 'Eezion'-style rear body, that could be lowered or raised on hydraulic rams, to load and transport the Rover-BRM gas-turbine 'Le Mans' racing car.

CHAPTER 24 – IIA and Beyond – Widening and Deepening the Range

The Series IIA Land-Rover family

The only Forward Control to go into production at this time would be the '109'. Utilising the current long wheelbase Land-Rover's 109-inch chassis, an additional 'body sub-frame' was placed on top, to support the cab and a new large 10ft. 3in. x 5ft. 3in. load platform.

First shown at the Commercial Motor Show at the Earls Court exhibition centre in October 1962, the '109' Forward Control was designed to carry a payload of 30-cwt. Enormous 9.00 x 16 dual-purpose tyres, on offset 6½-inch rims, gave it a full 10-inch ground clearance. But there was a downside – its overall weight. At 4,340lbs (2.043-tonnes) empty ('109' LWB, 3,294lbs), and 8,250lbs (3,742-tonnes) maximum GVW ('109' LWB, 5,905lbs), it would be seriously underpowered. The Forward Control was initially only offered with the existing 2¼-litre petrol engine, but despite this lack of power, it still managed to break its 'Rover' axle half-shafts. The other problem encountered with this high-sided vehicle was body roll.

To overcome these faults, a new IIB model was introduced on a 110-inch wheelbase chassis in 1966. The front axle had been moved forward an inch to accommodate Rover's 2.6-litre six-cylinder 'F-head' engine, installed to overcome the previous model's lack of power. ENV axles with wider 57½-inch track were used, and new stiffer rear springs sat above the back axle rather than below it. An anti-roll bar was added to the front. Rover's 2¼-litre diesel engine also became an option, with the 2¼-litre petrol engine now only available in the 'Export' market. Altogether, 3,193 IIA FC models and 2,305 IIB FC models were produced between 1962 and 1972, when production ceased.

307

LAND-ROVER – The Formative Years, 1947–1967

Technical spec of proposed 91-inch Lightweight

Girling data sheet for the L4

<u>T E N T A T I V E   S P E C I F I C A T I O N.</u>

DIMENSIONS.

Wheelbase.	91 ins. (7ft 7ins).
Track.	50 ins. (4ft 2ins).
Ground Clearance Fully Laden (General)	10 ins.) with standard
Ground Clearance Under Diff. -	9 ins.) 6.00 x 16 tyres.
Overall Length (Front Bumper To Rear Bumper).	141 ins. (11ft 9ins).
Overall Length With Spare Wheel.	145 ins. (12ft 1in).
Overall Width.	60 ins. (5ft 0ins).
Overall Height Fully Laden.	67 ins. (5ft 7 ins).
Front Overhang To Bumper.	22 ins. (1ft 10ins).
Rear Overhang To Bumper.	28 ins. (2ft 4 ins).
Standard Tyre.	6.00 x 16
Maximum Size Tyre (Without Snow Chains).	7.50 x 16
Cargo Space Width.	55 ins. (4ft 7ins).
" " Length At Waistline.	44 ins. (3ft 8ins).
" " Length At Floor.	50 ins. (4ft 2ins).
Approach Angle.	52°
Departure Angle.	36°
Turning Circle.	36 ft.
Front Wheel Movement:	
Fully Laden To Metal/Metal Bump.	3½ ins.
Total Movement M/M To Rebound.	7½ ins.
Rear Wheel Movement:	
Fully Laden to Metal/Metal Bump.	3 ins.
Total Movement M/M To Rebound.	7 ins.
Unladen (Kerb) Weight. (With 5 galls Petrol, Oil And Water).	2500 lbs.
Payload.	1000 lbs + 3 persons = 1500 lbs
Gross Weight.	4000 lbs.

The above weights are for a vehicle in standard form with cab and spare wheel.

Weight distribution will be similar to the 88 Land Rover but exact figures will depend on detail design.

TITLE :-		SHEET No.
	LIGHT LAND-ROVER BROCHURE.	

CHAPTER 24 – IIA and Beyond – Widening and Deepening the Range

BRAKE INSTALLATION DATA SHEET
GIRLING LTD.—BIRMINGHAM.

DATA SHEET No. **3651/1**
Neg. No. **199 B.T**

Customer: ROVER Model: 79" W.B. LANDROVER
Weight: 3050 LB GROSS.
Tyres. Front: 6.00 x 16 Eff. Radius: 13.5"
Tyres. Rear: " Eff. Radius: "
Braking Ratio at Tyre Radius: 58.7% F : 41.3% R
Retarding Force at Front Tyres: 1552 LB
Retarding Force at Rear Tyres: 1097 "
Total Retarding Force: 2655 lbs. for 2B Ft/Sec² Retardation
Type of Installation: HYDRAULIC

BRAKES. DRUM MATERIAL:- B.S.S. 1452 Grade 17 or Equivalent.
1st. Front Size: 9" x 2½" Type: H.L.S/S Opⁿ: HYD.
2nd. Front Size: — Type: — Opⁿ: —
1st. Rear Size: 9" x 1¾" Type: H.L./3 Opⁿ: HYD
2nd. Rear Size: — Type: — Opⁿ: —
Brake Factor (e.g. Drum Drag/Effort) Ft.: LININGS Wedge Angle Ft.:
Brake Factor " Rear: 4.35 Wedge Angle Rear:
Front: SHOE - TIP Effort per Brake: 1167 LB Travel (Foot Opⁿ):
Rear: " " Effort per Brake: 1524 " Travel (Foot Opⁿ):
Front: Travel (Hand Opⁿ):
Rear: LEVER Travel (Hand Opⁿ): .63
Shoe Centre Lift (Foot Operation) Front: .048" Rear: .048"
Pedal Effort: 119. Lbs. for Retardation of 2B Ft./Sec²
Pedal Ratio: 4/1 Pedal Travel at Foot Pad: 5½"
Handbrake Operates on: REARS
H/B to Hold on 1 IN 4 in Forward requires LEVER Effort of 153 Lbs. per Bk.
H/B to Hold on 1 " 4 in Reverse requires " Effort of 153 Lbs. per Bk.

HYDRAULIC OR PNEUMATIC DATA.
Ft. Brake Cyl ͬ Type: INT. S. ACTING Dia.: ⅞" Area: .1202 Sq. Ins/Bk.
Rr. Brake Cyl ͬ Type: " SAR Dia.: 1" Area: .1570 Sq. Ins/Bk.
Pipe Line Pressure Lbs./Sq. Inch Actual: 1020 Effective: 970
Master Cyl ͬ Dia. & Type: ¾" C.V. Eff. Area: .442 Sq. Ins.
Master Cyl ͬ Working Stroke: 1⅜" Max. Stroke: 1½"
Servo Type:

Special Remarks:

Compiled by: CB (BB) Date: 19. 3. 59 Data Sheet No.: 3651/1

Margin note: Present L.R. (88") Pedal Effort = 118/2B

309

CHAPTER 25
Air-Portable Lightweight The Closing Chapter

The Army's latest request was no longer for just a military vehicle capable of being airlifted by transport aircraft. They now wanted something that could also be transported by their new Westland 'Wessex' helicopters, and it also had to be capable of being airdropped by parachute too.

On 3 April 1964, a 'LIGHT LANDROVER GENERAL INFORMATION BROCHURE' was drawn up, describing the purpose of this latest vehicle, which gave its general overall specification. The brochure opened by stating 'This vehicle will be similar in shape to an 88 Land-Rover, but will be 6 ins. lower, 4 ins. narrower, and should be better looking'. It seems almost amusing that looks were to be taken into account when considering the specification for a military vehicle, but the vehicle did need to look right for the job. The standard Series IIA 88, in commercial form, was anything but lightweight.

The new lightweight design was to *'...have the same payload'* as its commercial counterpart, *'...but with slightly larger cargo space'*. Kerbside weight, however, was to be only 2,500 lbs (a military requirement), compared to a standard 88 Land-Rover's 2,900 lbs – a saving of 400 lbs or almost 14%. It was also hoped a more efficient engine and lower frontal area would provide a 25% improvement in petrol consumption. To provide the extra cargo space, a wheelbase of 91 in. - 3 in. more than the existing civilian model – was specified, but with a track of only 50 in. – 1.5 in. less than the standard 88.

The body would remain aluminium alloy and of similar construction to current models, but be modified *'...in the interests of economy'*, with items such as *'...galvanised cappings replaced by aluminium'*. Although it was stated that this vehicle was to be *'...more simple and economical'*, there were, however, some rather obvious contradictions – doors were to *'...have wind up windows'*, and there would be a cab and a separate steel frame used at the rear *'...to support the rear door carrying spare wheel'*. Not exactly lightweight components. It was decided the scuttle should also remain in steel, but with the bonnet now hinged from the front end.

The L4 project would have been based on parts from the new 1963 P3 Rover car, but not the engine because this was considered too large for that lightweight. But that same 2.0-litre 4-cyl. overhead camshaft P6 'Rover 2000' engine, along with its clutch, and drive transmitted through a 5-speed gearbox, was now being proposed for this new 91-inch lightweight. It would, of course, be de-tuned for the proposed 'Lightweight' Land-Rover, with special pistons fitted to allow it to run on 79 octane petrol.

Although the heading 'Gearbox and Transfer Box' is given, there is no mention of a transfer box, and only a single lever with additional lever operating operating two- or four-wheel-drive is mentioned, so there is some weight saving here.

Schematic drawing of Series II Lightweight showing general layout

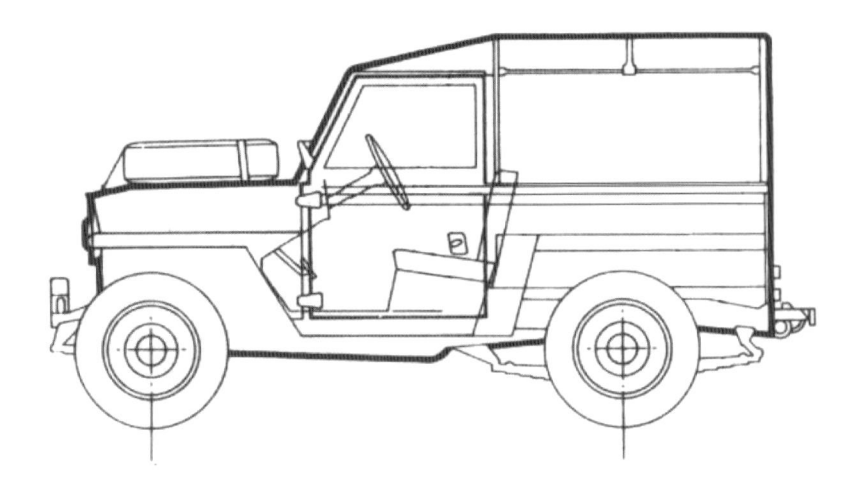

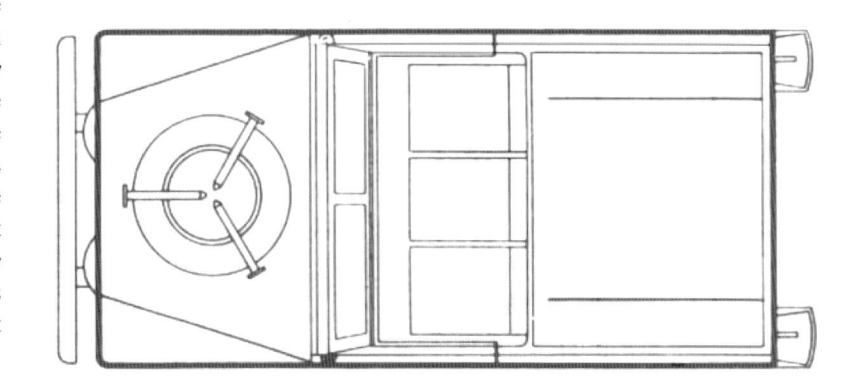

CHAPTER 25 – Air-Portable Lightweight – The Closing Chapter

Taking the plunge

Prototype Lightweight exits a Shorts Sc-7 Skyvan 2-100 Transport at RAF Andover, 1965

311

LAND-ROVER – The Formative Years, 1947–1967

Soft landing

Oops! Forgot to turn the mirrors round

All eight parachutes open

Half-shafts would have to be made strong enough to accept a differential locking device, which was to be offered as standard. The battery was to fit under the left-hand seat (a practice previously adopted for diesel models and the Rolls-Royce B40-powered Land-Rovers in 1950), while an 'L' shape fuel tank would sit under the right-hand seat, an idea originally proposed by Gordon Bashford for the 1948 pre-production Land-Rovers, but then abandoned when it was discovered it would be in the way of the 80-inch Land-Rover's exhaust system on RHD models.

Power take-off was to be optional, and although the current engine crankshaft drive for a front

CHAPTER 25 – Air-Portable Lightweight – The Closing Chapter

winch and usual propshaft drive to the rear are both mentioned, an alternative front drive from the gearbox, via chain drive and propshafts, is also mentioned, along with a chain drive from the rear PTO to provide drive for a powered trailer.

Gone was the idea of IFS (independent front suspension) using coil springs and wishbones, but instead a return to semi-elliptic leaf springs, which were to be lightweight in steel or fibreglass. Oddly, they were to have *'...shackles at the outer ends of the frame'*. This was the system originally used by the 80-inch Land-Rover to 1950, and the WW2 Jeep. Although this worked fine on the Jeep, as it had a central relay independently connected to each front wheel, it presented problems of wheel shimmy on the early Land-Rover with its offset relay connecting to only the right-hand wheel, the left wheel then connecting to the right. It seems this problem was now to be overcome by the use of a telescopic hydraulic steering damper, with 'no relay'.

The braking system was to be entirely 88 Land-Rover, incorporating any current improvements being made, and operated by pendant pedal as per the civilian model. The hand brake was to be *'...of compact size...'* and would also continue to act on the transmission at the rear of the gearbox. The possibility of a band brake was put forward for consideration.

By spring 1964 it was clear that the general concept of Rover's new military lightweight 'air-portable' Land-Rover had been clearly laid down. But even this particular design would never reach the production stage. The concept was now far nearer to the Lightweight Land-Rover that would eventually emerge off the production line than the original L4 project. Five years had now slipped by since that original inter-office memo of 19 December 1958, initiating the development of a 'Lightweight 4x4 Vehicle'.

By June 1964 the Rover Company had no less than 14 vehicles undergoing consideration as part of the new 'Light Land-Rover Project'. These included:

(i) the original L4 vehicle and an amphibious version using a GRP (glass reinforced plastic) 'hull containing as much of the machinery of the L4 as possible inboard', though a metal structure was considered as a possible alternative;

(ii) the 91-inch wheelbase model described above;

(iii) a variant on these involving the front of the 91-inch model and the rear of the 79-inch (L4) model, but on an 86-inch wheelbase;

(iv) a high, forward control version of the 91-inch vehicle;

(v) six 'semi-forward control' models on either 80-inch or 88-inch chassis, all of which were mid-engine vehicles;

(vi) two 'low-profile' vehicles with a 'wide track' of 64 in. – it was considered that 'In some areas of the world there is a requirement for wide-tracked light vehicles which can, with reasonable comfort, use the tracks made by the continuous passing of large vehicles' – one of the main criteria in the 'Africar' project of the 1980s;

(vii) a vehicle on the lines of the Austrian Steyr/Puch 'Haflinger' or the German Fahr/Chrysler 'Farmobil', both of which had recently come onto the world market.

The military lightweight that was to eventually emerge out of all this would be based on the 91 in. model now being considered but *'...will be similar in shape to an 88 in.'*. In the end it finished up as an experimentally modified 88-inch Series IIA Land-Rover in 1965, and was pretty much a complete return to the basic concepts embodied in the original 80-inch model of 1948. Even the width was back to 60 inches and everything considered as surplus could once again be easily removed. It appeared that the British Army was still looking to the same concepts Maurice Wilks embodied in the original 1948 Land-Rover in order to satisfy their needs.

The new design actually went one step further. Not only could doors, windscreen, side screens etc. be easily removed, but the upper sections of the rear body bin and tail board could also be removed. There was no fancy barrelling of the bodywork, as normally seen on a Series IIA of the period, and front wings were no more than shelves for a soldier's mug of tea.

Engine and transmission were all standard Series IIA Land-Rover, which meant existing military spares and technical expertise needed little updating, and drivers would also be familiar with the general layout too.

The Military's requirement was for an air-portable lightweight of no more than 2,500 lbs with basic structural strength maintained. In stripped-down form the Lightweight weighed 2,660 lbs. Although this was 160 lbs over the top, the Army was persuaded that if the internal load of a Wessex helicopter was reduced by roughly the weight of a man, it would be able to carry the new Lightweight Land-Rover.

Initial trials with the prototype Lightweight in 1966 proved successful, and in August 1967 the MoD placed a first order for 1,000 88-inch Lightweight Land-Rovers. These were delivered in 1968, but it seems they did not actually enter service until 1969. Designated 'Truck, ½-ton, Lightweight, Rover Mk1', the first 1,400 Series IIA Lightweights had their headlights in the radiator front panel. A further 1,589 Series IIA Lightweights then had their headlights in new modified front wings. Civilian Land-Rovers underwent a similar modification in 1968. The Series III Lightweight replaced the Series IIA model in 1972, a year later than civilian models. The Lightweight Land-Rover also became available equipped with Rover's diesel engine, but at a weight gain of more than 40 lbs. In the UK, Lightweight Land-Rovers were used by the Army, Royal Marines and the RAF. Overseas they were used by Belgium, Brunei, the Dutch Marines, Guyana, Hong Kong, Jamaica, and Libya.

LAND-ROVER – The Formative Years, 1947–1967

Land Rover

½ TON

CHAPTER 25 – Air-Portable Lightweight – The Closing Chapter

Technical details

Series III Lightweight brochure

Twenty years after the original launch of the Land-Rover, a major chapter in the Rover Company's history would finally come to a close. Following the inter-war depression of the early 1930s, the two brothers, Spencer and Maurice Wilks, had managed to rescue the Rover Company from drifting into obscurity. Then came the troubled aftermath of the Second World War when the allocation of steel to Britain's car manufacturers was to be solely determined by export performance. To solve this problem, they launched a brilliant new product, the Land-Rover, once again saving the company from oblivion.

The Wilks brothers went on to serve the Rover Company for more than 30 years. In 1957, elder brother, Spencer, or SB as he was affectionately known, became Rover's Chairman, before eventually retiring from active participation in the company's affairs in 1962. Together with J. Backhouse and A.J. Worcester, SB continued as a Production Consultant. Brother Maurice, who had originally been responsible for the Land-Rover concept, succeeded his brother, first as MD, and then as Chairman. But his time was cut short. In September 1963, while staying at his home on his beloved Anglesey, Maurice Wilks suddenly died of a heart attack. He was only 59. More than half his lifetime had been spent at Rover.

Maurice Wilks' sudden death marked the end of an era, the Wilks era. In less than four years, in March 1967, the Rover Co. an independent car company since 1904, became part of Leyland Motors. A year after that, in 1968, Leyland Motors merged with British Motor Holdings to become that ill-fated giant, the British Leyland Motor Corporation. Spencer Wilks died 3 years later in 1971, aged 79. With only Land-Rovers and Unipart showing a profit, by 1974 British Leyland was in a serious financial crisis and nationalised by the British Government the following year, bringing the 'Formative Years' of the Land-Rover firmly to a close.

The Illustrations

Most of the photographs, drawings, publicity material, and other illustrations contained in this book were begged, borrowed or bought from a wide variety of sources over the past 40 years. Many have been kindly provided by members of the Land-Rover Series One Club, and The Land-Rover Register (1948–1953). Others have been borrowed from the archives of the more serious collectors of motoring history, or purchased from dealers at classic car shows, autojumbles, and elsewhere.

A large number of photographs were generously provided by Stephen Wilks, from the Wilks' family archive. Without these, this book would be much the poorer. The late Gordon Bashford kindly provided various extracts from his personal ledger of the late 1940s, concerning the Land-Rover's initial development. The vast majority of illustrations within this book are known to be the old Rover Company's factory photographs, drawings, and other publicity material from the 1940s, 1950s and 1960s.

A number of factory photographs, together with George Middleton's letters, were kindly provided by James Taylor. Tony Hutchings, Les Lawrence and Pete Stringer also provided many old factory photographs from their own collections. Richard Lines provided a number of illustrations of the Turner diesel. Previously unpublished photographs of R02 on test in Wales were taken by Dick Ross, and along with the 'Road Tests', are courtesy of 'The Autocar'. All photographs depicting AA Land-Rovers are courtesy of the Automobile Association. The late Barbara Toy provided all photographs of Pollyanna. A number of illustrations, kindly lent by Brian Carvey, past Chairman of The Land-Rover Register, had previously been published in the LROC's magazine 'Review'. Tom Pickford kindly lent his excellent collection of early brochures depicting factory 'optional extra' equipment

All photographs in Chapter 2 were kindly provided by Stephen Wilks. Other photographs not of Rover Company origin are as follows: (p 65 top) Temple Press; (p 68 middle/bottom) Dick Ross; (p 71 bottom) Ann Welch; (p 75) Hamlin's News Services; (p p78) Stephen Wilks; (p 95 top) Roger Parker; (p 95 bottom) Derrey Ferdinando; (p 104/5 middle) Kent Messenger; (p 131 top) Claude Balteau; (p 137 bottom) Charles Cadogen; (p 152 top) the Post Office; (p 156/7) Cliff Petts; (p 158) Monica Rawlins; (p 164) Stephen Wilks; (p 167 top) Ivor Ramsden; (p 167 bottom) Scott Miller; (p 178 bottom) Hulton Press Ltd.; (p 215 top) Fernand Van de Plas; (p 220) Douglas Slocombe; (p 224 bottom) Stephen Wilks; (p 232 top) the Post Office; (p 242) Stephen Wilks; (p 248) Barrington-Brown; (p 255) 'The Motor'; (p 256/7) Ian Thompson; (p p283) 'The Autocar'. Most of the contemporary colour photographs, together with the drawings depicting the1947 hybrid centre steer prototype (p 40), the 1948 pre-production Land-Rover (p 81) and 'T' handle (p p84), the early 'Tickford' Land-Rover Station Wagon (p161), and the graph (p 107) and bar chart (p 277) depicting factory output, are by the author.

Several photographs included in this book are of unknown source, and while every effort has been made to uncover their origin, if there are inadvertent omissions in this acknowledgement, we offer our sincere apologies to those concerned.

The Illustrations

The family grows

The Rover Company

The foundations of the Rover Company can be traced back to 1877 when John Kemp Starley and William Sutton began manufacturing 'Ordinary' (Penny Farthing) bicycles at the Meteor works in Queen Victoria Road, Coventry. The 'Ordinary' bicycle was not a particularly safe machine, and in 1884 they started making tricycles in an attempt to make cycling a safer means of transport. The new machine was called the 'Rover'.

Starley dissolved the partnership with Sutton, and then went on to invent the world's first chain driven cycle, the 'Rover Safety Bicycle' in 1885. As the forerunner of the modern bicycle it was to end the days of the 'Ordinary' (Penny-farthing) forever, and made 'Rover' a household name.

In 1888 Starley built a motorised version of his tricycle, the 'Rover Electric Carriage'. It was Coventry's first motor-car, but he never put it into production. In 1896, the 'Rover Cycle Company' was formed as Starley progressed onto motorcycles. He finally formed the 'Rover Company Ltd' in 1904, when he went into production with Rover's first car, a good, solid, reliable 8 HP single cylinder machine designed by E W Lewis of Daimler. The famous Rover shield became the cars motive in 1907, together with the motto 'Aut Optimum Aut Nihil' – The Best or Nothing.

As well as the demise of the Penny-farthing, Rover can also be credited with bringing an end to the 'cycle car'. To compliment the 8 HP car a less expensive 6 HP car was introduced in 1905, followed by a more upmarket four-cylinder 12 HP model in 1911, designed by Owen Clegg of Wolseley. These were all good cars, and enabled the Rover Company to firmly establish itself as a motor manufacturer.

After the Great War, the Clegg car was again put into production Having already established their reputation, Rover were now out to capitalise on the population's new found experience of motorised transport brought about by the war. The end result was a new 'Rover Eight' in 1920. This was a cheaper, cruder, and less reliable car that anything they had so far been produced. Crude as it may have been, it was an advance on the various cycle cars now on offer, and at a competitive price, sold well. Rover were, however, soon to be beaten at their own game, when in 1922, four car manufacturers, Austin, Gwynne, Humber, and Talbot, all came up with the ingredients for a modern light car. The most successful of these was the 'Austin Seven', selling at around £15 cheaper than a Rover Eight.

Throughout the Twenties, Rover made various attempts to produce a suitable vehicle to beat the competition, but without success, and the company was extremely lucky to have survived those lean years - there were many that did not. A change in Rovers' fortune was to come about as a result of the activities of the Maidstone car dealers William and Reginald Rootes, who were Britain's largest car distributor in London and the Home Counties.

Captain S B Wilks, having courted and married one of William Hillman's six daughters, soon found himself in the motor industry, and by the late twenties became joint managing director with Captain J P Black. Hillman was right next door to Humber, in Humber Road, Coventry and a merger took place between the two firms in 1928. The two concerns faced a financial crisis the following year and received a large injection of capital from the Rootes Brothers, who then wanted to run the whole concern. Wilks and Black both knew it was time to make a move.

Spencer Wilks accepted an invitation from Rover to become works manager, and a number of other Hillman employees soon followed, including his brother Maurice, Robert Boyle, and Geoffrey Savage, who would eventually make up the other three cornerstones of the company. The opportunity to turn Rover into a going concern came in January 1933, when SB was appointed Managing Director and given a free hand to run the concern as he saw fit. He knew the major car manufacturers would be competing in the mass market for cheap vehicles, but there would always be those who could afford the fast or luxurious from the specialists. In between was a growing market of middle-class motorists - doctors, lawyers, civil servants, bankers - most of whom wanted good, solid, sober, reliable motoring, and Spencer Wilks was determined to satisfy their needs.

He immediately implemented a policy of 'quality before quantity' and it was not long before a deficit of £80,000 in 1931, which almost put the company into the hands of the receiver, was turned first into a small profit of £7,500 in 1933, and then a huge surplus of over £200,000 by 1937. Rover had at last re-established their reputation acquired in the early years before the Great War. The Second World War also brought its benefits. Rover received not only two new shadow factories from the government, gas turbine technology, and Ministry contracts for Meteor tank engines, but also had the reputation of their cars further enhanced. Those fortunate enough to be permitted to use a car in the war years on a 'make and mend' budget soon discovered that Rover was one of the more reliable makes that could outlast the 'duration', a fact which stood the company in good stead in the immediate post war period.

The post-war years leading up to the Sixties would be those for which the company will probably best be remembered - the P4 'Auntie' Rovers; the world's first gas turbine cars - Jet 1 and 'Le Mans'; the stylish' 3-litre Coupé'; and not least, the Land-Rover. They were exciting years. Rover's design department was at the peak of its career and at the height of prestige of not just Britain's, but the world's motor-industry. But Rover's years as an independent car manufacturer were already numbered. They were, in Maurice Wilks words *"... too big to be small, and too small to be big"*, and he was careful to persuade his sons away from the industry.

The purchase of Alvis in 1965 would have benefited both these independent motor manufacturers, with their mutual interest in research and development, quality motorcars and military vehicles. Their decision to accept an offer from Leyland Motors within 18 months resulted in what could have become one of Europe's best supercars for the American market, the smooth-lined mid-engine Alvis-Rover 'V8', P9 (a further development of the 1967 P6BS prototype), being axed for the inferior TR7 from Triumph's stable. For over 30 years the possibility of any merger with Triumph had been fortuitously avoided. Now that it was forced upon them, it resulted in the sort of decisions Rover's management feared most. The Rover Company was no longer its own master, and any success the Land-Rover continued to enjoy was firmly based on the solid foundations already set by the Wilks brothers.

The Land-Rover Series One Club

Every 'Series One' Land-Rover owner has a different tale to tell of how he or she first caught the 'bug'. As a teenager, I had taken a summer job working as a ghillie in Sutherland, where, at weekends, I was able to drive, unrestrained, all over the north of Scotland in a Series One estate car.

After discovering and rebuilding my very own Series One Land-Rover Station Wagon 12 years later, my Land-Rover and I joined the line-up of cars at the Yeovil Festival of Transport in 1977 and 1978. There, I met two other enthusiasts. *"We ought to have some sort of organisation to help people keep their Series Ones on the road." "That's a good idea. Who's going to do it?"*

Well, we did - and that's how the 'Land-Rover Series One Club' was born. That was the happy beginning to our helpful and cheerful club.

The plan, hatched in a pub, was that the Club's aims should be:

To further interest in the maintenance, use, and restoration of Series One Land-Rovers.

To produce information through research and technical help, and to assist in the location of spares and expertise.

To arrange meetings for members on an occasional basis.

To issue up to 6 Newsletters per annum.

To promote interest at motoring festivals etc. by displaying a variety of Series One Land-Rovers.

It was not long before all sorts of keen enthusiasts signed up, some taking on important roles that they continued doing for very many years.

The early shows the Club attended often had an agricultural basis, but as the classic car movement expanded, Land-Rovers became more acceptable at other venues. We, of course, all knew Series Ones were true classics, but with those extra abilities not found in lesser vehicles.

During the Club's 30 year existence, the magnificent 'Series One' has gone from strength to strength, and from small beginnings, the Club has grown enormously, with now over 2,000 members. New members brought new energy and abilities, enabling an even better service to be provided to members.

I'll never forget the phone call from one of the Commonwealth countries, where so many Land-Rovers were exported. The caller had found a 'Series One' and wanted to know if it was worth rebuilding. We talked of the pros and cons and the conversation ended with the warning that they were a disease. I wasn't believed. Some months later I received a letter telling me I was wrong. *"It's not a disease, it's an epidemic. I've got four of them."*

Be warned, reading John's book could lead to an even more severe infection.

Reverend Andrew Stevens
Vice President of the Land-Rover Series One Club

Erdington 2009

To join the LRSOC, please contact:

Membership Secretary
LRSOC
Maunsel Lock Cottage
Banklands
North Newton
Bridgwater
Somerset
TA7 0DH